# Treasures To Keep

## 365 DAILY BIBLE DEVOTIONALS

### *Revised Edition*

## EDNA HOLMES

**Published by**
**MAX HOLT MEDIA**

Published by:  Max Holt Media
303 Cascabel Place,
Mount Juliet, TN 37122
www.maxholtmedia.com
On facebook at www.facebook.com/maxholtmedia

Cover design by: © Max Holt Media
Cover art by:  © Litetender | Dreamstime.com - Pirate\'s Treasure Chest Photo

ISBN: 13: 978-1-944537-20-3

Other books by Edna Holmes:  Poems and More

# FOREWORD

*Treasures to Keep* was originally produced in 1998 under a different title, and with a different cover. After our retirement from the pastorate, I worked on revising much of the text, and changed the title. I am truly thankful that so many people over the years have found it to be a useful devotional guide. With this *Revised Edition* I have down-sized the book to make it the size of most bibles and to facilitate carrying and using it. To God be the glory. All the good in it is His alone. The rest is mine.

Since 2004 my husband and I have been retired from the pastorate in Grapevine, TX. Our ministry still continues on in our "old age" as we are doing what we love most without the responsibility of a pastorate. We thank our Lord for such a happy retirement and this ministry of "helps" as he preaches in various churches often, and I enjoy speaking at ladies' meetings and retreats. It was the hardest thing we ever experienced in our lives—to leave the church where we had served for forty-two years, and the people that we loved so much.

Peoples' lives constantly change with time and circumstances, but God's Word never does. It will keep us steady while all else around us is uncertain. Perhaps that's why this simple, easy to understand devotional book is still being read. It directs the reader to God's Word which is truly *Treasures to Keep.*

Edna Holmes

FOREWORD

# ACKNOWLEDGEMENTS

Quotes and illustrations from the Gray and Adams Commentary are used extensively throughout this devotional book and are used by permission from Zondervan Publishers.

The poem "With Jesus," by Martha Snell Nicholson is used by permission from Moody Press.

I am indebted to my friend, Yveatte Moore, for her invaluable work on the manuscript and preparing this document in the required format for publication. She made my work of revising the text much easier.

My son and daughter-in-law, Louis and Jan, are my ready helpers when I'm working with a computer. I'm grateful.

My husband helps me in so many ways, I can't name them all. He encourages me. He is attentive to my needs. I'm thankful for his love and consideration.

The women of Bethel Baptist Church in Grapevine, TX where we ministered for forty-two years are the reason this book was written in the first place. They urged me to do it and encouraged me all the way. I would not have attempted it otherwise.

NOTES:

The numbering of the daily devotionals provides the
reference needed to find each one. Therefore, no Table of
Contents is necessary.


Space has been provided at the end of each devotional for
your own personal notes.

# January 1

**"I rejoice at thy word, as one that findeth great spoil."**
**Psalms 119:162**

The *spoil* was the plunder taken from an enemy or captured city in time of war. Gold, silver, richly colored garments and other valuables were taken by the victors after the battle and became their property. The spoils were their treasures to keep. To obtain the spoils of war, men had to go to battle and be involved in the fight.

In our text verse the psalmist, David, compares the Word of God with 'great spoil' or treasure. Imagine a soldier, in a captured city, going into a house to collect the spoils and finding enough gold to make his family rich. He would say that it was well worth the battle to get such a prize.

Our battle is with the devil who tries to keep us from consistently reading the Word of God. He knows it will make us rich in faith and fill our hearts with treasures to keep that nothing can take away from us. The Word itself is the weapon to defeat the devil. The minute that you sit down with it each day to read it, think on it, and pray, you have won a major battle.

Consider these treasures we find in the Word of God.
**1. Light to walk by on the pathway of life. Psalm 119:105**
**2. It gives peace of mind and a right attitude. v.165**
**3. God's Word gives understanding about life. v.130**
**4. The Word 'cleans' our hearts; we must read it! Eph. 5:26**

When I became a Christian, I was fortunate to have a pastor's wife who loved the Word of God and taught the women to read it and live by its concepts. At first I couldn't understand the depth of its riches but through a lifetime of study it has become the most valuable thing in my life, after salvation. In time my own husband became a pastor and I felt the most important part I could do in our ministry was to also teach women the Word of God and urge them to make it the priority in their lives. My greatest joy and satisfaction as a pastor's wife was watching ladies "grow in grace, and in the knowledge of our Lord and Saviour Jesus Christ." II Peter 3:18

Be consistent in reading the Bible this year. You will be glad you did.

Additional Treasures: Psalm 138:2   Proverbs 30:5   Psalm 105:3

# January 2

**"Enter into his gates with thanksgiving, and into his courts
with praise: be thankful unto him, and bless his name."
Psalm 100:3-4**

The best habit to develop in this New Year is that of keeping a grateful heart toward God. Such a heart is *thankful.* The Lord pours so much good into our lives. We are accustomed to His blessings and take them for granted.

**How would it be if God deleted everything from your life for which you have not given thanks? What would be left of all you possess? Loved ones, friends, material possessions and things of the Lord are *life* to all of us, but do we ever say *thank you* to God?**

Gratitude toward God produces a valuable benefit. Praise will emerge as thankfulness overflows the heart. The garment of praise will lift the spirit of heaviness, which overcomes Christians at times.

"To appoint unto them that mourn in Zion, to give unto them beauty for ashes, the oil of joy for mourning, the garment of praise for the spirit of heaviness…" Isaiah 61:3

How does one put on the garment of praise? Start by writing down everything that comes to mind for which you are grateful and you will find that the longer the list gets, the less heavy and depressed you will feel in your heart. Express your thankfulness and admiration to the Lord. Instead of lying awake in the night or walking the floor with a heavy heart, do what the psalmist did for relief.

"At midnight I will rise to give thanks unto thee because of thy righteous judgments." Psalm 119:62

God's judgment of what circumstances He allows to come into our lives, *whether pleasant or not*, is always right. Our part is to praise and thank Him at all times, for that is the means of happiness and wellbeing for His children.

Additional Treasures:   Psalm 30:12   Psalm 118:29

# January 3

**"As we have therefore opportunity, let us do good unto
all men, especially unto them who are of the household of faith."
Galatians 6:10**

God's children are to *do good* unto all men. The Lord has done His work of grace in our hearts. Therefore, we desire to minister to others when we are living in obedience to Him.

"Who gave himself for us, that he might redeem us from all iniquity, and purify unto himself a peculiar people, zealous of good works." Titus 2:14

The world expects Christians to love and be kind even though it makes life difficult to bear. In Christ, we can do it.

"For we are his workmanship, created in Christ Jesus unto good works, which God hath before ordained that we should walk in them." Ephesians 2:10

However, our greatest door of opportunity is within the family of God. In the church we can share one another's burdens, pray and be willing to render aid in a practical way when the need arises.

**One of the things I especially liked to do was prepare a meal for a new mother on the day she came home from the hospital with the baby. I remember what those days were like! To have a nice dinner prepared and ready to eat is a wonderful blessing to the family. It was my opportunity to do a good thing.**

WHY WAIT

I would rather have one little rose, from the garden of a friend,
Than to have the choicest flowers when my stay on earth must end.
I would rather have the kindest words and a smile that I can see
Than a flattery when my heart is still and life has ceased to be.
I would rather have a loving smile, from a friend I know is true
Than the tears shed round my casket when this world I bid adieu.
Bring me all the flowers today whether pink or white or red,
I'd rather have one blossom now than a truckload when I'm dead.

Author Unknown

Additional Treasures: Philippians 2:3-4  Colossians 3:23

# January 4

**" And Jabez was more honorable than his brethren:
and his mother called his name Jabez, saying,
because I bare him with sorrow."
I Chronicles 4:9**

Jabez was tagged with a name meaning *sorrowful,* because his mother had a difficult time at his birth. Growing up he may have been reminded of that whenever he heard his name spoken. However that may have affected him, he was still more honorable than his brothers. As a man Jabez offered a fervent bold prayer to God, which made certain his happiness and prosperity in life.

We can learn from this dedicated man who lived in ancient Biblical history. He had a refreshing faith in God without the knowledge that we have today of the death of our Savior and the benefits of the written Word of God. He did have the record of Abraham, that man of God, who "believed God and it was accounted to him for righteousness." Gal: 3:6

Moses also left some footprints of faith for Jabez to follow. For "By faith Moses, when he was come to years, refused to be called the son of Pharaoh's daughter; choosing rather to suffer affliction with the people of God, than to enjoy the pleasures of sin for a season..." Hebrews 11:25

Jabez turned out to be more honorable than his brethren, because he put his faith in God and set his life on that course in the days when the glory of his nation was diminishing.

**"And all things, whatsoever ye shall ask in prayer, believing, ye shall receive."** Matthew 21:22

Jabez never saw this promise but he believed it because he did it. We have this and countless promises written down for us. Let us exercise faith; *faith simply believes God* as He speaks to us by His Word. Read it, believe it, and claim a precious promise for your present need. God loves you as much as He loved Jabez. He loves His children all the same. Trust Him.

Additional Treasures:    Romans 12:12    Hebrews 3:12

# January 5

**"And Jabez called on the God of Israel, saying, Oh that Thou wouldest bless me indeed, and enlarge my coast, and that Thine hand might be with me, and that Thou wouldest keep me from evil, that it may not grieve me!"**
**I Chronicles 4:10**

One must have a clear conscience to pray a prayer such as Jabez did in this scripture. What did this honorable man ask for in his petition to God?

**First, he asked God to bless him indeed:** in fact, in truth, and really! God can give *much* as easily as he gives *little*. Jabez's heart was full of faith.

**Second, he asked God to *enlarge his coast*.** God expanded his coast, or *borders*. There is a town named *Jabez* in I Chronicles 2:55 where the scribes dwelled. What about our borders; are we in a rut? Do we need to pray that God would 'enlarge our coasts', and enable us to expand and accomplish greater things for the Lord?

**Third, he asked God "that Thine hand might be with me."** God's hand moves obstacles out of the way, and we can accomplish anything He wants us to. Don't be afraid to try something that God has put in your mind to do. Just obey and you will be amazed how easy God makes it work for you.

**Fourth, Jabez asked God to keep him from evil,** "... that it may not grieve me!" Jabez knew in his day just as Christians know today that sin causes grief, and the finished product of sin is *death*.
Sin is a grief to man all of his living days and at death, unless he has been saved through faith in Christ, sin will grieve him forever...lost in eternity.

The Word of God fortifies us against sin. The more of it we have stored up in our hearts, the more "ammunition" we have to fire at the devil.
"Thy word have I hid in mine heart, that I might not sin against thee." Psalm 119:11

Make this your bold 'Jabez' prayer this year: **"Lord, keep me from evil."**

Additional Treasures:   I John 5:17   James 4:7-8

# January 6

**"Cause me to hear thy lovingkindness in the morning;
for in thee do I trust: Cause me to know the way wherein
I should walk; for I lift up my soul unto thee."
Psalm 143:8**

Lovingkindness is defined as kindness coming from love, affectionate tenderness, and consideration. That's what God has for His children. It has to do with Christ and His dying for us on the cross. God sees the blood, not our sins, for the blood covers the sins of those who have trusted in Him. That precious blood evokes the lovingkindness of God. He has affectionate tenderness and consideration for the redeemed of the Lord.

"How excellent is thy lovingkindness, O God! Therefore the children of men put their trust under the shadow of thy wings.

They shall be abundantly satisfied with the fatness of thy house; and Thou shalt make them drink of the river of thy pleasures." Psalm 36:7-8

If our eyes could be opened to see the countless ways in which the Lord tenderly guides us through each day and protects us from harm, we would be amazed. After all He has an army of angels, ministering spirits, which are sent forth for that purpose.

"Are they not all ministering spirits, sent forth to minister for them who shall be heirs of salvation?" Hebrews 1:14

**Whenever we hear something, it has been communicated to us, or passed along. We *hear* through reading God's Word, for by it He communicates everything to His children. Many of our prayers are answered through the Word of God. If we don't look in the Bible, the *answer column*, every day, we may miss the very key to solving a problem. It was a blessed thing when I discovered this fact: God specifically talks *to me* in His Word. Now I expect to find something special as I read, and have often been given answers to prayer.**

We should seek to hear His lovingkindness before the voices of the world and devil come clamoring into our minds each day. Lift up your soul to God by reading your Bible. You can *hear* its message of God's lovingkindness, and then go out and face the world with confidence.

Additional Treasures:   Jeremiah 31:3   Isaiah 63:7   Psalm 26:3

# January 7

**"The entrance of thy words giveth light;**
**it giveth understanding unto the simple.**
**Psalm 119:130**

Nothing can be more powerful, life-changing, and yet so easy and simple for us: as we read the Bible it will enlighten us. Whatever problem has entangled and perplexed us, God's Word can shed light on it and give us direction in the matter.

However, the Word is our spiritual food and we need a regular diet of it for the results we desire to come about. A person who seldom reads the Bible cannot flip it open and find answers to his problems like magic, no more than one who is physically weak and starved can eat one meal and be instantly healthy.

**Enlightenment means the illumination of the mind, information.** The Word of God illuminates, *makes clear,* knowledge and truth to our minds as we think about and desire answers to some situation or problem in our lives.

Where are we going to find enlightenment in the Bible? Reading the Word of God on a daily basis, you will find that perplexing things on your mind will be addressed by the Lord where you read or you will be reminded of other verses where the answer is revealed. It works that way!

"For thou wilt light my candle: the Lord my God will enlighten my darkness." Psalm 18:28

**Discovering that the Lord deals with our questions and problems in His Word, *as we read,* was a very great benefit to my life. Answers may not come the very day you ask. It may be days, weeks, or months, but they *will* show up and most likely in a place where you were not expecting it. It will be an advantage to your life to *keep faithfully reading the Word!***

Set a time and particular place in your home to meet with the Lord every day. Be consistent as possible, and soon it will be the most beneficial habit you ever formed in your life. Start in the gospels. Slowly read a chapter each day and think on what you are reading, as though you are following Jesus around watching Him minister to the people.

Additional Treasures:   Proverbs 6:23   Proverbs 22:20-21

# January 8

**"Dearly beloved, avenge not yourselves, but rather give place
unto wrath: for it is written, vengeance is mine;
I will repay saith the Lord."
Romans 12:19**

We should never try to *get even* when we suffer an injustice, but give place, that is, to yield in judgment or opinion, submit courteously...to wrath.

"To me belongeth vengeance, and recompence; their foot shall slide in due time; for the day of their calamity is at hand, and the things that come upon them shall make haste." Deuteronomy 32:35

So it is God's wrath. We are to give place to it, *stay out of the way,* and God will act. As long as we entertain revenge in our hearts, we will delay God's judgment on those who have wronged us.

God works all things together in perfect harmony with His will, so in *His* time, not ours, judgment will occur. "Vengeance is Mine..." the Lord said. Vengeance is the *inflicting of injury or punishment for a wrong.* We are not qualified and are forbidden to judge others. "Judge not, that ye be not judged." Matthew 7:1

Beside that command there is a solemn warning:

"For with what judgment ye judge, ye shall be judged: and with what measure ye mete, it shall be measured to you again." Matthew 7:2

**The particular meaning here is to criticize or condemn. The moment we engage in judging others in this way the wheel of judgment is set in motion. It rolls in reverse...over the judge!**

Trust all judgment to God, who knows all the intricate details of every human involvement. "...Shall not the Judge of all the earth do right?" Genesis 18:25

Our main concern should be to keep our own hearts clear of bitterness and a critical spirit which will eat away all joy of the Lord. When you are offended, for whatever reason, immediately turn it over to the Lord for His judgment alone. Then go on with a clear conscience and peace of mind.

Additional Treasures:    Romans 14:13    Psalm 96:13

# January 9

**"Then said he unto me, Son of man, hast thou seen
what the ancients of the house of Israel do in the dark,
every man in the chambers of his imagery?..."**
**Ezekiel 8:12**

These men were worshipping foul images portrayed on the walls of the secret chambers built into the court of the temple.

"The Lord seeth us not; the Lord hath forsaken the earth."
Ezekiel 8:12

They had convinced their own hearts that God Himself could not see their deplorable wickedness: 'He can't see us, because He is nowhere on the earth now!' They had lost their grasp of reality.

The chamber of our imagery, *imaginations,* is the mind; it is hidden from every living soul but not God.

"Thus saith the Lord; I know the things that come into your mind, every one of them." Ezekiel 11:5

We can never hide anything from God. Jesus read the thoughts of those around Him for He knew what was in man. How much more does the Lord search us by the Holy Spirit dwelling in us? Be very careful of the thoughts you allow to linger in your mind. Thoughts become words and words can stir us to action, good or bad.

We can learn from those ancients, supposedly learned men of centuries ago, who hid in the dark and worshipped evil images on the wall.

**Unconfessed sin in the heart can become your master, and you will do things you said you'd never do!**

**Keep your heart from becoming a *seed bed* of sinful thoughts by daily imprinting the Word of God on the walls of your mind.**

"Thy Word have I hid in mine heart, that I might not sin against thee." Psalm 119:11

Additional Treasures:   Luke 6:8   Luke 11:17   John 1:48

# January 10

**"And Noah went in, and his sons, and his wife, and his sons wives with him, into the ark....and of everything...There went in two and two... as God had commanded Noah.**
**Genesis 7:7-10**

Noah went in with his family first, and then the animals came into the ark unto Noah. The responsibility to round up animals, making sure none were overlooked, was not given to Noah. God put him inside the ark and had the animals come in. There was neither chaos nor confusion in God's program.

For God is not the author of confusion...I Corinthians 14:33

When your life begins to get chaotic, put *everything* into God's control and He will bring things back to an orderly function. We don't have to live on the edge all the time. God provided a peaceful life for us.

"And the peace of God, which passeth all understanding, shall keep your hearts and minds through Christ Jesus." Philippians 4:7

**Peace of God in the heart emerges, *comes out,* into the mainstream of your life.**

"A good man out of the good treasure of the heart bringeth forth good things: and an evil man out of the evil treasure bringeth forth evil things." Matthew 12:35

The peace of God generates quality of control in verbal expression. We may seem to be peaceable until we speak, for Jesus also said, "...out of the abundance of the heart the mouth speaketh." Matthew 12:34

We will be discerning if we believe this verse. *Listen* to people talk and you will know a lot about the condition of their hearts, and not only listen, but also *observe* the actions that characterize their lives. Human emotions *will be* expressed such as love, anger, hatred, compassion, and frustration. Pay attention, also, to *your own* actions and words for a day, a week, and discover the condition of *your* heart. God's Word proves to be true every time. "Keep thy heart with all diligence; for out of it are the issues of life." Proverbs 4:23

Additional Treasures: Luke 6:45   Psalm 119:165   Isaiah 26:3

# January 11

"...Whatsoever things are true...honest... just...pure...
lovely...of good report; if there be any virtue,
if there be any praise, think on these things."
Philippians 4:8

Whatsoever things are...

**True** - agreeing with fact; **Honest** - credible, commendable.

**Just** - right, proper; **Pure** - perfectly clean, without sin.

**Lovely** - beautiful in character.

**Of good report** - a good account of something seen, heard, read, or done.

**If there be any virtue** - moral excellence: goodness.

**If there be any praise** - commendation, acclaim, approval.

**Think on these things!**

This verse is a *plumb line* for the Christian as a guide for his thoughts.

*A plumb line* is a small weight used on the end of a line to test the vertical straightness of a wall.

To guard against negative thought patterns, display a copy of this verse as a reminder to keep your thoughts *plumb* with the Word of God. It will enable you to keep your thoughts in line: *straight.*

The mind is a battlefield where the devil wages war with the Christian every day. Fortify yourself with the Word. It is the Sword of the Spirit, which protects us. Keep it sharp and gleaming in your mind!

"I thought on my ways, and turned my feet unto thy testimonies."
Psalm 119:59

Additional Treasures:   Proverbs 12:5   Psalm 19:14

# January 12

**"And the children of Israel did eat manna forty years,
until they came to a land inhabited; they did eat manna,
until they came unto the borders of the land of Canaan."
Exodus 16:35**

Think of the number of days in forty years! Every day of the week, except the Sabbath, they gathered manna and baked their daily portion. On the sixth day they gathered twice as much and it stayed fresh. But they could not *hoard,* or gather extra at other times. It had to be gathered fresh each morning.

Jesus said "I am the living bread which came down from heaven: if any man eat of this bread, he shall live forever…" John 6:51

The manna was a type of Christ, and meant *gift from God.* The provision of manna was a tremendous, long-running miracle. God fed possibly two to three million people bread for 40 years. That was the Israelites, plus a *mixed multitude,* which was also a source of trouble.

"And the mixt multitude that was among them fell a lusting: and the children of Israel also wept again, and said, Who shall give us flesh to eat?"

Those attached to God's people today, such as the mixed multitude, benefit by the association. Blessings abound on the Lord's people and overflow to bless others connected with them. Jacob's father-in-law said:

"I have learned by experience that the Lord hath blessed me for thy sake." Genesis 30:27

**God has provided the *Living Bread*, the Lord Jesus. He died for our sins, was buried, and rose up from the grave on the third day. The Gospel, the good news of salvation, is for the whole world of sinners, *the mixed multitudes*, of the earth. Everyone can be saved by trusting Christ.**

Those who are saved should share the Bread of Life. The supply is sufficient for the whole world and will never diminish in the sharing.

Additional Treasures:  John 6:32-35     Romans 10:17

# January 13

**"Likewise, I say unto you, there is joy in the presence
of the angels over one sinner that repenteth."
Luke 15:10**

The salvation of one sinner is cause for rejoicing in heaven. Earth pays no attention and certainly does not rejoice. The world has only hatred for Christ. Jesus said, "If the world hate you, ye know that it hated me before it hated you." John 15:18

But heaven has a different view of Christ and His redemptive work.

### Joy In the Presence

**Faint words are flung out in a desperate cry
From the sea of humanity toward the throne:
*God...be merciful to me...a sinner.*
Heaven is transfixed in silence,
Beholding the face of the Savior.
A shadow of identification and love
Reflects in those fathomless eyes.
The Father nods His acceptance.
Heaven bursts forth in rejoicing,
And the angels watch in speechless wonder...
Another soul is redeemed for eternity.**
Edna Holmes

We should involve ourselves in the one thing that reaps great rewards and causes rejoicing in heaven, which is the winning of souls for the Lord.

"But we see Jesus, who was made a little lower than the angels for the suffering of death, crowned with glory and honor; that he by the grace of God should taste death for every man." Hebrews 2:9

Every man *can be* saved because Jesus died. Let us try to win souls personally, and help send missionaries to all parts of the earth where they may win the lost in the regions beyond.

Additional Treasures:    Matthew 28:19-20    Mark 1:17

# January 14

**"Yea, the darkness hideth not from thee; but the night shineth as the day: The darkness and the light are both like to thee."**
**Psalm 139:12**

The modern weapons of warfare now include a device which enables men to see at night. It is a tremendous asset.

**God has night vision.** The darkest part of the night and brightest part of the day are exactly alike to Him: midnight and noonday. He sees all over the entire earth at once, whether the sun is shining or not.

In the midnight of our trials and troubles, as we grope about in the darkness trying to *see* what to do, we should stop and be still and wait on God's directions. We see darkness...He sees light.

"....but all things are naked and opened unto the eyes of Him with whom we have to do." Hebrews 4:13

God sees and understands all about our lives...all the time.

"He revealeth the deep and secret things: he knoweth what is in the darkness, and the light dwelleth with him." Daniel 2:22

He knows what we need before we ask Him. He is never taken by surprise by our petitions, and He is our loving Heavenly Father.

"Be not ye therefore like unto them: for your Father knoweth what things ye have need of, before ye ask him." Matthew 6:8

When darkness obscures the light of understanding, go to the One who sees perfectly in the dark!

"Trust in the Lord with all thine heart; and lean not unto thine own understanding. In all thy ways acknowledge him, and he shall direct thy paths." Proverbs 3:5-6

Additional Treasures:  Isaiah 40:28    I Corinthians 2:16

# January 15

**"...Ye that are spiritual, restore...."**
**Galatians 6:1**

Many feel that being spiritual means to be occupied in the ministry of the church: visitation, teaching Sunday School, singing in the choir, etc. These are a necessary, vital part of the Lord's work in His church but all these good works combined could not make a person *spiritual*.

**A spiritual person is one whose spirit has been quickened, *made alive*, through believing on the Lord Jesus Christ. God's Holy Spirit comes in at the time of the new birth and we are made *spiritual* by His presence.**

"...he dwelleth with you, and shall be in you." John 14:17

We tend to measure the level of spirituality in others by whatever preconceived ideas fill our minds, with the top mark being "so". She is *so* spiritual! In reality, the quality of our spiritual life depends on our obedience to the Word of God. By that others can know that we are God's children. For obedience to what God says will make a difference in our lives.

Restoration is the *renewal* of something to its former state. Christians who have stumbled along the way and strayed away from the Lord need those who are stronger in the faith to *restore* them. The Word of God and prayer are the tools of restoration. The truth of the Word does wonderful things:

**Will make us free from sin and its entanglements.** John 8:32
**Cleanses our hearts, giving us joy and peace.** Ephesians 5:26
**Provides restoration for backslidden children.** Jer.3:22
**Reveals Christ, the Truth and the Way to us.** John 14:6

When we know the Truth, that is Christ, in the depths of our hearts, He effects a permanent change which shows we are *spiritual*. Do others see that change in you?
Additional Treasures: Matthew 6:14   Ephesians 1:7

# January 16

**"Order my steps in your word: and let not any iniquity
have dominion over me."
Psalm 119:133**

Our own sins or sins of others that put a lasting impression on our lives should not dominate us. That is *any iniquity*. That unkindness or cruelty you suffered many years ago could come into focus in your mind and ruin today, tomorrow, or any day in the future.

The devil knows that one of our weaknesses is our emotions. A memory can trigger our emotions into action and we may keep waging war in our minds over something that happened years ago. We should keep ourselves fortified with the Word of God, which has the power to deliver us from the enemy again *and again!*

"For the Word of God is quick, and powerful, and sharper than any two-edged sword, piercing even to the dividing asunder of soul and spirit, and of the joints and marrow, and is a discerner of the thoughts and intents of the heart." Hebrews 4:12

Our text verse is my *wake up* verse. Every morning I pray this prayer the first thing, usually before I'm out of bed. It was a particular help to me once during a difficult time, and I took it for my *wake up* verse. What sort of prayer was the psalmist praying?

**Order my steps in your word***: Lord, help me to walk obediently according to your Word.*
**And let not any iniquity have dominion over me***: And don't let any sin get control of me today.*

It is good to put at least one verse of scripture into our minds before our thoughts start going in all directions planning the day.

Ask the Lord to give you a *wake up* verse! Choose a prayer verse that has touched your heart before, and start your day with it. It will be very beneficial
and it's such an easy thing to do.

Additional Treasures:    Philippians 4:6    Matthew 6:25

# January 17

"Acquaint now thyself with him and be at peace.
Thereby good shall come unto thee."
Job 22:21

There is an advantage, at times, to having personal acquaintance with important people in this world. You may get help for various needs because of *who* you know. Some go to great lengths to cultivate friendship with the rich or famous.

However, personal acquaintance with the Lord will give you something that all others combined could never supply. That is peace of mind and heart.

To be at peace is the desire of every heart, but none will have it unless they are introduced to Jesus Christ the Lord.

"And, having made peace through the blood of his cross..."
Colossians 1:20

To be acquainted is the first step of having a close friendship with God. Acquaintance means "a person known to one, but not a close friend." At the time of salvation a person becomes acquainted with the Lord. Afterwards, as he learns and grows in the things of God, he comes to *know* Him and it develops into an intimate friendship.

**The greatest privilege imaginable is to have a personal friendship with God Himself, for we are by nature children of wrath and were estranged, *kept apart*, from Him because of our sin. It is the blood of Christ the Savior that brings us into that room of acquaintance with God.**

"Therefore being justified by faith, we have peace with God through our Lord Jesus Christ." Romans 5:1

The more we build upon our acquaintance with Christ by *searching the Word* and learning of Him, the more peaceful we become and the promised *good* then springs from that blessed peace which pervades our lives.

Additional Treasures:   Ephesians 2:14    Isaiah 27:5

# January 18

**"To whom God would make known what is the riches
of the glory of this mystery among the Gentiles;
which is Christ in you, the hope of glory: ..."
Colossians 1:27**

Christ living in the Christian is a mystery to the world. "How can He be in you?" This is very baffling to men, especially when they see a man who was once wicked turned into a godly person.

We, who are saved, understand that Christ dwells *in* us by His Holy Spirit who *changes us.*

"I am crucified with Christ: nevertheless, I live; yet not I, but Christ liveth in me: and the life which I now live in the flesh I live by the faith of the Son of God, who loved me, and gave himself for me."
Galatians 2:20

Christ dwelling in us comes by our believing in Him--His death, burial, and resurrection. If one believes the gospel of Christ, salvation follows and then His Spirit moves in to stay.

The presence of the Lord in us makes us new. "Therefore if any man be in Christ, he is a new creature: old things are passed away; behold, all things are become new." II Corinthians 5:17

**This truth compares to the first newborn baby in a household. Though the household is essentially the same as far as appearance, the presence of that new baby changes *everything,* so that life is never the same for the family.**

A change occurs in one that believes in Christ. It is true whether a sinner was known for being wicked, or as a *good* moral person. By that change others see *Christ in him*, as his words and actions testify of the Lord.

**Interest and desire toward the Word of God is one of the first identifying marks of a Christian.**

Additional Treasures:    I John 3:24    Psalm 119:72

# January 19

**"That he might sanctify and cleanse it with the washing
of water by the word."
Ephesians 5:26**

The Word of God does for us spiritually what soap and water does for us physically. Reading the Bible will make us clean when our hearts have been made dirty by sin. "Cleanse it with the washing of water by the word."

Generally we cleanse ourselves regularly with soap and water, particularly washing our hands frequently. We teach that good health habit to our children, hoping it will become a lifetime practice with them too. Women may have rough hands more so from washing than hard work.

We should have the same concern about keeping our *spiritual* hands clean. Any contact with the world necessitates the need for cleansing. The *"washing of water by the Word"* is the only means for that cleansing.

"Now ye are clean through the word which I have spoken unto you."
John 15:3

**The world is full of sin, and our daily walk in it causes an accumulation on us. It becomes *our* sin, just as dirt on our hands becomes ours. We wash our hands to be clean again, but we cannot clean our *spiritual hands* ourselves. That takes the blood of Christ our Savior.**

"But if we walk in the light, as he is in the light, we have fellowship one with another, and the blood of Jesus Christ his Son cleanseth us from all sin." I John 1:7

A good prayer for cleansing is found in Psalm 51:2. We should pray with King David, "Wash me thoroughly from mine iniquity, and cleanse me from my sin."

Before you lie down at night, take a *spiritual* bath, and you will have a more restful sleep with a good conscience.

Additional Treasures: I John 1:9   Psalm 51:1

# January 20

**"If we have forgotten the name of our God, or stretched
out our hands to a strange god; Shall not God search
this out: for he knoweth the secrets of the heart."
Psalm 44:20-21**

We can easily be distracted in this chaotic world. Some *good* thing may get our attention and time and soon we are drawn away from consistent devotion to the Lord. God's search often turns over many things in our lives until the cause of this is found. Yet the search is not for His benefit; He knows the secrets of the heart already, but we do not. The heart is untrustworthy and may be deceiving us when we feel certain that it isn't.

"The heart is deceitful above all things, and desperately wicked: who can know it?" Jeremiah 17:9

Since we don't really know our own hearts, it would be wise to consider with every inclination what the Word of God says.

"Trust in the Lord with all thine heart; and lean not unto thine own understanding; In all thy ways acknowledge him, and he shall direct thy paths." Proverbs 3:5-6

**Many years ago there was a dedicated young woman who was engaged to a man who made a half-hearted pretense of being a Christian, but only attended church to insure their engagement. However, the young lady felt in her heart that it was the right thing to do to marry him; they were so in love and he would surely change. The Sunday *before* they married was the last peaceable time that she got to attend the house of God. Her heart deceived her, because she leaned on her *own understanding* instead of the Word.**

Trust God. Don't think for a minute that your ideas will work better than what the Word of God says about the issues of life.

Acknowledge the Lord...and wait for His guidance.

Additional Treasures:    Jeremiah 29:13    Psalm 119:2

# January 21

"Pure religion and undefiled before God and the Father is this,
To visit the fatherless and widows in their affliction,
and to keep himself unspotted from the world."
James 1:27

The only religion that God approves is one that causes a love and concern for souls, conviction of sin, and an abhorrence of worldliness. That is a religion with Christ as its center of worship. Religions without Christ are false and have no help or hope for mankind. Religion, after all, is what men *do* in order to be holy. Some have outlandish practices, all to no avail.

*Pure religion and undefiled* will be the result of believing on the Lord Jesus Christ. The key is what Christ has done, and never the works men offer up, however impressive they may be. Nothing counts without Christ.

"By grace are ye saved through faith; and that not of yourselves: it is the gift of God: Not of works, lest any man should boast." Eph. 2:8-9

We should share our faith in the Lord. Unless our *religion* creates love and concern in our hearts for the lost, knowing they will perish forever without Christ, we are kidding ourselves about it being genuine.

"I said therefore unto you, that ye shall die in your sins: for if ye believe not that I am he, ye shall die in your sins." John 8:24

Concern for orphans and widows characterizes pure religion.

We are to share in the needs of others by giving out of our store of material goods, and then we show to others our faith by *works,* or actions toward them.

"Even so faith, if it hath not works, is dead, being alone."
James 2:17

And though we are in the world we should not let it *rub off* on us. A good testimony of faithfulness to our Savior is a precious treasure and that keeps our religion, as the world calls it, *pure.*

Additional Treasures:    James 1:22    Ecclesiastes 12:13

# January 22

**"Being then made free from sin,**
**ye became the servants of righteousness."**
**Romans 6:18**

We can never comprehend what degree of power it took to deliver us from the bonds of sin. Jesus had to *die* in order to accomplish our freedom from Satan.

"Being justified freely by his grace through the redemption that is in Christ Jesus..." Romans 3:24

Neither can we understand such love as the Lord has for us which compelled Him to die for our sins. Our lack of gratitude and love toward the Savior must be a grief to Him. How can we be so indifferent, and take for granted what the Lord did for us at Calvary? We cannot imagine the depth of His suffering, or the depth of the love which caused Him to endure it.

**In a time long ago, there was a young girl who was captured by a band of outlaws that made a slave of her. Her life was indescribable misery. Beside the hard labor and abuse, a favorite sport of the outlaws was to beat her unmercifully while laughing at her screams of pain and pleading. There was not a ray of light in her life. She was *dead* inside while she was living.**

**But one day the Crown Prince comes riding by that way. The outlaws were so surprised and frightened at his presence they scattered and fled...leaving the slave-girl standing there alone: ragged, dirty, and bruised from old and new wounds. She wanted to run and hide, but was rooted to the spot and utterly speechless.**

**The King's son looked down at her and spoke first. *"Would you like to be free?"* *"Oh yes...is it possible?"* she whispered. *"I have power to make it possible,"* said the Prince, and he reached down and lifted her up with himself, and took her to the King's palace. The slave-girl was adopted by the King, and soon learned the ways of a princess. --E.H.**

Can you imagine the new princess slipping out one day to go see the outlaws again? We would say with the apostle Paul: *"God forbid!"*

We cannot leave *obedience* to the Lord, and go flirt with sin, without grave consequences. Sin will overpower and make slaves of us! Be grateful to God and be faithful. *He is worthy.*

Additional Treasures:     Romans 6:6     I Thessalonians 5:22

# January 23

**"Know ye not, that to whom ye yield yourselves servants to obey,**
**his servants ye are to whom ye obey..."**
**Romans 6:16**

We will be servants either to *righteousness*, which is God's way, or *unrighteousness*, which is the devil's way. There is no *gray* area between.

This powerful chapter of Romans lets us know that Christ has delivered us from the bondage of sin. Sin has no effect on Him and it should have none on us, since we are in Christ.

"Likewise reckon ye also yourselves to be dead indeed to sin, but alive unto God through Jesus Christ our Lord." Romans 6:11

Sin can't dominate a Christian unless he yields to be its servant again. The tragedy is the failure of Christians to keep sin from invading their lives. They have forgotten that they don't have to yield to its power.

"For sin shall not have dominion over you: for ye are not under the law, but under grace." Romans 6:14

**Be armed!**
The old western fighters used to buckle on their guns to get ready for action. We must *buckle* the Word of God around our minds to get ready to fight sin and the devil every day. A soldier does not go into battle without his weapon. He would get killed or captured without it. **Opposing armies are not afraid of the men; they are afraid of the weapons they carry. Likewise, the devil is not afraid of us but he fears** *the Sword of the Spirit*. Buckle on the Sword!

**If you are captured the Word will free you!**
The Word tells us in John 8:32 "And ye shall know the truth, and the truth shall make you free." The devil cannot hold the Christian who prays to God for help, and then listens as God speaks to him in the Word.

Additional Treasures:    Romans 8:2    Nahum 1:7

# January 24

**"It is of the Lord's mercies that we are not consumed, because his compassions fail not. They are new every morning..."**
**Lamentations 3:22-23**

Knowing that the compassions of the Lord are new every morning should be a great comfort to Christians. Things new, according to the dictionary, *have never existed before.* Only God could have new compassion for us each day.

Another term for compassion is *sympathy*, or *pity*. What tender feelings the Lord has for His children. They never get worn and frazzled. They are new every day of our lives.

"The Lord is merciful and gracious, slow to anger, and plenteous in mercy. Like as a Father pitieth his children, so the Lord pitieth them that fear him." Psalm 103: 8,13

God has no limits in His store of things new. There have never been two alike of all the *trillions* of snowflakes that have fallen on the earth! Scientists have looked in vain trying to see a likeness in the intricate white flakes of ice crystals that float down so softly.

The clouds drifting over our heads are always different in design, and all plant life--trees, flowers, and other things of nature--are new each season. God doesn't have to bring out old designs to use in any facet of His creation.

Such an Omnipotent God is our Father, and His compassion is generated *new* for us each day. Why do we worry and fret and sometimes feel that no one cares and understands? *God does.*

"But thou, O Lord, art a God full of compassion, and gracious, longsuffering, and plenteous in mercy and truth." Psalm 86:15

We need the compassion and longsuffering of the Lord, because we sin every day of our lives. Even the "thought of foolishness is sin."
Proverbs 24:9
The Lord knew from the beginning the way we are and made provision. "If we confess our sins, he is faithful and just to forgive us..."I John 1:9

Additional Treasures:  Psalm 103:4    Psalm 78:38,39

# January 25

**"In that day when God shall judge the secrets of men
by Jesus Christ according to my gospel."
Romans 2:16**

I heard of a Judge whose wife was brought into his court for a traffic violation. She was confident that he would not fine *her*, but she was guilty, and the Judge charged her with the violation. Then he stood up, took off his robe, and came down from his place and *paid her fine himself!*

God's love for us cannot be fathomed by our finite minds. But along with that love, He cannot simply dismiss our sin. **We are guilty**! He charged us with the penalty, then Jesus the Savior left heaven and came down and paid the fine for us: **death.**

"The wages of sin is death but the gift of God is eternal life through Jesus Christ our Lord." Romans 6:23

The secrets of men, the *undercurrent of their lives,* will be revealed at the judgment.

**The *lost* will be judged,** and will acknowledge Christ as they bow the knee to Him, but it will be too late.
"That at the name of Jesus every knee should bow…And that every tongue should confess that Jesus Christ is Lord, to the glory of God the Father." Philippians 2:10-11

**The *saved* will appear at the judgment seat of Christ:**
"For we must all appear before the judgment seat of Christ; that every one may receive the things done in his body…whether it be good or bad. " II Corinthians 5:10

**Things done for God's glory will be rewarded.** Our own works will *go through the fire test* and be consumed.

"If any man's work abide which he hath built thereupon, he shall receive a reward." I Corinthians 3:14

Additional Treasures:    I Peter 1:17    Psalm 58:11

# January 26

**"Only take heed to thyself, and keep thy soul diligently,
lest thou forget the things which thine eyes have seen,
and lest they depart from thy heart all the days of thy life."
Deuteronomy 4:9**

The dictionary defines the heart of man as 'the seat of one's inmost thoughts and secret feelings,' soul and mind. It is also defined as 'the conscience and seat of emotions.'

**In the Bible, the *heart/mind/soul* are synonymous, the same. Our text bears that out: keep thy *soul,* lest thou *forget,* lest they depart from thy *heart.***

So the heart/mind/soul functions in the same framework of our innermost being. You can see that the heart is much more than we can imagine, and so important because it is the stronghold, or fortress, which controls our lives.

When Christ dwells in the *heart/mind/soul,* then one has the controlling factor that generates peace and happiness in the life. Without Christ there is no real protection for the heart. The devil knows how to crumble the defenses of morality, common sense, and any other standard people live by.

**Does Christ live *in the heart* of the believer?**

"That Christ may dwell in your hearts by faith…" Ephesians 3:17

"And the peace of God which passeth all understanding, shall keep your hearts and minds through Christ Jesus." Philippians 4:7

If the Lord has a place of honor and esteem in our hearts, we will have the strength of mind and soul to declare his presence with joy and to live in obedience to Him.

Our relationship with the Savior must be nourished by spending time with Him, talking (praying) and listening (reading the Bible) just as we nourish the relationship we have with others that we love. Talking and listening to one another is the way of friends. Are you and Jesus close friends?

Additional Treasures:   I Peter 3:15   Deuteronomy 4:29

# January 27

**"But now, after that ye have known God, or rather are known
of God, how turn ye again to the weak and beggarly elements,
whereunto ye desire again to be in bondage?"**
**Galatians 4:9**

The children of Israel, after being miraculously delivered from
slavery in Egypt, murmured and complained against Moses because they
didn't have the same things they'd had back in Egypt. They seemed to
forget that they were *slaves* there too!

"We remember the fish, which we did eat in Egypt freely; the
cucumbers, and the melons, and the leeks, and the onions, and the
garlick."
And they complained further: "But now our soul is dried away: there is
nothing at all, beside this manna, before our eyes." Numbers 11:5-6

God graciously made that wonderful bread, *manna,* appear fresh
every morning and they didn't appreciate that. They longed to return to
the weak and beggarly elements in a land of bondage. The *lust of the
flesh* can reduce a Christian to shame and dishonor in this world--a child
of the King eating slop with the hogs! It is imperative that we keep our
hearts with all diligence.

"Keep thy heart with all diligence; for out of it are the issues of life."
Proverbs 4:23

### UNSEEMLY

**A vagrant searched through garbage cans along an alley,**
**Looking for food...or things.**
***I pitied him.***
**My heart went searching, defiantly,**
**Through the world's garbage and polluted debris**
**Looking for something to satisfy.**
**It was so unseemly for a king's child.**
***All heaven pitied me.***
Edna Holmes

Additional Treasures:   Luke 9:62   Proverbs 14:14

# January 28

**"He that receiveth a prophet in the name of a prophet
shall receive a prophet's reward..."
Matthew 10:41**

God blesses those who show kindness to His preachers or any of His children, regardless of their place in the family of God. He is so pleased that He rewards such actions, even if the act of kindness is only a *cup of water* given to relieve someone's thirst. None should go to heaven without treasure when the gaining of rewards is so simple.

"As we have opportunity, let us do good unto all men, especially unto them who are of the household of faith." Galatians 6:10

"Bear ye one another's burdens, and so fulfil the law of Christ." Galatians 6:2

**During my years as a Pastor's wife, there were many who gave *cups of water* of kindness to me. The ladies of our church were especially kind in remembering my birthday, and thought of many unique ways to make it extra special. Year after year they continued being thoughtful and generous, and I was overwhelmed with gratitude! I can only pray that they reap many good things in life for the goodness they poured into mine.**

"And I entreat thee also, true yokefellow, help those women which laboured with me in the gospel, with Clement also, and with other my fellow labourers, whose names are in the book of life." Philippians 4:3

Start laying up some treasures in heaven by handing out some *refreshing water* to the thirsty. Witness to a lost soul. The *water of life* is Christ our Savior. Tell someone about Him.

A little *cup of kindness* that you offer may help another through a dark time of despair, and you will reap eternal rewards.

Christians can be rich in eternity! God rewards the smallest service, done in love and honor of the Lord. Start laying up treasure today.

Additional Treasures:    Mark 10:43-44    Luke 10:36-37

# January 29

**"And when he was come to the other side into the country
of the Gergesenes, there met him two possessed with devils,
coming out of the tombs, exceeding fierce...."
Matthew 8:28**

This incident with the demon possessed men occurred in the country of the Gergesenes, people living east of the Sea of Galilee. They were also called *Gadarenes or Gerasenes*, as told in the gospels of Mark and Luke. They narrate special circumstances concerning *one* of these two men who ran out of the tombs when Jesus came to their country. Matthew is exact on the *number* of men who came running out, *exceeding fierce*, the Bible says.

**These pathetic tormented creatures are an example of what the devil will do when he has full sway over human beings, *indwelling them* with evil spirits. They were tormented as they cut themselves with stones, cried out, and ran among the tombs or caves, where the dead were buried.**

God does just the opposite for Christians. His Holy Spirit comes into the believers to dwell and they have *peace and joy*.

The people had tried to tame the demonic men by binding them with chains, but they broke them. No human strength can contain or match the strength of evil spirits, but when Jesus came he was immediately recognized by these devils. *They had seen Him before, and they were afraid!*

Jesus could see the demons in the man, and they could see the Son of God in His human body. It is thrilling to read how Jesus, with a word, ordered them out of the man and they had to obey!

Read the four gospels: *Matthew, Mark, Luke,* and *John* continually. The more we learn of Jesus, the more we know of God and our faith increases. Jesus said...

"he that hath seen me hath seen the Father..." John 14:9

Think of the power that was in the words of Jesus as he spoke. He speaks to us today by His written word, which has power to change men's hearts and the way they live. It is our most precious treasure on earth. Do you read it?

Additional Treasures:     John 14:7     John 10:27-30

# January 30

**"...for thou hast magnified thy word above all thy name."**
**Psalm 138:2**

We can never over emphasize the importance of reading and holding the Word precious in the heart. It is impossible for us to grasp how highly God himself regards it, for the psalmist wrote, "thou hast magnified thy word above all thy name."

God's name, *Jehovah* or *Lord,* means the *Eternal One,* the One who makes promises, whose Word is His bond and One who enters into covenant relationship with us.

God holds His Word *above* that name! Each time we kneel in prayer and say *"Dear Lord,"* we are using that awesome name of God. We have a relationship with Him through Jesus Christ the Savior who died for our sins. Our Savior is *The Lord.*

Jesus said "he that hath seen me hath seen the Father..." John 14:9

Moses was the first man to whom God revealed His name Jehovah.

"And God spake unto Moses, and said unto him, I am the LORD: And I appeared unto Abraham, unto Isaac, and unto Jacob, by the name of God Almighty, but by my name JEHOVAH was I not known to them." Ex. 6:2-3

After a decisive battle with Amalek, in which God gave victory to the Israelites, Moses built an altar and called the name of it Jehovah Nissi, *The Lord Our Banner,* found in Exodus 17:15.

God reveals more of His name throughout His Word and that is another reason to read it, meditate on it and apply it to your daily living.

*Don't ever take that name in vain!* Exodus 20:7
*Remember God's estimation of His Word.*
*Focus on the eternal nature of the Word as you read.*
*Psa.119:89*

Additional Treasures:    Genesis 22:14    Judges 6:23-24

# January 31

**"Therefore I say unto you, Take no thought for your life,
What ye shall eat, or what ye shall drink;
Nor yet for your body, what ye shall put on."
Matthew 6:25**

Most Christians trust the Lord very little. It is evident in so many lives full of stress, worry, fear and anxiety. Why does this modern enlightened generation have so little faith in Jesus? I can think of one possible reason.

**The world has been very successful throughout the generations portraying the Lord as a *weak, anemic* type of person. Though some Christian artists now have painted a more masculine image of Jesus, most of us were brought up looking at pictures in Sunday School that cast Him as a feminine type of figure with long flowing hair, very soft features and pale, smooth hands. When I was a child looking at those pictures, He didn't look very strong to me. At the time I had no way of knowing that those images were the figment of someone's imagination, and not what Christ was according to the Biblical account of Him as a person. Many have those images still imprinted on their minds and even as they pray they think of the Lord in that way.**

Jesus was brought up as a carpenter's son as he was under the authority of Mary, his mother, and Joseph. He was a carpenter and no doubt his hands looked like it. It was hard work at which Jesus excelled. He was the perfect example in every facet of His life.

So His physical appearance was that of a working man, who also walked for miles on hot dusty roads with the sun beaming down on his head. He was no doubt physically robust, but the *source* of His power was God the Father, who was accomplishing His will and work through Him. *That is the reason we should not worry and fret!* Jesus is the Son of God and God the Son.

"Let all the earth fear the Lord: let all the inhabitants of the world stand in awe of him." Psalm33:8

"If I were hungry, I would not tell thee: for the world is mine, and the fulness thereof." Psalm 50:12

Additional Treasures:     Revelation 1:5     Hebrews 2:9

# February 1

**"...And every plant of the field before it was in the earth, and every herb... before it grew: for the Lord God had not caused it to rain upon the earth, and there was not a man to till the ground."**
**Genesis 2:4-5**

"And every plant...before it was in the earth, And every herb...before it grew..."

God's creation work was finished even though all the results were not visible.

We do not always see the results when God works in our lives through our prayers and obedience to His Word. However, our lack of perception and sight does not diminish His work. Some things are *never* made manifest to us, while others become evident when God causes the "rain" of whatever it takes to open our understanding and sight.

"For it is God which worketh in you both to will and to do of his good pleasure." Philippians 2:13

The first step we must take in doing the work of God is to put our faith in Jesus the Savior.

After salvation the work of God is operating in the life of every Christian because we are His workmanship.

"For we are his workmanship, created in Christ Jesus unto good works, which God hath before ordained that we should walk in them." Ephesians 2:10

**The first time I played a Christmas cantata for our church choir, it was so hard for me. I'd learned to read music as an adult, so was not adept at it like one trained from his youth. The Sunday morning we did it, I was so nervous and sent up some desperate prayers to the Lord. I was reminded of that verse. He gave me that "good work" to do and I was His "workmanship" to get it done. And God did enable me to do it.**

God is working in your life whether you see it or not. It is very likely that others may see it more than you do yourself.

Additional Treasures:     Titus 2:7     I Peter 2:12     Matthew 5:16

# February 2

**"When wisdom entereth into thine heart, and knowledge
is pleasant unto thy soul; Discretion shall preserve thee…"
Proverbs 2:10-11**

Wisdom is defined as knowledge and good judgment based on experience…or the right use of knowledge.

Wisdom comes from God, and one may ask for it specifically in any situation. See James 1:5.

Discretion is a by-product of wisdom and a protection for everyone, especially women in our society. In a reckless moment if a woman throws all caution to the wind, she may regret it for the rest of her life.

**A discreet person, according to the dictionary, is careful and sensible in speech and action; wisely cautious; showing good sense. The woman without discretion may look good, but her speech and behavior will soon betray her true character. To lose one's good name and reputation because of indiscretion is a sad loss indeed, and can rarely be reclaimed.**

"A good name is better than precious ointment…" Ecclesiastes 7:1

"As a jewel of gold in a swine's snout, so is a fair woman which is without discretion." Proverbs 11:22

Pray for wisdom, from which discretion develops. Then discretion will preserve and keep you in the ways of the Lord.

Abigail was a discreet, wise woman and it not only saved her life and that of her household, it paved the way for her to become the wife of David who later became Israel's most beloved king. Read the exciting story in I Samuel 25. In her tactful appeal to an angry warrior, she calmed him by her manner and added: *"but when the Lord shall have dealt well with my lord, then remember thine handmaid"*. David couldn't forget her! Discreet women are treasures on earth. *Be discreet.*

"A gracious woman retaineth honour…" Proverbs 11:16

Additional Treasures:    Psalm 112:5    Titus 2:4-5

# February 3

**"Which by his strength setteth fast the mountains; being girded with power: Which stilleth the noise of the seas, the noise of their waves, and the tumult of the people."**
**Psalm 65:6-7**

These verses depict God's power over the earth and the inhabitants that dwell on it. He stills the tumult of the people and controls the roaring waves of the oceans. The *tumult* is the noise, uproar, and commotion of humanity. We can see examples of such on television every day. Thank God for His strength to control the chaos in this world.

**When I first viewed mountains in Colorado, I was in awe and thought of how God *weighed the mountains in scales* as we weigh apples in the grocery store. I was very impressed at the power of God evidenced before my eyes by a heap of earth rising thousands of feet above everything else. *He setteth fast the mountains.* We don't see anybody moving mountains, though they may tunnel through or chisel around enough to carve out a road. Mountains stay right where God put them unless *He* moves one by an upheaval of nature, such as an earthquake.**

All of nature, and its impressive productions, functions under the power of God and is kept in check and harmony by Him. Why do we tremble and doubt when something in our lives goes amiss? He is *girded with power*; power is His clothing.

Touch the hem of His garment in prayer and experience the power of God in your life.

"The Lord reigneth, he is clothed with majesty; the Lord is clothed with strength, wherewith he hath girded himself: the world also is established, that it cannot be moved." Psalm 93:1

"And Jesus came and spake unto them, saying, All power is given unto me in heaven and in earth." Matthew 28:18

Additional Treasures:     Psalm 96     Psalm 97:6

# February 4

**"But do thou for me, O God the Lord for thy name's sake."**
**Psalm 109:21**

The scripture doesn't suggest to the Lord what to do; just *"do thou for me..."* Sometimes we are at a loss as to how to pray for others, for situations, or special needs in our own lives. God has given us a pattern for those *I don't know what to say* times when we are trying to pray. We can always pray after the pattern of the psalmist, *"do thou...Lord",* for whatever concern troubles our hearts. God has made a great provision in this matter of prayer.

"Likewise the Spirit also helpeth our infirmities: for we know not what we should pray for as we ought: but the Spirit itself maketh intercession for us with groanings which cannot be uttered."
Romans 8:26

No doubt some of our most fervent, effectual praying is done when our hearts are full and our mouths shut. It is those times when the burden is so great that you may have no words to express it. You can only present it to the Lord. *"Do thou for me..."*

We set our hearts in the attitude of prayer each day as we meet with the Lord for devotion and fellowship. That's how we may pray without ceasing as the Bible instructs us in I Thessalonians 5:17.

Prayer generates the power to live a satisfying, fruitful life for the Lord. The neglect of prayer robs the Christian life of all strength and vitality. With prayer all things are possible as God works in our lives.

"If ye abide in me, and my words abide in you, ye shall ask what ye will, and it shall be done unto you." John 15:7

**A Christian is not ready for the day until he has prayed. He needs a clear conscience, wisdom, and courage from the Lord to make decisions. Most of all he needs the peace that passes all understanding, which will keep his heart right. There is definitely a difference in the days that we start with the Lord in worship and the days that we find excuse to skip our devotional time altogether.**

Additional Treasures:    Luke 11:10    Isaiah 55:6

# February 5

**"But do thou for me, O God the Lord for thy name's sake:**
**because thy mercy is good, deliver thou me."**
**Psalm 109:21**

This verse is a great help when praying for *each other*. Not only should we pray as the psalmist, *"do thou for me,"* for the complex needs of our own lives, but in praying for others whose needs may be concealed. We can use this scripture for whomever we are praying and God will faithfully hear. The *only* thing that hinders our prayers is sin in the heart. We keep our hearts clean and clear by obedience to His Word.

"If we confess our sins, he is faithful and just to forgive us our sins, and to cleanse us from all unrighteousness." I John 1:9

With a clean heart we can pray wholeheartedly for God to "do for others" and also work in our own lives.

**Do Thou for Me Lord.**
**Help me to recognize and admit my own**
**Slothful neglect of devotion to You,**
**To gather my wandering thoughts as I read**
**Your Word and pray,**
**To make Your Word a reality in my life:**
***The song to sing,***
***The sword to swing,***
***The rock to keep me steady.***

**Do Thou for Her Lord.**
**Help her sort out thoughts and feelings**
**That may be churning in her heart.**
**Give her reassurance in prayer; renew her hope.**
**Reveal a precious promise to her heart**
**From Your Word:**
***A song to sing,***
***A sword to swing,***
***A rock to keep her steady.***
Edna Holmes

Additional Treasures:   Psalm 102:1-2   I John 3:22-23

# February 6

**"There is no fear in love; but perfect love casteth out fear:
because fear hath torment..."
I John 4:18**

**Fear:** a being afraid; **dread:** an uneasy feeling; anxious thoughts.
**Torment** means anguish, misery, and distress.

Everyone at some time has been caught in the grips of fear. Acute
fear is a tormenting thing.

**As a young child, I experienced fear whenever I heard my
parents argue. My fear was that they would separate, because they
did once for a brief period of time, and I'd been taken from home. I
had misery and great distress, even though the thing I feared did not
come about again.**

The *spirit of fear* comes from our enemy, the devil.

"For God hath not given us the spirit of fear; but of power, and of
love, and of a sound mind." II Timothy 1:7

Fear makes the mind unstable, unable to reason well. Resting in that
perfect love of God, trusting Him in all things, and in every situation of
our lives keeps that tormenting fear from us.

"Behold, God is my salvation; I will trust, and not be afraid: for the
Lord JEHOVAH is my strength and my song; he also is become my
salvation."   Isaiah 12:2

When our focus is on the Lord, there will be no room for the
debilitating fear that robs many of joy and peace.

**We are afraid to witness for the Lord.**   Proverbs 29:25
**We fear that the Lord won't meet our needs.**   Matthew 6:30
**We're afraid of failing to be good Christians.**   II Thess. 3:3

"God is faithful, by whom ye were called unto the fellowship of his
son Jesus Christ our Lord." I Corinthians 1:9

Additional Treasures:   II Timothy 2:13   Psalm 27:1

# February 7

**"For the work of a man shall he render unto him,
and cause every man to find according to his ways."
Job 34:11**

We can't get away from the law of the harvest. In the ancient days of Job they understood it; the law was in force then as it shall be as long as the earth stands. The workings of that law in nature are a pattern for the greater part: the law of sowing and reaping in the lives of human beings.

"Be not deceived; God is not mocked: for whatsoever a man soweth, that shall he also reap." Galatians 6:7

The Christian should see this law as very encouraging. When a man lives to honor God, being obedient to His Word in everything, *God is not mocked*, the law works; he shall reap good things in his life. This means a life free from care and worry, since he is resting in the promises of God with confidence that He will honor His Word.

We can never guess how the Lord will meet our needs. He can surprise us every time.

**Many years ago when our church had expanded the first little auditorium, we wondered how we could get pews to fit our space. Meanwhile, another church we had never heard of enlarged their auditorium and had their old furnishings for sale. Word came to our church and we bought them. It was made to order! Even the choir pews fit perfectly, and every piece of furniture was like *new*; not one scratch was on any of it and it was priced so reasonably. *God did that for us.***

God can supply every need you will ever have, and He delights to care for His children. Sow good things, and see how God will give you a blessed harvest.

"Give and it shall be given unto you; good measure, pressed down, and shaken together, and running over, shall men give into your bosom..." Luke 6:38

Additional Treasures:     Galatians 6:8-9     Ephesians 6:8

# February 8

**"Great peace have they which love thy law: and
nothing shall offend them."
Psalm 119:165**

The Lord gives an illustration of the meaning of "offend" in the text
verse as He taught a parable about how people receive the Word.

"And these are they likewise which are sown on stony ground; who,
when they have heard the word, immediately receive it with gladness;
And have no root in themselves, and so endure but for a time: afterward,
when affliction or persecution ariseth for the word's sake, immediately
they are offended." Mark 4:16-17

Those who love God's Word will continually put it into their hearts.
When afflictions and persecutions come *for the word's sake,* that Word
will keep them strong. They will not be offended...that is to stumble and
give up living for Christ. Reading and applying the scriptures in our daily
living infuses us with wisdom and understanding for every trial of our
faith.

**Peace is a gift from the Lord, which is incorporated into all the
blessed benefits we continually receive as children of God.**
"The Lord will give strength unto his people; the Lord will bless
his people with peace." Psalm 29:11

**Peace is connected to God's Word and obedience to it.**
"Oh that thou hadst hearkened to my commandments! then had
thy peace been as a river, and thy righteousness as the waves of
the sea:" Isaiah 48:18

So the love of God's Word will bring growth and change, because
we all give time and attention to the things we truly love. The Word
conforms us steadily to the image of Christ, and a great peace that
nothing disturbs will be maintained. Not of our doing or by our own
struggle, but the power of the Word in our hearts will accomplish this for
us.

Additional Treasures:     John 14:27     Philippians 4:7

# February 9

**"Looking diligently lest any man fail of the grace of God;
lest any root of bitterness springing up trouble you,
and thereby many be defiled."
Hebrews 12:15**

Those who have a troubling *root of bitterness* will invariably affect others around them *defiling* them with the unrighteousness that bitterness generates.

A vital thing for the Christian is to never fail of the grace of God. That means to immediately apply God's grace when we are offended; forgive others and thereby keep bitterness from taking root in our hearts. Roots of bitterness spread out into our lives and defile all that we touch.

"Let all bitterness, and wrath, and anger, and clamour, and evil speaking, be put away from you, with all malice: And be ye kind one to another, tenderhearted, forgiving one another, even as God for Christ's sake hath forgiven you." Ephesians 4:31-32

**Bitterness emerges from the heart and shows up in the outward motions of one's life. The sparkle of happiness goes out of the eyes and this enemy of joy and peace will affect the beauty of the countenance. I have witnessed the effect of bitterness in old people who would not resolve the conflict, but carried it to the end being miserable and wretched. The Lord said *put it away from us!***

"But if ye have bitter envying and strife in your hearts, glory not, and lie not against the truth. This wisdom descendeth not from above, but is earthly, sensual, devilish." James 3:14-15

Bitterness will generate all kinds of misery if you harbor it in your heart. *Forgive* when you are offended, *before* the awful effects of bitterness take root and make a place to stay in your life. The devil can control the heart that is filled up with bitterness. Don't give him the opportunity.

Additional Treasures:   James 3:17    Mark 11:25

# February 10

**"And Jesus said unto him, no man, having put his hand
to the plough, and looking back is fit for the kingdom of God."
Luke 9:62**

A man plowing in a field must keep his eyes straight ahead, usually on some distant immovable object which is his guide. That enables him to plow straight, orderly furrows. If he looks around or behind, the furrows will be crooked.

**A Christian, who constantly looks back to the old life before salvation changed him, will *plow a crooked furrow* and mess up his life. He will not be happy and blessed in the new way so is not *fit* to be an example of God's great love and grace on this earth.**

We are not to look to the world for anything we need and desire, for God has promised to take care of us.

"But seek ye first the kingdom of God, and his righteousness; and all these things shall be added unto you." Matthew 6:33

To be unsettled in our commitment to live for Christ affects our success in every area. "A double minded man is unstable in all his ways." James 1:8

We must never look back with longing to the old life, or the new life in Christ will get out of line like a crooked furrow.

"For ye were sometimes darkness, but now are ye light in the Lord: walk as children of light...." Ephesians 5:8

**Christ has no hands but our hands To do His work today;
He has no feet but our feet To lead men in His way;
He has no tongue but our tongues To tell men how He died;
He has no help but our help To bring them to His side.**
(From The World's Bible, by Annie Johnson Flint)

Focus on Christ and what He means to you and you will 'plow a straight furrow' which is a good testimony for the Lord.

Additional Treasures:     Hebrews 13:9     Luke 16:13

# February 11

**"God is our refuge and strength, a very present
help in trouble."
Psalm 46:1**

A very present help is one that is *already* there. Because God lives in
us by His Holy Spirit, He is more than present; He is *very* present with
us.

Refuge means *protective place;* strength is *power,* and those things
are present with us. God has equipped us for anything we may face.

"Be thou my strong habitation, whereunto I may continually resort:
thou hast given commandment to save me; for thou art my rock and my
fortress.*"* Psalm 71:3

Thanksgiving in the heart plays a vital part in the readiness of the
Lord to deliver us in time of trouble.

"Offer unto God thanksgiving; and pay thy vows unto the most
High: And call upon me in the day of trouble: and I will deliver thee, and
thou shalt glorify me." Psalm 50:14-15

Are you truly thankful to the Lord? Are you honest and truthful in
all your dealings with Him? Then you can expect much from His *very
present* help in time of trouble.

**PRESENT HELP**

**We do easily forget,
As trouble looms ahead
With intimidating, threatening brow
Blocking where we are led.**

**Before we take the time to think,
To quiet our panic with prayer,
Or look toward heaven in our plight;
Help is present...*He is there.***
Edna Holmes

Additional Treasures:    Psalm 28:7    Proverbs 14:26

# February 12

**"Draw thee waters for the siege, fortify thy**
**strongholds..."**
**Nahum 3:14**

When an army besieged a city, none could go in or come out of that place. The siege could go on for months and sometimes for years. The enemy encamped around the walls and waited. That's all they had to do to eventually capture the city. The people inside would slowly starve to death, and many horrible acts took place during those times when a city was in dire straits because of a siege. Certainly, a city could not sustain its people unless the water supply was secure *inside* the walls for them.

Our enemy, the devil, has us under siege all the time. We should never be so foolish as to allow our *water supply* to dwindle. We would then be too thirsty and weak, spiritually, to resist the temptations of the devil.

"Put on the whole armour of God, that ye may be able to stand against the wiles of the devil." Ephesians 6:11

One of his wiles, or tricks to deceive, is to keep Christians from the *water of the Word,* which will keep them strong and able to endure the siege and to fight the good fight of faith. We should draw in a supply every day to keep our hearts ready for any attack by the enemy. We cannot defend ourselves if we are thirsty and dry spiritually.

**In my childhood, we lived in a place with only an outside well for the water supply. We drew out water with a bucket and rope attached to a pulley. When winter weather threatened, we had to draw a good supply of water to have inside the house. To go out in freezing weather to get water was a miserable experience.**

*"Draw thee waters for the siege...."* Be sure you have a ready supply of the Word to fortify your heart for the daily siege by your enemy, the devil. He will *never* give up trying to keep you from being faithful to God.

**Don't allow yourself to get *too busy* to read the Bible every day.**

Additional Treasures:   Psalm 119:42   Psalm 119:110

# February 13

**"Jesus said unto them, If ye were blind, ye should have no sin:
but now ye say, We see; therefore your sin remaineth."
John 9:41**

Some verses are difficult to fully understand and explain to others. This one falls into that category for many people.

Every word our Lord spoke is worthy of careful consideration. Many are like jewels whose luster is concealed by a screen, and they certainly were baffling to the religious leaders of the day who hated Jesus and despised his words.

Once when officers were sent to arrest Jesus, they listened to Him teach and then didn't arrest Him. "And some of them would have taken him; but no man laid hands on him." John 7:44

The officers went back to the Pharisees who demanded to know why they had not brought Jesus with them.
"The officers answered, Never man spake like this man." John 7:46

Our verse follows the episode of the man born blind being healed by Jesus on the Sabbath day. The religious leaders angrily questioned the man. He gave Jesus praise for healing his eyes and they cast him out of the synagogue. He couldn't go back there to worship.

Later, Jesus found the man and told him that He was the Son of God. The man believed, and received *spiritual sight* in addition to his physical sight.

By their question to Jesus, the Pharisees demonstrated their spiritual blindness. Jesus told them it would be better if they were blind, then they would not have the sin of seeing and then rejecting Him. Their attitude was that they could "see" and didn't need Jesus. Therefore, Jesus told them that their sin remained.

The 'new birth' is the only way we get 'spiritual' sight. There is no other way. It opens our eyes to the things of God and His Word. That is the results of having *spiritual sight*. Thank God each day for your 'spiritual sight'. Tell someone this very day how you came to 'see' and be saved.

Additional Treasures:   John 3:19    John 15:22

# February 14

**"Commit thy works unto the Lord, and**
**thy thoughts shall be established."**
**Proverbs 16:3**

We have all heard this comment: "I wish I could keep my mind on what I'm supposed to be doing."

The Lord gave a solution to that little problem that we all have at times. Whatever activity engages us should be committed to the Lord. Do it as "unto the Lord" and see how much better your attitude will function in that light.

**We are serving God in performing even the mundane duties of housework: laundry, scrubbing floors, dusting, and vacuum cleaning, cooking, and generally keeping the household in order. God designed us to fulfill that role and it's the Lord's work for wives and mothers, for the most part, even in this modern generation. Commit it to Him and He will enable you to establish your thoughts.**

Some women must do the chores after they have worked all day on a job outside the home. God knows all about our lives, and the difficulties we have to endure for a season. The Bible still gives the simple answer for being content and keeping our minds on our business: "Commit thy works...and thy thoughts shall be established..."

In every area of life it is always difficult to keep focused on the Lord and His Word. Even our personal Bible study must be committed to Him, or our thoughts will scatter in all directions with the least little distraction. It's easy to give up for the day and close the Book in frustration. That's just what the devil wants us to do...*every day!*

Commit your works, *everything you do*, to Him and allow the Lord to establish your thoughts in a continual faithful pattern.

I find it helpful to commit my day to the Lord at the beginning and ask Him to help me think according to reality and truth. That way, my thoughts aren't running around in the past drudging up something to sidetrack me, or daydreaming into the future about what might be. If I keep that prayer in the forefront of my mind, I have a more productive, satisfying day.

Additional Treasures:    Proverbs 3:6;    Job 42:2;    Psalm 139:2.

# February 15

**"And while he lingered, the men laid hold upon his hand...**
**the hand of his wife, and upon the hand of his two daughters...**
**and they brought him forth, and set him without the city."**
**Genesis 19:16**

The great mercy of God was demonstrated in the matter of Lot and his family. They *lingered* in that city designated to be destroyed according to God's judgment. That is, they *delayed, hesitated, and dawdled* until the angel had to pull them bodily out of the place. They hated to leave Sodom!

Even when Lot begged to go to Zoar, another city of the plain marked for destruction, God again shows His infinite mercy to this weak, unfaithful believer. He allowed him to flee to that place, and spared it for Lot's sake.

Lot was given first choice when he and his Uncle Abraham had parted company, and he chose the well-watered plains of Jordan. He eventually moved his household into the wicked city of Sodom. They grew accustomed to the sins of the people, and though Lot was vexed with their sinful practices he stayed there and tolerated it, which brought his family to ruin.

"And delivered just Lot, vexed with the filthy conversation of the wicked..." II Peter 2:7-8

God lets us know by that word in the New Testament, that Lot *was* righteous because of his faith in God, just as Abraham, but his life reaped bitter fruit because of his disregard for God's Word.

Many Christians do not consult God about decisions they make and reap untold troubles which leave them wondering 'what went wrong'. God is infinitely interested in us; He even has the hairs on our heads numbered. Only God could do that impossible thing. Matthew 10:30

With such love and care of His children, we can trust Him to work in every detail of our lives. Let Him be your chief consultant and never go against His Word. It is for your well-being and good.

**Do we sometimes *linger in* and *yearn after* the world that is designated for destruction? If we live close to the world we will soon embrace it, be swept into it, and lose our influence for Christ. Our interest and love should be directed to the One who will someday come for us and take us *bodily* from this place!**

Additional Treasures:    I Thessalonians 4:16-18    Matthew 16:26

# February 16

**"And therefore will the Lord wait, that he may be
gracious unto you."
Isaiah 30:18**

The Lord is not affected by our impatience for quick answers to our prayers, or by our desires to know how He will work in our lives. He will wait, and He *will be gracious* because God has a criterion, or standard, by which He acts in regard to His children.

"And we know that all things work together for good to them that love God, to them who are the called according to his purpose."
Romans 8:28

> **Certainty** - *And we know...*
> **What** - *That all things work together...*
> **How** - *For good...*
> **For whom** - *To them that love God...*
> **Design** - *To them who are the called according to his purpose.*

**The Word of God is immutable, *unchanging*. It will always be His standard for perfecting His work in our lives to conform us to the image of Christ our Savior. He wants us to have a family likeness.**

At times, we may have immediate answers to prayer:

"And it shall come to pass, that before they call, I will answer; and while they are yet speaking, I will hear." Isaiah 65:24

God reads the heart before prayer ever moves our lips, and if His purpose is fulfilled in granting our petition *before we call* or while we are *yet speaking*, it shall be done.

Better to wait upon the Lord, as He waits, that He may be gracious to us. To put feet to our prayers, to make things happen, will only bring us heartache.

"They that wait upon the Lord shall renew their strength..."
Isaiah 40:31

Additional Treasures:   Psalm 25:5    Isaiah 8:17

# February 17

**"Withhold not correction from the child;
for if thou beatest him with the rod, he shall not die."
Proverbs 23:13**

In our generation this verse is certainly misunderstood and even when the meaning is understood, it is generally rejected.

The means of discipline and correction is referred to as the *rod*.

"I am the man that hath seen affliction by the rod of his wrath." Lamentations 3:1

"What will ye: shall I come unto you with a rod, or in love, and in the spirit of meekness?" I Corinthians 4:21

The apostle Paul certainly didn't mean he would come in and literally beat the people with a big wooden stick! But he would use the *authority*, which Christ gave to him as an apostle, to correct and exhort them concerning discipline in the church and to practice sound doctrine.

For Moses, his rod was a symbol of authority from God. The Lord verified that authority by signs and wonders involving the rod when Moses stood before Pharaoh in Egypt, warning him to let God's people go. The rod meant power, God's power, at the disposal of His servant Moses. We know what it accomplished.

**The rod of power, given to parents to train and correct their children, should be used with wisdom and love in obedience to God's Word. Our children are the greatest treasures we have on earth: *our life* continuing on after we are gone.**

"Only take heed to thyself, and keep thy soul diligently, lest thou forget the things which thine eyes have seen, and lest they depart from thy heart all the days of thy life: but teach them thy sons, and thy sons' sons." Deuteronomy 4:9

Additional Treasures:    Deuteronomy 31:13    Proverbs 19:18

# February 18

**"Thou shalt beat him with the rod, and shalt
deliver his soul from hell."
Proverbs 23:14**

The word *switch* is not in the Bible, but this rod in Proverbs can translate to *switch* in our day.

**The rod was a limb, large or small, cut or broken off from a tree. Most people of older generations certainly know what *switches* are as a means of discipline. My parents helped to keep the young trees around our place pruned by breaking little limbs off for switches. It was one of the best things they did for their large brood of seven sons and three daughters. All turned out to be respectable citizens, with some in the ministry. With many hindrances in their lives, my parents still accomplished this by obedience to God's Word in that matter. That took courage and consistency, for which I'm grateful.**

The rod of *discipline and correction* does not necessarily mean a spanking, or switching, each time the child disobeys. Parents soon learn by experience the best way to correct their own children, and teach them to respect and obey.

There's a very good reason to be obedient to this command as parents. In using the rod of discipline, parents contribute to saving the child from hell. Teaching children to respect parental authority and to learn obedience leads them to respect God's Word and authority, which will direct them to Christ and they can be saved...*saved from hell!*

So much depends on the diligence of parents to obey God's Word in the matter of rearing their children. Many have reaped a bitter harvest because they neglected to discipline their offspring in some manner. When they are grown, it's too late.

"There is a way that seemeth right unto man, but the end thereof are the ways of death." Proverbs 16:25

Additional Treasures:   Proverbs 20:7   Proverbs 22:6

# February 19

"The rod and reproof give wisdom: but a child left to himself
bringeth his mother to shame."
Proverbs 29:15

The rod is more than just a tool of discipline or correction because exercising the rod produces valuable fruit in the lives of children. Wisdom is its special gift; we know that wisdom is *the right use of knowledge*. When children learn by the rod of correction the right use of knowledge in regard to the matters of life, they will be spared much grief and pain.

**I remember when I was taught that it was wrong to steal. At the age of five years, I climbed upon a dresser and took a coin from my mother's purse without permission, then ran down to the store to buy bubble gum. The storekeeper wisely sent me back home with the coin. *I must have looked sneaky.* Just as I was replacing the coin, my mother caught me and I spent the rest of the day regretting that I'd become a thief! She knew just how much *switching* it took to convince a little child that stealing was a very bad thing to do. My life of crime *started* and *ended* in the same day.**

The rod certainly taught me some valuable wisdom at that time in my young life. What I learned is that *the way of the transgressor is hard.* Sin will be punished!
"…The way of transgressors is hard." Proverbs 13:15

Parents do their children a great injustice when they do not teach them this truth. Left to himself, a child does not learn this and may grow up having a troubled life and heartbroken parents because he lacked the discipline that imparts the right use of knowledge.

More can be taught *in love* than any other way. To children, time equals love, and it's not *quality* time as we hear referred to so much that is important; it is simply time--seconds, minutes, hours spent with a child. Whatever part in his waking hours that a child has of his parents' time and attention is precious to him.

Additional Treasures:    Proverbs 29:17    Deuteronomy 31:12

# February 20

**"Submit yourselves therefore to God.**
**Resist the devil, and he will flee from you."**
**James 4:7**

"Resist the devil and he will flee from you" is a familiar exhortation. We hear this verse partially quoted so much that the first part is nearly forgotten. *"Submit yourselves therefore to God..."* In reality, one cannot resist at all until the condition stated in the first part is met. Strength for the resisting is in the submission to God. Submit, resist, and the devil flees! That's the order.

**Any element of rebellion in our hearts toward God and His Word will weaken our ability to stand against the *wiles of the devil.* When there is only disappointing defeat and frustration going on in our daily lives, we need to ask the Lord to search our hearts and show us the cause.**

"Search me, O God, and know my heart: try me, and know my thoughts: And see if there be any wicked way in me, and lead me in the way everlasting." Psalm 139:23-24

When the Lord searches, He always finds what we have hidden in the heart that depletes our spiritual strength. We may not be aware of the thing ourselves for sin often has a deceptive appearance. God uncovers sin and gives us the remedy:

"He that covereth his sins shall not prosper: but whoso confesseth and forsaketh them shall have mercy." Proverbs 28:13

**As long as Christians try to cover up their sins they will suffer the consequences. The Lord *never* tolerates sin, though His judgment may not come immediately when one disobeys. *But it will come.* Sin will cut off our prospering because sin leaves a wake of devastation. We oftentimes cling to the thing that is destroying us. *Confess and forsake it.***

**Submission...Resistance...Victory...**that is God's order.

Additional Treasures: Jeremiah 17:9-10    Psalm 29:110

# February 21

**"Whoso keepeth his mouth and his tongue
keepeth his soul from troubles."
Proverbs 21:23**

The first thought in reading this verse may be 'if we don't constantly fill our mouths with food, we won't have the health problems that go with being overweight.'

That is not the meaning of the verse though the statement draws a sensible conclusion. Too much food equals excess pounds for most people. It's common knowledge that it can eventually lead to trouble with physical health.

The most *difficult* discipline in the world is keeping your mouth and your tongue. Most people go through life regretting impulsive words they have spoken. "Why did I say that? Why didn't I keep quiet?"

In James 3, *the whole chapter,* we learn all we need to know about the detriment of the tongue. Not one compliment is written, but warnings about this deadly member of the body.

"But the tongue can no man tame; it is an unruly evil, full of deadly poison." James 3:8

These solemn words should subdue our inclination to talk unless it is absolutely necessary. Let us take warning and use the Word of God in helping us to control the most unruly member of our bodies.

**When you wish to make a positive impression by *not talking too much* in the company of others, just read the third chapter of James beforehand. The Word will do more than your own determination, because no man is able to tame the tongue...*but God can.***

"Let the words of my mouth, and the meditation of my heart, be acceptable in thy sight, O Lord, my strength, and my redeemer." Ps.19:14

Additional Treasures:    Colossians 4:6    Proverbs 17:27

# February 22

**"Holding faith, and a good conscience; which some having put away concerning faith have made shipwreck."
I Timothy 1:19**

On a list of rules for good mental health I saw a simple exhortation: "Maintain a good conscience."

**Conscience** - ideas and feelings within a person that tell him when he is doing right, and warn him of what is wrong.

That is a *good* conscience. The challenge is to maintain it: to keep, to support, to keep supplied or in repair. The Word of God does all this for us.

Our ideas should be governed by what God says. We can't allow our hearts to be our guide, for we will certainly be deceived.

"The heart is deceitful above all things, and desperately wicked: who can know it?" Jeremiah 17:9

**One can expect a *shipwreck* on the sea of life if he fails to keep a good conscience. It steers the soul through storms and dangers because it is the *warning system* that keeps us on track. The apostle said some put away the good conscience concerning faith, and went down shipwrecked!**

Maintain a *good* conscience about your faith.

**Express your faith verbally:** *Say something about it!* Speak a word for the Lord and more courage will come, enforced by that good conscience.

**Live your faith:** Our behavior and conversation in this world should always be "...as it becometh the gospel of Christ." Philippians 1:27

**Keep sins confessed, *up to date!*** That's the best advice of all to maintain a good conscience. I John 1:9

Additional Treasures:    Romans 13:1-5    Hebrews 9:14

# February 23

**"Ye are our epistle written in our hearts, known and read of all men... written not with ink, but with the Spirit of the living God; not in tables of stone, but in fleshly tables of the heart."**
**II Corinthians 3: 2-3**

Those without Christ in this world cannot understand things about God and His Word. That's why the Ethiopian eunuch, when asked if he understood what he was reading said, "How can I, except some man should guide me?" Acts 8: 30-31

The things of God are spiritually discerned and cannot be understood by those outside of Christ.

"But the natural man receiveth not the things of the Spirit of God: for they are foolishness unto him: neither can he know them, because they are spiritually discerned." I Corinthians 2:14

The unsaved gets no pleasure in reading the Bible for that reason, so God gave the world of unbelievers something that they *could* read: *Christians.* Ready or not, when you step out into the world each day in view of other people, *you are being read* or observed.

We are *living letters* and the ink never dries. There are daily additions as the Holy Spirit faithfully records in our hearts what we are, and what we are becoming in our walk with the Lord. Then He shows everybody! *Known and read of all men.*

"...for out of the abundance of the heart, the mouth speaketh..." Matthew 12:34

**We should examine ourselves each day, before others read and observe us, to see if we need anything *erased* or *added* in order that they might see Christ in us more clearly.**

"...ye are manifestly declared to be the epistle of Christ..."

Additional Treasures:    Proverbs 3:3    Romans 2:15

# February 24

**Now faith is the substance of things hoped for,**
**the evidence of things not seen.**
**Hebrews 11:1**

This is the first verse of scripture that ever lodged in my heart. It didn't mean anything to me at the time, but I did remember it. Many years later, after I was saved, I understood a little of the depth of that verse.

When you have faith, you *believe* God. We know of God by His written Word, but without the written Word His works and wonders in creation are evidence that *God is.*

Yet sinners cannot find Christ through the wonders of nature. They find Him through *believing*, that is, putting their faith in what God says in His Word. Once that faith is established in the heart, everything about the things of God begins to make sense.

**"Faith is the substance of things hoped for..."**
**Substance** - the real meaning: to stand under, to support, something that subsists by itself. So faith is the real meaning of our hope and assurance of heaven. It *stands under and supports that hope...*without needing any help.

**"The evidence of things not seen..."**
**Evidence** - whatever makes clear the truth: an indication, or sign. Or you may say it simply means *conviction.* Faith is the conviction in the believer's heart that the things of God are true.

Faith is to a Christian what a foundation is to a house; it gives confidence and assurance that he will stand. Faith enables us to stand in this present evil world.

**Faith is the <u>sixth</u> sense for Christians. We just know some things in our hearts, supported by the facts of God's Word.**

Additional Treasures:   <u>Ephesians 6:14</u>   <u>Hebrews 11:6</u>

# February 25

**"Through faith we understand that the worlds were framed by the Word of God, so that things which are seen were not made of things which do appear."**
**Hebrews 11:3**

Having looked into the definition of faith so that we may relate to it, we can easily understand why so many in our world today deny the things of God, especially the creation of all things as Genesis chapter one tells us. It takes *faith* in the heart to know that it all came about just like God said.

"By the word of the Lord were the heavens made, and all the host of them by the breath of his mouth."   Psalms 33:6

For the child of God, that verse stirs a feeling of wonder in the heart because he *knows* by faith that it is a fact.

"Let all the earth fear the Lord: let all the inhabitants of the world stand in awe of him.  For he spake, and it was done; he commanded, and it stood fast."   Psalms 33:8-9.

The unbelievers have a problem with creation as the Bible describes it because they have no foundation for understanding it. *They have no faith.*

Since the things created are clearly visible, then they must concoct some theory as to how it all got here. '*A big bang perhaps?* The universe and the process of creation *suddenly* began; then things just evolved somehow...' Such ridiculous ideas are prevalent in our world today.

People who make that theory the foundation of their belief are "likened unto a foolish man which built his house upon the sand: And the rain descended, and the floods came, and the winds blew, and beat upon that house; and it fell: and great was the fall of it." Matthew 7:26-27

**We should diligently teach our children and grandchildren the facts of what God's Word says about creation. Genesis, chapter one, should be as familiar as the pledge of allegiance to the flag!**

Additional Treasures:   Psalm 104:5-6   Psalm 104:24   Psalm 102:25

# February 26

**"And God saw that the wickedness of man was great in the earth,
...And it repented the Lord that he had made man
on the earth, and it grieved him at his heart."
Genesis 6:5-6**

Did the Lord do something that He was sorry for? Did He make a mistake? Certainly not, as the scripture clearly bears it out.

"And also the Strength of Israel will not lie nor repent: for he is not a man, that he should repent." I Samuel 15:29

"God is not a man, that he should lie; neither the son of man, that he should repent: hath he said, and shall he not do it? Or hath he spoken, and shall he not make it good?" Numbers 23:19

It obviously does not mean that God made a mistake that he had to later correct. "As for God, his way is perfect; the word of the Lord is tried: he is a buckler to all them that trust in him." II Samuel 22:31

Rather, the Lord speaks in a way to accommodate our limited ability to understand God and His ways. He describes Himself as clothed with bodily members, as eyes, ears, hands, etc., yet we know that "God is a Spirit, and they that worship him must worship him in spirit and in truth." John 4:24

He speaks of Himself as waking and rising early, yet He neither slumbers nor sleeps. Psalm 78:65   Jeremiah 7:13

**When God institutes a change in His dealings with men, He describes His course of conduct as *repenting*. To repent is to *turn*.**

"We know that in the Lord's dealings with us, His grace and mercy prevail. "But where sin abounded, grace did much more abound..."
Romans 5:20

"For he knoweth our frame; he rememberth that we are dust."
Psalm 103:14

Additional Treasures:   Romans 11:32-33

# February 27

**"But seek ye first the kingdom of God, and his
righteousness; and all these things shall be added unto you."
Matthew 6:33**

Those who keep things in their lives organized do *first things first.* In
the matter of salvation it is *first the kingdom of God, and his
righteousness.* That righteousness is obtained by trusting in Jesus Christ
who died on the cross for our sins to make it possible.

"For he hath made him to be sin for us, who knew no sin; that we
might be the righteousness of God in him." II Corinthians 5:21

The *first* step a person takes to go to heaven is the step toward the
Savior, for without Him there can be no righteousness of God. Jesus
imparts, *gives to us*, that righteousness the moment that we are born
again by trusting Him as our personal Savior. Christ died for the whole
world, but the sinner must realize that it was for him personally that Jesus
died, and he must *personally* receive the gift of salvation.

**The grandstand was packed; the hometown baseball team was
playing the championship game with their rivals, who were ahead 4
to 3. In the bottom of the last inning, the home team was batting,
had 3 men on base, and the last player, *their best hitter,* came up to
bat. He hit a homerun! The crowd went wild as all four men ran
across home plate! But, the umpire was shaking his head 'NO'.
Finally, when he could be heard as the crowd quieted, he said "He is
out...he didn't touch first base."**
I was a good church member, yet without salvation, for many years.
I thought I'd made a homerun until God convicted me of my lost
condition. I had to go back and touch *first base.* That is Christ. Things
such as service, growth, and maturity can only follow *after* salvation.

If you have always had a vague, uneasy feeling about whether you
are saved, just go back and touch first base. Push your pride away, take
that first step, and then *run* back to where Christ is waiting with
outstretched arms!

**Be sure that you are saved. Nothing else really matters.**

Additional Treasures:    John 3:3-7    John 3:36    Acts 4:12

# February 28

**"And they said unto Moses, Speak thou with us and we will hear:**
**but let not God speak with us, lest we die."**
**Exodus 20:19**

The people of Israel had not seen *anything* like Sinai, quaking with thunders, lightning, smoke and the exceeding noise of a trumpet signifying the presence of the Lord on the mountain. They removed from it and stood afar off. They were afraid to be close enough to God to hear His voice for themselves. In reality they were saying, "Moses, you go hear what God has to say and come back and tell us, and we will listen. We are afraid that if He speaks to us personally we will die!"

**That attitude still prevails in many of God's people. They want the pastor to hear God and relay the message or someone else they may hear or read from, but they do not desire to spend time with God alone for themselves and hear Him *personally*. It could alter their lives! They may die--to things that keep them from being fully surrendered to God.**

A common fear among Christians is that God may require from them some hard thing if they dedicate themselves to Him. He may send them to some remote corner of the earth to be a missionary, make them stand on a busy street corner and witness while being ridiculed, or make them dress in a frumpy fashion so that everyone will laugh.

We should know where such unreasonable thoughts about the Lord come from. The devil wants us to think that God mistreats His children. We know differently. The Lord has given us a Bible full of such amazing promises such as this one from the Psalms. "Delight thyself also in the Lord; and he shall give thee the desires of thine heart." Psalm 37:4

That means if we are thrilled at the Lord's presence in our life, and spend time with him as with a best friend, there is no limit to what He will give us.

"For I know the thoughts that I think toward you, saith the Lord, thoughts of peace, and not of evil, to give you an expected end."
Jeremiah 29:11

Additional Treasures:   Ephesians 3:20   Ephesians 2:4-7

# February 29

**"For to him that is joined to all the living there is hope:
for a living dog is better than a dead lion."
Ecclesiastes 9:4**

Those who say the Bible is dry and dull have surely never given themselves to the study of it. The scriptures are the most interesting reading on earth! God says simply, "...a living dog is better than a dead lion." Why?

The dogs of Palestine were not *housedogs*. They were commonly vicious and ran in packs. Remember that they ate Jezebel as Elijah's prophecy stated in I Kings 21:23. This wicked woman worshipped Baal and had the true prophets of God killed. She had the man, Naboth, killed so her husband, King Ahab, could have his vineyard. For that, she was destined to die with an unusual judgment...to be eaten by the dogs! Jezebel is a name that is always associated with evil.

The lion has always been regarded as the noblest of beasts in history. There is no comparison to dogs and lions, yet the Bible says that *a living dog is better than a dead lion.*

The message is 'where there is life there is hope.' The living knows things the dead will know no more.

**Death is coming.** Hebrews 10:27
**Life is uncertain.** James 4:14
**It is blessed to live one's life for God's glory.** Psalm 145:9
**Opportunities end at death.** II Samuel 14:14

The living still possesses what death takes away:

**The opportunity to repent and receive God's gift of salvation.**
**Opportunity to live for Christ and honor Him in all things.**
**Opportunity to show love to others and share your faith.**

"Keep yourselves in the love of God, looking for the mercy of our Lord Jesus Christ unto eternal life." Jude 21

Additional Treasures:    Psalm 31:23    Deuteronomy 10:12

# March 1

**"Thou preparest a table before me in the presence of mine enemies: Thou anointest my head with oil; my cup runneth over."**
**Psalm 23:5**

In forty-two years as a Pastor's wife I attended scores of funerals, and this Psalm is used most to comfort families at the time of death. Not only is it used frequently for the grieving, it is also very meaningful all the time in the life of a Christian.

**God's love and care for us is demonstrated in the role of the shepherd as he tended the sheep. In the appropriate season the Shepherd anointed the sheep's heads with oil. In the summer nasal flies tormented the sheep. They buzzed around their heads and laid their eggs in the damp moisture of the sheep's nose. Later, little worm like larvae hatched out and burrowed up into the sheep's head causing misery for the animal. It is said that the sheep have literally killed themselves in butting their heads against rocks or trees trying to alleviate the torment.**
**At the outset of the season, a good shepherd treated his sheep by anointing their heads with a mixture of oil and medicine, which kept the flies from bothering the flock. They could graze in peace. Pity the sheep whose shepherd never bothered to *anoint his sheep* with the protective oil.**

Our Shepherd, the Lord Jesus Christ, has anointed us with the oil of the Holy Spirit who is our protection and comfort because He dwells *in* us.

The *flies* of sin buzz us every day, seeking to burrow into our hearts and cause trouble and torment for us. The blessed 'oil' of the Holy Spirit protects us and strengthens us when we resist the temptations the devil puts in the way.

"And I will pray the Father, and he shall give you another Comforter, that he may abide with you forever." John 14:16

"Know ye that the Lord he is God: it is he that hath made us, and not we ourselves; we are his people, and the sheep of his pasture."
Psalm 100:3

Memorize this little Psalm. It will be a treasure stored in your heart.

Additional Treasures: John 10:4,14   Ephesians 4:30

# March 2

**"Because they met you not with bread and with water
in the way, when ye came forth out of Egypt."
Deuteronomy 23:4**

The ancient people of the Ammonites and Moabites, descendants of Lot, could not enter into the congregation of the Lord until their tenth generation. *Why*? They refused to give bread and water to the weary, traveling Israelites coming out of Egypt beside their country. Also these two brother nations hired Balaam, the prophet, to put a curse on God's people. God turned that to good and the half-hearted prophet had to utter a blessing instead.

"Behold, I have received commandment to bless: and he hath blessed; and I cannot reverse it." Numbers 23:20

God names first the cruel act of refusing bread and water to Israel. The wheel of judgment would roll over them for ten generations for that heartless treatment of God's suffering people.

**In our day, we see a similar attitude of indifference to the need of those who lack the bread and water of life: the Lord Jesus Christ. Those of us who are saved often hesitate to share the good news of the gospel with those who are lost. Weary sinners are plodding through this world in our generation, hungry and thirsty for something that will satisfy the emptiness inside them. Most Christians are sitting on the well of the water of life watching them go by!**

Do you lack courage to witness for the Lord? *Prayer* will make the difference. Confess that sin of not caring for the lost. Jesus loves the whole world of sinners, should we not care for the comparatively few who will pass through our lives? With sincere prayer, we will see opportunities open up for witnessing which we never dreamed possible.

Don't be heartless and cruel by hoarding the Bread and Water to yourself, as if there were not an abundant supply for everyone. The lost will perish forever without it, and God will judge our selfish unconcern.

"I am the way, the truth, and the life…" John 14:6

Additional Treasures:   II Corinthians 4:3-4   Ephesians 3:20-21

# March 3

**"I am the vine, ye are the branches: He that abideth in me,
and I in him, the same bringeth forth much fruit:
for without me ye can do nothing."
John 15:5**

Sometimes a simple ordinary statement can impress on our hearts the most sublime truth. One night my husband invited a missionary to preach who said, "God *must* be in *his* work." That truth dawned in my understanding, and from that time made a difference in my life. Later, after teaching at a Ladies' Retreat the Lord reinforced it a bit more and showed me this solemn word from the Lord: *"for without me ye can do nothing."*

If we accomplish anything at all which honors God, it will be because we did it *with* Him and not by our own ability.
"For it is God that worketh in you both to will and to do of his good pleasure." Philippians 2:13

How can we be sure that God is in His work?

**The work is not difficult if it is God leading you in doing it.
The praise and glory will all go to God.
There will be some fruit or results from His work.**

"All thy works shall praise thee, O Lord; and thy saints shall bless thee." Psalm 145:10

### WITHOUT ME...NOTHING

**Heaps of *nothing* are piled around us.
To our shame, praise of men is such a welcomed sound
To our prideful hearts, that for a display of *nothing*,
We accept acclaim.
Lord, help me see that hoarded collection
Of doings, mine alone, for what it is:
*Nothing*...designated to be consumed.
I repent now, remembering God's warning:
*For without me, ye can do nothing.*
Edna Holmes**

Additional Treasures:   Psalm 50:23   John 12:43   I Corinthians 3:13-15

# March 4

**"Therefore shall they eat of the fruit of their own way, and
be filled with their own devices."**
**Proverbs 1:31**

There's a sowing and reaping principle active in every facet of our lives. It's the law of the harvest:

"...for whatsoever a man soweth, that shall he also reap."
Galatians 6:7

In the same verse God says, *"be not deceived..."* Don't be fooled! It will come about just like God says in His word. Sow *whatever* and you reap *whatever;* it's that simple. God said that He is not mocked. He won't be made fun of or ridiculed in the matter of this law. It is going to operate perfectly as life sets it into motion.

**As a youth on the farm, I worked *halfheartedly* when we planted the cotton crop, because I dreaded the harvest: pulling a long cotton sack between rows picking the cotton by hand. It was hard, backbreaking work. But my childish attitude didn't affect the results one bit after that seed was planted in the ground. The cotton came up *wholeheartedly* in time and produced its harvest. Wishful thinking does nothing to alter or deter the harvest of whatever is planted, whether it is literal seed or the seeds of our thoughts and actions.**

Christians may forget what they have sown, or perhaps not consider sin to be sin. While they are *eating the fruit of their own way,* they complain to God as though He has forgotten to be gracious to them.
"The foolishness of man perverteth his way: and his heart fretteth against the Lord."        Proverbs 19:3

The fruit of sin is bitter. The devices, or plans and schemes which are perpetrated by those living their own way instead of God's way, will come back and fill up their lives with misery.

*We reap what we sow...More than we sow...Later than we sow.*

Consider what you *think*, what you *speak* and what you *do* because it will most certainly come back to you, multiplied, in the law of the harvest.

Additional Treasures:   Galatians 6: 8-9   Luke 6:38   Colossians 3:25

# March 5

**"When Jesus therefore had received the vinegar, he said,
It is finished: And he bowed his head and gave up the ghost."
John 19:30**

In reading through the Bible every year, I'm always amazed when I get to the account of the building of the tabernacle in the wilderness with all its intricate detail. The law was also very complicated with its many rules and regulations, but it was absolutely necessary. The law caused men to realize they were sinners.

"Moreover the law entered, that the offence might abound. But where sin abounded, grace did much more abound..." Romans 5:20
"Therefore by the deeds of the law there shall no flesh be justified in his sight: for by the law is the knowledge of sin." Romans 3:20

**When that law entered their lives, the people not only realized that God was holy and they were sinners, but also that they *could not* keep the law perfectly no matter how hard they tried. Only one person ever kept it. That was the Lord Jesus Christ.**

"But when the fullness of time was come, God sent forth his Son, made of a woman, made under the law, To redeem them that were under the law, that we might receive the adoption of sons..." Galatians 4:4-5
"Wherefore the law was our schoolmaster to bring us to Christ, that we might be justified by faith." Galatians 3:24

Jesus fulfilled the law and paid its penalty for sin by His death on the cross: the perfect sacrifice, once and for all. *"It is finished..."*
"For Christ is the end of the law for righteousness to everyone that believeth." Romans 10:4

**Read through Exodus and Leviticus and you will come out with a greater appreciation of the grace of God. Jesus is the One to be praised!**

"Let everything that hath breath praise the Lord. Praise ye the Lord." Psalm 150:6

Additional Treasures:    Galatians 6:14    I John 5:12

# March 6

**"And the man of God said, Where fell it? And he shewed**
**him the place. And he cut down a stick, and cast it in thither;**
**And the iron did swim."**
**II Kings 6:6**

This illustrious story from the Old Testament is used in preaching about the power of God, and how it is impossible to accomplish anything for the Lord without it. Nobody can use an axe if the head is gone from the handle. That is the vital part of the tool...*the power*.

The man lost the axe-head, but he knew where he lost it so it could be retrieved. After consideration, we can usually pinpoint the place where the power of God has slipped away from us. We find ourselves *chopping* away in our Christian life, and there is no power to make anything work...*it is gone*.

*Where fell it?* We must show God the place before He retrieves His power for us. "If we confess our sins, he is faithful and just to forgive our sins, and to cleanse us from all unrighteousness." I John 1:9

**The place may be a *friendship* that was cultivated, which has affected your attitude toward the things of God.** James 4:4 Proverbs 22:24

**The place may be an *activity* that soon involved too much valuable time and attention.**
Psalm 28:3-5

**The spot may be a *misunderstanding* where you were offended or you offended another.** Ephesians 4:31-32

**The place may be a *bad attitude* that's taken root in your heart.**
Psalms 51:10
**It may be *neglect* or *indifference* settled into your life and now you skip reading the Bible, praying, and faithful attendance to the Lord's house. Psalm 85:6**

These things slip in and the power of God is soon gone, as the axe-head was flung off the handle. *Where fell it?* If you know the place, confess it to God then He can bring the power back into view in your life.

Additional Treasures:     Proverbs 28:13     Proverbs 4:23

# March 7

*"Although the fig tree shall not blossom, neither shall the fruit be in the vines; the labour of the olive shall fail, and the fields shall yield no meat; the flock shall be cut off from the fold, and there shall be no herds in the stalls: Yet I will rejoice in the Lord...."*
Habakkuk 3:17-18

The prophet, Habakkuk, paints a very dismal picture--a *'what if'* situation as a test. Everything in the picture was necessary for life and sustenance of the people. What was he going to do if everything at once went wrong? "Yet I will rejoice in the Lord, I will joy in the God of my salvation." He said in verse 19, *"The Lord God is my strength..."* And that is the secret of keeping calm in the midst of a bleak situation.

These verses may not touch us at all since we don't need figs and olives and sheep to exist. But if we transfer it to our time slot in this world, it would be a dismal picture for us too. We would say, "How are we going to survive*?"*

**There are no fruit and vegetables available in the stores, no cooking oil; the electricity is off indefinitely, the clothing industry has stopped producing; there are no dairy foods available and the garage is empty...there is no more transportation! With those circumstances, could we *rejoice* in the Lord?**

Since this present generation has known little hardship in their lives that comes close to this illustration, we can only hope that the Christians would be strong in faith in such an adversity. The only way to do that is to keep our eyes fixed on the Lord. "My heart is fixed, O God, my heart is fixed..." Psalm 57:7

A few years ago my son composed a chorus for his church with reference to this wonderful verse.

**My heart is fixed on You, My heart is fixed on you...**
**I will sing and I will praise, For my heart is fixed on you.**
Louis A. Holmes

Additional Treasures:   Psalm 123:1   Psalm 124:8   Psalm 138:7-8

# March 8

**"God is a Spirit: and they that worship him
must worship him in spirit and in truth."
John 4:24**

Were you ever talking with someone in a room where others were also conversing, and the person to whom you were speaking was obviously listening to all the other conversations as well as your own? Perhaps we all have done that at one time or another, pretending interest in a conversation when we had none.

Jesus was a *sincere* listener. He gave His whole attention to one at a time, as well as the multitudes as He preached to them. It is said that some of the Lord's greatest utterances were delivered to a congregation of one or two people!

**He told the Samaritan woman this tremendous truth.**
*God is a Spirit.* The fact that God is Spirit (not flesh as we are) and, therefore, can only be worshipped *in spirit and in truth* was one of the greatest statements ever heard by human ears, and He told it to this poor fallen woman! Only those who are in Christ, *made spiritual,* can truly worship God.

**Jesus told Nicodemus another startling truth, as this ruler of the Jews came to see Him alone at night.**
*Ye must be born again.* Nicodemus could only say in disbelief, "How can these things be?" It seems that he was born again, later, for he is named with the one who took Jesus' body down and buried it. John 19:38-39

**Jesus gives personal attention to His children individually.**

We can cast our burdens upon Him in prayer. He cares. I Peter 5:7
He loves us unconditionally.   I John 3:1
He works all things *together* for good in our lives. Romans 8:28

Jesus speaks to us personally if we read His Word with the purpose of 'hearing' what He has to say to us.  Start your day listening to His voice first.

Additional Treasures:    Colossians 1:26-27    Psalm 57:2

# March 9

**"Search the scripture; for in them ye think ye have eternal life:
And they are they which testify of me."
John 5:39**

The most profitable time we will ever spend is in the reading and study of the Word of God. It is the Word that reveals the Lord to us, increases our knowledge of Him, and thereby motivates us to prayer and consistent faithfulness. Other books about Him may be helpful in some area, but in the Bible we see Jesus and we see ourselves as in a mirror. What God's Word reveals about us is true, and He uses the same Word to correct the flaws.

The Bible won't be dull if you will just start and continue in *searching the scriptures.* It will become a vital part of your life as its truth begins to lodge permanently in your heart.

**The story is told of a young woman who was given a book which, when she read it, she found dull and uninteresting. She put it aside after reading only a few chapters.**
**A few months later she went on a cruise and met and fell in love with a young man. One day she said to him, "You know, I have a book in my library written by a man with a name just like yours." "What's the name of the book?" he said. When she told him he said, "That's not so strange. I wrote that book."**
**When she returned home she immediately located the book, dusted it off, and read it from cover to cover. She found it to be the most interesting book she ever read. What was the difference? She had met and fallen in love with the author.**

It will make our reading of the Word very interesting if we fall in love with the Author, the Lord Himself, and the benefits are more than we can imagine. Many of those benefits are listed in Psalm 119, which is like a treasure chest overflowing with gold.

**It gives insight concerning things in life. v. *130.***
**It makes you *alive* to the things of God. v. *93***
**It will keep you from sinning. v. *11***
**Great peace and a calm spirit come through the Word. v. *165***

Additional Treasures:    John 6:63    Luke 4:32

# March 10

**"For I am poor and needy, and my heart
is wounded within me."
Psalm 109:22**

We live in perilous days. Sin is rampant in the world, and in the wake of its devastation there are many wounded.

**The *lost* are mortally wounded**. They will die without Christ unless the saved reach them with the good news of salvation in Him. Sadly, the emptiness and despair in the hearts of the mortally wounded does not stir compassion in us as it should.

"I looked on my right hand, and beheld, but there was no man that would know me; refuge failed me; no man cared for my soul." Psalm 142:4

That is the silent cry of many mortally wounded...the lost sinners. The world has this generation of Christians *bound and gagged* in the matter of witnessing to the lost. Few souls are being saved today. Do we feel any grief about that fact?

**Many Christians are also wounded**. It may be unresolved conflict from the past. It's hard to function well in adult life when one is still emotionally troubled about childhood or about difficulties of any nature in the past.

Situations in life such as divorce or separations because of marital conflict have grievous consequences that sweep through the family and hurt many. There will be wounds and scars which will hinder emotional development in children, and also hinder Spiritual growth later in adulthood. God's Word is the key for resolving such conflicts. It heals and restores the soul. God made us; He can repair us when we are 'broken'.

"The Lord upholdeth all that fall, and raiseth up all those that be bowed down." Psalm 145:14

The Lord moves among the wounded, holding them in His arms and gently helping them up. Can we fathom that? *May His name be praised!*

Additional Treasures:    Psalm 23    Psalm 69:16-17

# March 11

**"He restoreth my soul: he leadeth me in the paths**
**of righteousness for his name's sake."**
**Psalm 23:3**

Christians need to be *restored* from time to time because we tend to stray from the paths of righteousness. That's why the Good Shepherd must lead us along; we are sheep.

"Know ye that the Lord he is God; it is he that hath made us, and not we ourselves; we are his people, and the sheep of his pasture." Psalm 100:3

Sheep are in danger when they wander away from the flock. They are more vulnerable to predators. God's people can slip into the habit of missing church services and become a statistic, a *'used to go to church'* person. It's so easy to become indifferent. We must keep God's exhortation fresh in our hearts.

"And let us consider one another to provoke unto love and to good works: Not forsaking the assembling of ourselves together, as the manner of some is; but exhorting one another..." Hebrews 10:24-25

A shepherd leads his sheep out to the best grass to feed so they will be healthy and content. God has given His Word to feed our hearts so that we may be strong in the Lord and have peace and joy. When we neglect it we have no defense against the devil, making it easy for him to defeat us.

Church attendance has steadily declined. Many Christians have lost their focus on the things of God, and have been led into the world. King David strayed off the path, and though God restored his soul when he repented, that sin cost him more than he could ever have imagined.

Psalm 51 was David's song of sorrow and prayer of repentance after his sin with Bathsheba. "Create in me a clean heart, O God...." V. 10.

True to His Word, God always forgives our sins when we confess and forsake them; *but He does not cancel the consequences.* We should keep that solemn fact in our minds because temptations will always be with us.

Additional Treasures:    Proverbs 3:5-6    Psalm 56:3-4

# March 12

**"I have showed you all things, how that so labouring ye ought to support the weak, and to remember the words of the Lord Jesus, how he said, It is more blessed to give than to receive."**
**Acts 20:35**

My little nephew ran out of the kitchen with a fresh baked cookie in each hand. His dad asked him for one. He looked at both cookies, took a big bite of one, and then gave *that* one to his father.

God's people will never experience the blessedness of *giving* until they actually *do* it. A devious attempt to claim this promise won't work. God reads us from the *inside* out. He looks into the depths of the heart and observes the attitudes and motives lurking there.

"Every man according as he purposeth in his heart, so let him give; not grudgingly, or of necessity; for God loveth a cheerful giver." II Cor. 9:7

When a man gives grudgingly, he takes some for himself first then gives the leftover to God. His *'tithes and offerings'* are never quite complete. He is reluctant to give the *whole* thing. He takes a big bite out of it first for himself.

In the early church, the Lord made an example of two believers who deliberately dishonored Him in such a manner. They agreed, and lied so they could keep back part of the money they had promised to God. Ananias and his wife died within three hours of each other...*in church.* Acts 5:1-11

A generous soul gives out a full measure from every area of his life, which comes back to him again. God's Word will come to pass as surely as the sun and moon function in the heavens, day and night.

"Give, and *it* shall be given unto you; good measure, pressed down, and shaken together, and running over, shall men give into your bosom. For with the same measure that ye mete withal it shall be measured to you again." Luke 6:38

The key word in that verse is 'it'. Give *it* and *it* will come back to you, not always in the same like substance, but God will give back to you abundantly.

Additional Treasures:    Proverbs 19:17    Galatians 6:10

# March 13

**"These six things doth the Lord hate: yea, seven
are an abomination unto him…"
Proverbs 6:16**

We don't have to wonder about what God hates. He made a list for us to read in His Word. He does *not* hate the souls that are guilty of these things. It's the *sin* that God hates; He will judge it wherever it makes an appearance.

An abomination is a *shamefully wicked action*--anything that arouses strong disgust--a revolting thing. That's what sin is to God. *He is Holy!*

First on the list is: **A proud look.**     Proverbs 6:17

The most devastating thing about the attitude of pride is its affect in the matter of salvation. Pride keeps people from being saved. They will not humble themselves and admit they are lost sinners in need of salvation. I remember my struggle with pride, having been a church member long before I was actually saved. It was a battle!

"Pride goeth before destruction, and an haughty spirit before a fall".
     Proverbs 16:18

Because of pride, some people will live beyond their means causing sorrow and strife in the home as they struggle under the pressures of debt.

Many couples come to the brink of divorce over credit card debt more than any other reason.  It should be thought of as a 'debt' card instead of a credit card.  It can pile up debts so quickly because it seems like 'money in hand'.

Pride causes disdain for others according to appearance or social standing.  James 2:1-4

**Pride in our hearts displeases the Lord, in fact, He hates it! We should fear to harbor the attitude of pride for God will take it out of us in one way or another. He loves us and always deals with our sins.**

"For all that is in the world, the lust of the flesh, and the lust of the eyes, and the pride of life, is not of the Father, but is of the world." I John 2:16

Additional Treasures:     Proverbs 11:2     Proverbs 13:10

# March 14

**"A proud look, a lying tongue, and hands that shed innocent blood, an heart that deviseth wicked imaginations..."**
**Proverbs 6:17-18**

We continue with the list of things that God hates. The second hated element listed is: **A lying tongue.**

It is truly an outstanding person who has it in his heart to be truthful in his words and actions. In my father's generation, a man's word was his 'bond' and most could be trusted to be truthful in all his dealings. No so today! This generation seems to regard lying as a way of life. Yet God says He hates it and will judge that abominable sin.

"Lying lips are abomination to the Lord: but they that deal truly are his delight." Proverbs 12:22

A lying tongue indicates sin in the heart. "...for out of the abundance of the heart the mouth speaketh." Matthew12:34

Lying can have many respectable guises. People may *insinuate* something is true with hints or suggestions. A look or even a shrug of the shoulders may help perpetrate a lie. Even silence sometimes is party to lying...to the hurt of others. God looks right into our hearts and sees the motive for every word we speak or agree to.

The third abomination God hates is: **Hands that shed innocent blood.**

This scripture implies *heartless cruelty*. We can't imagine the magnitude of cruelty inflicted in this generation and the innocent blood that has been shed. The world has legalized killing the unborn: the most 'heartless cruelty.'

It is a horrendous act to take another's life; yet our prisons are already full and untold numbers are awaiting trial for the act of murder. Shedding blood! We are not safe anywhere, unprotected, because of the lawlessness of the land.

We are living in the generation that definitely does not want to retain God in their knowledge. The result is unrestrained evil. Romans 1:28

How can we be happy with the wickedness of this world swirling around us? We can by "Looking unto Jesus the author and finisher of our faith" and staying focused on Him. He is certainly looking after us. Hebrews 12:2

Additional Treasures:    Romans 14:12    II Peter 3:7

# March 15

**"An heart that deviseth wicked imaginations,**
**feet that be swift in running to mischief,"**
**Proverbs 6:18**

In a further study of things God hates, we consider the *heart* and *feet.*

### A heart that deviseth wicked imaginations.

That kind of heart is fertile with evil intent and hatches out sinful schemes which cause pain and grief for others. This is the reason for the necessity of keeping, or guarding the heart with all diligence.

"Keep thy heart with all diligence; for out of it are the issues of life." Proverbs 4:23

The *'issues* of life' which come from the heart are not troubles and trials which are common in life. What comes from the heart is our *attitude* by which we deal with those things, our outlook. A well-kept heart will have the fruit of the Spirit growing in it. Love, joy, and peace etc. will present a good attitude no matter what comes. Keep your heart in good shape with the Word of God. It is desperately needed because of the nature of the human heart.

"The heart is deceitful above all things, and desperately wicked: who can know it?" Jeremiah 17:9

### Feet that be swift in running to mischief.

"Their feet run to evil, and they make haste to shed innocent blood: their thoughts are thoughts of iniquity; wasting and destruction are in their paths." Isaiah 59:7

That is business as usual for sinful man. God hates it! He gives His own children instructions by His Word how to avoid that sinful practice.

"Ponder the path of thy feet, and let all thy ways be established. Turn not to the right hand nor to the left: remove thy foot from evil." Prov. 4:26-27

Walk away from the place of temptation...*remove thy foot from evil.*
Beware of the 'respectable' sins which can be swift and deadly...
Gossip and slander have very eager feet, running to hurt someone.
A bad attitude has swift feet; how *quickly* everyone is notified!

Additional Treasures:     Proverbs 10:18     Proverbs 5:21

# March 16

**"A false witness that speaketh lies, and he that
soweth discord among brethren."
Proverbs 6:19**

God's list of things He hates continues as we come to the subject of *lying as a witness* and *sowing discord* among Christians.

### A false witness that speaketh lies.

"Thou shalt not bear false witness against thy neighbor." Exodus 20:6

This is one of the Ten Commandments. Something *false* is misleading, and in essence a *lie.* Therefore, a false witness *lies.*

God put a safeguard on the function of witnesses, especially in matters of life and death. There had to be at least two or three to condemn a person to death. "At the mouth of two witnesses, or three witnesses, shall he that is worthy of death be put to death; but at the mouth of one witness he shall not be put to death." Deuteronomy 17:6

Much strife would be avoided if every witness would be *true* in the report of things. A sensible guideline is to tell only what you have seen and know to be a fact. That means no embellishment, or making the report more "interesting" with your own slant on things.

### He that soweth discord among brethren.

"Behold, how good and how pleasant it is for brethren to dwell together in unity."     Psalm 133:1

Those who slander, gossip, or try to disrupt unity among Christians in other ways is on God's 'hate' list. Don't allow your ears to be used for garbage cans! Flee the temptation to listen to gossip or slander. Guard your ears as well as your tongue and pray fervently for your church if it comes under Satan's attack by those sowing discord. It must be the devil's favorite method to disrupt the work of the Lord. It works so well. Beware!

Additional Treasures:     Psalm 31:20     I Corinthians 1:10

# March 17

**"The heavens declare the glory of God; and the firmament
showeth his handywork.  Day unto day uttereth speech,
and night unto night showeth knowledge."
Psalm 19:1-2**

A young Christian girl when viewing the moon and stars one clear
night said of heaven, "How lovely the inside must be; the outside is so
beautiful."

The sun shining by day, the moon reflecting the sun's light at night
and the stars twinkling in the depth of space are silently *speaking* to the
inhabitants of earth: *God is!*  Only He could create the great wonders you
view in the heavens.  In every remote corner of the globe, they're
speaking.

"There is no speech nor language, where their voice is not heard."
Psalm 19:3

**Man cannot approach the sun; it is unthinkable. The moon,
being closer, has been reached and *touched* by men, that is, through
the trappings of their space suits, which have a life support system to
sustain them away from earth. They couldn't pull off their shoes and
wiggle their toes in the dirt on the moon! So in reality men were
there, but didn't literally *touch* it. They saw a dry, dusty, silent *dead*
place fit for only one thing--what God created it to do: *to reflect the
light of the sun on the earth.* The moon is our *night-light* that keeps us
from being in total darkness when the sun goes down.**

We were *"dead in trespasses and sins..."* until Jesus, the Light of
the world shined in our hearts giving us life. Now we are reflectors of the
Son!

"For ye were sometimes darkness, but now are ye light in the Lord:
walk as children of light."  Ephesians 5:8

God's glory in creation reminds us of His glorious work in
redemption. The moon is dead and dark without the sun.  Men are dead
and in darkness without the Son of God.  Be a *night-light* in this dark
world for the glory of God. Let *your* light shine.

Additional Treasures:   I Thessalonians 5:5   Matthew 5:14

# March 18

**"Glory and honor are in His presence; strength
and gladness are in his place."
I Chronicles 16:27**

Many decades ago, as new Christians, we were reluctant to let go of Sunday; we enjoyed the day so much. Often, we would meet with other young couples for a little more fellowship after church. We would gather at each other's' homes...whichever couple had the best leftovers of food to snack on. "What do you have at your place?" was the basic question.

We desperately need to meet with the Lord at His place each day. He has what we need there--*Strength and gladness!*

**Strength** - The quality or condition of being strong; power.
**Gladness** - This translates for us *joy and delight!*

God has something exceptional to offer at His place, and He waits for us to come by so that He can impart what we need for the day--strength, *spiritual power,* to be obedient to Him. Then He freely gives us *joy* and *peace* to keep our hearts *glad* all day.

**Where is it?** God's place is anywhere that you meet with Him to read His word and pray--the place where you have your "devotions."

**How long should you stay?** That's up to you and God. Even one minute to read a verse and ask God to bless your day is better than ignoring God and His place altogether.

**Why is it so important?** The Word of God is our *bread and water!* That's what the Lord serves us to keep us healthy spiritually, and full of peace and joy for our happiness. It's our *fuel* that keeps us going.

**What we profit from meeting with the Lord:**

The Word *reveals answers to our prayers.* Psalm 119:170
The Word *cleanses* us. Psalm 51:2
The Word *increases our faith.* Romans 10:17
The Word *keeps us from sinning.* Psalm 119:133

Additional Treasures:  Psalm 138:2  Psalm 42:1-2

# March 19

**"...And his name shall be called Wonderful, Counsellor,
The mighty God, The everlasting Father, The Prince of Peace."
Isaiah 9:6**

There are no words to expound the fullest meaning of these names of Christ prophetically given here in Isaiah. The great German composer, George Frederick Handel, set this verse to music in *The Messiah.* That music plays in the background of my mind whenever I read this awe-inspiring verse.

We have many *counselors* today, for our world is full of troubled people. Disregard for God is causing the whole structure of our society to crumble. Professionals may do all they can to help those who need counsel, but they have *no power* to generate healing as our Counselor, the Lord Jesus Christ.

The *privilege* of having such a Counselor as the Lord is more than we can adequately appreciate. And it cost us nothing. Jesus paid for it Himself when He died for our sins at Calvary. Wonderful benefits come with having our Lord as our personal Counselor.

**He loves us with an everlasting love.** Nothing will change it.
> "The Lord hath appeared of old unto me, saying, Yea, I have loved thee with an everlasting love: therefore with lovingkindness have I drawn thee." Jeremiah 31:3

**He can change circumstances and our own hearts.**
> "...but with God all things are possible." Matthew 19:26

**He knows and understands all about us.**
> "Thou compassest my path and my lying down, and art acquainted with all my ways. For there is not a word in my tongue, but, lo, O Lord, thou knowest it altogether." Psalm 139:3-4

"Are you weary, are you heavy-hearted? Tell it to Jesus, Tell it to Jesus;
> Are you troubled at the thought of dying? Tell it to Jesus alone."

Additional Treasures:    Matthew 11:28    Psalm 69:16-17

# March 20

**"And he carried me away in the spirit to a great and high
mountain, and shewed me that great city, the holy Jerusalem,
descending out of heaven from God."
Revelation 21:10**

For a few months I visited a terminally ill woman each week and
read the Bible to her. In the last weeks of her life her interest gravitated
to the twenty-first chapter of Revelation. She loved to imagine heaven
and the holy city coming down when all things are made new. Her eyes
would shine with delight as I read, and we would try to picture together
the beauty and reality of the place. I came away each time more focused
on the things of God.

With such a blessed future awaiting us in the end, we should keep
our priorities in order down here so that the Lord may be glorified
through our lives. The devil succeeds in keeping us befuddled and very
distracted much of the time. We must *make choices* as Mary did.

"But one thing is needful: and Mary hath chosen that good part,
which shall not be taken away from her." Luke 10:42

**Choose** to be consistent in reading and studying the Bible.
**Make it a priority** to spend time in prayer each day.
**Make it a rule**: the family faithfully attends church *every time.*
**Decide now**: be obedient to the Lord in all things.

When these things are implemented in your life, you'll have
something precious that can't be taken away from you. Jesus said that of
Mary with her choice of sitting at His feet and listening to His words.

The Bible is the source of news concerning the future. Read it to
keep focused on the big picture. *The Word is true!*

"Thy word is true from the beginning: and every one of thy righteous
judgments endureth forever." Psalm 119:160

Additional Treasures:   I Peter 3:15   Revelation 21

# March 21

**"But as he which hath called you is holy,
so be ye holy in all manner of conversation."
I Peter 1:15**

With God as our Heavenly Father, what are we supposed to be like? Here it says that we are to be holy in all manner of conversation. That is not just our 'talk' as we equate the word with verbal communication, but the archaic or Biblical meaning is *manner of living*, or behavior. That takes in everything!

Thoughts often turn into words. We must be constantly aware of how we are thinking as words and actions go hand in hand...which becomes behavior. How can we keep a holy standard as the Lord instructs us to do?

"Because it is written, be ye holy; for I am holy."      I Peter 1:16

Something happens to us when we spend time with the Lord. If we read His Word daily, we *will* pray; it will come automatically...a natural response. As God's Word becomes a part of our thinking, it will affect spiritual maturity in time. Becoming like Christ is a process because we start out as "newborn babes". Babies aren't walking and talking in a short time. They must grow to walk and talk...a process. Older godly saints will always humbly admit that they are still "learning and growing" in the things of God.

The 'knowledge of God' is a great ocean and we discover that when we begin to learn of Him. You will never know all the depths of the His Word but what little you take in day by day will amaze you with its effect on your life. The days that "start with God" are altogether different from the ones where we hit the ground running and put the Lord off because we don't have time for Him on a busy day. When we grieve Him, we are not going to have a happy day. I have had to learn that over and over.

Christ is in us, and He is our life. We have reason to *be holy* for He is with us, and *in us*. That is the greatest mystery in the entire world. He abides in His Children. Such love and grace should motivate us to live by His word of exhortation: "Be ye holy; for I am holy."

"To whom God would make known what is the riches of the glory of this mystery among the Gentiles; which is Christ in you, the hope of glory...." Colossians 1:27

Additional Treasures:     I Thessalonians 5:22     Galatians 5:22-23

# March 22

**"He that answereth a matter before he heareth it,**
**it is folly and shame unto him."**
**Proverbs 18:13**

It is hard to carry on a conversation with an individual who has the trait of answering a matter before he hears it! He interrupts the other to express his own thoughts, though he doesn't know the whole of the issue.

**This is folly** - lack of sense; unwise conduct.
**And shame** - disgrace, discredit, dishonor.

There is lack of discipline in the character of one who has not learned to control his tongue from expressing impetuous thoughts. His lack of good sense and consideration for others makes him known.

"Seest thou a man wise in his own conceit? There is more hope of a fool than of him."  Proverbs 26:12
"Woe unto them that are wise in their own eyes, and prudent in their own sight!" Isaiah 5:21

We should always listen, and then *think* before we speak. We've heard of rash advice given by older women to younger about marriage, especially if the former is embittered about the matter. Without knowing the whole of the situation the advice flows:

**"I'd leave him right now!  You should pack your bags!"**
**"Don't clean the house and do laundry; see how he likes the mess!"**
**"He's trying to make a doormat out of you!"**

It is folly and shame to sow such things in the minds of young wives who will certainly have adjustments to make in marriage as two learn and grow together. God will judge the wickedness of *sowing discord* in a marriage.

**Listen…give thought to what you hear…speak with discretion.**

Additional Treasures:   Proverbs 20:3   Proverbs 18:2

# March 23

**"Even those men that did bring up the evil report ...died by
the plague before the Lord. But Joshua...and Caleb...lived still."
Numbers 14:37-38**

The children of Israel listened to the evil report given by ten of the
twelve spies after they had searched out Canaan. God had said they could
go in and take the land, and He *knew* what was there. Two of the twelve
gave a good report, but it was rejected. The two were Caleb and Joshua.
For their obedience in following the Lord fully, they were allowed to live
and enter the land forty years later.

**But the ten men, with an evil report, set the nation of Israel back
forty years! That's how long they would wander in the wilderness
until the generation that didn't believe God, died off.**

We think of these men as brightly clothed figures being moved about
on a flannel-graph board in Sunday school, carrying a big cluster of
grapes. But these men were real people, and they are named:
Shammua, Shaphat, Caleb, Igal, Oshea, Palti, Gaddiel, Gaddi,
Ammiel, Sethur, Nahbi, and Gevel. Oshea was later called Joshua.

These men were rulers. For that reason, the people respected them.
They had seen all the miracles and wonders God had done along the way,
but these *except Joshua and Caleb,* didn't believe God could take them
into Canaan.

And they discouraged the people, causing them to disobey God. The
result of that wickedness was their death sentence. V.37

Always *encourage* others in the things of the Lord. Discouraging
words may destroy the joy and confidence others have to do something
for God.

"A man hath joy by the answer of his mouth: and a word spoken in
due season, how good is it!" Proverbs 15:23

**Be encouragers, ready to speak a good word *"in due season."***

Additional Treasures: Matthew 12:37    Matthew 17:20

# March 24

**"For this cause I bow my knees unto the Father of our Lord Jesus Christ, Of whom the whole family in heaven and earth is named."**
**Ephesians 3:14-15**

All over the world God's people are called *Christians.* They are named after Christ their Savior. The family of God is scattered around the globe. Whenever those from one country meet some from the opposite side of the earth, it is like meeting kinfolk. There is a bond between them since the Holy Spirit lives in *every* child of God.

In visiting many Mission fields with my husband, it has always been a delightful experience to meet and fellowship with women so totally opposite in their culture, yet very much the same *in Christ.*

**In Papua New Guinea, the Missionary's wife conducted classes for the women and interpreted the lessons as I taught. The women sat on the bare ground, many holding nursing babies or tending other small children, yet they were so attentive to the Word of God.**
**It was a privilege to meet my sisters in that remote corner of the earth. They carry wood on their heads, babies on their backs and live in the most primitive conditions imaginable, yet they are content as God's children--Christians! I felt as though there was a string running through all our hearts connecting us together.**

"For ye are all the children of God by faith in Christ Jesus."
Gal. 3:26

The Holy Spirit reveals Christ to believers; that's why they recognize each other wherever they meet. There is a common bond which is soon apparent, and stronger than culture and language.

Christians make up a very large family, scattered all over the earth. Our standard of conduct toward each other is given in God's Word, with our own local church being the starting place. "And be ye kind one to another, tenderhearted, forgiving one another, even as God for Christ's sake hath forgiven you." Ephesians 4:32

Additional Treasures: I John 4:10-11    I Thessalonians 5:5

# March 25

**"Therefore we ought to give the more earnest heed to the things which we have heard, lest at any time we should let them slip."**
**Hebrews 2:1**

Few things that we hear spoken make a great impression on us. It helps if we *see* as well as hear, since this television generation is visually oriented. We remember a sermon better if the preacher illustrates it in a clever way.

If we don't give *earnest heed* when we hear God's truth, it will slip away from our minds and be gone.

**Earnest** means sincerely zealous: strong and firm in purpose and serious.
**Heed** is to give careful attention to: take notice of or regard.

The devil does not want us to heed the Word of God ever. God reveals Himself to us through His Word. Satan will send distractions when a person is taking notice of a message being preached or taught. He snatches the Word out of the heart before it can lodge there.
"...then cometh the wicked one, and catcheth away that which was sown in his heart. This is he which received seed by the way side." Matt.13:19

Many people fall into the *way side* category of listeners. You might say that the Word goes in one ear and out the other before it affects the heart. This will be the case every time unless there is a deliberate purpose of heart to get something from the preaching. To give earnest heed, we need to use more than just our eyes and ears.

**Have a Bible that you can underline verses in and make notes.**
**Follow the scripture references during the message.**
**Have a little notebook or something for taking notes.**
**Listen carefully, and *write down something* that is meaningful.**

This is how I began to gain knowledge of the Word. I've maintained that habit through the years, which helps me to continue learning.

Additional Treasures:    Psalm 119:18    Titus 1:3

# March 26

**"Receive, I pray thee, the law from his mouth, and lay up his words in thine heart."**
**Job 22:22**

Before this modern era of so many conveniences, people had to lay up supplies of food for the winter. They canned food and also preserved it in other ways, storing it in their cellars and pantries. My parents also stored corn in the barn for the horses, and also for the family. Whenever we needed cornmeal someone went to the corncrib, shucked a few ears of corn, shelled the corn off, and ran it through the grinder: *fresh cornmeal!*

**Many Christians live defeated lives, because there is a famine in their hearts. They have not laid up a supply of God's Word to nourish them. That Word feeds the soul and protects the Christian from the adversary, the devil. It is the Holy Spirit's weapon. When we are tempted, He reminds us of its warnings to keep us out of trouble which sin causes. We grieve Him by having little, or none, stored in our hearts.**

"For the Word of God is quick, and powerful, and sharper than any two-edged sword, piercing even to the dividing asunder of soul and spirit, and of the joints and marrow, and is a discerner of the thoughts and intents of the heart." Hebrews 4:12

"And grieve not the Holy Spirit of God, whereby ye are sealed unto the day of redemption." Ephesians 4:30

If Job had not loved God's Word and had it stored in his heart, he could not have endured his afflictions with such faith. He clung to his faith in God while his friends offered Job discouragement instead of comfort.

"In all this Job sinned not, nor charged God foolishly." Job 1:22

Store the Word of God in your heart, for the *lean* times will come: times of disappointment, trials and problems of life. Be prepared by having a good supply of spiritual food for defense and nourishment.

Additional Treasures:    Deuteronomy 11:18    Jeremiah 15:16

# March 27

**"But sanctify the Lord God in your hearts: and be
ready always to give an answer to every man that asketh..."
I Peter 3:15**

A statement overheard was "Be sure you talk to a responsible person when you call the company..." A responsible person has qualifications:

**He has made it his business to *know* all about the company.**
**He *believes* in the company and can answer questions intelligently.**
**He *upholds* company policies and *defends* them with confidence.**
**He will *recommend a higher authority* to get a problem solved.**

How responsible are we in representing our *company,* the Lord Jesus Christ and His church? We are called *Christians* after Christ, the Head of the company.

Do we have knowledge of our company to answer inquiries should the occasion arise? Would we panic or be calm with what we know?

Do we believe with all our hearts that the Word of God is true and absolutely reliable to solve every problem of the heart?

Would we uphold the company *policy*? For example: There is only one way to be saved and that is through Jesus the Savior.

Would we heartily recommend that people come to the Lord, assure them that He loves them, and that He has the power to help?

The Lord must have a special permanent standing, *or place*, in your heart and mine, a place of honor and esteem. Only then can we be *responsible* persons in representing our Lord and His church. We will have confidence to speak up and give an answer of what we know at any time.

"Let your speech be always with grace, seasoned with salt, that ye may know how ye ought to answer every man." Colossians 4:6

Additional Treasures:    Matthew 5:16    Colossians 1:10; 18

# March 28

**"And these are the days of the years of Abraham's life
which he lived, an hundred threescore and fifteen years."
Genesis 25:7**

Abraham died in a good old age, an old man and full of years. We would say that 175 years certainly was a good old age! By Abraham's time, men had stopped living hundreds of years, such as Adam. However, the age span was very impressive.

Abraham was faithful to God and is the ancestral father of the nation of Israel, through whom Jesus came to be the Savior of the world. He is also the "father of all them that believe, though they be not circumcised; that righteousness might be imputed unto them also…" Romans 4:11.

In reading the Bible, remember that the characters were ordinary people in that day as we are today. *They were.* God worked through faithful men then just like today. Our greatest blessing is in having the written Word. By it we know that Abraham was called the Friend of God.

"…Abraham believed God, and it was imputed unto him for righteousness: and he was called the friend of God." James 2:23

**Abraham was grandfather to Esau and Jacob. They were 15 years old when Abraham died. But having him as their grandfather did not make them godly. I'm sure Abraham *instructed* them to walk with God, but Esau grew up to be flippant about the things of God: *he sold his birthright for a bowl of stew.* Jacob also used deceit to get what he wanted so was the same as a thief.** Genesis 27:19

Jacob came to be a man of faith after years of toil and disappointments as he learned the hard way that a man 'reaps what he sows'. He had bitter trials and troubles, yet God gave him twelve sons who were heads of the twelve tribes of Israel, the nation that God promised to Abraham. God patiently works His purpose and plan through those who learn obedience to Him.

In every generation ordinary people accomplish great things for God, not by accident, but by faith. They tap into God's power. Whatever you wish you could do for God is entirely possible. Try Abraham's secret, which is revealed to us in the Bible. He *believed* God and was obedient.

Additional Treasures:   Genesis 26:24   Galatians 6:7-8

# March 29

**"How forcible are right words!   But what doth your arguing reprove?"  Job 6:25**

We know that wrong words can be harmful and make a lasting impression, but we tend to forget that right words have a most unique power. They are *forcible*, that is, *powerful, forceful and potent.*

"A man hath joy by the answer of his mouth: and a word spoken in due season, how good is it!" Proverbs 15:23

**Sincere words of comfort for grieving or troubled people are *right* words, and leave a positive influence on the heart.**

Those who can most effectively offer words of comfort in afflictions have been there themselves. They have suffered and learned by experience how precious right *words* are to the ears and heart.

"Who comforteth us in all our tribulation, that we may be able to comfort them which are in any trouble, by the comfort wherewith we ourselves are comforted of God." II Corinthians 1:4

The Word of God has given me such comfort through the years. I have been amazed at its power to enlighten and help me in some difficult times and afterwards I've used what I'd learned to minister to others.

**Words of encouragement for the weary are *right* and *forcible.***

Sometimes just hearing  encouraging words such as "You can do it!"
is enough to cause a tired worker to keep on with renewed energy. It takes so little time or effort to speak a right and forcible word to someone who needs it. Watch for opportunities to spread those good kinds of words to others.

**Words of witnessing to the lost are *right* and *forcible.***

The power is in the gospel, not in the messenger who carries it. The most timid soul who speaks those *right* and *forcible* words, the gospel of Christ to a lost man, can set off an explosion of conviction in his soul! The gospel is *potent.* Speak those words to someone often. Pray for opportunities. Nothing is as satisfying to the soul as sowing the good seed of the gospel or leading a person to Christ.

Additional Treasures:   II Corinthians 1:3    Romans 1:16

# March 30

**"I stretch forth my hands unto Thee:**
**my soul thirsteth after thee, as a thirsty land. Selah."**
**Psalm 143:6**

The word 'Selah' is a musical term found seventy-one times in the Psalms. 'Selah' means *pause and calmly think of that.* Christians have many treasures in Christ which cause their hearts to rejoice. *Selah!*

I am a child of God through faith in Christ. *Selah.*
I talk to God Himself through the privilege of prayer. *Selah.*
"I can do all things through Christ, which strengtheneth me." *Selah.*

**The work of God in human hearts is the most amazing thing on earth. When we think on the wonder of knowing God in a personal way through Christ, and how that relationship changes us from the inside out, we cannot express it. The term 'Selah' seems suitable.** *Pause and calmly think of that.*

Christians also need time with the Lord each day. We are a thirsty land and need the watering of the Word to sustain spiritual growth in us. If we skip the watering for a single day, something will shrivel and die. Daily reading of the Bible is so vital for our spiritual health. Every Christian should have a plan which enables them to give undivided attention to the Lord *every* day. Some read the Bible through each year. That's my favorite plan, and I've discovered how to avoid the pitfalls which gets one off track. When I miss a day or more for some reason, I've learned not to try and catch up by reading all the back chapters. I start with whichever day it is, and continue on. That way I don't get discouraged and want to drop the schedule, and I have a specific place to start reading each day.

Prolonged neglect of God's Word will have devastating results.

**The joy of the Lord will wither away very soon.**
**The desire to pray will be dried up.**
**Eagerness to attend the house of God dies out.**
**Assurance of eternal life is affected by draught in the soul.**

We should always keep *outstretched* hands toward the Lord. To have robust spiritual health, we must not neglect Him for a single day. *Selah!*

Additional Treasures:     Psalm 42:1-2     Psalm 119:57

# March 31

**"Cursed be he that doeth the work of the Lord deceitfully,
and cursed be he that keepeth his sword from blood."
Jeremiah 48:10**

Some go through the motions of working, but are not working at all. Others may pretend to be in the fight, but never get the sword out of the sheath. Such can be a great hindrance and discouragement to others who are depending on them for assistance in the work of the Lord, and help in fighting spiritual battles that challenge Christians.

**Doing the work of the Lord deceitfully** is being *fraudulent*, or making others believe a lie about one's service. But the heart is not in it.

**Keeping the sword from blood** means that one is not going to really be involved in the good fight of faith. The Word of God, *the sword,* will stay in the sheath or lay-up unread, instead of in hand to be used in telling the gospel to the lost.

Churches struggle in this world today because we have so many *cursed* people in this generation. Worldliness has a stranglehold on Christianity; the Bible is generally ridiculed all over the world, and the standards of decency and honesty are gone. This has affected the people of God. Many have become weak, anemic Christians.

Doing the work of God deceitfully is a hypocritical pretense. We should listen to the Word and keep deceit out of our lives. If we really have no interest in being involved in reaching lost people or serving the Lord where it will take some of our precious time, it can be remedied by praying for a burden from the Lord. He can put the desire in our hearts and make us wonder why we never really cared about it before. The Lord's work is exciting! Being involved will fill the heart with joy, which will overflow when one begins to see results along the way.

"But have renounced the hidden things of dishonesty, not walking in craftiness, nor handling the word of God deceitfully; but by manifestation of the truth commending ourselves to every man's conscience in the sight of God." II Corinthians 4:2

Additional Treasures:     II Corinthians 13: 5     Ephesians 2:10

# April 1

**"For the Lord our God, he it is that brought us up
and our fathers out of the land of Egypt."
Joshua 24:17**

There's a saying passed down from long ago: "You ought to dance with the one that brought you!" The meaning has nothing at all to do with *dancing*, though it probably initially started with such an incident.

**Some country boy worked hard for money to take a girl to the dance. While there, she proceeded to dance with others while the one that brought her was left standing on the sidelines. No doubt people there shook their heads in disapproval and murmured: "You ought to dance with the one that brought you." This saying is about *gratitude, respect and loyalty.***

The children of Israel were not in Canaan very long before they forgot the Lord who had miraculously brought them to that place.
"And they forsook the Lord God of their fathers, which brought them out of the land of Egypt, and followed other gods..." Judges 2:12

It is incredible that they forgot what the God of Israel had done.

**God parted the Red Sea for Israel to pass over.**  Exodus 14:29-31
**Their clothes didn't wear out in that 40 years!**  Deut. 8:4
**God provided manna, their bread, each morning.**  Exodus 16:15
**He fought their battles for them, insuring victory.**  Deut. 20:4

They were *ungrateful, disrespectful, disloyal,* and for their wickedness they were eventually driven out and ruled by other nations.

Do we show gratitude, respect, and loyalty to the One who brought us? Jesus did what it required to deliver us from the power of sin and the devil. He died for our sins on Calvary. "In whom we have redemption through his blood, even the forgiveness of sins..." Colossians 1:14

Let us be thankful and loyal to our Blessed Savior. *He brought us!*

Additional Treasures:     Psalm 95:2     II Corinthians 9:15

# April 2

**"Because sentence against an evil work is not executed speedily, therefore the heart of the sons of men is fully set in them to do evil."**
**Ecclesiastes 8:11**

Men cannot understand the longsuffering of God. That is the '*long and patient endurance of trouble, pain, or injury*' as defined in the dictionary, but it falls far short of describing the longsuffering of our God.

"The Lord is not slack concerning his promise, as some men count slackness; but is longsuffering to us-ward, not willing that any should perish, but that all should come to repentance." II Peter 3:9

Men may assume slackness when God doesn't do something the minute they sin against Him; therefore they do not fear judgment. If God were of that nature, to immediately punish, there would be few sinners left on this earth. But God is *longsuffering* in His love and grace, waiting patiently for men to repent and be saved through Christ.
"For my name's sake will I defer mine anger, and for my praise will I refrain for thee, that I cut thee not off." Isaiah 48:9

It seems that evil is winning on this earth, but remember that God is longsuffering to all. He does not tolerate sin; He has a long waiting period before judgment. Men have ample time to repent of their sins. All sin will be judged...*all*. Let us rejoice and be thankful as Christians that our sins have already been judged in our Savior, Jesus Christ.

Nobody is getting away with anything! How ignorant and foolish men are to think that they are frustrating God and His dealing with their wicked ways.
"For He remembered that they were but flesh; a wind that passeth away, and cometh not again." Psalms 78:39

Christians are safe from God's judgment for sin, but as God's children, we are in line for chastisement when we disobey Him. Besides losing our peace of mind, sin will diminish the flow of God's blessings. Good parents do not reward misbehavior in their children, and our Heavenly Father certainly does not. Jesus said "If you love me, keep my commandments." John 14:15

Additional Treasures:    Ezekiel 18:20    Matthew 12:36

# April 3

**"Therefore whosoever heareth these sayings of mine, and doeth them, I will liken him unto a wise man, which built his house upon a rock..." Matthew 7:24**

The wise man acted in the right way with the knowledge he had of the Lord. Wisdom is the right use of knowledge. The wise man entrusted all his life and future into the Lord's keeping: *he built his house upon a rock.*

"...for they drank of that spiritual Rock that followed them: and that Rock was Christ." I Corinthians 10:4

The Lord also describes the foolish man: "And everyone that heareth these words of mine, and doeth them not, shall be likened unto a foolish man, which built his house upon the sand:
    And the rain descended, and the floods came, and the winds blew, and beat upon that house; and it fell: and great was the fall of it."    Matt. 7:26-27

**The two men built their houses in the same environment, but they chose different foundations. The *rock* represents Christ. The *sand* represents the world and its ways. The wind, rain, and floods came alike on the two houses; the one built on the rock stood, while the other fell.**

All around us we see the houses of the *foolish* crumbling in a heap on the sands of this world. We are in the world, though not of the world, and the same adversities will come to Christians as to others. The wind, rain, and floods of trouble and trials beat on the house of the Christian the same as the unsaved. It's the *foundation* that keeps him steady and safe.

Witness to others by keeping your house*, your life,* steady and firm on the foundation which is Christ. Opportunities will come to explain what makes the difference.

**Once while visiting an old veteran friend of my husband in New York, we stayed overnight with him and his wife, a stranger to us. The next morning when I came down to the kitchen, and the men were outside, she said suddenly, "So what makes you different like you are?" God had flung the door of opportunity wide open and I was able to talk to her about the Lord and His salvation.**

Additional Treasures:    Isaiah 28:16    I Timothy 6:19

# April 4

**"I say unto you, Though he will not rise and give him, because he is his friend, yet because of his importunity he will rise and give him as many as he needeth."**
**Luke 11:8**

Jesus is teaching about prayer, and He stressed the importance of being persistent. The man who came to get bread from his friend at midnight wouldn't have been successful without importunity. *Importunity* means persistency in asking.

"And I say unto you, Ask, and it shall be given you; seek and ye shall find; knock, and it shall be opened to you." Luke 11:9

Only one thing will hinder our prayers and that is sin in the heart.

"If I regard iniquity in my heart, the Lord will not hear me." Psalm 66:18

A Christian cannot pray effectively when he has sin in his heart. It is wise when you go to your special place each day to meet with the Lord, to pray "Create in me a clean heart, O God; and renew a right spirit within me." Psalm 51:10

Even the thought of foolishness is sin, so it is impossible for us to go any length of time without need of cleansing. Remember that we come before our Heavenly Father, holy beyond our imagination, to talk to Him about the things on our hearts. The presence of Jesus is the key to our success in prayer, for He makes intercession for us.

"And whatsoever ye shall ask in my name, that will I do, that the Father may be glorified in the Son. If ye ask anything in my name, I will do it." John 14:13-14

**Persistence is continuing on, whether results are visible or not. Some have prayed for loved ones to be saved for decades...and finally saw the miracle! Pray faithfully, pray fervently, and pray persistently.**

I am the heartbeat of success; I dictate which man wins,
I overpower all reasoning; I outlast to the end.
I don't burn in the furnace, And I do not wear away.
The essence of achievement, Persistence always pays!
From: Persistence, by John A. Holt

Additional Treasures:     I Chronicles 16:11     Luke 18:1

# April 5

**"Forasmuch as ye know that ye were not redeemed with
Corruptible things, as silver and gold..."
I Peter 1:18**

God emphasizes the tremendous cost the Lord paid for the redeemed. It was not with things the world would count as valuable.

"But with the precious blood of Christ, as of a lamb without blemish and without spot:" I Peter 1:19

Since we have been purchased at such a cost to Christ our Savior, we should freely surrender ourselves to Him and not hold back any part of our lives.

"For ye are bought with a price: therefore glorify God in your body, and in your spirit, which are God's." I Corinthians 6:20

Most Christians do not let go of their lives but give God a token part, ignoring the claim He has on the *total* purchase.

**Picture an exclusive department store full of very valuable, expensive merchandise. There was something you wanted very much and you saved money diligently, and finally had enough to purchase the special item you longed for. You go in and buy it, *cash money*; it is wrapped nicely and put into your hands. However, to your great surprise the saleslady holds on to the package...you pull and she hangs on! You drag her to the front door, her feet sliding on the floor holding on to your package. You yell at this person, "Let go! I bought and paid for this, what is your problem?"**
**The manager comes and pries her fingers loose, and holds her while you run out the door with your treasure! You would *never* go back in that place to purchase anything again. --*E.H.***

Only God has the means to purchase the precious souls of men. He redeemed us at a great cost--*the death of Christ, His Son.*

Are we clinging to our lives to keep Him from having control of His purchase? He *will* pry our fingers loose and claim His property.

Have you surrendered yourself to the Lord, holding nothing back?

Additional Treasures:   I Peter 1:23    Exodus 19:5

# April 6

"That the trial of your faith...more precious than of gold that perisheth, though it be tried with fire, might be found unto praise and honour and glory at the appearing of Jesus Christ."
I Peter 1:7

Christians do not enjoy having their faith tested, but the trial of faith is more precious than gold.

When we come through tests with our faith intact and stronger, it brings glory to God. We know how we are doing in our spiritual growth when we are tested frequently.

God does not need the information from any test because He already knows what we will do or not do in any circumstance of life. The testing is for our own benefit, so we will know where adjustments need to be made to keep our lives on track for the Lord.

**Once I walked upon a scene where it was apparent that many people had just been given a test in patience and failed. It was at a produce area in the grocery store. Evidently, the plastic bags would not come open with ever so much pulling, tugging, stretching, ripping, and probably some chewing with the teeth. Bags were flung everywhere! If frustration could be measured, I'm sure it would have been knee-deep. But in the midst of the chaos one lady remained, patiently poking at the end of a plastic bag with her fingernail, finally pulling it open. She's the only one that passed the test.**

Remember that longsuffering is *patience.* Our patience is frequently tested, but God is on our side in all our trials and testing.

"Knowing this, that the trying of your faith worketh patience."
James 1:3

"There hath no temptation taken you but such as is common to man: but God is faithful, who will not suffer you to be tempted above that ye are able; but will with the temptation also make a way to escape, that ye may be able to bear it." I Corinthians 10:13

Additional Treasures: Hebrews 2:18 James 1:12

# April 7

**"These were more noble than those in Thessalonica, in that they received the word with all readiness of mind, and searched the Scriptures daily, whether those things were so."**
**Acts 17:11**

These Christians in Berea were nobler than the others because they searched the Scriptures daily. They desired to see the words of truth with their own eyes, *whether those things were so.*

We can be noble which is having *good character* and *greatness of mind* by doing the same as the Bereans: search the scriptures daily discovering what precious things the Lord has for us in His Word. It will make us more faithful to God from our thoughts to our deeds.

Job was the highest example of dedication and devotion to God in his day, and the scriptures tell us what Job said during the awful trial that engulfed his life.
"Neither have I gone back from the commandment of his lips; I have esteemed the words of his mouth more than my necessary food..."
Job 23:12

Job esteemed, *highly regarded,* the Word of God and kept it faithfully. It made Job be more than a noble man. His character, even in this present time is impeccable. The Word gives us a description of such a godly man.
But his delight is in the law of the LORD; and in his law doth he meditate day and night.      Psalm 1:2

**The first apparent change in me after I was saved was a desire to read the Bible, and really know what it said about God and everything. As an unsaved church member, I did read it, but it meant little. It was only words and verses I used at times. The difference could compare to reading another's letter of no interest to me, and then reading my own letter from a loved one.**

**I eagerly learned the books of the Bible, writing them in order, learning to spell and later memorizing them. It was a whole new thing being 'in Christ' instead of just near, but not knowing Him. That was fifty years ago, and I still haven't gotten over the wonder of becoming a child of God.**

Additional Treasures:    Psalm 119:97    Jeremiah 15:16

# April 8

**"He that hath no rule over his own spirit is like a city
that is broken down, and without walls."
Proverbs 25:18**

A city broken down without walls was defenseless. People in such a city were easy prey without the protection which the walls afforded.

The Word tells us that "he that has no rule over his own spirit" is just like that city--*easy prey.* The devil can use the least little thing to trigger the reaction of one with no self-control.

### His temper can be set off, and anger flares up unchecked.
"He that is soon angry dealeth foolishly…" Proverbs 14:17
Anger can cause a man to make a fool of himself very quickly, and the impression on others will last a lifetime! Once he gets a reputation of one with a nasty temper, it will never go away. And the Bible has a strong warning in regard to angry people. "Make no friendship with an angry man; and with a furious man thou shalt not go." Proverbs 22:24

### The untamed tongue is set to wagging with a subtle coaxing.
"If any man offend not in word, the same is a perfect man, and able also to bridle the whole body." James 3:2
If you control your tongue, you have mastered the utmost in self-control.
Verbal expression gets people into more trouble than anything else.

### Jealousy is unleashed with a slight provocation.
"For jealousy is the rage of a man....." Proverbs 6:34
When this *green monster* springs into action it makes so much misery for others in its wake. It is defined as 'resentfully envious' as well as suspicious of another. It is a most miserable trait in persons, and is sure to cause others to avoid their friendship. Marriages have been destroyed, homes broken up and little children devastated by jealousy. May God give us the desire to keep our hearts with all diligence. If we plant the fruit of the Spirit and tend it daily by the Word of God and prayer, we won't have the ugliness of jealousy affecting our lives. God's Word is like a wall that protects!

Don't be easy prey for the devil because of lack of discipline and control. We must remember where our strength and protection comes from.
Additional Treasures:     Ephesians 3:16     Psalm 28:7

# April 9

**"The entrance of thy words giveth light; it giveth understanding unto the simple."**
**Psalm 119:130**

When a darkened room is suddenly opened to the sunlight, one can see hidden dust and dirt and the need for cleaning. I wonder if that's the way spring-cleaning originated, when people opened up doors and windows of their houses after winter, so the fresh air and sunlight could flood in and freshen the place.

**Spring-cleaning did become a practice, and long ago that meant a thorough operation. My great-grandmother used to put fresh straw in the mattresses. The countrywomen of that generation also diligently saved the goose down from their geese to make feather beds to lay on top of the straw mattresses. It took a lot of work to freshen up things in those days.**

We should give our hearts a spring-cleaning often with the Word of God. The scripture is the light that reveals every nook and corner of our hearts and reveals what has lodged there at times when we let down our guard.

"For the commandment  is a lamp; and  the law is light; and reproofs of
instruction are the way of life..." Proverbs 6:23

Jesus told us what sin would do if we tolerate it. If the *light* in us becomes darkness, how great is that darkness! Nothing is more pitiful than a Christian whose light has become obscured by sin. So many stumble in that darkness, it is described by the Lord as *great* or intense. The devil is constantly tempting Christians to wander out into sin so that glorious light of the gospel in them can be at least diminished, if not hidden from view. He hates it so!

"The light of the body is the eye: if therefore thine eye be single, thy whole body shall be full of light.  But if thine eye be evil, thy whole body shall be full of darkness.  If therefore the light that is in thee be darkness, how great is that darkness!" Matthew 6:22-23

Set aside a day this spring to check on the condition of your heart, with the Bible in your hands.  Clean out any clutter of sin.

Additional Treasures:     John 3:19     I Thessalonians 5:4

# April 10

**"But if thine eye be evil, thy whole body shall be full of darkness. If therefore the light that is in thee be darkness, how great is that darkness!"**
**Matthew 6:23**

Before Jesus uttered these words, He had already said that the light of the body is the eye. We understand that one who is physically blind lives in darkness because he can't see. Sin can cause a Christian to become *spiritually* blinded in part and be engulfed in a peculiar kind of darkness. His eye is evil, affected by sin. Things of the Lord are not seen and understood as before sin entered into the life.

Remember that the *unsaved* are not just spiritually blind, but dead in trespasses and sins; the darkness is not less or greater, it is *total* darkness for the lost.

Darkness of sin in a Christian's heart will cause others to stumble. It is important to let the light of God's Word in when one begins to see things with an indifferent attitude. Sin has crept in and impaired the spiritual vision.

**Begin with prayer.**

"Search me, O God, and know my heart: try me, and know my thoughts." Psalm 139:23

**Get a *spiritual* bath.**

As a young child I helped do the family washing on the rub-board. That was our *washing machine!* It was hard on knuckles, arms, and the back but it got the clothes clean. I think of this 'thorough washing' as somewhat like the rub-board affect. Jesus has done all the hard work; all we do is accept what He did and confess and repent of our sins.

"Wash me thoroughly from mine iniquity, and cleanse me from my sin." Psalm 51:2

**Get rid of heart clutter and use time wisely.**

"Let all bitterness, and wrath, and anger, and clamour, and evil speaking, be put away from you, with all malice..." Ephesians 4:31

Joy and peace is crowded out of the heart with these poisonous things. Confess and forsake them to restore your heart to a happy state.

"See then that ye walk circumspectly, not as fools, but as wise, redeeming the time, because the days are evil." Ephesians 5:15-16

Additional Treasures:    Psalm 90:12    Colossians 4:5

# April 11

**"And I have led you forty years in the wilderness: your clothes are not waxen old upon you, and thy shoe is not waxen old upon thy foot."**
**Deuteronomy 29:5**

Imagine wearing the same outfit for forty years, and it stays like new in appearance. The shoes remained 'new' on their feet. What a miracle, seeing that they *walked* in those shoes for forty years!

**We would be appalled if God suggested that we wear the *same* clothes and shoes forty years. A great deal of our lives is taken up with the matter of what to wear and how to get more, though the closets may be stuffed full. We have outfits for every occasion and don't want to be seen wearing the same thing too often.**

The Lord *proved* He could take care of the needs of His people on their journey to the Promised Land of Canaan. We have a record of that proof to support our faith in this present time as we journey through this world on our way to heaven. The precious blood of Christ, God's Son, has redeemed us. Our Heavenly Father will take care of us in every way.

"Therefore I say unto you, Take no thought for your life, what ye shall eat, or what ye shall drink; nor yet for your body, what ye shall put on. Is not the life more than meat, and the body than raiment?"
Matthew 6:25

As simple as it is, this verse still washes right over our hearts without making a lasting impression. We are not to be anxious and fretful about clothes and food. Jesus is saying to us *"don't fret about those things; you will have them as you need them."*

Halfway through forty years, the Israelites had no doubt stopped worrying about food and clothing. They *knew* God would provide for them.

As we mature in the study of God's Word, we will stop fretting about many things of life that tend to trouble us. *"Tis so sweet to trust in Jesus."*

Additional Treasures:    Ecclesiastes 12:13    Matthew 6:28-31

# April 12

**"All that the Father giveth me shall come to me; and
him that cometh to me I will in no wise cast out."
John 6:37**

People may be fearful about whether or not they were really saved
when they came to Jesus. The Lord said if you come, He will not turn
you away! That is a promise that has comforted many fearful souls.

**Salvation is so simple because Jesus made it so. But it is not to
be taken lightly. Jesus paid dearly for everyone who calls upon His
name. He can take away the darkness from a heart and fill it with
light because His blood has the power to remove that blackness of
sin.**

Many years ago there was an older couple in our church who went to
sales and auctions regularly and often found unexpected treasures at flea
markets. They came by our house one day and handed us a brown paper
sack and said, "We were told this was good stuff but we don't want to
bother with it; you may keep it if you like, or just throw it away."

I looked in the sack, and decided I'd throw it out later since it
contained a large jumble of knives, forks and spoons all very severely
blackened with tarnish. There was nothing about the looks of it that
indicated it had any worth at all.

But one evening, we decided to clean a piece of it to see what it
looked like. We were very surprised! It turned out to be a classic set of
*real* silverware, and after being polished, it was so beautiful we decided
to keep it. With all the tarnish on it we could not see anything but trash;
with the black removed, it would grace the loveliest of dining tables.

When a sinner comes to Jesus, the Lord removes the blackness of sin
from his spirit and soul and makes him new.

"Therefore if any man be in Christ, he is a new creature: old things
are passed away; behold, all things are become new." II Corinthians 5:17

Stay *clean and polished* by reading and listening to the Word of
God. It has power to restore us and keep us fit for service.

Additional Treasures:     Acts 3:19     Psalm 51:10

# April 13

**"For she said, If I may touch but his clothes I shall be whole."**
**Mark 5:28**

This timid frightened woman had faith, *sincere belief,* that Jesus could heal her even if He didn't see her! She meant to press forward through the crowd and touch His garment without anyone knowing. When she did, the power of healing from the Lord immediately surged through her body, and Jesus knew that someone had touched Him by faith.

"And He looked round about to see her that had done this thing." v.32

Jesus already knew her, but she needed to see His face and confess her faith in Him and to hear the Lord's voice speaking directly to her.

"But the woman fearing and trembling, knowing what was done in her, came and fell down before him, and told him all the truth.
And he said unto her, Daughter, thy faith hath made thee whole; go in peace, and be whole of thy plague." Mark 5:33-34

**Virtue is moral excellence, the power to produce effects.**
Such was the virtue of Jesus; He could heal all that came to Him.
"And the whole multitude sought to touch him: for there went virtue out of him, and healed them all." Luke 6:19

**Faith *always* brings results, even very little faith.**
"...for verily I say unto you, If ye have faith as a grain of mustard seed, ye shall say unto this mountain, Remove hence to yonder place; and it shall remove; and nothing shall be impossible unto you. *"* Matthew 17:20

**God's Word is the foundation of strong faith.**
We may approach the Lord with confidence because He always honors our faith. Believe what He says, and that will delight Him.
Use the scriptures when you pray. I often use Psalm 31:19 as I pray daily for our children and their families. They do "fear the Lord, and trust in Him before the sons of men." Therefore there is *goodness* laid up for them according to what God says. I claim that promise. Choose your own from God's rich store and let its power work for you in prayer.

Additional Treasures:    Romans 10:17    Mark 9:23

# April 14

**"So likewise, whosoever he be of you that forsaketh not
all he hath, he cannot be my disciple."**
**Luke 14:33**

The most common name for the followers of Jesus is *disciples.* The
Lord makes a distinction between salvation and discipleship.

**Salvation:** believing on the Lord Jesus Christ. It is a 'new birth'
which makes one a member of God's family, and the beginning of a
whole new life.

**Discipleship:** Christians following Jesus to learn of Him and serve
Him.

"Then said Jesus to those Jews which believed on him, If ye
continue in my word, then are ye my disciples indeed..." John 8:31

Continuing in God's Word is the prerequisite of being a disciple.
The Word causes spiritual growth and maturity which makes a believer
strong and desirous to be a disciple indeed, consistently following the
Lord.

A Christian cannot travel two roads at the same time. That's where
*forsaketh all* comes into focus. If we follow the Lord in a dedicated life
we *must* get off the other road! A definite choice has to be made.

"And whosoever doth not bear his cross, and come after me, cannot
be my disciple." Luke 14:27

**Make Bible reading a priority in your life.** It won't happen by
itself. You must set a time to be with the Lord and read His word or there
will be too many other things which will demand time and attention and
crowd it out.

**Obey the Word when you *'get it'* or understand it.** When it has
enlightened you mind, then use it. Store it in your heart to refer to often.
Tell someone what wonderful thing you have learned from God's Word.

**Talk to God every day in sincere prayer.** Many Christians really
don't know how to pray. They can talk to others, but cannot talk to God.
A simple method of prayer is to pray as you read the Bible. Great men
of faith have used this method. Open your Bible and start reading.
Something will come to mind you need to talk to God about as you read
along. Stop, and pray. Then continue reading etc. That is conversation
on the highest level. God is speaking to you and you are prompted to
speak to Him. What a privilege!

Additional Treasures:     Luke 18:29-30     Philippians 3:8

# April 15

**"The kings of the earth, and all the inhabitants of the world,
would not have believed that the adversary and the enemy
should have entered into the gates of Jerusalem."
Lamentations 4:12**

The entire known world at that time had heard of the nation of Israel,
and of Israel's God. They heard how He made a path through the Red
Sea for them to pass over, and how He fought for Israel. God had put the
fear of Israel in the hearts of all other nations. But when the people
forsook the Lord and turned to idols, Israel became as vulnerable and
weak as one of the lesser nations of the world. Sin *always* deletes the
good from our lives and replaces it with the bad. That includes secret sins
we may have hidden in our hearts.

The nations of the world were astonished when God's people lost it
all after possessing power and prestige for generations. And nobody
came to the rescue!

"As for us, our eyes as yet failed for our vain help: in our watching
we have watched for a nation that could not save us. They hunt our steps,
that we cannot go in our streets: our end is near, our days are fulfilled; for
our end is come." Lamentations 4:17-18

God had warned Israel when He brought them into the Promised
Land not to forsake Him and turn to the idols and the ways of the people
of Canaan. They promised, but did not keep their word. They prayed, but
it was too late.

"Turn thou us unto thee, O Lord, and we shall be turned; renew our
days as of old. But thou hast utterly rejected us; thou art very wroth
against us." Lamentations 5:21-22

Christians cannot flirt with sin and come away unharmed. The devil
makes it appear harmless while he slips the chains and shackles around
them. Then they start paying the price that sin costs. The greatest mistake
is when people think that they will be the exception to the rule. When
God says something, it will be exactly as He says. He will not be
'mocked' as one who is powerless to perform his word. So His warning
is *don't be deceived!*

"Be not deceived; God is not mocked: for whatsoever a man
soweth, that shall he also reap." Galatians 6:7

Additional Treasures:    Deuteronomy 28:67    I Thessalonians 5:22

# April 16

"When they were filled, he said unto his disciples,
gather up the fragments that remain, that nothing be lost."
John 6:12

The feeding of the multitudes is recorded in all four gospels: Matthew, Mark, Luke and John. There are things to learn from this miracle of the Lord, such as give what you have to the Lord and let Him do something tremendous with it as the little lad who gave up his lunch, which was used by the Lord to feed five thousand!

It matters to the Lord what we do with the little bits and pieces of our lives. Nothing of us should be wasted: our time, talent, and various skills which we possess. The leftovers were precious to the Lord. The people would have left them scattered on the ground. Let us not waste one little thing of our lives, but use all for the glory of God.

### FRAGMENTS THAT REMAIN

Fragments, that's all I received that night,
Words that pierced with deadly aim.
They lodged in my heart with purpose.
I was saved because fragments remained.

There are countless sermons
I've heard with dutiful heart.
They left nuggets of truth in the washing,
The fragments becoming my part.

Fellowship sweet with God's children,
Refreshing as needed rain,
Sweet memories lingering sustain me...
Those fragments that remain.

They are the gracious bounty of God...
Gathered up for spiritual gain,
For we really can't contain the whole,
Only the fragments that remain.

Edna Holmes

Additional Treasures:    John 6:13    Mark 6: 41-44

# April 17

**"And all these blessings shall come on thee, and overtake thee,
if thou shalt hearken unto the voice of the Lord thy God."
Deuteronomy 28:2**

The blessings of God are literally pursuing His children, and in accordance with their obedience to Him can easily overtake them. Then the blessings become their own possession. Sin, *disobedience*, gives speed to the child of God if he wanders off the path of righteousness. Therefore blessings cannot overtake him.

Jonah hurriedly arranged things to get away from God's plan. Every little detail fell into place for this stubborn preacher who did not want to go preach in the city of Nineveh as God had said.

**The ship was right there ready to sail.
Jonah had money to pay the fare.
The ship was going in the opposite direction from Nineveh!**

Things often seem to go smoothly in the way of disobedience, and that always disarms the Christian. He may think he is being blessed in the way he is going away from God's will, when he is really being set up by the devil for trouble and sorrow. Because the Lord is longsuffering and does not always punish sin immediately, the saved and unsaved alike forget that God is holy and He *will* judge wickedness, especially in His children.

"Because sentence against an evil work is not executed speedily, therefore the heart of the sons of men is fully set in them to do evil."
Ecclesiastes 8:11

Jonah spent three days and nights in a whale's belly with seaweed wrapped around his head *before* his stubborn will surrendered. He had to repent of his sin and get back to obedience to God. You'd think that he would have repented by the time he hit the water and was swallowed. But he endured three days in a whale's belly before being willing to obey God. Keep a clear mind and heart in tune with God's Word, and the blessings will catch you!

*Obedience* **gives speed to blessings that overtakes the Christian.**
*Disobedience* **will hinder the blessings, or stop them altogether.**

Additional Treasures:    Jonah 2:1-10    Psalm 68:19

# April 18

**"Therefore shall they eat of the fruit of their own way,
and be filled with their own devices."
Proverbs 1:31**

People who will have no part of God and His salvation shall indeed eat of the fruit of their own way, and it is a sorrowful way.

"Even as I have seen, they that plough iniquity, and sow wickedness reap the same." Job 4:8

"In the day shalt thou make thy plant to grow, and in the morning shalt thou make thy seed to flourish: but the harvest shall be a heap in the day of grief and of desperate sorrow." Isaiah 17:11

Life may appear to be going well, but when the harvest comes in it will show the desperate foolishness of ignoring God and His salvation. Then the unsaved will realize that *their own way* was their undoing.

"Fools, because of their transgression, and because of their iniquities, are afflicted." Psalm 107:17

"Good understanding giveth favor: but the way of transgressors is hard." Proverbs 13:15

Those who have believed on Christ have a different kind of fruit to enjoy because of the Holy Spirit of God that dwells within the innermost being of every Christian. *He* produces fruit that enriches the life and gives a bountiful harvest of blessings.

"But the fruit of the Spirit is love, joy, peace, longsuffering, gentleness, goodness, faith, Meekness, temperance: against such there is no law." Galatians 5:22-23

The Lord gives us instructions to keep our hearts with all diligence. The reason is to have good soil for the Holy Spirit to produce His fruit in us for our own blessing and to attract others to the Savior. There will be some impressed by love, joy, and peace flourishing in a Christian's life. By that souls may be rescued from the fruit *of their own way* and brought to salvation. You may not be able to speak the words to witness to a lost sinner, but you can keep your heart free from weeds of sin which hinders good fruit from growing. God's Word will do that for you. It is the only tool. Don't neglect it. All we can do is to *display* the fruit; the Holy Spirit alone produces it in us.

Additional Treasures:     Isaiah 3:10     Proverbs 4:23

# April 19

**"But the fruit of the Spirit is love…"**
**Galatians 5:22**

God names *love* first of the fruit the Holy Spirit produces in the Christian. He gives a description we can read in the 'love' chapter:    I Corinthians 13.

**Love suffereth long**. Love understands and will wait.

**And is kind**: looks for a way of being constructive.

**Envieth not**: does not feel discontent at others' good fortune.

**Vaunteth not itself** - it is not haughty or boastful..

**Not puffed up** with pride or anger.

**Doth not behave itself unseemly**: always exhibits good manners.

**Seeketh not her own**: does not demand her own way or rights.

**Is not easily provoked**: is not touchy, fretful or resentful.

**Thinketh no evil**: does not keep account of offenses.

**Rejoiceth not in iniquity**: is not glad over others' misfortunes.

**Rejoiceth in the truth**: love is glad when goodness triumphs.

**Beareth all** things: strong in faith enduring all things with patience.

**Believeth all things**: love is always ready to believe the best.

**Hopeth all things**: love is optomistic.

**Endureth all things**: love remains under the load: love is strong.

**Love never faileth**: everything else will fail, but love never will.

This amazing fruit can freely grow and flourish in any Christian who will keep his heart fit for its cultivation. We cannot produce this fruit on our own no matter how hard we try to emulate it. We can only yield ourselves to God who is able to develop these traits in us.  It is called *spiritual growth* and it is a process which should be going on constantly in each one of us.

**Keep your heart *with all diligence* and allow love to grow there.**

Additional Treasures:    John 3:16    I John 3:1-2

# April 20

**"But the fruit of the Spirit is love, joy, peace, longsuffering, gentleness, goodness, faith, Meekness, temperance..."**
**Galatians 5:22-23**

The characteristics of the fruit of the Spirit are combined with love. Only God Himself can produce such a harvest in the lives of His children. He is patient and persistent in the production, and this process in us is called *spiritual growth.*

These qualities are being developed in those who have been saved:

**Joy** is that inward peace and sufficiency that is not affected by outward circumstances. It comes from the presence of God.
"... in thy presence is fulness of joy..."   Psalm 16:11
**Peace** is produced by love and joy together: *peace,* the peace of God "which passeth all understanding."   Philippians 4:7
**Longsuffering** is patient endurance of trouble, pain or injury. The Lord is longsuffering with everyone. He waits long before judgment because of this lovely part of His character.
**Gentleness** is exhibited as *kindliness* in the character.   God's gentleness made King David great.   Psalm 18:35
**Goodness** is love in action.
"...the earth is full of the goodness of God."   Psalms 33:5
**Faith** perceives as true and real, simply believing God!
   Hebrews 11:1
**Meekness** - Having a mild, patient disposition--not easily angered.
**Temperance** - Self-control, self-restraint.  Proverbs 25:28

Warning! The devil produces the works of the flesh.

There are other things which spring up in the absence of the fruit of the Spirit. It is the 'works of the flesh' and they sound like something out of a horror story.  "Now the works of the flesh are manifest, which are these; Adultery, fornication, uncleanness, lasciviousness, Idolatry, witchcraft, hatred, variance, emulations, wrath, strife, seditions, heresies, Envyings, murders, drunkenness, revellings, and such like..." Galatians 5:19-21
**Listed above are seventeen good reasons to prayerfully take up God's Word each day and yield our hearts for Him to develop His fruit in us.**

Additional Treasures:   Ephesians 2:10   Philippians 1:11

# April 21

**"And he said also unto his disciples,
There was a certain rich man, which had a steward..."
Luke 16:1**

A steward was someone who managed another's wealth. The most important thing was that he served his master faithfully.
"Moreover it is required in stewards, that a man be found faithful."
I Corinthians 4:2

The steward had to remember the riches he oversees belonged to his master, not to him, and must be managed in a way to please and profit the owner. This steward of whom Jesus spoke had forgotten this and began to act like the estate was his own; he began to spend foolishly and wasted his master's wealth. We would judge this steward harshly and rightly so, yet God has made each of His children a steward. He has entrusted us with valuable things to oversee and use for a profit for our Heavenly Father.

**We are stewards of time.**
"See then that ye walk circumspectly, not as fools, but as wise, redeeming the time, because the days are evil." Ephesians 5:15-16
The phrase *redeeming the time* means buying up the opportunity.

**We are stewards of gifts and abilities.**
"As every man hath received the gift, even so minister the same one to another, as good stewards of the manifold grace of God." I Peter 4:10

When we started in the pastorate decades ago, we had many new Christians who were excited about doing something for the Lord. One lady decided she would get a small organ for the church and learn to play it herself, so we could have organ music with the piano. It was a labor of love for this woman had no musical talent to help her. She strictly learned by rote, just tirelessly practiced until she could follow the music and use the foot pedals right. She wrote chords on all the pages of her hymnbook so she could follow. She was willing to serve beyond her ability, and God honored her desire.

If we make ourselves available to God and stay 'prayed up' it will be amazing how opportunities open up for us to do something for the Lord. We all have something that is uniquely ours that God can use.

Additional Treasures:   I Corinthians 3:13-15

# April 22

**"Let your speech be always with grace, seasoned with salt,
that ye may know how ye ought to answer every man."
Colossians 4:6**

We all wish to say the right thing whenever something needs to be said. How many times have we felt frustrated because we couldn't come up with that perfect answer at the time we needed it so much?

Fortunately, we do have access to the source that does have the right answers for everything. The Word stored in our hearts prepares us for every situation; we may converse intelligently in a way that honors God, and at the same time answer questions that others may pose to us. There are some good guidelines to follow.

### Keep sins confessed *up to date.*
"If we confess our sins, he is faithful and just to forgive us our sins, and to cleanse us from all unrighteousness." I John 1:9
We need a good conscience to think clearly and make right decisions in the matters of life. Sin is a stumbling block, and we must daily open our hearts and allow God to clear out the sin that creeps in, which hinders our ability to think and act in a God-honoring way.

### Read the Word of God daily to learn and grow.
"But grow in grace, and in the knowledge of our Lord and Saviour Jesus Christ…" II Peter 3:18
We will *not* grow apart from the Word. It is our link to spiritual health and well-being. The Scriptures have the answers and impart to us the needed wisdom and attitudes to answer any challenge.

### Pray without ceasing.  I Thessalonians 5:17
When prayer becomes vital for you to start the day, the quality of *praying without ceasing* will follow as communication with the Lord has been opened and established. I used to wonder how one could pray 'without ceasing' for it seemed an impossible thing. But as I learned and developed the early morning start with the Lord, I discovered how it works. After I pray initially, during the rest of the day it is easy to communicate with Him continually, sometimes speaking aloud, sometimes just a thought. I sense His presence more as I go about the work of the day.

Additional Treasures:   Psalms 37:30    Isaiah 50:4

# April 23

**"For consider him that endured such contradiction of sinners against himself, lest ye be wearied and faint in your minds."**
**Hebrews 12:3**

The suffering of Jesus was far more than the horrible death that He endured for us on the cross. He endured the 'contradiction of sinners' against Himself. We are to consider what He did for us when we are disturbed by the injustices we suffer in this wicked world because we are Christians.

**Contradiction** is denying what has been said; saying the opposite.
**Endure** is to undergo; bear; tolerate; to suffer patiently.
We know from the Word that Jesus suffered the contradiction of sinners. They followed Him around and constantly tried to find fault with His teaching and actions. They denied the truth that He spoke and ridiculed His claim of being God's Son. Jesus *tolerated* that when He could have zapped them off the face of the earth with a thought!

Jesus focused on His goal to die for sinful men, that they might have eternal life. So He endured everything this wicked world could hurl at Him, and in the end died for it.

"Looking unto Jesus the author and finisher of our faith; who for the joy that was set before him endured the cross, despising the shame, and is set down at the right hand of the throne of God." Hebrews 12:2

When we get discouraged in the Christian life, we should first of all consider Jesus and all that He patiently endured on this earth for us.

"For we have not an high priest which cannot be touched with the feeling of our infirmities; but was in all points tempted like as we are, yet without sin." Hebrews 4:15

When the devil tempted Jesus in the wilderness, the Lord answered him each time with "It is written..." He then quoted the scriptures to rebuke the devil. I've taught women to use this phrase whenever they are tempted. Just quote it aloud, if need be, and remind the devil what God says! It will protect us if we will only use it. "It is written" is the tip of the mighty Sword!

Additional Treasures:     James 5:8     John 15:9

# April 24

**"Blessed is the man that heareth me, watching daily
at my gates, waiting at the posts of my doors."
Proverbs 8:34**

Being watchful and obedient is the way of happiness for Christians. Many are caught in the miserable consequences of not obeying the Word of God and the prompting of the Holy Spirit within them. Satan is watching and continually tempting the Christian to venture out from that protection, which obedience to God provides for him.

"Every word of God is pure: he is a shield unto them that put their trust in him." Proverbs 30:5

In our generation, these two commandments have been increasingly ignored by the world which has caused untold suffering and tragic consequences.

**Thou shalt not kill.**

Murder is very commonplace today, and many of the *murderers* are even found among the youth of our land! The influence of the church has about disappeared altogether. Many youth have never even heard of the Ten Commandments or attended a church Sunday School.

**Thou shalt not commit adultery.**

The structure of our society is steadily crumbling away as this command is ridiculed and absolutely rejected as old-fashioned and irrelevant for this generation. Many little children are being drowned in the 'sea of adultery' as their lives are turned upside down by the sins of the parents. They are neglected, often cruelly abused, and sometimes killed to get them out of the way. No wonder the judgment seat of God will be a fearful time.

We cannot comprehend the devastation and misery among the people of this world because of ignoring these laws of God. Our land is a crime and disease ridden jungle where no one is safe.

Let us hold fast to the Word of God, and directly follow what the Lord
would have us do. The name of the Lord is like a strong tower...*safety!*

"The name of the Lord is a strong tower: the righteous runneth into it, and is safe." Proverbs 18:10

Additional Treasures:    Psalms 27:1    Psalm 112:7

# April 25

**"But be ye doers of the word, and not hearers only deceiving your own selves."**
**James 1:22**

If there is no *doing* on our part after we hear God's Word, then we are deceiving ourselves. The Word always stirs up the heart and affects us in some way.

**It is quickening**, so has the power to generate life to the souls that hear it and believe on the Lord Jesus Christ.

**It is cleansing**, and keeps us *washed* and free from the holds of sin as we read and meditate daily on the Word.

**The Word gives answers to questions and difficulties.**
Understanding that the Bible gives answers to questions and problems has been a great discovery in my Christian life. The Word is full of wisdom for us. As we read it, answers will show up in verses or chapters where we would least expect them.

People, who read the Bible but are *never* motivated to do something for the Lord as a result, are not listening to what they read; they are not allowing it into their hearts to move them.

**How does the Word move us? What are we supposed to do?**

**Confess** and forsake the sins that it uncovers in our hearts.
**Obey** the prompting of the Holy Spirit as He leads us.
**Pray** as the Word stirs our hearts to talk to the Lord.
**Go** and tell someone else of God's love and salvation.

Once when my daughter's two children were very small they were watching a television movie one evening which suddenly turned very scary for them. Jeanne turned the TV off and put the children on her bed where they sat around the Bible as she read Psalm 91, explaining the meaning on their level of understanding. Soon they were calm again and with that incident, even as children, they could see that God helps and protects us with His Word. We should consider the Bible our most valuable possession. It is!

Additional Treasures:     Luke 6:47-49     John 13:17

# April 26

**"And, behold, one came and said unto him, Good Master,
what good thing shall I do, that I may have eternal life?"
Matthew 19:16-22**

This rich young ruler came to Jesus with perhaps a sincere desire to know how to be saved, but his approach to salvation was centered on works and not faith in Christ. "What good thing shall I do...?"

Jesus, first of all. made the young man think about what he had just said to the Lord, calling Him *good.* "Only God is good," Jesus said, which meant *'Do you believe that I am good and therefore I am God?'* He was testing the man's heart: what he really believed about the Saviour.

Mankind is definitely not in the category of *good.*

"They are all gone out of the way, they are together become unprofitable: there is none that doeth good, no, not one. "Romans 3:12

If Jesus was *good*, then He was God and the young man should have heeded what the Lord said to him.

The Lord refers him to the law not for salvation, but to show the rich young ruler that he was a sinner. That's what the law does.

"Therefore by the deeds of the law there shall no flesh be justified in his sight: for by the law is the knowledge of sin." Romans 3:20

**The law is a mirror that reveals what we are. Jesus held up the Word and showed the man his heart, uncovering *covetousness* rooted deep within. The young man loved his riches more than his own soul, and unless he repented later he will forever be separated from Christ in eternity.**

Those who trust in their riches, or anything other than Christ, will ever see heaven. In the end, nothing will matter but Jesus and what He has done for us at Calvary. "Let every thing that hath breath praise the Lord." Psalm: 150:6

Additional Treasures:　　I Timothy 6:10　　Psalms 34:8　　Nahum 1:7

# April 27

**"So are the ways of every one that is greedy of gain;
which taketh away the life of the owners thereof."
Proverbs 1:19**

Greed in the soul will show up eventually in one's life. It cannot be hidden or disguised for long.

The dictionary defines greed as the 'quality of wanting more than one's share; extreme or excessive desire; covetousness.'

Greediness in the family can lead to indebtedness and great stress in the home as that excessive desire for things craves to be satisfied. In my early days as a pastor's wife, I soon learned the ways of some among the congregation who had not outgrown this hindering characteristic: greedy of gain.

**We lived in the little parsonage behind the church and were barely getting by on the meager salary with which we had started. One day an older affluent lady drove back to the house, got out and raised the trunk lid of her car and invited me to pick out anything I needed of numerous things from bedding to clothing items, used, but in excellent condition.**

**I was very naïve, and gathered up an armload of stuff *assuming* that she was giving it to me to help out. Then she told me the price! I was too embarrassed to dump it all back into the car and tell her I couldn't afford any of it, so I suffered the consequences of my pride and ignorance, paid her with my grocery money, and scrimped to feed the family the rest of the week. As she drove off around the corner of the church building, I mentally attached a sign to the back of her car: BEWARE!**

"And he said unto them, Take heed, and beware of covetousness: for a man's life consisteth not in the abundance of the things which he possesseth." Luke 12:15

There are many promises in God's Word referring to being a generous soul instead of having a spirit of greed. Some Christians have taken God's Word to live by, in the matter of giving, with startling results. They are practicing bountiful givers and life is an adventure as their needs are met and there is always an overflow of blessings coming back into their lives.

"Give, and it shall be given unto you; good measure, pressed down, and shaken together, and running over, shall men give unto your bosom." Luke 6:38

Additional Treasures:     II Corinthians 9:6     Proverbs 11:25

# April 28

**"Go to the ant, thou sluggard;
consider her ways and be wise..."
Proverbs 6:6**

Whether we consider ourselves to be sluggards or not, we would do well to review the characteristics of this little insect and think carefully about how it does things, in order to decide how we may improve ourselves, to be wiser.

We can learn valuable lessons in life if we consider what God says to consider. The meaning of the word is to 'think carefully about in order to decide; deliberate.'

The lowly little ants can instruct us in the way of wisdom, yet they will never speak an audible word to us. We must watch them and consider.

### The ant is a self-starter.

Nobody is coaxing, leading, pushing, chiding or pleading for the little ant to do what he is supposed to do. He just does it, *diligently.* "Which having no guide, overseer, or ruler..." *v.7*

### The ant works while he can.

There is a country saying, "Make hay while the sun shines..."
You can't bale hay when it's raining and storming.
"Provideth her meat in the summer, and gathered her food in the harvest." Proverbs 6:8

**The ants have a goal in mind** and will not be turned from it.

Preparation for winter, the time when there is no food outside, is his goal. When winter is in force, the ants are burrowed deep in the ground with food stored in abundance, ready when needed.

Prepare for winter in your Christian life. That's the time when the productive cycle is stopped; you must draw on what you have stored up in your heart, constantly going back to the verses that have blessed you before. *Wintertime!*

Take in the Word of God at every opportunity; *it is your life.*

Additional Treasures:     Proverbs 30:25     Jeremiah 15:16

# April 29

**"This book of the law shall not depart of out thy mouth;**
**but thou shall meditate therein day and night…"**
**Joshua 1:8**

The verse here continues to reveal a very precious promise connected with reading and meditating on the Word of God.

"…for then thou shalt made thy way prosperous, and then thou shalt have good success."

There is great success and prosperity for our lives if we obey what God says. It is not 'money' prosperity referred to, but the riches which come with a happy Christian life. One rich in faith is prosperous.

"But his delight is in the law of the Lord; and in his law doth he mediate day and night. And he shall be like a tree planted by the rivers of water that bringeth forth his fruit in his season; his leaf also shall not wither; and whatsoever he doeth shall prosper." Psalm 1:1-3

**Excel in wisdom and understanding.**
   "O how love I thy law! It is my meditation all the day… for thy
   testimonies are my meditation." Psalm 119: 97, 99
**Discover how to live.**
   "He taught me also, and said unto me, Let thine heart retain my
   words; keep my commandments and live." Proverbs 4:4
**Have new power over sin.**
   "Wherewithal shall a young man cleanse his way? By taking
   heed thereto according to thy word…Thy word have I hid in my
   heart that I might not sin against thee." Psalm 119: 9, 11
**Success will be obvious to all!**
   "Meditate upon these things; give thyself wholly to them; that
   thy profiting may appear to all." I Timothy 4:15

I read the testimony of a man who is a great teacher and instructor in the Bible. As a youth when he took time to read his Bible every morning before he went to school, he made better grades! Once he slacked off just to see if that had anything to do with it for sure, and it did. His grades came down again. So he continued the practice of reading scripture before school on into his college years. God's Word makes the mind more alert. Try it and see.

Additional Treasures:     Psalm 37:31     Luke 21:33

# April 30

**"Who is among you that feareth the Lord, that obeyeth
the voice of his servant, that walketh in darkness, and hath no light?
let him trust in the name of the Lord, and stay upon his God."
Isaiah 50:10**

Among the Lord's people, there are always those who have
difficulty in simply trusting God in all things. Even those who truly *fear
the Lord* and *obey His voice* may stumble as though they have no light in
the darkness.

One of these areas is the lack of assurance of salvation. Our
assurance is in the Word of God. A fearful Christian is ignorant of the
scriptures or reads them with doubt.
"These things have I written unto you that believe on the name of the
Son of God; that ye may know that ye have eternal life, and that ye may
believe on the name of the Son of God."    I John 5:13

Some people wonder if they *said the right words* when they called
on the Lord for salvation. God looks into the heart and reads the words of
faith there before *anything* is spoken. But some folk have stumbled over
such things for years and can't seem to settle it. Whatever the cause,
every difficulty must be dealt with in the light of the Word until all
doubts and fears are driven out of the heart. There can be no peace in the
heart until the assurance of salvation is as sure as the sun and moon over
our heads!

'Tis a point I long to know;  oft it causes anxious thought;
Do I love the Lord or no?  Am I His or am I not?
If I love, why am I thus?  Why this dull, this lifeless frame?
Hardly, sure, can they be worse,  Who have never heard his name.
When I turn my eyes within,  All is dark and vain and wild;
Filled with unbelief and sin,  Can I deem myself a child?
Could I joy His saints to meet,  Choose the way I once abhor'd;
Find at times the promise sweet,  If I did not love the Lord?
Lord decide the doubtful case,  Thou who art Thy people's sun:
Shine upon Thy work of grace, If it be indeed begun.
Let me love Thee more and more,  If I love at all I pray;
If I have not loved before,  Help me to begin today.
John Newton

Additional Treasures:    John 3:36    John 10:27-28

# May 1

**"While the earth remaineth, seedtime and harvest,
and cold and heat, and summer and winter,
and day and night shall not cease."
Genesis 8:22**

This was the promise of God, after the flood on the earth in which Noah and his family came through safely inside the ark.

After the ark came to rest on the mountain of Ararat, Noah came out on dry ground, and he built an altar unto the Lord. He took of the clean animals and worshipped God with a sacrifice. The Lord was pleased and gave a wonderful declaration.

"And the Lord smelled a sweet savour; and the Lord said in his heart, I will not again curse the ground any more for man's sake; for the imagination of man's heart is evil from his youth; neither will I again smite any more every thing living, as I have done." Genesis 8:21

**In addition, the Lord gave the promise concerning the cycle of seasons on the earth. Some folks contend that in time the seasons will run together with no distinction between them. We know that's not going to happen. God says in His Word. *"While the earth remaineth..."* As long as the earth hangs in space, its seasons will come and go as God has ordered.**

In the beginning God created all and established the laws of nature, which are vital to life on the earth.

"The day is thine, the night also is thine: thou hast prepared the light and the sun. Thou hast set all the borders of the earth: thou hast made summer and winter." Psalms 74:16-17

The first chapter of Genesis is the "seed plot" of the Bible. That is where it all begins in this little room of 'time' in the universe. "God created" is a reassuring statement which will encourage your faith when you think on it.

One year, the ladies' in the church worked on memorizing Genesis chapter one. We had memorized chapters before, but this one was a little more difficult. However, I finally mastered it and was able to recite it at a Ladies' Retreat to demonstrate how, at any age, the scripture can be committed to memory. I retyped the chapter and sectioned it off by days, underlining key phrases. It is true that if you repeat something over and over for a period of time, you will memorize it. Try it!

Additional Treasures:   Hebrews 11:3   Nehemiah 9:6

# May 2

**"... although I have scattered them among the countries,
yet will I be to them a little sanctuary..."
Ezekiel 11:16**

When God's people had settled in the Promised Land, they began to enjoy all the blessings of their possession and soon forgot the Lord.

"And they forsook the Lord God of their fathers, which brought them out of the land of Egypt, and followed other gods, of the gods of the people that were round about them, and bowed themselves to them, and provoked the Lord to anger." Judges 2:12

Eventually the whole nation was broken up and taken into captivity, being scattered into several countries. And God said, *"I will be to them a little sanctuary..."*
God is merciful, and forgives His children when they repent.
"If we confess our sins, he is faithful and just to forgive us our sins and to cleanse us from all unrighteousness." I John 1:9

**God is also kind and understanding of His children. He humbles Himself to be a *little sanctuary* for us. We could not function in the light of His glory if He did not scale it down to '*little*' for us.**

While in London England, my husband and I went to see the great Westminster Abbey where kings and notable men are buried and where the present queen was crowned. It is a *grand sanctuary* and we gazed in awe at the interior of that historic old cathedral. I didn't feel inclined to kneel and pray at all for it seemed to be only a magnificent showplace.
Once in Colorado with my daughter's family, I visited a chapel in the woods with an old pump organ and rustic pews. The keeper invited me to play the organ, and those who were present gathered around and sang several old hymns until the woods were full of the sounds of praise in song! That Church was a *little sanctuary* and we were comfortable worshiping there.

God accommodates our limited ability to understand His greatness and glory. He makes Himself *a little sanctuary*...for our praise and worship.

Additional Treasures:  Psalms 113:5-6   Acts 17:28

# May 3

**"Enlarge the place of thy tent, and let them stretch forth
the curtains of thine habitations: spare not,
lengthen thy cords, and strengthen thy stakes."
Isaiah 54:2**

It is said that this verse gave William Carey, that great missionary to India, a world vision. Many such men had a *text* verse that changed their lives. God's Word has such power.

"For the word of God is quick, and powerful, and sharper than any twoedged sword, piercing even to the dividing asunder of soul and spirit, and of the joints and marrow, and is a discerner of the thoughts and intents of the heart." Hebrews 4:12

Do you have a text verse that is marked in your Bible because it has spoken to your heart and changed you? Every Christian should have this important verse underlined.
"For whosoever shall call upon the name of the Lord shall be saved." Romans 10:13

If you know the date of your salvation, pencil that in also. It is a good reminder to read if the devil tries to tempt you in the area of assurance of salvation. You *can* rely on God's Word. He promised to save all that come to Him.
"...and him that cometh to me I will in no wise cast out." John 6:37

Another verse to mark in your Bible is one that encourages and comforts Christians in time of trials and temptations.
"There hath no temptation taken you but such as is common to man: but God is faithful, who will not suffer you to be tempted above that ye are able; but will with the temptation also make a way to escape, that ye may be able to bear it." I Corinthians 10:13

We are not at the mercy of the devil. We are under the protection of God according to His Word. Get some verses *personalized* today.

Additional Treasures:    Hebrews 4:15-16    Jeremiah 23:29

# May 4

**"My soul shall be satisfied as with marrow and fatness; and my mouth shall praise thee with joyful lips: When I remember thee upon my bed, and meditate on thee in the night watches."**
**Psalms 63:5-6**

This clearly gives us some idea of what to do when we can't sleep and are worn out with trying. It will be satisfying to the soul and give joy to the heart when we remember the Lord upon our beds and then meditate, or ponder, on the things that we know of Him.

To meditate means to *reflect, think on,* or *contemplate.* We have such solemn subject matter to think about; it would be a beneficial habit to bring God's Word up in our thoughts at any given time, and especially when sleep eludes us in the night.

**Remember the conviction of The Holy Spirit, and the events in your life leading up to the time and place where you were saved.**

My husband likes to reflect on the great mercy of God in allowing him to come through the Korean War. He was not a Christian at the time, yet served for months on the frontlines of battle in constant danger of being killed, as many soldiers were. But God spared his life in that place, and in a few years saved him and placed him in *God's army* where he has already served 54 years, including 42 as a pastor. The people in our church knew my husband's testimony of salvation very well; he told it so much through the years. He loves to reflect and tell about how and when he became a Christian.

**Meditate on the tender blessings of God,** which fill your life day by day in faithful succession. *Count them!* If you are awake in the night, this is a soothing effective way to make one feel calm and relaxed enough to drop off into a peaceful sleep.

"My meditation of him shall be sweet: I will be glad in the Lord."
Psalms 104:34

Additional Treasures:     Psalms 19:14     Philippians 4:8

# May 5

**"But we all, with open face beholding as in a glass
the glory of the Lord, are changed into the same image from
glory to glory, even as by the Spirit of the Lord."
II Corinthians 3:18**

What we constantly see will eventually affect us. That's why most any fashion in hair and clothing will catch on; people tend to mimic what they continually look at.

Parents now have a dreadful time-slot in history for raising their children. In my childhood there was no 'peer-pressure' to worry about. When our children were young computers were not commonplace, television was not a river of violence and pornography, and peer-pressure was not prevalent. But now parenting has all these things to contend with. I admire parents who are desperately trying to raise their children in all the muck and mire of this generation. Children are bombarded every waking minute with temptation to conform to some other image besides 'descent and normal'. Christian parents have a greater challenge than ever before. But they have the same tool to help them succeed and that is the Word of God. God knew all about this generation before He ever created the first one! His Word has the same power to guide and protect His children in the world. Teaching children from the day they are born is the key to success. Parents are the first ones children will imitate. Blessed are the Christian parents who have the image of Christ reflected in their own lives.

"For whom he did foreknow, he also did predestinate to be conformed to the image of his Son...." Romans 8:29

**The more we look on the image of Christ in the Word, the more like Him we will become. See then how very important it is to pursue the study of the scriptures. We cannot change ourselves. However, through the power of His Word God will do it for us.**

It is not a change in physical appearance, obviously, but a change in our thought patterns which forms our attitude as the things taking root in the heart start growing and showing up on the outside. Those 'things' will be nuggets of truth we learn day by day from reading the Bible.

Additional Treasures:    II Corinthians 4:6    Romans 6:11

# May 6

**"And the ark of the Lord was in the country
of the Philistines seven months."
I Samuel 6:1**

The Philistines defeated Israel in battle, and took the ark of the Lord away into their own country. They *knew* the ark represented Israel's God, so they took it to the temple of their god, Dagon, and set it by him. The next morning they had quite a surprise.

"And when they of Ashdod arose early on the morrow, behold, Dagon was fallen upon his face to the earth before the ark of the Lord. And they took Dagon, and set him in his place again." I Samuel 5:3

Those heathen picked their god up, brushed him off, and set him in his place again. The next day when they came into their temple they found Dagon was in a lot more trouble.

"....Dagon was fallen upon his face to the ground before the ark of the Lord; and the head of Dagon and both the palms of his hands were cut off upon the threshold; only the stump of Dagon was left to him." V.4

**After that they took the ark from one city to another as "the hand of the Lord was heavy upon them." They finally realized they were doomed if they kept it, and prepared a kingly offering of gold to go with the ark as they returned it to Israel. They had taken it with boldness and confidence, and returned it with fear and meekness.**

We can rejoice if we have a personal relationship with the only true God through the death, burial, and resurrection of the Lord Jesus Christ.

We visited many mission fields while my husband was a pastor and we were in countries where idols were worshipped. We saw sincere people bowing before them, and I was thankful at the time that we had dedicated missionaries living there to witness to those lost souls. Our country is not the 'Christian nation' it once was, but it still has the light of the gospel more than any other country in the world. We should thank God daily for the privilege of living here, and not only thankful but motivated to give of our means so the gospel of Christ can be preached in other lands where spiritual darkness rules. Ask God to burden your heart today. You may not go, but you can give generously so that missionaries can go in your place.

Additional Treasures:     Psalms 115:3     Mark 4:39

# May 7

**"And they of Bethshemesh were reaping their wheat harvest
in the valley: and they lifted up their eyes,
and saw the ark, and rejoiced to see it."
I Samuel 6:13**

The Philistines schemed to the last, hoping that it was by chance that the plagues came upon their cities. They *feared* God, but did not want Him.

They put the ark on a *new* cart, harnessed two young cows that had never been yoked, tied them to the cart and shut up their calves at home. In that way they would know, because a cow *will not* leave her little calf or calmly pull in a yoke for the first time.

Bethshemesh was a city near the border, and the cows went along the highway, lowing as they went, and stopped in a field near where men were working in the wheat harvest. The Philistines following turned back when they saw the ark arrive safely. The men immediately offered up a sacrifice unto the Lord for the return of the ark, and there was great rejoicing.

However, tragedy struck quickly for in their joyous mood they forgot what the ark represented. They were not supposed to even touch it, but some of the men *opened it and looked inside!*

"And he smote the men of Bethshemesh  because they had looked into the ark of the Lord..." v. 19

Inside the ark were the commandments of the law. The covering was the mercy seat where the blood was applied by the high priest for the sins of the people. The men of Bethshemesh boldly gazed at the law, without the blood on the mercy seat between to shield them from certain death.

Jesus took our *death* as prescribed by God's holy law when He died on the cross for our sins.  His blood will forever be between the saved and judgment.  "Let us therefore come boldly unto the throne of grace, that we may obtain mercy, and find grace to help in time of need." Hebrews 4:16

Additional Treasures:     Exodus 25:21-22     Psalms 33:8

# May 8

**"For what is a man profited, if he shall gain
the whole world, and lose his own soul?" Matthew 16:26**

This is a solemn question addressed to every living person on earth. In the loss of the soul, *all is lost indeed.* When one is facing the door of eternity waiting to go through, nothing else matters but the certain knowledge and assurance of salvation in Christ.

Years ago when our pastor's wife was ill and near death, we visited with her often. I wanted to just sit near her and hear what this remarkable Christian lady would say. She was the most knowledgeable person I knew concerning the Word of God. The book of Psalms was her favorite, and she had most of it memorized. You could start any verse and she could finish it by memory.

But the nearer she came to the time of her passing, the more she rejoiced in the simple fact of her salvation. I'd ask her what she was thinking about, and she would reply, "I'm just so thankful for the assurance in my heart that I'm saved." She was not concerned about her years of service and the accomplishments of her life, but only what Jesus had done to make it possible for her to enter heaven. As a young pastor's wife I was impressed, and learned something then as I had so many times before when she had taught me.

**Our faith in Christ is the foundation of our lives. All the motions of life revolve around that truth. If we feed that faith it will grow and sustain us all through life and unto death...with perfect peace.**

The following Psalm has been prescribed to calm a troubled spirit. It's to be read three times a day for one week to restore peace of mind and heart. Memorize it and you will always have the 'medicine' with you to take as needed. It has been proven to be effective.

"The Lord is my Shepherd; I shall not want. He maketh me to lie down in green pastures: he leadeth me beside the still waters. He restoreth my soul: he leadeth me in the path of righteousness for his name's sake. Yea, though I walk through the valley of the shadow of death, I will fear no evil: for thou art with me; thy rod and thy staff they comfort me. Thou preparest a table before me in the presence of mine enemies: thou anointest my head with oil; my cup runneth over. Surely goodness and mercy shall follow me all the days of my life: and I will dwell in the house of the Lord for ever." Psalm 23

Additional Treasures:    John 20:31    I John 3:23    Philippians 3:9

# May 9

**"...for there is no restraint to the Lord
to save by many or by few."
I Samuel 14:6**

Jonathan, the son of King Saul, because of his fearless faith in the Lord was able to roust the opposing army encamped against Israel, causing them to flee in confusion and disarray. All had seemed hopeless because Israel's army had no weapons except the king and his son, and they were greatly outnumbered. Then Jonathan, full of faith in God, made a bold move.

"And Jonathan said to the young man that bare his armour, Come, and let us go over unto the garrison of these uncircumcised: it may be that the Lord will work for us: **for there is no restraint to the Lord to save by many or by few.**" v 6

The Lord did work according to Jonathan's faith. He, with his armor bearer alongside, surprised the enemy and overcame twenty men in battle. The rest of the enemy camped nearby became terrified by the noise and fled.

"But our God is in the heavens: he hath done whatsoever he hath pleased." Psalms 115:3

We often pray with little faith and expectation because we feel that conditions are not favorable for God to work on our behalf. We put some imaginary restraint on the ability of God, but in reality nothing can hinder *whatsoever* except our unbelief. Reading God's Word, with our focus on the greatness of the Lord, will increase our faith.

"Fear thou not; for I am with thee: be not dismayed; for I am thy God: I will strengthen thee; yea, I will help thee; yea, I will uphold thee with the right hand of my righteousness." Isaiah 41:10

Do you have problems in your life that you feel hesitant about presenting to God? Don't waste another moment. *There is no restraint with God.* He is interested in the smallest details of your life. Write this old saying at the top of your prayer list or somewhere to be seen. Focus on it as you pray. It's true.

**"Nothing is too hard for Jesus; no man can work like Him."**

Additional Treasures:     Luke 1:37     Matthew 8:26

# May 10

"Favour is deceitful, and beauty is vain: but a woman
that feareth the Lord, she shall be praised."
Proverbs 31:30

Favor, the condition of being liked, accepted, or approved is as changeable as the wind. Beauty is also a transient thing when applied only to the physical appearance. Many rich and famous people struggle after their youth to maintain both favor and beauty by spending fortunes on the maintenance and pampering of their physical bodies.

**In the month of May, when the mothers of our land are honored, the things that are recalled about them by their children are generally not in the category of favor or physical beauty. What endears a mother to her children is her unconditional love and caring, and the sacrifices so willingly made, which she invested in her offspring.**

Christian mothers who have the fear of the Lord in their hearts also provide many beneficial examples of God's love and grace to their children.

"The fear of the Lord is the beginning of wisdom: and the knowledge of the holy is understanding." Proverbs 9:10
"The fear of the Lord prolongeth days: but the years of the wicked shall be shortened." Proverbs 10:27
"The fear of the Lord is the beginning of knowledge: but fools despise wisdom and instruction." Proverbs 1:7

A mother with the fear of the Lord in her heart will teach her children by words and conduct things that will help them make better decisions, gain more knowledge, and generally live longer.
Mother, keep your heart. Make sure the *fear of the Lord* is the ruling factor, and you will honor God in your role as a mother.

**Though I was raised in a family with ten children and helped take care of younger siblings all my young life, when I had my first child it was totally different. Motherhood starts a new life when you hold your own 'flesh and blood' in your arms. It's a miracle and a wonder that you never get over.**

Additional Treasures:     Proverbs 31:10-11     Psalms 112:1

# May 11

**"Then saith he to the disciple, Behold thy mother!
And from that hour that disciple took her unto his own home."
John 19:27**

As Jesus was dying on the cross, He spoke words to John regarding his mother. He provided for Mary a home with John, the beloved disciple, who took her unto his own household that day.

"Honour thy father and mother; which is the first commandment with promise; That it may be well with thee, and thou mayest live long on the earth." Ephesians 6:2-3

God said that things will go better for those who honor parents, and also promises a longer life for them. That promise was given as one of the Ten Commandments in Exodus 20:12.

It is a privilege to grow up having both parents. Some have missed that in life and had to grow up with incredible hardship. Both of my parents lost their mothers at an early age. That loss greatly affected their lives. They had difficulties that caused hardship for their own children later in life.

In the year my mother died I wrote a poem about *her* mother. She had told me some things she remembered about Belle, my grandmother, whom I never had the privilege of knowing. The loss still affects me, when I think of the suffering that my mother endured without her.

### Grandmother Belle

**Was she tall? Yes, and so graceful, or maybe she just looked that way
To a wee little girl my mother was in those wonderful long ago days**

**When her *mama* was there, sweet memories, cut off at the age of nine
When suddenly, it was a common tragedy, Belle and a new baby died.**

**After that, life was hard for a little girl not yet ten.
How do you fill up the awesome space where a mother's love has been?**

**But she grew up, tenacious of life, with talents that amaze us still.
The things passed down can't be explained, unless they came from Grandmother Belle.**

Additional Treasures:     Proverbs 11:16     Exodus 35:25

# May 12

**"Sorrow is better than laughter: for by the sadness of the countenance the heart is made better."**
**Ecclesiastes 7:3**

When the countenance, or face, reflects sadness it indicates sorrow in the heart and *the heart is made better.* We do not enjoy it as we do laughter, but it is more beneficial for our lives to have the sorrowful times scattered here and there throughout the years.

"For our light affliction, which is but for a moment, worketh for us a far more exceeding and eternal weight of glory…" II Corinthians 4:17

"Now no chastening for the present seemeth to be joyous, but grievous: nevertheless, afterward it yieldeth the peaceable fruit of righteousness unto them which are exercised thereby." Hebrews 12:11

Sorrow and affliction yields fruit, the peaceable fruit of desiring to do what is right before the Lord which is *righteousness.* A heart full of sorrow is more profitable than a mouth full of laughter. If we could only remember that when we are in the middle of sorrowful times!

I walked a mile with pleasure, she chattered all the way,
And left me none the wiser, for all she had to say.
I walked a mile with sorrow, and ne'er a word said she.
But oh the things I learned from her, when sorrow walked with me.
**Author Unknown**

**By trusting the Lord and believing His Word, we can welcome the trials and afflictions that come because we have a sure promise.**

"For his anger endureth but a moment; in his favour is life: weeping may endure for a night, but joy cometh in the morning." Psalm 30:5

Perhaps one of the reasons for our afflictions is that they cause us to seek the Lord and pray. When everything is going well, it is far easier to skip our fellowship and prayer time with God. When we are hurting, we long for His comfort and help and we are eager to communicate with Him.

Additional Treasures:    Psalms 28:7    Matthew 10:30-31

# May 13

**"Mine eyes fail for thy word, saying,
When wilt thou comfort me?"
Psalms 119:82**

Perhaps you have searched the Word until your eyes were too tired and strained to see because of some grievous trial in your life. Your heart cried for relief from your misery, *"Lord, when wilt thou comfort me?"*

Mary and Martha could not understand why the Lord tarried longer when He got their message that Lazarus, their brother, was very sick.
"When he heard therefore that he was sick, he abode two days still in the same place where he was." John 11:6

When Jesus did return to Bethany, Lazarus was dead and his sisters were grieved and a little *put out* with the Lord.
"Then said Martha unto Jesus, Lord, if thou hadst been here, my brother had not died." John 11:21

Then the Lord took the occasion to teach Martha and Mary about the resurrection.
"Jesus said unto her, I am the resurrection, and the life: he that believeth in me, though he were dead, yet shall he live: And whosoever liveth and believeth in me shall never die. Believest thou this?" *v.25-26*

Jesus also displayed his power and glory in raising Lazarus after he had been dead four days! Those sisters would never have seen the miracle if they'd not had the grief of their brother's dying and the deliberate delay of the Lord in getting there.

We naturally want the Lord to hurry when we are in dire straits. But because He loves us with an everlasting love, He will only do as His Word tells us. He will "work all things together for good" and our crying and complaining won't change His mind. If the Lord did as His children beg Him to do all at once, the spiritual realm and our lives would be in constant chaos and confusion. But God will not do anything contrary to His nature. "For God is not the author of confusion, but of peace...."
I Corinthians 14:33

Additional Treasures:   II Chronicles 16:9   Psalms 34:7

# May 14

**"Also day by day, from the first day unto the last day,
he read in the book of the law of God."
Nehemiah 8:18**

Nehemiah had been called of God to do a work, a difficult task, needing all the strength of his faith in the Lord to accomplish it. He got permission from the king to go to Jerusalem and rebuild the walls of the city, after his fervent prayer in chapter one. His burden was great, and he knew also that God had put it in his heart to do this monumental task.

"And I arose in the night, I and some few men with me; neither told I any man what my God had put in my heart to do at Jerusalem.""Neh 2:12

He was also burdened about the Word of the Lord being neglected. He gathered the people together out in a big open place in the street so that Ezra the priest could read the book of the law aloud to them.

"And Ezra the scribe stood upon a pulpit of wood, which they had made for that purpose;...And Ezra opened the book in the sight of all the people (for he was above all the people) and when he opened it, all the people stood up:.....So they read in the book of the law of God distinctly,... and caused them to understand the reading." Neh. 8:4-8

The first thing to do when revival is sought is to get back to the Word of God. With the Word, hearts must return to prayer. The churches may have a program planned in order to *have a revival,* but the power will only come when people yield their hearts to God and pray. Prayer equals power. When a Christian prays the devil trembles. If a child of God goes to pray with all sins 'confessed up to date' and nothing hindering, then God Himself listens and considers what is to be done for His child. We can hardly imagine the reality and wonder of it. We can bring revival into our lives, and our churches. Are we willing?

After Christians are revived, their hearts become concerned for the things that matter to God. He is "not willing that any should perish, but that all should come to repentance." Witness to lost people: precious souls to God.
II Peter 3:9

Additional Treasures:    I Chronicles 16:11    Hebrews 4:12

# May 15

**"And we have seen and do testify that the Father
sent the Son to be the Saviour of the world."
I John 4:14**

When our daughter was a young teenager, she asked her Dad about the time of some event that was scheduled. He said "Jeanne, don't you listen to the announcements?" Without hesitation she replied, "Daddy, I *live* in the announcements!" And certainly, pastors' children do live in such proximity to the work of the ministry they are right in the middle of it, or as our daughter put it, "live in the announcements."

God has made some very important announcements:

**Christ, the Son of God, was born into the world.**
And the angel said unto them, Fear not: for, behold, I bring you good tidings of great joy, which shall be to all people. For unto you is born this day...a Saviour, which is Christ the Lord." Luke 2:10-11

**Christ the Saviour died for our sins on the Cross of Calvary.**
"Who his own self bare our sins in his own body on the tree, that we, being dead to sins, should live unto righteousness: by whose stripes ye were healed." I Peter 2:24

**Christ the Lord arose from the grave on the third day.**
"He is not here: for he is risen, as he said, Come, see the place where the Lord lay." Matthew 28:6

**Christ is coming back again.**
"...this same Jesus, which is taken up from you into heaven, shall so come in like manner as ye have seen him go into heaven." Acts 1:11

Christians live in these announcements! Let us be faithful in proclaiming the good news to others who do not know and so live our lives that they may see the reflection of Christ in us. That is the most effective witness of all.

Additional Treasures:     I Corinthians 15:3-4     I Thessalonians 1:9-10

# May 16

**"And he took his staff in his hand, and chose him five smooth stones out of the brook....and his sling was in his hand..."**
**I Samuel 17:40**

We all know the story of the shepherd boy, David, who was brave enough to take on the giant Goliath. He had confidence that he could defeat this enemy of the Lord and of Israel, because there was a good cause.

"...that all the earth may know that there is a God in Israel." v.46

There were other reasons for David's confidence. The Lord had helped him before, and he had some things consistent in his life. One was his habit of meditating on the greatness and glory of God. It filled his heart and gave David strong faith.

So this youth chose five stones out of the brook to use with his sling as a weapon. Through time, these rocks had been worn smooth by the running water. The outcome was glorious, for Goliath was slain with one stone out of David's sling. I Samuel 17: 49-51

God's people are in constant warfare, and our preparedness determines the outcome in the battles. When we are facing some Goliath trial in our lives we must take up some *smooth* stones for weapons, those worn smooth by constant use and the washing over of the water of the Word.

**Clear conscience.** Keep sin out of the heart.     I Timothy 1:19

**Word of God stored up in the heart.**     Hebrews 4:12

**Habit of prayer in your life.**     I John 3:22

**Faithfulness to God's house.**     Luke 4:16     Hebrews 10:25

**Fellowship with godly people.**     Proverbs 17:17     Psalms 119:63

"Finally, my brethren, be strong in the Lord, and in the power of his might." Ephesians 6:10

Additional Treasures:     Ephesians 6: 12-13     II Corinthians 10:3-5

# May 17

**"And he answered, Fear not: for they that be
with us are more than they that be with them."
II Kings 6:16**

Elisha, the man of God, was feared because the power of the Lord was with him. The king of Syria was defeated on every turn because Elisha gave counsel to the king of Israel as to where the Syrian army would be encamped. The Syrian king didn't know who was telling, so he called a meeting of his servants and said:

"Will ye shew me which of us is for the king of Israel?" II Kings 6:11

One of the king's servants wisely replied, "None, my lord, O king: but Elisha, the prophet that is in Israel, telleth the king of Israel the words that thou speakest in thy bedchamber." I Kings 6:12

The king of Syria said in essence, "Somebody among us is telling my plans to the other side!" And the wise servant said, "It's not us! It's that man of God, Elisha. He knows everything, even what you say in your bedroom."

So the king found that Elisha would be in Dothan, and the Syrians surrounded the city. The servant saw the mighty army early in the morning, and cried out to Elisha, "Alas, my master! How shall we do?"

Elisha prayed for his servant to see God's army surrounding the place!
"And the Lord opened the eyes of the young man; and he saw: and, behold, the mountain was full of horses and chariots of fire round about Elisha." II Kings 6:17
God's protection is constantly around us, or we would be consumed in a moment.
"The angel of the Lord encampeth round about them that fear him, and delivereth them." Psalms 34:7

**I love the Old Testament stories such as this one, all true, though they sound like a fictitious tale to many people. But they teach us something about our God. He will protect us as He did Elisha and his servant. Just think, we pray to the same God as Elisha! God is the same, yesterday, today and forever. Blessed be His name.**

Additional Treasures:     Psalm 125:2     Psalm 91:4

# May 18

**"...but the soul of my lord shall be bound in the
bundle of life with the Lord thy God."
I Samuel 25:29**

David and his men had protected the servants and sheep of Nabal
while they were encamped near his fields. Nabal, a wealthy, crude man
refused to give them some food to eat. David and his men lived off the
land as they hid from the king's army. King Saul was determined to do
away with David.

They had earned the food, and when their request was scorned David
set out to destroy Nabal's entire household. One of the servants quickly
explained the situation and danger to his wife, Abigail, who was a godly
woman with discretion and understanding.

"...David sent messengers out of the wilderness to salute our master;
and he railed on them. But the men were very good to us, and we were
not hurt, neither missed we anything, as long as we were conversant with
them, when we were in the fields...

Now therefore know and consider what thou wilt do; for evil is
determined against our master, and against all his household: for he is
such a son of Belial, that a man cannot speak to him." I Sam 25:14-15, 17

**In this fascinating story Abigail takes food and goes to meet
David and his men, graciously offers the food, and soothes David's
temper. She knew of David's faith in God and said in verse twenty-
nine:**

**"...but the soul of my lord shall be bound in the bundle of life
with the Lord thy God." She was saying that David had a glorious
future!**

Abigail's bundle of life contained wisdom and discretion. By it, she
saved her household and her unworthy husband at that time. God blessed
this woman, and she later became King David's wife.

Jesus died for our sins so He could wrap us in the *bundle of life* with
Himself. Salvation cost more than all the riches in the world; that is why
it cannot be purchased by any means. Jesus paid it all... I Peter 1:18-19

Additional Treasures:     Proverbs 12:4     Proverbs 11:16

# May 19

**"Consider the lilies of the field, how they grow;
they toil not, neither do they spin:"
Matthew 6:28**

Because we have a tendency toward anxiety about things in this life, the Lord patiently taught on the subject. He points to the lilies of the field as an example of His care and provision.

**Consider the lilies:**
The lilies do absolutely nothing but grow. However, they are gloriously arrayed, *or clothed,* Jesus said. When we feel anxious about having suitable clothes to wear, we should give consideration to the lilies and other flowers of the field. We worry about shoes and clothing etc. But it's not about a need. It's about our desire to get more to add to the abundance we already have.

"Wherefore, if God so clothe the grass of the field, which today is, and tomorrow is cast into the oven, shall he not much more clothe you, O ye of little faith?" Matthew 6:30

**Consider the heavens!**
"When I consider thy heavens, the work of thy fingers, the moon and the stars, which thou hast ordained; What is man that thou art mindful of him?" Psalm 8:3-4

The Bible does not tell us anywhere that God loved the sun, and moon and stars, even as glorious as those created hosts of heaven are in their distant realm. We should remember that and consider how *God loves us!* John 3:16

**Consider Him.**
"For consider him that endured such contradiction of sinners against himself, lest ye be wearied and faint in your minds." Hebrews 12:3

When we are having a difficult time of it in our lives, we should remember all that Christ endured for us so that we could have the gift of salvation. We don't have it in us to fully understand what it cost Jesus in pain and suffering to pay our sin debt. He was God; he felt the agony of having our sin touch Him as our sins were 'laid on Him'. Then because He was the "Son of Man" living on this earth in a body of flesh, He felt the acute physical pain and torture which the crucifixion inflicted on Him. Words cannot paint a picture of His death. It is indescribable. He loves us that much; is there any evidence in your life that you love Him? Take inventory today. *Consider Him,* Who deserves all of our consideration.

Additional Treasures:     I Samuel 12:24     Haggai 1:5

# May 20

"Now I Nebuchadnezzar praise and extol and honour
the King of heaven, all whose works are truth, and his ways
judgment: and those that walk in pride he is able to abase."
Daniel 4:37

This great heathen king of Babylon had to go through a lot before he would realize the truth of our text. He was walking in pride, and had such power and majesty one could not have imagined that he would be humbled before God. But he was only a servant in God's purpose.

**God used this king to punish Israel for their sins.** II Kings 24:1-3
When the people of Israel forgot God, they turned to the idols of the land and surrounding nations. God was long-suffering, but in time they paid for their disobedience. They were taken into captivity, and they never regained the glory they had as a nation.

**The king chose Daniel and others for special training.** Daniel 1:3-8
Daniel was to be God's choice servant in the history of that time where he came to be a very important figure in Nebuchadnezzar's kingdom. He is also a major prophet of the Old Testament. His writings contain prophecies having to do with the end times.

**The King was extreme in his pride and worship of idols.** Daniel 3:1-3
The king in his pride and foolish vanity made a huge image of himself and ordered all people to worship it. He had it set up in the plain of Dura in the province of Babylon. This was the time when the three Hebrew children were thrown into the fiery furnace because they would not fall down and worship the image. God was glorified through that act!

**God made a believer out of Nebuchadnezzar!**
"Nebuchadnezzar the king, unto all people, nations, and languages, that dwell in all the earth; Peace be multiplied unto you. I thought it good to shew the signs and wonders that the high God hath wrought toward me. How great are his signs! And how mighty are his wonders!"
Dan. 4:1-3
The king was humbled and later proclaimed his faith in the God of heaven and earth. He bowed his knee to the King of Kings.

"Humble yourselves in the sight of the Lord, and he shall lift you up." James 4:10

Additional Treasures: Daniel 4: 34-36   Colossians 3:5-6

# May 21

**"Jesus saith unto him, I am the way, the truth,
and the life: no man cometh unto the Father, but by me."
John 14:6**

It is a fact of life that if we are going to some particular place, we must know the way to get there. We have road maps that outline the way to any given destination in the country.

Jesus said, "I am the way, and the life..." The Lord had told His disciples that great truth when they inquired about heaven, and how to get there where Jesus was preparing a place for those who would trust in Him as Savior.

The way to heaven is through Jesus Christ. Nobody will get there without a personal relationship with Him. The Word reveals Christ. When it is believed, it makes the most remarkable, permanent change in one's life.
"...faith cometh by hearing, and hearing by the Word of God." Rom 10:17

What a blessed thing to hear and believe, and be saved through faith in Christ. Then the believer is on the way to heaven, and he *knows the way*.

**A few months after we were married, my husband got out of the army and we visited my family, then living in East Texas, before we settled into a permanent place of our own. We went into town one evening in my father's old dilapidated truck, and it was late when we left town to go back the sixteen miles through the dark piney woods to the farm. On the edge of town as we drove out, the headlights went out! We were thankful that the moon was bright and there were no other cars on the road at that time. I drove the vehicle because I was familiar with it, and I also *knew the way* even though I couldn't see all the details of the road in the dark. We arrived safely because of that fact.**

If you know Christ, the way to heaven, you can give directions to those that are lost and do not know the way. You don't have to know every little detail of the road, just that it is "straight and narrow" and only the saved are traveling on it. Study the Bible to know Jesus better and pray that God will give you opportunities to tell others what you know about 'the way'.

"But grow in grace, and in the knowledge of our Lord and Saviour Jesus Christ. To him be glory both now and forever. Amen." II Peter 3:18

Additional Treasures:     I Timothy 1:15     Luke 19:10

# May 22

**"Let your light so shine before men, that they may see
your good works, and glorify your Father which is in heaven."
Matthew 5:16**

All the light that we possess is a reflection from Christ and His glory. We may let it shine or obscure the light, depending on our obedience to the Lord through the Holy Spirit and the Word of God.

Obedience in all things of the Lord brings a bright reflection of Christ in our lives. It's as the full moon, reflecting the brightness of the sun in an unclouded night sky. This is the effect of sunshine on the moon, earth's great reflector of light.

**There is a phenomenon known as *earthshine* that affects the moon. This *earthshine* is defined as the faint light visible on the part of the moon not directly illuminated by the sun: *earthlight*. It is due to the light that the earth reflects on the moon and is seen at its best about four days before or four days after the new moon.**

**Those of us who have noticed this *earthshine* on the moon see a very dark reflection. That's all the earth can offer at best...*darkness*.**

Christians who do not live in such a manner to reflect the light of Christ will have the darkness of *earthshine* upon them. Worldliness will tarnish the reflector, and the things of the earth will quickly diminish the reflection of God's glory in one's life.

"But we all, with open face beholding as in a glass the glory of the Lord, are changed into the same image from glory to glory, even as by the Spirit of the Lord." II Corinthians 3:18

We should live blameless lives as children of God, "without rebuke, in the midst of a crooked and perverse nation, among whom ye shine as lights in the world." Philippians 2:15

In the world the light of the gospel is not shining gloriously because there are so few bright reflectors among Christians. Sin and darkness have overtaken us, and *earthshine* instead of *Sonshine* is settled on the church.

Additional Treasures:     Philippians 3:20-21     Colossians 1:10

# May 23

**"And they took knowledge of them, that they
had been with Jesus."
Acts 4:13**

The most telling thing about an individual is the company he keeps. People endeavoring to live godly lives will not keep company with those who despise God and His church. The two have no basis for friendship.

In our text the disciples were out preaching the gospel of Christ, and the religious leaders could not contain their anger when they were reminded of the Lord. They put the disciples in prison.

"And they laid hands on them, and put them in hold unto the next day: for it was now eventide." Acts 4:3

The next day the whole swarm of religious leaders descended on the place to examine the disciples and to threaten them with punishment to silence them on the subject of Christ.

"Now when they saw the boldness of Peter and John, and perceived that they were unlearned and ignorant men, they marvelled; and they took knowledge of them, that they had been with Jesus." Acts 4:13

## WITH JESUS

**Do they know I have been with Jesus?
Those who are walking with me
On the everyday paths of life's journey
When they look at me, what do they see?**

**Do they know I have been with Jesus?
Is the light of His love on my face?
Does my every action bear witness
To the depths of His infinite grace?**

**Do they know I have been with Jesus?
Dear Lord, I pray that they do,
That their hearts may be touched with longing
To know Thee and be with Thee too!
Martha Snell Nicholson**

Additional Treasures:    Philippians 3:8    I Peter 2:7

# May 24

**"And he came to Nazareth, where he had been brought up: and, as his custom was, he went in to the synagogue on the Sabbath day, and stood up for to read."**
**Luke 4:16**

We are creatures of habit, and even the Lord in His earthly ministry had a habit, a custom, of going to the house of God on the day set aside to worship. Back in that time it was the Sabbath, the seventh day of the week. For us it is Sunday, the first day of the week on the calendar, as that is the day that Jesus was resurrected from the grave.

Someone once said that if we do something consecutively for twenty-one days, it becomes a habit. It seems to be easier to form *bad* habits in that way than good ones! The world has such a strong appeal with which to tempt us.

"For all that is in the world, the lust of the flesh, and the lust of the eyes, and the pride of life, is not of the Father, but is of the world."
I John 2:16

Women may become addicted to television programs or reading books, such as novels, that are a detriment to the mind. They don't measure up to the Bible guidelines for how Christians should think.

"Finally, brethren, whatsoever things are true, whatsoever things are honest, whatsoever things are just, whatsoever things are pure, whatsoever things are lovely, whatsoever things are of good report; if there be any virtue, and if there be any praise, think on these things."
Philippians 4:8

Anything that passes the test of that verse is acceptable to watch on television or read in books and magazines. Things that appeal to us can be habit-forming in our lives. Ask the Lord to help you develop good habits.

**Bible reading and prayer every day without fail. Set your time.**
**Attendance in Sunday School and worship on the Lord's day.**
**Tell the gospel to others. Ask God to give you opportunities.**

Additional Treasures:    Hebrews 10:25    Romans 6:11

# May 25

**"Thy word is very pure: therefore thy servant loveth it."**
**Psalm 119:140**

The best habit of all we could cultivate is that of reading the Bible, the Word of God. It is the foundation for Christian living, and is our only weapon and defense in the world that opposes all which is holy and right.

"For the word of God is quick, and powerful, and sharper than any twoedged sword, piercing even to the dividing asunder of soul and spirit, and of the joints and marrow, and is a discerner of the thoughts and intents of the heart." Hebrews 4:12

With all the power of the Word, we should *never* leave our homes without some of it in our hearts each morning. But that habit must be formed and nourished continually because the devil opposes the reading of the Bible so much. He knows it is the tool with which we are building and maintaining our life and testimony for the Lord.

**Set aside a regular time to read every day.**
The time must be scheduled or things will distract you from the important exercise of reading the Word of God. Imagine that you have a date with the Lord and for that few minutes you *must* keep that date.

**Have a Bible with large enough type to read easily.**
Some Bibles that are not used much have small type and would strain the eyes of anyone, young or old. Your Bible should have a type that is comfortable for you to read, and be one in which you can underline verses and make notes on the page. It must be a *study book* to you so that you can make the most of all the benefits the Lord provides in His Word.

**Read the Word with confidence.**
The Holy Spirit dwells in us and is our teacher. Remember that you know the author, and that makes it *personal* to you.

**Develop the Bible Reading habit and never break it!**

Additional Treasures:    Jeremiah 23:29    Ephesians 6:17

# May 26

**"If ye then be risen with Christ, seek those things which are above, where Christ sitteth on the right hand of God."**
**Colossians 3:1**

To seek means *to try to find; search for.* The things above where Christ is sitting at the right hand of God are certainly worth seeking for. It could be termed as the 'riches of Christ' and Christians, by searching the Word of God to learn, will find those things like precious jewels and nuggets of gold. As we grow richer in faith, we love 'seeking' and add daily to our treasures.

**The things which are above are eternal things.**

"…for the things which are seen are temporal; but the things which are not seen are eternal." II Corinthians 4:18

The things which we can't see are the things we should seek. Things of the earth can be seen and will someday pass away. Things of the Lord are *spiritual,* such as the new birth and salvation it provides. Those things are invisible, though one can see the affects in Christians. By faith those things are understood and applied. Faith is a most precious treasure which increases in our hearts as we 'seek' and 'search' God's Word for these precious things that are 'above'.

**Christ is there interceding for us continually.**

"Seeing then that we have a great high priest, that is passed into the heavens, Jesus the Son of God, let us hold fast our profession." Hebrews 4:14

We have nothing to fear. Our Savior is there to intercede for us at the throne of God the Father. Sometimes we don't know how to pray when we are in a troubled state of mind. The Lord even provides for that dilemma. He tells us in His Word the most amazing thing He does for His children:

"...for we know not what we should pray for as we ought: but the Spirit itself maketh intercession for us with groanings which cannot be uttered."
Romans 8:26

"Let us therefore come boldly unto the throne of grace, that we may obtain mercy, and find grace to help in time of need." Hebrews 4:16

Seek eternal things. Be thankful for Christ representing us, and praise God for the grace and mercy that is ours in time of need.

Additional Treasures:   Hebrews 2:17   II Corinthians 5:17-18

# May 27

**"And Naomi said unto her two daughters in law,**
**Go, return each to her mother's house: the Lord deal kindly**
**with you, as ye have dealt with the dead, and with me."**
**Ruth 1:8**

This woman, Naomi, was a model mother-in-law. Her two sons had married women in Moab, a heathen nation, after her family had moved there because of the famine in Israel. Naomi's husband and two sons had died and she was returning to her own land a widow, old and heartbroken. Her daughters-in-law loved her and clung to her, desiring to go too, but she encouraged them to go back, marry again and go on with their lives with her blessing. One did return, but Ruth would not go back from following her mother-in-law.

"And Ruth said, Intreat me not to leave thee, or to return from following after thee: for whither thou goest, I will go; and where thou lodgest, I will lodge: thy people shall be my people, and thy God my God..." Ruth 1:16

We know that Naomi had sown the seed of faith in Ruth's heart, because of her confession and acceptance of God. "thy people shall be my people and thy God my God..."

Naomi believed in God's law concerning the kinsman redeemer who could help her and Ruth, her daughter-in-law.
"Then Naomi her mother in law said unto her, My daughter, shall I not seek rest for thee, that it may be well with thee?" Ruth 3:1
Knowing the law of God, Naomi told Ruth what to do in order to become the wife of Boaz, who redeemed the land and took Ruth as his wife to raise up children to inherit the land of Naomi's sons.

Naomi had the joy of seeing a son born to Ruth and Boaz which would be counted as her own grandchild, heir to her son's inheritance.
"And Naomi took the child, and laid it in her bosom and became nurse unto it." Ruth 4:16
Naomi played a key role in Israel's history by trusting God in returning to the land, and trusting Him to provide for her and Ruth. The son born was named Obed, who was Jesse's father, who was King David's father!

Additional Treasures:    Ruth 4:14-15    I Peter 1:18-19

# May 28

**"In the same hour came forth fingers of a man's hand,
and wrote over against the candlestick upon the plaister of the
wall of the king's palace: and the king saw...."
Daniel 5:5**

There are so many common sayings passed down through
generations and the source in many instances is the Bible. "I can see the
handwriting on the wall" was probably taken out of the book of Daniel.

**In this setting Belshazzer, called the son, though he was the
grandson of Nebuchadnezzar, is now king of the great Babylonian
Empire. He has no regard for God, whom Nebuchadnezzar came to
acknowledge before the end of his reign. To show his disdain for the
God of Israel, he brought out the golden and silver vessels taken
from the temple in Jerusalem and used them as drinking utensils for
his big feast.**

While the assembly of people drank and made merry praising the
gods of gold, silver, brass, iron, wood, and stone, there came the fingers
of a man's hand and wrote a message for the king on the wall!

We know he called Daniel in to interpret the writing. After Daniel
reminded him of the lesson the king's grandfather had learned the hard
way, he rebuked him:

"And thou his son, O Belshazzar, hast not humbled thine heart,
though thou knewest all this; but hast lifted up thyself against the Lord of
heaven..."

Daniel interpreted the writing: in essence... You are finished!
"In that night was Belshazzar, king of the chaldeans slain."  Daniel 5:30

We see the *handwriting on the wall* concerning our lives when we
get slack in the things of the Lord. Disobedience, whether great or small,
brings the chastisement of God upon us. He is our faithful, loving Father
and He will not do contrary to His Word. He cannot let sin go
unpunished.

"For whom the Lord loveth, he chasteneth..." Hebrews 12:6

Additional Treasures:   Hebrews 12:11   Colossians 3:5-6

# May 29

**"Give, and it shall be given unto you... For with the same measure that ye mete withal it shall be measured to you again."**
**Luke 6:38**

Giving ties in with the law of the harvest of sowing and reaping. Whatever you sow will come back in greater abundance than what was sown. Very little seed goes into a crop of wheat, cotton, or corn, compared to the great amount yielded in the harvest.

**If we think in terms of *generous* when we are sharing with others, and giving unto the Lord, then we can expect a *generous* return of blessings in the form of whatever we have sown. "Give and it shall be given unto you."**

The great woman of Proverbs 31 had a very generous spirit and reaped bountifully for her affluent household.
"She stretcheth out her hand to the poor; yea, she reacheth for her hands to the needy. " Proverbs 31:20

There were women with loving, generous hearts who ministered to the needs of Jesus as He went about preaching. What blessings must have been heaped upon their lives!
"And many women were there beholding afar off, which followed Jesus from Galilee, ministering unto Him..." Matthew 27:55

Another, who no doubt reaped from her generous spirit of giving was Lydia of Thyatira, a convert of the apostle Paul. She ministered to Paul and the other missionaries of that day.
"And when she was baptized, and her household, she besought us, saying, If ye have judged me to be faithful to the Lord, come into my house, and abide there. And she constrained us." Acts 16:15

It is God who established the law of the harvest and it will never fail. Whatever is sown in a field is what comes up. It is so in the realm of giving. What we give or 'sow', it will come back into our own lives in some manner.

"And God is able to make all grace abound toward you; that ye, having all sufficiency in all things, may abound...." II Corinthians 9:8

Additional Treasures:    II Corinthians 9:6-7    Galatians 6:9-10

# May 30

**"That this may be a sign among you, that when your children ask their fathers in time to come, saying, What mean ye by these stones? Then ye shall answer them..."**
**Joshua 4:6-7**

When God parted the river Jordan, as he did the Red Sea for the children of Israel to go through safely, Joshua was instructed to take twelve stones out of the middle of the river and stack them up for a memorial. A memorial is something that causes people to remember.

**In our state, today is the legal holiday for honoring deceased servicemen, observed by decorating graves and memorials: *Decoration Day*. It is fitting and proper that men who gave their lives for our country should be remembered at least one day out of the year.**

On Sunday of each week we come together to worship the Lord, remembering His death, burial and resurrection. It is the Lord's Day, a memorial for our Savior.

We should establish some of our own memorial stones, and when our children or grandchildren say, "What do these stones mean?" we can tell them that our faith is in Christ and He is the foundation of our lives. If you have the stones stacked up, you can prove what you say.

**Bible reading and prayer.** Do your children or grandchildren ever see you reading the Bible and praying? It will make an impression on their memory...*they won't forget that stone.*

**Church attendance.** Kids notice how you attend God's house, and also what you say *before and after* you are there. Tell your family: "*we* are to be faithful to the house of God." Hebrews 10:25

**Seeking the lost.** Jesus died for sinners, and just as He saved us He longs to save others who are lost. Pray always for opportunities to witness, and set up that stone of love and caring for lost people.

Additional Treasures:     I Corinthians 13:1-8     Joshua 24:15

# May 31

"O God, thou art my God; early will I seek thee:
my soul thirsteth for thee, my flesh longeth for thee in a dry
land, where no water is.."
Psalm 63:1

We should have another memorial stone established in our lives that is obvious to our children...a personal devotion to the Lord.

Our family, *especially,* knows if we are really devoted to God or if we are pretending. Our loved ones know what we are really like.

This stone is very important; it affects us personally. We become like what we gaze upon continually. We know that a Christ-like person has been sitting at the Lord's feet looking at Him by faith.

Don't get into some system of Bible reading which makes it difficult for you to keep up. Just simply *read the Bible through* at your own pace, where each day you start at the place where you stopped. Don't bog down! If you are stuck where you aren't getting anything, simply go to the next chapter or book, or from the Old to the New Testament. It is so important to stay with it and read your Bible, and it will be a fountain of blessing in your life.

### God's Unchanging Word

For feelings come and feelings go,
And feelings are deceiving;
My warrant is the Word of God,
Naught else is worth believing.
Though all my heart should feel condemned
For want of some sweet token,
There is One greater than my heart
Whose Word cannot be broken.
I'll trust in God's unchanging Word,
Till soul and body sever:
For, though all things shall pass away,
His Word will stand forever.
**Martin Luther**

Additional Treasures:    Psalm 5:3      Psalm 119:2

# June 1

**"This is a great mystery: but I speak**
**concerning Christ and the church."**
**Ephesians 5:32**

The great mystery of which the apostle Paul speaks is the relationship of a man and woman in marriage because it is a type of a greater union, that of Christ and His church.

"For no man ever yet hated his own flesh; but nourisheth and cherisheth it, even as the Lord the church: For we are members of his body, of his flesh, and of his bones. For this cause shall a man leave his father and mother, and shall be joined unto his wife, and they two shall be one flesh."Eph. 5:29-31

June is called the Bride's month because of its weddings. However, marriage is not taken as seriously as it used to be. Many people have the attitude; 'We will try it and if it doesn't work, we will just get a divorce.'

Some women do take marriage seriously, but have the mistaken notion that marriage is going to make them happy at last and every problem will be left behind. I have taught women on the subject of marriage for years, and I emphasize the fact that marriage cannot make a woman happy if she is not already happy *before* she gets into the marriage relationship.

**Dearly Beloved...and as the ceremony begins the bride makes her vows to her husband, and with that she may feel that all of her insecurities and other hang-ups are *symbolically* removed in this new relationship. Not so! Marriage is new, yes, but the people are not. In time the *old* comes out again *affecting everything* as usual, and especially the new relationship shared with another who *also* has a store of normal or abnormal hang-ups.** Bible Study Notes...'97 E.H.

The joy of the Lord in the heart provides the wisdom and strength needed to meet the wonderful challenge of marriage.

"Ask, and ye shall receive, that your joy may be full." John 16:24

Additional Treasures:    Nehemiah 8:10    Psalm 16:11

# June 2

**"And the Lord said unto Moses, Stretch out thine hand
toward heaven, that there may be darkness over the land
of Egypt, even darkness which may be felt."
Exodus 10:21**

We cannot imagine darkness that may be felt unless we have an actual experience of it. It is no wonder the Egyptians didn't move out of their places while the darkness prevailed in the land.

"They saw not one another, neither rose any from his place for three days: but all the children of Israel had light in their dwellings." Ex. 10:23

**I could imagine this happening after I'd experienced darkness where nobody would dare move. Our church gave us a very nice gift for our thirtieth anniversary in the pastorate. It was a trip to the beautiful state of Virginia, and we saw many historic places and other attractions as well. During a drive around the Smoky Mountains, we visited an underground cavern with a group, and in the depths of that place the lights were turned off to show us *darkness*! I *felt* that darkness and thanked God for light when it came on.**

In complete darkness, one feels disoriented as darkness engulfs the body. That's why the people of Egypt could not escape the darkness by running to Israel's dwelling places where there was light. *They couldn't move.*

**The way of sin is described as *darkness.***
"The way of the wicked is as darkness: they know not at what they stumble." Proverbs 4:19
"The night is far spent, the day is at hand: let us therefore cast off the works of darkness, and let us put on the armour of light." Romans 13:12

**Stay out of the darkness of sin! God made provision for us.**
"But if we walk in the light, as he is in the light, we have fellowship one with another, and the blood of Jesus Christ his Son cleanseth us from all sin." I John 1:7
Sin is the darkness to be afraid of. Stay in the light!

Additional Treasures:    Matthew 6:23    Jeremiah 23:12

# June 3

"But ye, brethren, are not in darkness, that that
day should overtake you as a thief."
I Thessalonians 5:4

The apostle Paul taught the Christians at Thessalonica about the Lord's coming in the clouds to take the church out, *the rapture,* and their need to stay ready for that event. Their readiness would depend on their right relationship to Christ, being obedient in all things.

"Therefore let us not sleep, as do others; but let us watch and be sober." I Thessalonians 5:5

Most people sleep in the darkness of nighttime; that is the normal time for physical rest and sleep. Christians also sleep in *spiritual* darkness when sin has overtaken them. Their spiritual vision is impaired in the darkness and they do not *see* the importance of the things of God as they once did in the light of obedience. They will not be watching and longing for the coming of the Lord.

Unbelievers are lost in *paralyzing darkness*, pictured in the darkness of Egypt before the exodus of God's people from that land. They cannot move because they are dead spiritually.

"And you hath he quickened, who were dead in trespasses and sins."

The gospel of Christ, news of His death, burial and resurrection is the only thing with power to reach into that spiritual darkness and make the dead *alive* in Christ! It is our responsibility to share that light so the lost will not perish forever in the eternal darkness of hell.

There is nothing that brings joy to the heart like telling someone about Jesus and seeing him respond and trust Christ as his Savior. Always remember that you are the messenger; the power to convict a lost sinner is only in the  message. Our stories, illustrations or power of persuasion has no power whatever to 'win' a sinner. Only the message of Christ can do it.

Rescue the perishing, Care for the dying,
Snatch them in pity from sin and The grave;
Weep o'er the erring one, Lift up the fallen,
Tell them of Jesus the mighty to save.
Rescue the perishing, Care for the dying;
Jesus is merciful, Jesus will save.
Hymn by: Fanny J. Crosby

Additional Treasures:    I John 5:12    Daniel 12:3

# June 4

**"Even so the tongue is a little member, and boasteth
great things. Behold, how great a matter a little fire kindleth."
James 3:5**

The scriptures tell us in plain words that our tongue is the worst problem we have and that no man can tame it. Therefore, we must be serious about relying on the Lord for the strength to deal with it continually.

God says it plainly: "But the tongue can no man tame; it is an unruly evil, full of deadly poison." James 3:8

Jesus preached a very pointed sermon to the religious leaders that followed Him around hoping to catch Him in an error. What folly! They poured out religious words constantly which sounded pretty to the ear, but in their hearts it was a different picture altogether, and Jesus could see the depths of their hearts. He saw all their hypocrisy and wickedness.

"Even so ye also outwardly appear righteous unto men, but within ye are full of hypocrisy and iniquity, "Woe unto you scribes and Pharisees, hypocrites!"  Matthew 23:28-29

When the mouth is like a fountain that has both sweet and bitter water flowing from it, something is very seriously wrong. We cannot call back one word that we utter, though we may apologize for it many times.

> **Boys flying kites haul in their white winged birds;**
> **But you can't do that when you are flying words.**
> **Thoughts unexpressed may fall back dead,**
> **But God Himself can't kill them...once they are said.**
> Author unknown.

Christians should always give thought to their words *before* they express them. Saying the first thing that pops into your head may cause a lot of grief for someone, and the Lord's hand of discipline in your life. God's word of warning in the scriptures should motivate us to keep our tongues in check.

But remember that a word is always a 'thought' before it is verbalized. Don't think that the respectable sin of ungodly thoughts will stay hidden. God sees them and eventually when you're off guard, out they will come in words!

"Whoso keepeth his mouth and his tongue keepeth his soul from troubles." Proverbs 21:23

Additional Treasures:  Titus 2:7-8   Proverbs 17:27

# June 5

**"And many false prophets shall rise, and shall deceive many."**
**Matthew 24:11**

We certainly have many *false prophets* in our day. Leaders of cults and various groups called by religious names have led their followers even to death by suicide. It is appalling that so many in the world believe false prophets, those who indoctrinate others with their philosophy and teaching.

In these last days Jesus said many *antichrists,* those pretending to be the Lord Himself, would come on the scene and we have seen this in our generation. It will get worse as the coming of the Lord draws nearer.

"For there shall arise false Christs, and false prophets, and shall shew great signs and wonders; insomuch that, if it were possible, they shall deceive the very elect." Matthew 24:24

Each time someone sets a date for the Lord's coming, *the very day,* it is a false alarm, and the world becomes more indifferent to the truth.

**Once I was in a Nursing Home visiting a lady that I read to occasionally, and as I was leaving her room an alarm went off in the building. The shrill sound was so loud people were holding their ears, and the fire alarm lights along the hall started flashing. When I got out to the big waiting area, several of the staff people were sternly rebuking a little lady in a wheelchair who had *set off the fire alarm!* She seemed unresponsive to their rebuke because she was enjoying all the commotion it had caused.**

The danger in false alarms is that one may be indifferent to a *real alarm,* when action must be taken immediately in an emergency situation.

We must warn people of their need to be saved while there is still time before the Lord comes. False alarms going off in the world do not alter the truth in the slightest. Christians must stay alert too!

"Let no man deceive you with vain words: for because of these things cometh the wrath of God upon the children of disobedience." Ephesians 5:6

Additional Treasures:    Ephesians 5:11-12    John 4:35

# June 6

**"I know that, whatsoever God doeth, it shall be for ever:
nothing can be put to it, nor any thing taken from it:
and God doeth it, that men should fear before him."
Ecclesiastes 3:14**

If the work of God has begun in your heart, you can be sure it is an eternal work. This should be a verse of great assurance for the timid souls that cannot lay hold of the fact that they are saved eternally, if they are saved at all. From the moment that a person believes on the Lord Jesus Christ, a seal is put on his soul: *This soul is preserved for eternity.*

"In whom ye trusted, after that ye heard the word of truth, the gospel of your salvation: in whom also after that ye believed, ye were sealed with that holy Spirit of promise..." Ephesians 1:13

After our new birth into God's family, our Heavenly Father begins a work in us to conform us to the image of Christ. He wants us to have a family resemblance so we can be easily identified. God's children on earth!
"For whom he did foreknow, he also did predestinate to be conformed to the image of his Son, that he might be the firstborn among many brethren." Romans 8:20

God is patient and persistent in His work in us, and He doesn't back down in defeat because we may at times become indifferent about the things of the Lord. That only brings correction into our lives until we are willing to focus again on things that matter and get back to 'growing in grace and knowledge.'

God is immutable, *unchanging*, and what He begins He finishes. We can have perfect assurance in our hearts, if we believe God's Word, since that is the foundation for our faith.

"Verily, Verily, I say unto you, He that heareth my word, and believeth on him that sent me, hath everlasting life, and shall not come into condemnation; but is passed from death unto life." John 5:24

Additional Treasures:    Romans 8:1    John 3:36

# June 7

**"Thou hast bought me no sweet cane with money,
neither hast thou filled me with the fat of thy sacrifices..."
Isaiah 43:24**

Sweet cane was one of the ingredients making up the holy anointing oil used in the service of the tabernacle.

"Take thou also unto thee principal spices, of pure myrrh five hundred shekels, and of sweet cinnamon half so much...and of sweet calamus two hundred and fifty shekels...and thou shalt make it an oil of holy ointment...and it shall be an holy anointing oil." Exodus 30:23, 25

The *sweet calamus* was sweet cane according to the Bible references and commentaries. Our text indicates that sweet cane was connected with the offering of sacrifices in worship. It was a part of the sweet incense used in anointing the tabernacle and everything in it, including the ark of the testimony where God met with His people.

"And I will meet with thee there, and I will commune with thee from above the mercy seat, from between the two cherubims which are upon the ark of the testimony..." Exodus 25:22

**As a child, I remember my father making syrup from the sugar cane that we grew on the farm. He had a syrup mill set up in the pasture where he processed our own and that of others who had no mill.**

**It was a childish delight to watch the mule, harnessed to a pole, go around and around all day as people fed the cane into a grinder to extract the juice that ran down a trough into the huge cooking pan over a fire. My father stood there cooking and stirring constantly until the juice turned into syrup, with *just the right* consistency. There was a sweet odor that permeated the air as the syrup cooked.**

*Prayer* is the nearest thing to a sweet cane offering on earth today. Offer to the Lord today your prayer of praise and thanksgiving for His great love which made a way for our salvation. Your prayers are kept in heaven!

"And when he had taken the book, the four beasts and four and twenty elders fell down before the Lamb, having every one of them harps, and golden vials full of odors, which are the prayers of the saints." Revelation 5:8

Additional Treasures:  John 15:7  Matthew 21:22

# June 8

**"And he said unto them, Follow me, and I will
make you fishers of men."
Matthew 4:19**

The Lord did not command his followers to be fishers of men; He commanded them to *follow Him*, and He would *make them* fishers of men.

Jesus won individual souls, as well as the multitudes. He said to Zacchaeus after He called him down from the tree:
"...This day is salvation come to this house, forsomuch as he also is a son of Abraham. For the Son of man is come to seek and to save that which was lost." Luke 19: 9-10
Jesus does the work of salvation, but he allows Christians to be used in the *seeking* by being witnesses. That's telling the gospel, *the good news,* to the lost: that Christ died for our sins, was buried, rose the third day, and every soul can be saved that will believe it and trust in Him.

Everyone who has *received* God's salvation should be willing to tell others so they can receive it too. These things are needful:

**Be *sure* of your own salvation.**
If you don't *personally* know a person, you can't introduce him to others. The apostle Paul said "For I know whom I have believed..."
II Timothy 1:12
To be sure, trust in Him...and believe God's Word!

**Have a working knowledge of the Word.**
The most timid individual can use the *Romans Road* to present the gospel of Christ to a lost soul. If you aren't familiar with it, ask your pastor or a mature Christian to show you how to use it.

We should pray for courage to witness to the lost around us. My pastor's wife over fifty years ago was an effective soul-winner. She never hurried, and was so patient with people until her opportunity came to give them the gospel. She said the secret was prayer. The more time she spent in prayer, the more results were seen in witnessing. Let us learn from those who have been very successful in the area of soul-winning.

Additional Treasures:    Psalm 126:6    Proverbs 11:30

# June 9

"Being born again, not of corruptible seed, but of
incorruptible, by the word of God, which liveth and abideth
forever."
I Peter 1:23

It is clear that the Spirit of God uses the *incorruptible seed* of the Word of God in the fertile soil of a heart in order to produce the new birth. No one can be saved without it. That's why it is imperative to know something of the Word, and be willing to share it.

**The Word, which is seed to the sower,** *the one who witnesses,* **becomes bread to the eater,** *the lost one who gets saved.*

"For as the rain cometh down, and the snow from heaven, and returneth not thither, but watereth the earth, and maketh it bring forth and bud, that it may give seed to the sower, and bread to the eater: So shall my word be that goeth forth out of my mouth: it shall not return to me void, but it shall accomplish that which I please, and....prosper in the thing whereto I sent it."

In the matter of sowing the good seed, understand that there *will be* results because of the power in the seed. Our part is to sow it; God said that He would prosper it. It won't come back void, or empty. We may not *see* the results, but they will be produced in time by God's power. In heaven all the results will be evident. What rejoicing takes place there!

"Likewise, I say unto you, there is joy in the presence of the angels of God over one sinner that repenteth."     Luke 15:10

It has always been of interest to me to hear soul-winning experiences told by pastors and missionaries. In the pastorate, we had many occasions to talk with them and hear unique stories of salvation. My brother, a missionary in Papua New Guinea for years, tells of driving 500 miles back into the 'bush' country to a remote village to answer an old chieftain's questions. He had sent for him to come. A young native of that village had attended their Bible College and gone back there preaching the gospel. The old man asked was it really true that God would forgive all his sins. Frank began with repentance and explained salvation. Later the old chief and several more men of the village were saved. God's servants all over the world, obedient to His call, are winning souls one by one...trophies of God's amazing grace.

Additional Treasures:     Acts 4:13     John 4:36

# June 10

**"Whoso findeth a wife findeth a good thing,
and obtaineth favour of the Lord."
Proverbs 18:22**

I'm glad it is my husband's opinion that he found a *good thing* when we married on this day sixty years ago. We were married on a Sunday afternoon in the Baptist church of our little town, and since then life has never been the same.

So it is when one believes on the Lord Jesus Christ. The presence of the Holy Spirit indwelling the Christian forever changes his life.

"Therefore if any man be in Christ, he is a new creature: old things are passed away; behold, all things are become new." II Corinthians 5:17

**A few years after we were married we became Christians, and later my husband was called to preach. In time, he was also called to be a pastor and that brought another great change in our lives, which now included a son and daughter. We understand now that God had a plan and purpose for our lives...together.**

One thing that has been a source of strength for me in the work of the ministry is the fact that *I know that my husband is called to preach.*
I was there when the struggle was on and God dealt with his heart until he surrendered to preach the gospel. He has always been consistently faithful.

## THE GOD-CALLED PREACHER

**Who can describe that inward bent,
The call of God on the man He's sent?
He lives and serves in the Lord's design,
Not a shallow thing such as *change of mind*.
Like a mighty oak of many generations,
A long-time preacher is a prized possession.
With roots grown deep in strength of the Lord,
He understands the power of the Word.
As the body grows older, not heart and mind,
God's call stays vibrant, ageless in time.
Decades of dedicated service commend
The God-called preacher...faithful to the end.**
Edna Holmes

Additional Treasures:    Romans 8:28    I Corinthians 15:58

# June 11

**"Be not deceived; God is not mocked: for whatsoever
a man soweth, that shall he also reap."
Galatians 6:7**

This truth is not applied to the marriage and family as much as other areas, but the home is the most important field in which to sow.

I've heard this saying so much: *The grass is greener on the other side of the fence.* In reality, the grass is greener where it has been watered. If more people would tend to their own field instead of looking over the fence, many homes would be happier places where the family could thrive in love and security. Children feel secure where there is obvious love and contentment.

**God Himself performed the first marriage ceremony.**
"And the rib, which the Lord God had taken from man, made he a woman, and brought her to the man. And Adam said, This is now bone of my bones, and flesh of my flesh: she shall be called Woman, because she was taken out of Man. Therefore, shall a man leave his father and his mother, and shall cleave unto his wife: and they shall be one flesh." Genesis 2:22-24

Marriage is very important, for God instituted it. For those of us who are married, it is a good field in which to sow good things in abundance.

Seeds of love, kindness, respect, courtesy, and forgiveness produce harmony and happiness. With these qualities being planted constantly, there will always be evidence of a harvest in the home.

Make up your own little bundle of *happiness seeds* and start sowing and watering on *your* side of the fence. It will be conducive to maintaining the right attitude for both husband and wife, according to the Bible.
"Submitting yourselves one to another in the fear of the Lord."
Ephesians 5:21
Early in our marriage we decided that we would never call each other by derogatory names when we got upset and the notion just evolved over time that we would also be courteous to one another. That has been a tremendous factor in our marriage. It has soothed feelings and set the tone for a reasonable discussion about matters needing attention. Plant your 'happiness' seeds!

Additional Treasures:    Ephesians 5:33    I Thessalonians 5:15

# June 12

**"Neither have I gone back from the commandment of his lips;
I have esteemed the words of his mouth more than my necessary
food."
Job 23:12**

In the aftermath of World War II, there were many homeless, starving orphans in war-torn Europe and orphan homes were established to rescue these little children. In one such place, the workers had a perplexing problem. They fed the children daily all they could eat, bathed them at night and put them to bed, but they *would not go to sleep.* The caretakers tried everything they could think of to get the children to relax, reassuring them that when they awoke there would be food for them. But the orphans still struggled against sleep. Then someone had an idea. They put a piece of *bread* in each child's hand when he was put to bed. The results were amazing! Every child went  to sleep, clutching his bread, only confident of food for tomorrow *if* the bread was in his hand.

**In our country of plenty we do have a lack of bread, *that spiritual bread,* the Word of God, although it is stacked up all around us. Families and churches should partake of it by making its inspired words their rule in conduct and worship. In these last days we should be *devouring* the bread of God's Word, *holding it in our hands,* for tomorrow we may not have it!**

"Behold, the days come, saith the Lord God, that I will send a famine in the land, not a famine of bread, nor a thirst for water, but of hearing the words of the Lord. And they shall wander from sea to sea, and
from the north even to the east, they shall run to and fro to seek the word of the Lord, and shall not find it." Amos 8:11-12
"Thy words were found, and I did eat them: and thy word was unto me the joy and rejoicing of mine heart: for I am called by thy name, O Lord God of hosts." Jeremiah 15:16

Make sure that the Word of God is present in your mind and heart before you lay down for sleep each night and be diligent to seek the Lord's face early each morning to prepare your heart for the day. I try to maintain that good habit. I still regret all the time wasted in fruitless days when I didn't understand that the time with the Lord would make the day profitable, my heart happier, and I'd make better decisions as a result of putting Him first. If you don't meet Him early, start today. It's never too late to learn good habits.

Additional Treasures:    Romans 15:4    Colossians 3:16

# June 13

**"Moreover the law entered, that the offence might abound.
But where sin abounded, grace did much more abound."
Romans 5:20**

Sin will always abound in this world. It is Satan's territory. Jesus referred to the devil as the *prince of this world.* "Hereafter I will not talk much with you: for the prince of this world cometh, and hath nothing in me." John 14:30

Satan is also the prince of the power of the air. "Wherein in time past ye walked according to the course of this world, according to the prince of the power of the air, the spirit that now worketh in the children of disobedience." Ephesians 2:2

We cannot take lightly the power of sin and its devastation to the life of a Christian who gets slothful in his devotion to the Lord, and is taken in by sin's deceitfulness. The devil always works through deceit.

Sin is overspreading the whole earth, and we must encourage one another to be faithful to God. "But exhort one another daily, while it is called today; lest any of you be hardened through the deceitfulness of sin." Hebrews 3:13

**While living in West Texas, we occasionally had a *sandstorm.* You could see it approaching on the horizon, a huge cloud of *dirt* rolling toward us, and all we could do was watch as it came. It made no difference how new or old the house might be or how airtight the windows and doors, the dust got in and covered things. The cloud of sand engulfed the town and continued on until it gradually ran its course.**

Sin has engulfed the world and affects all of the inhabitants, even the Christians who have the Holy Spirit dwelling in them. We must stay inside the *shelter of obedience* to God and as quickly as the fallout of sin touches us, confess it and claim God's promise for cleansing. "If we confess our sins, he is faithful and just to forgive us our sins, and to cleanse us from all unrighteousness." I John 1:9

That verse is one of the most powerful in the Bible, an extraordinary promise for our benefit. When we sin, *and we will,* God says for us to confess it. That means admit and agree with Him that we have done wrong, and He will forgive us. Christians who won't 'confess' it will be corrected or chastised by the Lord. He won't allow sin to be hidden away for long.

Additional Treasures:  II Thessalonians 3:3   Psalm 32:10   Psalm 34:22

# June 14

**"Preach the word; be instant in season, out of season;
reprove, rebuke, exhort with all longsuffering and doctrine."
II Timothy 4:2**

The Word is not referring to the seasons where work is done in planting, cultivating and harvesting crops in the literal sense of the word. That would mean no preaching in winter; *that's out of season.* But instead we are to understand that whether the time is convenient, favorable or pleasing to us personally, we are to be ready and willing to do the work of the Lord that He has appointed us to do.

"He that observeth the wind shall not sow; and he that regardeth the clouds shall not reap." Ecclesiastes 11:4

If we wait for that perfect time to come along to do some service for the Lord, that *just right* opportunity, we will never do anything.

**"The call to meet someone's need comes in an hour that we think not. The door of opportunity opens suddenly, unexpectedly; and unless one is ready on the instant to pass through, the door closes again."** Spurgeon

God's people must first be willing to do whatever the Lord puts in their way, and then the out of season factor will not matter.

The first difficult *out of season* thing I was asked to do as a pastor's wife helped me realize that I was willing in my heart to do whatever the Lord had for me to do. We don't *know* about our faith until it's tested.

On a winter night years ago a young mother called me at 1:30 in the morning. She asked me to come and stay with two little children, while she and her husband took the sick baby to an emergency room in another town. Sleet was pelting the windows, mixed with freezing rain, and the bed had *never* felt so warm and comfortable. *God's call* on our lives is what pulled me out of that bed and made me dress and go out in that winter weather, drive across town, and stay awake and alert until they returned.

**Be sensitive to the Holy Spirit in you.
Seize the opportunities that come into your life.**

Additional Treasures:     Matthew 25:44-45     Romans 14:12

# June 15

"A man's pride shall bring him low: but honour
shall uphold the humble in spirit."
Proverbs 29:23

Pride is defined as *a high opinion* of one's own worth or possessions.
This is one of the traits that God hates in human beings. It causes so much sorrow and devastation in their lives. "These six things doth the Lord hate: yea, seven are an abomination unto him: a proud look...."
Proverbs 6:16-17

Pride keeps people from coming to Christ when the Holy Spirit convicts their hearts. They do not want to *humble* themselves and admit their need for the Savior. Pride causes families to spend far beyond their means. In many cases debt overwhelms them, and the stress and trouble generated by it destroys the family.

Pride is common among many rich people. They disdain those who are poor in material possessions and feel superior to them. Blessed are those who though they may be rich, have a humble, thankful attitude toward God and a right spirit toward their fellowmen.

**My great uncle and aunt became wealthy when oil was discovered on their land many decades ago. I remember how big and beautiful their home looked to me as a little girl. In the large sitting room there were plush chairs and couches to sit on, but in front of the fireplace were two cane-bottom straight-back wooden chairs where the owners of that beautiful furniture sat. These had the prominent place, and were well worn by use. It showed the character of these humble country folk. The circumstance of wealth did not alter them. They controlled their wealth; it did not control them.**

In the present day, occasionally somebody may become extremely rich by winning the lottery, a phenomena which has sprung up in modern days. It is an amazing thing what happens to many of these recipients of a fortune that most people can only dream of. Very few handle it wisely. Most manage to spend it all within a year or two and come out being bankrupt. It is a classic demonstration of the truth of the Bible. "By humility and the fear of the Lord are riches, and honour, and life." Proverbs 22:4

Additional Treasures:    James 4:6    Luke 14:11

# June 16

**"The Lord will destroy the house of the proud:
but he will establish the border of the widow."
Proverbs 15:25**

This verse is a comfort for widows. It is a promise of God's special attention and care to one whose spouse has died, who then faces life alone. "...but he will establish the border of the widow."

A border is defined as a *boundary*, and a boundary is a protective factor in God's design. A widow who fears the Lord and honors Him with her life is surrounded as Elisha was in Dothan, when the Syrian king was out to kill him because he was God's prophet.
"And Elisha prayed, and said, Lord, I pray thee, open his eyes, that he may see. And the Lord opened the eyes of the young man; and he saw: and, behold, the mountain was full of horses and chariots of fire round about Elisha." II Kings 6:17

Every child of God is precious and beloved in His sight, and He is no respecter of persons. "Then Peter opened his mouth, and said, Of a truth I perceive that God is no respecter of persons." Acts 10:34

As surely as the prideful walk the path of destruction, the widows and orphans are encircled with God's protection and care. The Lord connects 'pure religion and undefiled before God' with ministering to the fatherless children and widows.
"Pure religion and undefiled before God and the Father is this, to visit the fatherless and widows in their affliction, and to keep himself unspotted from the world." James 1:27

It is easy to think that the heart of that verse in James is the 'visiting the widows and orphans' part. That's not hard at all. But keeping ourselves from becoming spotted, or stained, by the sins of the world is another factor altogether. Our "religion", as we think of it, will not amount to anything if there are obvious sins attached to our testimony before others. That requires diligence in our world today. Technology has brought every kind of immoral thought and practice right into our homes by computers and televisions. We need the purity of God's Word to keep our hearts cleansed. Stay 'unspotted'.

Additional Treasures:   Isaiah 1:17   Exodus 22:22   Deuteronomy 26:12

# June 17

**"For I know the thoughts that I think toward you,
saith the Lord..."
Jeremiah 29:11**

Some have the mistaken notion that God may get weary in well doing and not help during our troubles and trials. *We* need the reminder from the Word, but God does not! "And let us not be weary in well doing: for in due season we shall reap, if we faint not." Galatians 6:9

We cannot put a number to the thoughts that God thinks toward us. Earth does not contain that knowledge. God's thoughts are more in number than the grains of sand by the seas.
"How precious also are thy thoughts unto me, O God! how great is the sum of them! If I should count them, they are more in number than the sand: when I awake, I am still with thee." Psalm 139:17-18

We could not count the grains of sand in the palm of a hand, much less on the seashore. We should be thankful, comforted, and ever praise the Lord for His love in thinking toward us. It is amazing to learn that our God is capable of such thing, thinking of us more than we can compute into numbers. How can that be? He is God and that's what the One and only God can do. That's why the more we learn of Him, the more peaceful our soul remains. Nothing will ever disturb Him and He is thinking about us, His children.

God is delighted when His children think of Him. He keeps what we would call a scrapbook, a book for precious memory items.
"Then they that feared the Lord spake often one to another: and the Lord hearkened, and heard it, and a book of remembrance was written before him for them that feared the Lord, and that thought upon his name." Mal. 3:16

God thinks about us, and He values our thoughts about Him. He even keeps a memory book of them. Is your page in God's book full of worshipful thoughts, or is it sparse or blank? Think of Him often. At night look up and think on His creation of the universe. Watch a sunrise, gaze on a sunset, look at everything around you in nature growing, but best of all consider what happened when God saved your soul. Think on that.

Additional Treasures:    Malachi 3:17    Isaiah 55: 8-9

# June 18

**"And he hath put a new song in my mouth,
even praise unto our God..."
Psalm 40:3**

When our thoughts continually dwell on the Lord, the heart produces music. It will be a new song of praise unto our God!   The works of the Lord and His thoughts toward us cannot be *reckoned up in order* or numbered.

"Many, O Lord my God, are thy wonderful works which thou hast done, and thy thoughts which are to usward: they cannot be reckoned up in order unto thee: if I would declare and speak of them, they are more than can be numbered." Psalm 40:5

We are to direct our thoughts not only to the Lord, but also toward each other. "Let this mind be in you, which was also in Christ Jesus." Phil. 2:5

## THINKING OF YOU

It's a comforting message from His Word,
As things go right, or wrong.
Molehill troubles turn to mountains,
Yet, "I think toward you" says the Lord.

My heart was full, silently pleading.
You passed by, too distracted to see
One longing for a touch, or a smile;
The moment passed...do you think of me?

I meant to call, but was busy that day;
Other opportunities slipped away.
Coldness pierced me like a sword,
And I ran cringing to God's Word,
Was warmed by His love...And thought of you.

Edna Holmes

The lack of love and compassion in God's people for each other is appalling.  We don't want to be bothered with others' needs or problems. But we should take time to *listen* with our hearts, and pray with genuine concern.

Additional Treasures:    Proverbs 12:5    Philippians 4:8

# June 19

**"Watch therefore; for ye know neither the day nor
the hour wherein the Son of man cometh."
Matthew 25:13**

In this context, *watch* could be defined as *to look or wait (for) with
care and attention.* Jesus said He was coming, and we do not know
when. Therefore, we must live each day as though it is *the* day. It will
have a purifying effect on our lives.

"Beloved, now are we the sons of God, and it doth not yet appear
what we shall be: but we know that, when he shall appear, we shall be
like him; for we shall see him as he is. And every man that hath this hope
in him purifieth himself, even as he is pure." I John 3:2-3

While we watch we are to occupy, or be involved in the work of the
Lord on earth. "And he called his ten servants, and delivered them ten
pounds, and said unto them, Occupy till I come." Luke 19:13

In Mark, the Lord said: "Watch ye therefore: for ye know not when
the master of the house cometh, and what I say unto you I say unto all,
Watch." Mark 13: 35, 37

**When my husband worked in the oilfield, before we had
children, we *night-watched* when the oilrig was down (not being
worked) for a few days. It was situated on a huge range called
*Waggoner's Pasture*, and there were numerous cattle-guard type
gates to keep in the cattle, which grazed in various parts. Our duty
was to be there from sundown until sunup, so we'd take food and
bedding, drive out to the oil-rig, park nearby and spend the night in
our car. Once as we dozed with the windows down slightly, listening
to music on the radio, we heard soft snorts and shuffling. We looked
out upon a small herd of cows gathered around us, contentedly
listening. They had gravitated to the music so quietly, we didn't hear
them coming. It was a good thing they weren't thieves!**

Don't be caught unaware at the Lord's coming. He said, "Watch".

Additional Treasures:    Matthew 24:28-29    Luke 21:34

# June 20

**"And Samuel said, Hath the Lord as great delight in
burnt offerings and sacrifices, as in obeying the voice of the Lord?"
I Samuel 15:22**

*Disobedience* is not as harsh a word as *rebellion*, but they are the same in God's estimation. "Behold, to obey is better than sacrifice, and to hearken than the fat of rams. For rebellion is as the sin of witchcraft, and stubbornness is as iniquity and idolatry..." I Samuel 15: 22-23

This verse tells us that disobedience is *rebellion* and *stubbornness*. So when Christians will not do what the Word of God clearly teaches them to do, they are being rebellious and stubborn. These sins are always very costly. It cost King Saul his kingdom and much unhappiness before his rule was finally ended by his own death. The prophet, Samuel, told the king of God's sure judgment because of his disobedience: "Because thou hast rejected the word of the Lord, he hath also rejected thee from being king." v.22

King Saul was the first king of Israel. He was an outstanding man and could have been a hero like David, but he *rebelled* and did not completely obey God in the matter of the sacrifice. He later became insanely jealous because David was a hero to the people for killing the giant Goliath and being courageous in battle. Sin robbed King Saul of everything because he did not confess that first little spark of rebellion that sprung up in his heart. It could have stopped right there. But he didn't. Other sins were added to cover the rebellion. Now his name is blight in Israel's history.

In any instance, disobedience is costly. Christians are deprived of the blessings simple obedience brings because of their own foolishness. They do not 'mind' as good children, but fail to do what they know God would have them do. There is usually a 'fretting' about the troubles they experience.
"The foolishness of man perverteth his way: and his heart fretteth against the Lord." Proverbs 19:3

Call disobedience what it is—*rebellion*, and don't listen to others who make light of being obedient to God. It does matter! It grieves the heart of God, and He will judge and correct it in His children.

Additional Treasures:     Ephesians 5:6     I Samuel 12:15

# June 21

"And a curse, if ye will not obey the commandments
of the Lord your God, but turn aside out of the way which I
command you this day..."
Deuteronomy 11:28

A curse was a pronouncement of evil or harm, and it was conditional. As a result of disobedience, a curse came upon Israel even after they had witnessed the great miracles of the Lord as he brought them out of the slavery of Egypt. When we read of the wonders God did for them in the journey to the Promised Land, we feel dismay at their deliberate turning away from Him in disobedience after He plainly warned them not to. Their sin cost Israel all that they had gained after being delivered from Egypt! They went back into the bondage of sin. They never imagined that it would happen. "Our necks are under persecution: we labour, and have no rest."     Lamentations 5:5

**Today, disobedience is encouraged in all levels of our society, and every act of disobedience against God automatically starts the wheel of judgment turning.   There doesn't have to be a special pronouncement of it; it's already in force. It is important to teach little children to obey at an early age for even their disobedience can bring about devastation.**

Many years ago a mother let her little boy out to play, and instructed him as usual not to play near a covered well in the back yard.  She then lay down to take a nap.  A neighbor, washing dishes at her kitchen window, looked up just in time to see that child tumble into the well that he had uncovered.  Not wasting a moment, she ran out and jumped down into the well to hold his head above water so he wouldn't drown. She was chin deep in cold water, and held the child up with her arms while they both screamed for help until they had no voice left.  After a while the mother of the boy awakened, came out, discovered the open well and quickly called for help. As they were lifted from the well, the boy was all right, but the woman had a stroke and died there with her arms frozen in that position of holding the child up above the water.   Irresponsibility and disobedience caused that horrible tragedy. Let us not be guilty of either in our regard for the Word of God.

Be obedient to the Lord in everything. It is the key to happiness.

Additional Treasures:     John 15:10     James 1:25

# June 22

**"For the wages of sin is death; but the gift of God**
**is eternal life through Jesus Christ our Lord."**
**Romans 6:23**

With all the suffering on earth because of sin, people still have not understood the devastation that sin leaves in its wake. Christians having the scriptures open to their understanding, are still indifferent to the facts of sin and its affect. Sin is deceptive, and it can fool any Christian who is not daily fortified with the Word of God. That is his weapon against the devil.

"For the word of God is quick, and powerful, and sharper than any two-edged sword, piercing even to the dividing asunder of soul and spirit...and is a discerner of the thoughts and intents of the heart." Hebrews 4:12

**Enticing sins.—There is said to have been kept in the halls of the Inquisition a beautiful statue of a virgin. The white arms were undraped and extended wide, as though to embrace; the countenance was beautiful. The professing penitent was led into this fair presence, and commanded to advance and embrace the figure.**

**As soon as he drew near the fair white arms encircled him with the vice-like clutch of vengeance. The bosom opened, and the lips expanded, and a hundred gleaming knives shot from the figure, transfixing the victim with a hundred scarlet stabs; the parted lips pushed forth a barbed tongue, and showed fanged teeth to lacerate and tear—in short, the beauty was transformed into a beast whose every charm concealed a dagger, and whose every grace was death. And so it is with sin.**

That horrible scene depicted from an early century is a very apt description of what sin is really like. To play around with a 'harmless' little sin is very foolish for it may look beautiful, promising, and innocent while the daggers and fangs are concealed right below the surface, waiting for its victim to walk into the trap. Sin may change its appearance often, but its nature remains the same. *It will never change.* In time, sin always reveals exactly what it is. For many it is too late; they have already 'embraced' it.

As the devil deceived Eve in the beginning, he still deceives men today. He makes sin appear so harmless and wonderful until his victim is in the trap. Many are *chewing on gravel,* regretting their sin. "Bread of deceit is sweet to a man; but afterward his mouth shall be filled with gravel." Proverbs 20:17

Additional Treasures:    Numbers 32:23    Ecclesiastes 12:14

# June 23

**"And she gave the king an hundred and twenty talents of gold, and of spices great abundance, and precious stones: neither was there any such spice as the queen of Sheba gave king Solomon."**
**II Chronicles 9:9**

The queen of Sheba gave of the best of her riches to Solomon, who already had worldwide acclaim for his wealth. It was unthinkable to offer a king a lesser gift. Gold, precious stones and exotic, precious spices were great riches; the queen brought lavish amounts of these to King Solomon. *One talent* of gold was worth a fortune and the queen brought many. The spices had worth similar to gold; they were so difficult to obtain from foreign lands.

Shoddy gifts were not given to kings or important acquaintances. The richer the recipient, the richer the gifts! That is common in this world. People would not think of giving a wealthy friend or acquaintance something they had found 'on sale' or at a bargain table. Even if they must go in debt to impress those who already have all they can possibly desire, they will do it because they want the rich recipient of their gift to be impressed. Christians should be relieved to know that the Lord has no such standard. Everything in the universe is His and He is the Creator; yet He was impressed with the tiny amount the widow put into the treasury, much more than the impressive amount the rich folk were putting in.

"And he said, Of a truth I say unto you, that this poor widow hath cast in more than they all; for all these have of their abundance cast in unto the offerings of God but she of her penury hath cast in all the living that she had." Luke 21:3-4

The difference in the givers was love. Jesus looks straight into the heart and sees the motives of our actions. Devotion is what impresses the Lord, not elaborate gifts which are given for show.

**Jesus is the King of Kings and Lord of Lords!** What kind of things do we offer Him to show our love? Those who love give *something.*

The first, and most important thing anyone can give to the Lord is his heart. It will follow that other acts of devotion and love will come naturally. We do things for people we love, for love cannot be hidden. We should do things for the Lord to demonstrate our love and gratitude for His unspeakable gift of salvation.

Additional Treasures:    I Chronicles 29:3-4    Romans 12:1

# June 24

**"Every wise woman buildeth her house: but the
foolish plucketh it down with her hands."
Proverbs 14:1**

The word pluck means to pull at or jerk. People who grow up on a
farm understand that definition because that's how a chicken is cleaned
before cooking it. The feathers are plucked off by pulling and jerking
with a mixture of energy and aggravation. It was an unsavory chore for
me, and I've never met a person who enjoyed plucking a chicken.

**In *plucking*, something is pulled at, jerked away or torn down.**
**In *building*, something is constructed, added to, or improved
overall.**

There are three types of houses a woman is busily building or
plucking: Spiritual house...Physical house...Home and family.

The building of her *spiritual house* has more effect on a woman's
happiness, and the happiness of those connected with her. If her faith is
strong from diligently reading and learning from God's Word, she will be
a happy well-adjusted lady whose family will thrive in her love and good
attitude. Blessed is the mother whose children or husband will ask her to
pray about something. That means her testimony is vibrant to those daily
observing her life. There is the greatest benefit and joy in building your
spiritual house. The fruit of the Spirit will grow in your heart and show
up on the outside.
"But the fruit of the Spirit is love, joy, peace,..." Galatians 5:22

**Building blocks for the wise woman's *spiritual house*:**
**Assurance:** There must be assurance of salvation before the building can
ever begin. Ask God to settle any doubt, confusion or whatever clouds
your mind about salvation. Stay with facts, not your feelings. Trust the
Lord.
    **Diligence in reading the Bible.** Keep firmly in mind that God's
Word is not optional. It is 'water and food' for your soul. Without it you
will be weak spiritually and have a vague unsatisfied feeling.
    **Obedience to God in everything.** As the song title "Trust and
Obey" suggests, that should be our motto for life. The old fashioned
parent used to say 'just mind me!' to the children, for their own good.
Our lives will be more pleasant if we will only trust and obey Him.

Additional Treasures:   I John 2:3    I Peter 3:1

# June 25

**"And when she had done giving him drink, she said,
I will draw for thy camels also, until they have done drinking."
Genesis 24:19**

A woman is wise who gives thought to the maintenance of her physical house. The Lord gives us a good reason: "What? Know ye not that your body is the temple of the Holy Ghost which is in you, which ye have of God, and ye are not your own? For ye are bought with a price: therefore glorify God in your body, and in your spirit, which are God's." I Corinthians 6:19-20

Your body is the 'vehicle' that carries you around, and reasonable care should be given to keep yourself fit enough to glorify God in your body, living your life in obedience to Him. People do as much for their cars, because they consider that to be very important. "That's our transportation," they say. So the physical body is the Christian's mode of 'transportation' and dwelling place. We certainly can't do without it on earth.

**Women who tend their physical health reap benefits and blessings that others, who are indifferent to fitness, never realize.**
Consider what Rebekah gained. She was physically fit enough to water the camels of Abraham's servant. That was a tremendous feat!
"And she hasted, and emptied her pitcher into the trough, and ran again unto the well to draw water, and drew for all his camels." v.20
Rebekah impressed the messenger with her willing attitude, and with her energy in watering thirsty camels. She was chosen to marry Isaac and was instantly rich, and became the mother of a nation through Jacob her son.

**Be wise in feeding your body; eat a balanced diet.** We all know the difference in good food and 'junk' food. Certain foods zap my energy and I know it a short time after indulging my impulse to eat them.
**Exercise to keep fit.** Daily work is not the 'exercise' that helps the body to keep fit. Some excuse it with "I work hard!" Regular walking is an excellent way to keep fit, doesn't cost anything but shoes to walk in, and is a good time to catch up on prayer as you go.
**Get enough sleep at night.** Watch the traps that keep you up too late at night, rob you of sleep, and causes fatigue when you need energy for the day. If it can be avoided, do it. It is more beneficial for you to feel well and alert in the day than to be entertained late at night.

Additional Treasures:    Genesis 24:53    Proverbs 31:25

# June 26

**"She looketh well to the ways of her household,
and eateth not the bread of idleness."
Proverbs 31:27**

Proverbs' ideal woman took care of her household. In this chapter we read of this remarkable wife and mother who, though obviously rich, was up early and late overseeing the business of her home and family. The next verse sums up all the reward that her heart would ever desire. *"Her children arise up, and call her blessed; her husband also, and he praiseth her."* v.28

It is considered old-fashioned and outdated in society today to be a dedicated mother and housewife at home. But God still blesses His Word and those who obey it. He gives wisdom, a great asset, to the godly women who are endeavoring to live according to the Word of God.

"Every wise woman buildeth her house: but the foolish plucketh it down with her hands." Proverbs 14:1

When a woman has wisdom, she uses the knowledge she has in the right way and that makes all the difference in the building up of her house.

In the building of her home, the simple things are the best building blocks to insure happiness and harmony in the family.

**Accept your spouse** and don't try to change him. People are born with a certain nature and disposition which stays essentially the same. The only true change in anybody will come by being born again into God's family. When that old nature has to live with the Holy Spirit, that causes a change which makes others exclaim, "What happened to him?"

**Teach your children to obey**, showing them from the Bible why they are to follow your rules. True...they should obey just because you say so, but it is good for them to learn that their parents have a reason for the way they are training their children. It teaches them to trust God too.

**Keep order in your house.** Someone has suggested that the order in the house reflects the condition of the mind of the housekeeper. That should inspire all of us! You can think better, and will certainly feel better if your house is generally clean and uncluttered.

Additional Treasures:     Proverbs 12:4     Proverbs 19:14

# June 27

**"All flesh is not the same flesh: but there is one kind
of flesh of men, another flesh of beasts,
another of fishes, and another of birds."
I Corinthians 15:39**

This verse does away with the theory that we all evolved from the same life form eons ago. Animal life is divided into different categories and the Lord said "is not the same flesh."

Animals communicate only with their own kind. That is evident in that man can tame the animals and train them to respond to his commands, but cannot communicate with them as he does humans.

"And God made the beast of the earth after his kind, and cattle after their kind, and every thing that creepeth upon the earth after his kind: and God saw that it was good." Genesis 1:25

**When our children were young, they were given a squirrel that had been raised from a baby, kept in the house, and had only human contact. It had a cage where it could run about, and we let it out in the house occasionally where the kids let it perch on their shoulders. They also fed it bits of food by hand. Once, for some reason, the cage was set outside and after that the little squirrel was not the same. The next time he was out of the cage, he ran under a sleeper sofa and hid up in the metal framework. We could not get him out with food, water, coaxing, or any other thing we tried. My husband got some men to help him carry the sofa out into the backyard, and carefully unfolded it to free the squirrel. As soon as the little creature was on the ground he was gone! We hardly saw the streak of brown fur and bushy tail as he disappeared--*going to his own kind!***

Just as the animals cannot communicate with humans because they are not of the same flesh, so man cannot communicate with God because he is *not of the same Spirit.* He must be *born again* into God's family, then he will have God's Spirit *in him* and he can finally communicate with God Himself. God sent Jesus to be our Savior so that He could redeem us and change us into His own kind. *"Behold what manner of love is this…"*

Additional Treasures:   I Corinthians 2: 12, 14   John 3:5-6

# June 28

**"For where your treasure is, there will your heart be also."**
**Matthew 6:21**

The affection of our hearts is tied to the things we love and are most precious to us. It is easy to discern because we talk about the things we love, and busy ourselves with maintaining our treasures. If they are of the wrong kind, we can lose them when we least expect it. Jesus gave us warning:

"Lay not up for yourselves treasures upon earth, where moth and rust doth corrupt, and where thieves break through and steal:
But lay up for yourselves treasures in heaven, where neither moth nor rust doth corrupt, and where thieves do not break through and steal."
Matthew 6: 19-20

**A rich nobleman was showing a friend a great collection of precious stones, whose value was almost beyond counting. There were diamonds, pearls, rubies, and gems from many countries, gathered by great labor and expense. "And yet," he remarked, "they yield me no income."**
**His friend replied that he had two stones, which cost him very little yet they yielded him a very considerable income. And he led him down to the mill, and pointed to the two toiling grey millstones. They were laboriously crushing the grain into flour, for the use of hundreds who depended on this work for their daily bread. Those two dull homely stones did more good in the world and raised a larger income than all the nobleman's jewels. So it is with idle treasure everywhere. It is doing nobody any good. While souls are dying of thirst, money is hoarded and hid away which might take the water of life to them.** Commentary

God's children might have more earthly wealth if they would not set their hearts on it. King David acquired great riches, and gave praise to God for that privilege afforded to him.
"Both riches and honor come of thee, and thou reignest over all; and in thine hand is power and might; and in thine hand it is to make great, and to give strength unto all." I Chronicles 29:12
Someone has said "don't love anything that can't love you back". That is good advice. We should not wrap our hearts around inanimate things. If they are lost, stolen, or just wear out we are unduly upset about it. Be wise.

Additional Treasures:     Ecclesiastes 5:19     Deuteronomy 8:18

# June 29

**"Thus saith the Lord God of Israel, That which thou
hast prayed to me against Sennacherib king of Assyria I have
heard."
II Kings 19:20**

This cruel Assyrian king had Israel terrorized, and the king of Israel
did the most sensible thing he could have done: he earnestly prayed to
God for help. Sennacherib sent Hezekiah a blasphemous letter which he
took and showed to the Lord!

"And Hezekiah received the letter of the hand of the messengers, and
read it: and Hezekiah went up in the house of the Lord, and spread it
before the Lord." II Kings 19:14

God's reply to his prayer is our text above. He said, "...*I have
heard.*" What followed was the destruction of King Sennacherib's army
by a great miracle of God. After the king returned to his land in defeat,
his own sons assassinated him as he worshipped his heathen god in the
temple.

**In high school, our English class studied a poem by Byron
entitled *The Destruction of Sennacherib*. I was not a Christian at that
time, but that poem made a lasting impression on my mind. When I
read the last line I felt a thrill in my heart and wondered at the great
power of God, whom I did not know. Here's an excerpt, including
the last verse.**

For the Angel of Death spread his wings on the blast,
And breathed in the face of the foe as he passed;
And the eyes of the sleepers waxed deadly and chill,
And their hearts but once heaved, and forever grew still!

And the widows of Ashur are loud in their wail,
And the idols are broke in the temple of Baal;
And the might of the Gentile, unsmote by the sword,
Hath melted like snow in the glance of the Lord!
George Gordon, Lord Byron

Lay every problem, difficulty or fear in your life out before the Lord
in prayer. He hears and has power to work a solution. Never let
difficulties pile up to a 'worrying' state. Write them down, pray over
them, and trust God.

Additional Treasures:     II Kings 19:32-36     II Chronicles 16:9

# June 30

**"My soul, wait thou only upon God;
for my expectation is from him."
Psalm 62:5**

When we look to God for our needs and not depend on any human connection, we will have greater peace and contentment in our lives. The One who can meet all of our expectations has *all power* with which to do it.

"And Jesus came and spake unto them, saying, All power is given unto me in heaven and in earth." Matthew 28:18
"Now unto him that is able to do exceeding abundantly above all that we ask or think, according to the power that worketh in us." Ephesians 3:20

Job learned through his terrible affliction that left him with nothing on earth but an unsympathetic wife and judgmental friends, that God was the only source of comfort and power for his life. His *expectation* was in the Lord. He believed in the coming Savior and the resurrection.

"For I know that my redeemer liveth, and that he shall stand at the latter day upon the earth:  And though after my skin worms destroy this body, yet in my flesh shall I see God..."Job 19: 25-26

**King David discovered the Lord early in his life and developed a strong unwavering faith in God's power and ability. His *expectation* was focused on the Lord when he faced the wild beasts which were after his father's sheep, and when he faced the giant, Goliath, who challenged the army of Israel.**
"David said moreover, Thy Lord that delivered me out of the paw of the lion, and out of the paw of the bear, he will deliver me out of the hand of this Philistine..." I Samuel 17:37

We would do well to do as these saints before us and enumerate the reasons why our *expectation* is in the Lord. Have you learned that God is faithful and your expectation of His promises is always rewarded? Keep a list in your mind; tell others what God has done for you so your heart will stay vibrant with faith. I have learned that counting blessings is better than 'counting sheep' when I can't go to sleep at night. It also keeps my thoughts lined up in the right way. God is worthy of our praise, night and day.

Additional Treasures:    Philippians 4:19    Isaiah 41:10

# July 1

**"And ye shall know the truth, and the**
**truth shall make you free."**
**John 8:32**

Most of the world's population is not free today because they do not know the Truth, which is the Lord Jesus Christ.

"Jesus saith unto him, I am the way, the truth, and the life: no man cometh unto the Father, but by me." John 14:6

Blindness caused by religion is especially prevalent in countries like India, with many among its huge population being followers of Hindu.

**My husband and another pastor were in India on a Mission trip and stopped in Calcutta, on the Ganges River. They saw Hindu mothers dip their babies in the filthy waters of the Ganges, and old men and women immerge themselves. It is the most sacred river in India, and it plays an important part in the Hindu religion. Temples line its banks along the river, and there are stairways leading down to the river for people to have access to its waters. The sick and crippled come, hoping the water will cure them. Others come *to die in the river*, for Hindus believe those who die in the Ganges will be carried away to Paradise.**

**An astounding thing they saw was the people baptizing their gods! Some poor people had made their gods out of straw tied together with paper glued on the surface. As they immersed them, some came apart and later one could see the straw and paper floating down the river.**

So many people in the world are groping about in spiritual blindness.

"In whom the god of this world hath blinded the minds of them which believe not, lest the light of the glorious gospel of Christ, who is the image of God, should shine unto them." II Corinthians 4:4

Through missions, preachers are sent all over the world to preach the gospel of Christ. That message lifts men out of spiritual darkness and gives them light and hope. "Go ye therefore, and teach all nations..." Matt. 28:19

We must send someone or go ourselves! All of us have the responsibility.

Additional Treasures:     Acts 1:8     I Corinthians 3:11     Mark 16:15

# July 2

**"Teach me to do thy will; for thou art my God:
thy spirit is good; lead me into the land of uprightness."
Psalm 143:10**

The will of God will always be the way of righteousness, and by that we may know whether or not we are keeping to that path. There is not a particle of imperfection in God's character, so *His will* is going to reflect His glory in the things accomplished by obedience to it. It is necessary for the Christian's happiness and wellbeing to focus on the reality of God's will as the source of wisdom and stability for his life.

"If any man will do his will, he shall know of the doctrine, whether it be of God, or whether I speak of myself." John 7:17

Doing God's will gives us certain knowledge and spiritual discernment. We are not to make a show to others of our obedience to God's will, but obedience should come from our hearts because we love the Lord.

"Not with eyeservice, as menpleasers: but as the servants of Christ, doing the will of God from the heart..." Ephesians 6:6

**The will of God is always *obedience* in the things of God.**

"And be not conformed to this world: but be ye transformed by the renewing of your mind, that ye may prove what is that good, and acceptable, and perfect will of God." Romans 12:2

**The will of God at work in us will cause us to reach out to the lost.**

The Lord is not slack concerning his promise, as some men count slackness; but is longsuffering to us-ward, not willing that any should perish, but that all should come to repentance." II Peter 3:9

**The will of God may mean suffering for our faithfulness.**

"Wherefore let them that suffer according to the will of God commit the keeping of their souls to him in well doing, as unto a faithful Creator." I Peter 4:19

Christians today have not known suffering like the saints of centuries ago, though some are suffering now in countries where freedom of worship is not allowed. The thing is, will we be true to God if His will brings some 'misunderstanding' from friends, or ridicule from others sources? Decide now to obey Him and let Him handle the resulting consequences in your life.

Additional Treasures:     Exodus 19:5     Psalm 116: 7-9

# July 3

**"I found no rest in my spirit, because I found not Titus
my brother: but taking my leave of them, I went
from thence to Macedonia."
II Corinthians 2:13**

Everyone has to cope with disappointment once in a while. At times it may be a *big* disappointment, which churns in our hearts day and night; we are like the apostle Paul in our text: *I found no rest in my spirit.*

**We can be sure of one very important thing: God is with us.**
"Fear thou not; for I am with thee: be not dismayed; for I am thy God: I will strengthen thee; yea I will help thee; yea, I will uphold thee with the right hand of my righteousness." Isaiah 41:10

What are we to do when devastated by disappointment?

**Get encouragement from God's Word.**
The psalms of David reveal how oftentimes he was cast down in his soul, and was revived by looking up to God for encouragement.

"Deep calleth unto deep at the noise of thy waterspouts: all thy waves and thy billows are gone over me. Yet the Lord will command his lovingkindness in the daytime, and in the night his song will be with me, and my prayer unto the God of my life. " Psalm 42: 7-8

David describes his disappointments as *waves and billows* washing over him as in an ocean, yet he looked to God, Who always held him up and gave him strength in every trial he passed through.

**Keep going on with your life, being faithful in all things.**
Paul was keenly disappointed when his helper did not show up as he expected, and he had no rest in his spirit. But he went on his way to preach in Macedonia, and God gave him great victory in his soul. "Now thanks be unto God, which always causeth us to triumph in Christ…" II Corinthians 2:14

No matter how 'down' we may feel we can arise each day and know that God made it and we are to 'rejoice and be glad in it!' Every day will have new experiences with opportunities for us to show love and gratitude to God.

Additional Treasures:   Isaiah 41:13   Proverbs 13:12

# July 4

**"For the law of the Spirit of life in Christ Jesus
hath made me free from the law of sin and death."
Romans 8:2**

Each year we celebrate on this day to commemorate the signing of
the Declaration of Independence for our country. It was a bold statement
for a new nation, largely unexplored and underdeveloped at that time.

The enemy later hounded the men, who had the courage to sign that
declaration of freedom. They lost property, families and their own lives
because of love for their country and the desire to live as free men. Their
sacrifice and suffering is the reason we have a great nation today! There
is always a price for freedom.

**Jesus came to set men free from the penalty and shackles of sin.
He read the prophetic passage about Himself in the book of Isaiah as
He began to preach in His earthly ministry.**

"The Spirit of the Lord is upon me; because the Lord hath anointed
me to preach good tidings unto the meek; he hath sent me to bind up the
brokenhearted, to proclaim liberty to the captives, and the opening of the
prison to them that are bound…" Isaiah 61:1

**The freedom that Jesus purchased for us cost more than we can
ever comprehend, because of sin's penalty *He tasted death* for every
man.**

"But we see Jesus, who was made a little lower than the angels for
the suffering of death, crowned with glory and honour; that he by the
grace of God should taste death for every man." Hebrews 2:9

**Our Lord came to the world for the purpose of redeeming lost
humanity. There was no other way, for the sacrifice had to be perfect
and acceptable to God.**

"And ye know that he was manifested to take away our sins; and in
him is no sin." I John 3:5

Every day of our lives we should thank God for our salvation
through the Lord Jesus Christ. *He paid it all.*

Additional Treasures:    John 10:11    Titus 2:14    Ephesians 5:2

# July 5

"Those that be planted in the house of the Lord shall
flourish in the courts of our God. They shall bring forth fruit…"
Psalm 92: 13-14

The plants growing in our individual homes are those that we have planted or placed there. God does the planting *in His house*, and those that He does not plant are referred to as tares or weeds. They look just like God's plants but they are not, and someday they will be rooted up and discarded.

"Another parable put he forth unto them, saying, The kingdom of heaven is likened unto a man which sowed good seed in his field:
But while men slept, his enemy came and sowed tares among the wheat, and went his way…
Let both grow together until the harvest: and in the time of harvest I will say to the reapers, gather ye together first the tares, and bind them in bundles to burn them: but gather the wheat into my barn."
Matthew 13:24-25, 30

In the Lord's house, there are always some that talk like, look like and act like Christians in many ways. However, they have not trusted Jesus *personally*, and therefore are not *born again* into God's family. He has not planted them, and in time it will be evident in the lack of spiritual growth and desire for the water of the Word. *Are you planted?*

**Are you planted,**
      **Your roots growing toward, seeking out,**
      **And desperately desiring the water?**
**Are you planted,**
      **Swaying in fierce winds of adversity,**
      **Thrashed about in storms of life,**
      **Yet clinging to the soil, determined to survive?**
**Are you planted,**
      **Notched by the axe for destruction**
      **Yet sending roots deeper as tears heal the wounds,**
      **Though the scars remain?**
**Are you planted,**
**Gnarled, bent, roughened by time but laden with fruit, Sweetened with maturity? Are you planted?**    Edna Holmes

Additional Treasures:  Matthew 13:23   Ephesians 2:19   Romans 8:14

# July 6

"But he that is spiritual judgeth all things,
yet he himself is judged of no man."
I Corinthians 2:15

We think of *spiritual* people as those doing and talking a certain way about the things of the Lord. Actually, we can't *do* anything that will make us spiritual. Christ is our way to being spiritual. He said that we must be born again to get into God's kingdom, the realm of the *spiritual.*

"That which is born of the flesh is flesh; and that which is born of the Spirit is spirit. Marvel not that I said unto thee, Ye must be born again." *John 3:6-7*

Trusting in Jesus as your Savior and believing that He died on the cross for your sins, personally, will make a *new creature* out of you; a *born again* one in God's family, just as a new baby enters its family by the physical birth. It is by that means we are made spiritual.

As we serve the Lord, some of the tasks that are necessary at times may not seem very *spiritual*, but God's work overall has that unique category.
The ministry is involved with people so there is humor along the way.

**One Sunday morning early in our ministry just as the preaching started, an elderly lady became ill. I had to take her home and get back in time to play the piano for the invitation. My husband gave me a *'hurry up and get back'* look, so with the help of another lady I quickly got her out to the car and drove across town to her house. There we stalled at the front door because she couldn't find her key. She dug in her purse; *we dug in her purse,* searching every little nook. I began to feel panic! The minutes were rushing toward 12:00, but I couldn't leave her on the porch.**
**Then she suggested we try the front window. It was unlocked, and with me in a straight skirt and high heels the other lady boosted me up where I managed to wiggle through the window, get in, and open the front door. The elderly lady just then pulled a long string out of her bosom, and at the end dangled the key! She had finally remembered. As we left, she was settling into her chair chuckling and muttering to herself what a funny sight it was to see her pastor's wife climbing through that window.**

Additional Treasures:    Romans 8:9-11    I Corinthians 3:16

# July 7

**"On that night could not the king sleep, and he commanded
to bring the book of records of the chronicles;
and they were read before the king."
Esther 6:1**

King Ahasuerus had signed a decree to have the Jews destroyed throughout his kingdom; he was *not aware* that his beautiful young queen, Esther, was a Jew nor was he aware that Esther's uncle, Mordecai, was also a Jew. It was in that situation that God revealed some things to the king, which led to a definite turning of events.

Haman the wicked enemy of the Jews was distraught because Mordecai *would not bow* to him as the king's servants did. Therefore, upon learning that Mordecai was a Jew, Haman devised a scheme to rid the country of God's people. He had an audience with the king as a favored one, and presented his proposition.

"...There are a certain people scattered abroad ...in all the provinces of thy kingdom; and their laws are diverse from all people; neither keep they the king's laws: therefore it is not for the king's profit to suffer them.

If it please the king, let it be written that they may be destroyed..."
Esther 3:8-9

The king made the decree and the plan went into action. It only remained for the new law to reach all the provinces of his vast kingdom. Fasting and prayers were begun for Queen Esther's success in petitioning the king on behalf of her people.

As God's people prayed, *the king could not sleep!* The chronicles were read to him, and he heard how Mordecai had reported a scheme and stopped an attempt on the king's life. He immediately sent to honor Mordecai, and soon Haman came to an untimely death, being hanged on the gallows he had built for his enemy, Mordecai.

You will notice that God worked all things together for good for His people then as He does His children today. God *never* changes. When we read Esther, we see how God foils the schemes of men to bring about His purpose in history. "The king's heart is in the hand of the Lord, as the rivers of water: he turneth it whithersoever he will."
Proverbs 21:1

All of God's Word is meaningful to us today because God is in it! We can learn from every page of it. Read, read, read it; it is of more worth than you can imagine to your health and happiness in this world.

Additional Treasures:     Isaiah 26:3     Psalm 135:6

# July 8

**"…and so I will go in unto the king, which is
not according to the law: and if I perish, I perish."
Esther 4:16**

The king of Persia could not be approached without permission, and unless the king chose to be merciful it meant certain death, even for his wife, if she comes into his presence uninvited.

**Esther, knowing that the decree had been issued to destroy the Jews, had fasted and prayed for three days and nights with her maidens. Then she prepared herself and went to the king's royal house where he sat upon his royal throne. Esther *knew* she had to do something; it was all or nothing. She determined to take her chances and go directly into the king's presence saying, " *if I perish, I perish."***
**We cannot imagine the real danger that Esther faced, for if the king had been in a bad mood or irritated about something, he could just as easily have refused her his favor and she would have been killed immediately for her intrusion into his court. Three *days of prayer and fasting* is the thing that gave Esther the courage to face the king.**

"And it was so, when the king saw Esther the queen standing in the court, that she obtained favour in his sight: and the king held out to Esther the golden sceptre that was in his hand. So Esther drew near, and touched the top of the sceptre." Esther 5:2
Through prayer and fasting, Esther knew what she would do to gain the king's favor, get the decree overturned, and expose the wicked Haman at the same time.

In the end the beautiful young queen won the victory, but it was not her beauty or her position. It was the power of God in answer to fervent prayers. He turned the heart of that powerful heathen king to *do His will*, thereby protecting His people. Again we emphasize the power of our God to turn kings and circumstances to serve His purpose. We should not worry about powers in this world that seem to affect our lives while we can do seemingly nothing. God is the One who is looking out for us, and there is no limit to His love for us, or His power to do us good in all circumstances.

"The king's heart is in the hand of the Lord, as the rivers of water: he turneth it whithersoever he will."       Proverbs 21:1

Additional Treasures:     Hebrews 4:15-16     Psalm 57:1

# July 9

**"If any man's work shall be burned, he shall
suffer loss: but he himself shall be saved..."
I Corinthians 3:15**

The Lord Jesus Christ paid for salvation, and nothing can be added to it or taken from it. His work is perfect and complete, and every soul that trusts in Christ shall be eternally saved. There will be no judgment before the Great White Throne of God for those who have been *born again* into God's family. Their names were recorded at the time of their *spiritual birth.*

"And whosoever was not found written in the book of life was cast into the lake of fire." Revelation 20:15

The judgment of Christians has to do with their service for the Lord. There will be no mistakes in the accounting; the heavenly book-keeping is accurate in every detail. What and why we are doing some service will all be laid out starting from the observation of the depths of our hearts. That is why a close relationship with the Lord is imperative. He keeps our hearts right, and that's the thing that will keep our works right.

"Every man's work shall be made manifest: for the day shall declare it, because it shall be revealed by fire; and the fire shall try every man's work of what sort it is." I Corinthians 3:13

Our works will go through the *fire test*, and many that we consider valuable may not make it through the fire without being consumed. Only the works done for the glory and honor of Christ will remain as treasures.

**Early in our marriage, on the day we were to move into our first apartment, the house where we were staying burned to the ground and all of our earthly possessions with it! It was a sad day for us as we searched through the ashes looking for anything that remained of our things, but the fire destroyed all and we had to start over. God used that tragedy to turn our lives in a different direction, ultimately bringing us to the place where we would become Christians.**

None of our material possessions were fireproof. They burned just like kindling wood, and so will the worthless activity which engages our time and attention but does not bring glory to God. We can start afresh every day to serve the Lord in sincerity with a true heart, but after this life we will face the Judgment Seat of Christ.

Additional Treasures:    James 4:14    Zechariah 13:9

# July 10

**"Yea, though I walk through the valley of the shadow
of death, I will fear no evil: for thou art with me..."
Psalm 23:4**

In our modern world of instant communication worldwide, we are constantly being bombarded with news of *death*. A tragedy can happen in the most remote part of the earth and somehow news people get there and begin telecasting it into our homes--earthquakes, floods, fires, train wrecks and airplane crashes.

For Christians the fear of death has been diminished for all time, for the Lord Jesus has removed the *sting* of death itself by His resurrection from the grave. "O death, where is thy sting? O grave, where is thy victory? But thanks be to God, which giveth us the victory through our Lord Jesus Christ." I Corinthians 15:55, 57

## The Ship

**I am standing upon the seashore. A ship at my side spreads
Her white sails to the morning breeze and starts for the blue ocean.**

**She is an object of beauty and strength, and I stand and watch her
Until at length she is only a speck of white cloud just where the sea
And sky meet, and mingle with each other.
Then someone at my side exclaims, "There, she's gone!"**

**Gone where? Gone from my sight, that is all.
She is just as large in hull and mast and spar as she was when she left
My side, and just as able to bear her load of living freight
To the place of her destination.
Her diminished size is in me, not in her.**

**And just at the moment when someone at my side says,
"She's gone," There are other eyes watching for her coming
And other voices ready to take up the glad shout, "There, she
comes!"
And that is dying.**
Henry Van Dyke

Additional Treasures:    I Corinthians 15:54    Psalm 116:15

# July 11

**"Now we know that God heareth not sinners: but if any man
be a worshipper of God, and doeth his will, him he heareth."
John 9:31**

God does not *attend* to the prayers of unsaved people. However, because he is God, He certainly knows every word that is uttered on earth. He gives light to those seeking after Him, as in the case of Cornelius.

"There was a certain man in Caesarea called Cornelius, a centurion of the band called the Italian band, A devout man, and one that feared God with all his house, which gave much alms to the people, and prayed to God always..." Acts 10:1-2

The Lord led Cornelius to send for Peter so that he could hear the good news of salvation through believing on the Lord Jesus Christ.

"He lodgeth with one Simon a tanner, whose house is by the sea side: he shall tell thee what thou oughtest to do." v 6.

Cornelius' prayers and good deeds could not save him. He had to be *born again* into God's family. Peter was sent to preach the gospel to Cornelius, his family, and friends he had gathered together to hear that good news. They were all saved that day!

**In the days following the Sunday my husband became a Christian, he witnessed to everyone around his workplace and began to bring men to our pastor's home, to be saved, after work in the evenings. He didn't yet know how to lead one to Christ by himself. We lived on the same street, and I could see when our car stopped in front of the pastor's house and he'd take another man in to be saved. One evening, my husband brought one who lived in another town. He also was saved, and in a few weeks asked if the pastor would come and preach to his family one night in their home. My husband accompanied the pastor to the man's home. He had gathered his relatives together and his house was filled with people. It was an extraordinary experience, and some believed on the Lord that night because of that new Christian's concern for his family in having the gospel preached to them.**

Pray for the "Cornelius" kind of concern for your family and others.

Additional Treasures:    John 1:48    II Timothy 2:19

# July 12

**"I am the good shepherd, and know my sheep,
and am known of mine."
John 10:14**

God knows His children and *they know Him,* personally. That knowledge comes by the Holy Spirit who dwells in us as a result of the new birth. There is no other way to God, yet people will argue.

A common assertion is *"God answered my prayer!"* In a crisis unsaved people may pray. If things turn out well they think God answered and therefore they must be Christians. No assumption could be more foolish.

**In my years as a church member, without Christ, I clung to such ideas. As the Holy Spirit began to convict my heart, I didn't want to face the truth of my need for salvation. I remembered times that I had prayed and God surely answered I thought, because things turned out all right.**

When I was nine years old, one Saturday my father came home from town with a *goat* in the back of our old truck. I don't remember why he got it, but it was out of place on our farm and created a problem as soon as its feet were on the ground. Daddy tied it on a long rope by the pond in the pasture where it could graze and also reach the water. It upset the mules, which showed such threatening behavior toward the goat that my dad put them in a separate part of the pasture with a fence between them and the little strange, smelly creature. They walked the fence line as close as they could get, snorting and stomping, which frightened me terribly. I had a horror of those mules jumping the fence and killing that goat.

A few days later I was playing near the barn, keeping an eye on the goat, when it suddenly got loose and headed right to the fence where the mules were waiting! I fell to my knees, and as children do, got right to the point in prayer: *Dear Jesus, please don't let the mules hurt that goat.*

As I raised my head, it jumped the fence *between the mules*! It scampered off as they scrambled around clumsily trying to find it in the shuffle. The goat escaped unharmed and I was convinced that God answered my prayer.

Regardless of the circumstances which seem to reinforce someone's idea that he or she is a Christian, without a *personal* relationship with Christ there can be no salvation.

"I am the door: by me if any man enter in, he shall be saved..."
John 10:9

Additional Treasures:    Romans 10:9    I Timothy 2:4    John 5:24

# July 13

**"Enter into his gates with thanksgiving, and into his courts
with praise: be thankful unto him, and bless his name."
Psalm 100:4**

It must be a grief to the Lord that His children are so ungrateful in their hearts. We are blessed daily and, for the most part, take it for granted.

"Blessed by the Lord, who daily loadeth us with benefits, even the God of our salvation. Selah." Psalm 68:19

We should notice that this is a *Selah* verse. We are instructed by that word to *pause and calmly think of that.* If our Lord did not deliver the load of blessings to us for one day, we would be awakened out of our indifference. Our sense of wellbeing is linked to gratitude.

"To appoint unto them that mourn in Zion...the garment of praise for the spirit of heaviness..." Isaiah 61:3

There should never be a debilitating gloom in our lives, for expressing thanks to the Lord will turn that spirit of heaviness into gladness.

**While a preacher of long ago was once traveling, he suddenly dismounted, delivered his horse to the care of his servants, and retired to a particular spot at some distance from the road where he knelt down and continued for some time in prayer. On his return one of his attendants took the liberty of asking his reason for this singular act. The man of God said that when he was a poor boy he traveled over that cold and bleak mountain without shoes or stockings, and that he remembered disturbing a cow on the identical spot where he prayed, that he might warm his feet and legs on the place where she had lain. His feelings of gratitude would not allow him to pass the place without giving thanksgiving to God for the favors He had shown.** Commentary

Does gratitude ever fill your heart to overflowing? We should pray and render thanks to God for the numberless blessings He 'loads' us with each day. We can't possibly think of all of them, but the ones that you do remember...name them! A grateful heart is not easily drawn away from God. Gratitude expressed also lifts the 'heavy' spirit, or as we would say it, a feeling of depression. Making a 'thanksgiving' list will bless your soul. The longer the list gets, the better you will feel.

Additional Treasures:     I Thessalonians 5:18     Psalm 107:22

# July 14

"The Lord is my shepherd…"
Psalm 23:1

This is the most well-known psalm in the Bible and as much as learned men have studied, digging out its treasures, there is still much to glean from its few verses. Men will never be able to discover all of its richness.

This psalm has been prescribed as *spiritual medicine* for troubled Christians and has been known to solve much heartache when taken, *read*, three times a day for a week.

Someone has listed the perfect benefits in the lines of Psalm 23.

**The Lord is my Shepherd – Perfect Salvation.**
**I shall not want – Perfect Satisfaction.**
**He maketh me to lie down in green pastures – Perfect Rest.**
**He leadeth me beside still waters – Perfect Refreshment.**
**He restoreth my soul – Perfect Restoration.**
**He leadeth me in the paths of righteousness – Perfect Guidance**
**I will fear no evil – Perfect Protection.**
**Thou art with me – Perfect Company.**
**Thy rod and Thy staff – Perfect comfort.**
**Thou preparest a table – Perfect Provision.**
**Thou anointest my head – Perfect Consecration.**
**My cup runneth over – Perfect Joy.**
**Surely, surely – Perfect confidence.**
**Goodness and mercy shall follow me – Perfect Care.**
**I will dwell in the house of the Lord forever – Perfect Destiny.**

This psalm is short and can be easily committed to memory. Put it into your heart, and consider what wonderful spiritual nourishment you will have laid up for any time. Opportunities for you to help someone come when you least expect them, you may not have a Bible handy, but you'll have Psalm 23 ready to be 'read' from memory to comfort or calm a soul. I love 'reading' it to myself during exercise walking. I never tire of its beautiful expressions.

"This is my comfort in my affliction: for thy word hath quickened me."  Psalm 119:50

Additional Treasures:   Psalm 119:105   Psalm 5:11-12

# July 15

**"In the beginning was the Word, and the Word
was with God, and the Word was God."
John 1:1**

It is said that in the book of Matthew, Jesus is set forth as a *King*, in the book of Mark as a *Servant*, in the book of Luke as the *Son of Man*, and in the book of John as the *Son of God*.

"And the Word was made flesh, and dwelt among us, (and we beheld his glory, the glory as of the only begotten of the Father,) full of grace and truth." v. 14

Since the Word was God, and the Word was made flesh and dwelled among human beings on earth, we know without a doubt that the Lord Jesus was God in the flesh. John the Baptist was born for the purpose of pointing out Jesus to Israel.

"He said, I am the voice of one crying in the wilderness, Make straight the way of the Lord, as said the prophet Esaias. The next day John seeth Jesus coming unto him, and saith, Behold the Lamb of God, which taketh away the sin of the world." John 1:23, 29

The saved from all ages have endeavored to express the wonder of our Savior, Who loved us so much He left heaven to become *flesh,* as we are.

> Before the heavens were spread abroad,
> From everlasting was the Word;
> With God He was, the Word was God,
> And must divinely be adored.
>
> But lo! He leaves those heavenly forms;
> The Word descends and dwells in clay,
> That He may converse hold with worms,
> Dressed in such feeble flesh as they.
> Isaac Watts

Jesus could never have communicated with humans had He not become one of them. He never ceased to be God, but He condescended to live on this earth in a body of flesh as the Son of man. No comparison can really be made to do it justice, but look down at an ant-bed and consider how it would be to go from what you are to one of them so you could communicate with them.

Additional Treasures:　　John 6:48-51　　John 10:27-30

# July 16

**"But godliness with contentment is great gain."**
**I Timothy 6:8**

Contentment is a beautiful attitude of the heart. It stands out in this frantic world of humanity where money is a god, and people are destroying themselves and others in order to accumulate more of it. Even God's children fall into temptation of desiring many things, and it immediately causes a *discontented* feeling which must be dispelled by the truth of the Word of God.

"And he said unto them, Take heed, and beware of covetousness: for a man's life consisteth not in the abundance of the things which he possesseth." Luke 12:15

The word *contentment* means satisfaction, being pleased, and peace of mind. Things gotten by us will not bring the desired affect if we have the wrong motive. No matter how much or little the Christian possesses, he must keep the right perspective.

"For ye are bought with a price: therefore, glorify God in your body, and in your spirit, which are God's." I Corinthians 6:20

The world thinks of Christianity as keeping one *dull, ignorant and poor.* Satan started that lie back in the Garden of Eden with the first temptation. Eve listened! But it is recorded that the Lord has pleasure in the prosperity of His servants.

"Let them shout for joy, and be glad, that favour my righteous cause: yea, let them say continually, Let the Lord be magnified, which hath pleasure in the prosperity of his servant." Psalm 35:27

The Word instructs us to be content. Contentment is the greatest gain of all, that of being satisfied. Obedience to the Lord brings prosperity to a Christian which can't be measured by money. A home and family with love, peace, and harmony in it is priceless. Having a close relationship with Christ is wealth beyond our imagination. We can tell Him everything in our hearts and He listens with consideration. That is true wealth! When we pray we are talking to the One who hung the moon and sun out there in the universe to "give light on the earth". We could never estimate the value of that privilege. But that isn't all. God does give His children money and material things and the wisdom to use them right if they read His Word. Christians, on all levels of the prosperity scale, are the most fortunate people on earth.

Additional Treasures:    Hebrews 13:5    Philippians 4:11

# July 17

**"When goods increase, they are increased that eat them:
and what good is there to the owners thereof, saving
the beholding of them with their eyes?"
Ecclesiastes 5:11**

Those who are not rich in this world's goods may imagine how wonderful it would be to be *wealthy* and get anything in the world that they desire. Of course they imagine that they wouldn't let the riches interrupt their peace and tranquility, or otherwise affect their lives in an adverse way.

Actually, there is a phenomenon connected with the increase of riches or goods; *they are increased that eat them.* That has been made a reality as we have viewed the fantastic palatial homes of the rich and famous on television, and they told how many servants were required to take care of the house and grounds of these showplaces.

**A few years ago I accompanied my two sisters on a trip to a beautiful historic part of the country. While there we toured a lovely mansion built in the last century, a three-story structure full of antique furnishings. I was reminded of our text verse as I looked at all the things that had to be maintained perfectly at all times in a house like that. The mistress of that place, in its original time period, had to be like a general commanding a small army of servants. What a responsibility! I'm sure it took a fortune each year to maintain that wealthy place.**

The Lord would have us to be content and trust Him for all that we require to live comfortably in this life. With the Lord as our Shepherd, *we shall not want,* or lack, anything.

"And having food and raiment, let us be therewith content." Tim.6:8

"Riches and honour are with me; yea, durable riches.." Prov. 8:18

The riches that the Lord gives in salvation cannot be measured. t is enough that we have the *peace of God, which passes all understanding.* Sadly enough, most very rich people will not exercise faith in God. Their lives are wrapped up in what they possess. Jesus said "that a rich man shall hardly enter into the kingdom of heaven." Matthew 19:23

Jesus also said..." but with God all things are possible." v. 26

Additional Treasures:     Proverbs 10:22     Ephesians 3:8

# July 18

**"If we live in the Spirit, let us also walk in the Spirit."**
**Galatians 5:25**

How blessed we are to have the Holy Spirit of God actually living *in us!* He is our security for all eternity, and our guide and keeper here on earth in our journey of faith. He convicts us of sin and helps us understand the Word of God. Without the Holy Spirit revealing it to us, the Bible would be meaningless and we'd never grasp its divine message.

"But the Comforter, which is the Holy Ghost, whom the Father will send in my name, he shall teach you all things, and bring all things to your remembrance, whatsoever I have said unto you." John 14:26

The Holy Spirit cultivates His blessed fruit in our hearts, and it shows up in our lives. He is patient, but persistent, when we carelessly destroy the precious fruit in the bud. He starts the growth process over as many times as it takes to develop these godly characteristics in us.

"But the fruit of the Spirit is love, joy, peace, longsuffering, gentleness, goodness, faith, Meekness, temperance: against such there is no law." Galatians 5:22-23

These fruits are produced by the Holy Spirit of God and Him only in the heart of a Christian. They cannot be produced by pretending. Only one whose heart is kept 'diligently' can enjoy growth of these characteristics.

"Keep thy heart with all diligence; for out of it are the issues of life." Proverbs 4:23

My family lived on a farm with a large vegetable garden when I was a child. There was a fence around it to keep out the large animals such as cows or horses if they happened to get out and wander near the garden. The small animals could do a lot of damage, too, and there was no way to keep them out. They sneaked right under the fence. It is the same way with our hearts if we are not diligent in keeping them. The big "awful" sins such as murder and adultery have a high fence to break through; we guard against those! But the little "respectable" sins, such as neglecting God's Word or an unforgiving spirit, come in under the fence and we don't notice until the damage is done. Let God search your heart daily to see if any little thing is lurking there eating away at the good fruit in your heart.

Additional Treasures:    I Corinthians 2:13    Ephesians 4:30

# July 19

**"...And they shall take them captives, whose captives they were; and they shall rule over their oppressors."**
**Isaiah 14:2**

The people of God were taken captive and dispersed abroad because of their disobedience to God. But in time they would be restored, and it is then that they would take their *captors* captive even as they were captive.

"And it shall come to pass in the day that the Lord shall give thee rest from thy sorrow, and from thy fear, and from the hard bondage wherein thou wast made to serve..." Isaiah 14:3

Many elements in our lives at different times may *hold us captive.* We find ourselves either giving up, or locked in a warfare that keeps us drained of strength and the joy of the Lord.

### Thoughts:
The mind is under attack by the devil constantly. He knows that if he can get the Christian to thinking unholy thoughts for just a minute, it will be very difficult to stop. The only weapon is the *Word of God, the Sword.*

For the word of God is quick, and powerful, and sharper than any twoedged sword..." Hebrews 4:12

"Casting down imaginations, and every high thing that exalteth itself against the knowledge of God, and bringing into captivity every thought to the obedience of Christ." II Corinthians 10:5

We must make a conscious effort to keep our thoughts on the right track. One verse that helps is "Commit thy works unto the Lord, and thy thoughts shall be established." Proverbs 16:3

That is so simple. As you start the day, tell the Lord right then that you are doing what the verse says, committing your day's activities to Him and trusting that your thoughts will be established on the right things. Of course you can invoke that verse anytime, even in the heat of the battle up in the day. The thing is to keep up the good fight! Remember that thoughts evolve into words and eventually actions. Guard your mind and heart!

### Bitterness and Anger
"Let all bitterness, and wrath, and anger, and clamour, and evil speaking, be put away from you, with all malice: And be ye kind one to another, tenderedhearted, forgiving one another, even as God for Christ's sake hath forgiven you." Ephesians 4:31-32

Additional Treasures:    I John 1:9    Matthew 6:14

# July 20

**"For precept must be upon precept, precept upon precept;
line upon line, line upon line; here a little, and there a little."
Isaiah 28:10**

It seems here that the Lord is laboring a point with us. But that's the way of learning. We go over and over words of knowledge until we learn what's being taught.

That is the secret of spiritual growth. The Bible is our textbook, and we learn its truth by reading it constantly. It gives instructions in the way of righteousness. As we go through each day and meet with difficulties, we can immediately apply the *precepts* we remember from the Word and that it keeps us faithful and encouraged.

Many Christians keep records by marking verses in the Bible that have worked for them at some particular time. Some use the T.P. sign. That means *tried and proven!* It is encouraging as we graze through the scriptures at times, and see our notes and remember what the Lord has done for us. And there is a wonderful promise from God for those who *delight* in His Word in this manner. "Delight thyself also in the Lord; and he shall give thee the desires of thine heart." Psalm 37:4

**I loved getting letters from my husband before we married. We wrote to each other every day, and hardly a day passed that I didn't get one or more letters. I read them over and over and never grew tired of reading his words. I imagined how his hand held the pen, and how he smiled as he wrote about some event of the day. Every letter was a treasure. How I delighted in them!**

The Lord says that if we *delight* in His Word, He will give us the desires of our hearts. If we set our hearts on Him in that manner, our desires will soon line up with what the Word is teaching.

Some give the excuse for not reading the Bible saying that 'they just don't like to read.' To this reasoning I always use the illustration of personal letters from loved ones. Everyone loves to read personal mail! The reason for not reading could be ignorance of God's Word and not realizing that it is personal to us as though we pulled a portion of it out of the mailbox each day with our name on it. Only God could address His Word to all of His children and it be personal to each one individually. A miracle! Read your part today.

Additional Treasures:     Proverbs 30:5     Psalm 119:127-128

# July 21

**"Hast thou not known? Hast thou not heard, that the everlasting God, the Lord, the Creator of the ends of the earth, fainteth not, neither is weary? there is no searching of his understanding."**
**Isaiah 40:28**

Someone has said that an hour spent with God is worth more than a lifetime spent with a man. The more that we meditate on His words, the more we understand the things of the Lord. But learned men have told us that after a lifetime of serious study of God's Word, they still knew so little and felt that they had only *scratched the surface* of knowledge about our Lord: the everlasting God, the Lord, the Creator of the ends of the earth!

Christians often misunderstand the workings of the Lord when they are going through trials and temptations. He knows everything that is happening, yet He seems indifferent and distant to us at times when we are struggling the most. We need to exercise faith like the prophet, Habakkuk, when every blessing was dried up.

"Yet I will rejoice in the Lord, I will joy in the God of my salvation."
Habakkuk 3:18

**God moves in a mysterious way  His wonders to perform;**
**He plants His footsteps in the sea  And rides upon the storm.**

**Deep in unfathomable mines  Of never-failing skill,**
**He treasures up His bright designs,  And works His sovereign will.**

**Ye fearful saints, fresh courage take;  The clouds ye so much dread**
**Are big with mercy, and shall break  In blessings o'er your head.**

**Judge not the Lord by feeble sense,  But trust Him for His grace;**
**Behind a frowning providence  He hides a smiling face.**

**Blind unbelief is sure to err,  And scan His work in vain;**
**God is His own interpreter,  And He will make it plain.**
*Light Shining Out of Darkness* – William Cowper

Additional Treasures:   Proverbs 3:5-6   Psalm 73:25-26

# July 22

"For the wrath of God is revealed from heaven against
all ungodliness and unrighteousness of men
who hold the truth in unrighteousness."
Romans 1:18

Many people have a wrong attitude about the wrath of God. The Bible speaks much of that wrath and helps us to better understand His holiness.

"For which things' sake **the wrath of God** cometh on the children of disobedience..." Colossians 3:6

"He that believeth on the Son hath everlasting life: and he that believeth not the Son shall not see life; but **the wrath of God** abideth on him." John 3:36

**God's wrath is a fixed attitude opposing unrighteousness. This attitude never changes. It will culminate, *come to a head,* in righteous judgment upon all that finally and completely reject God's offer of love and salvation.**

We can't understand God's wrath because we don't understand His holiness. God hates sin! He loves sinners, but He will not condone sin. When Jesus, God's own son, had our sins on Him while He was dying, God turned away. It brought the most desperate words that Jesus uttered: "MY GOD, MY GOD, WHY HAST THOU FORSAKEN ME?" It is folly for Christians to harbor sin thinking it won't matter. It will, and not only that, but the chastisement will come as sure as the sun and moon are real. Sin devastates; that is its nature. God loves us and He has numberless ways of prying sin out of the hearts of His children. Sometimes, even as they suffer the results of sin, Christians refuse to repent and forsake them. They don't see the true nature of sin until it's too late.

I read about a family that raised a python snake from a baby and the children grew up petting it, and caring for it like one of the family. But one day the rest of the family came home to find that the huge full grown python had coiled around their teenage son and killed him. The snake acted according to its nature. Being a pet all its life didn't change what it was. So it is with sin. It may seem harmless, innocent, beautiful or appropriate at the time, but the end results of sin will bring sadness and regret.

Let not sin therefore reign in your mortal body..." Romans 6:12

Additional Treasures: Psalm 37:8 Colossians 3:8

# July 23

**"Cease from anger, and forsake wrath: fret
not thyself in any wise to do evil."
Psalm 37:8**

Man's wrath is connected with evil, whereas God's wrath is connected with His righteousness. He cannot observe evil passively as man does. "Thou art of purer eyes than to behold evil, and canst not look on iniquity..." Habakkuk 1:13

**There are some important facts concerning God's wrath:**

**God's wrath was revealed at Calvary** when Jesus laid down His life for lost sinners. The moment that He "became sin" for us the wrath of Almighty God turned on Jesus. Can we ever fathom such love that was demonstrated when Jesus took our sins in His own body and died that we might be saved?

"...that he by the grace of God should taste death for every man." Hebrews 2:9

**God's Wrath is against all evil: all inclusive.**

Sin is sin to God! We put sin into categories with some bad, and some not so bad. But all unrighteousness is sin, even our foolish thoughts. It is impossible to be right with God apart from Christ. He paid for our sins, and is now in heaven making intercession for us as we live in a world that is wicked and contaminates us. Sins must be confessed to God and Jesus clears them up...He has already paid for them. A failure to confess our sins will bring, not God's wrath, but His correction as a loving Father to his erring children.

"The thought of foolishness is sin..." Proverbs 24:9

**God's wrath is absolutely inescapable.**

Where could one possibly go to hide from God? He is omnipresent! In the end time men will desperately try to hide from His wrath when they will say to the rocks and mountains "Fall on us, and hide us from the face of him that sitteth on the throne, and from the wrath of the Lamb: for the great day of his wrath is come: and who shall be able to stand?" Revelation 6:16-17

**God's wrath is justifiable.**

If men refuse to take Jesus as their Savior, God's wrath cannot be held back in their judgment. Christ is the 'hiding place' we all must run to in order to escape the deserved wrath of God. Now, there is grace, mercy and God's long-suffering. Someday, there will only be His wrath. "For the wrath of God is revealed from heaven against all ungodliness and unrighteousness of men, who hold the truth in unrighteousness..." Romans 1:18

Additional Treasures:   Hebrews 4:2   Jude 14,15

# July 24

**"For they loved the praise of men more
than the praise of God."
John 12:43**

Chief rulers of the synagogue had believed on the Lord, but did not confess it before the people because they did not want to be put out of the synagogue. They loved the praise, being chief rulers, and they knew to be identified with Jesus would mean the end of that acclaim.

People refuse Christ in our day because they would lose the praise of men in this world. And Christians will often serve the Lord with eye service, that is, hoping others will *see* what they are doing and give them praise for their efforts. The flesh loves recognition! But we should be willing to serve our Lord, as good servants are instructed to serve their masters with whom they are employed.

"And whatsoever ye do, do it heartily, as to the Lord, and not unto men; Knowing that of the Lord ye shall receive the reward of the inheritance: for ye serve the Lord Christ." Colossians 3:23-24

Jesus stooped so low to come to earth and redeem us. We should be willing to do anything on earth for Him, and serve with gladness.

**"Father, where shall I work today?"
And my love flowed warm and free.
He pointed out a tiny spot,
And said, "Tend that for me."**

**I answered quickly, "Oh, no, not that.
Why, no one would ever see,
No matter how well my work was done.
Not that little place for me!"**

**And the word He spoke, it was not stern,
He answered me tenderly,
"Ah, little one, search that heart of thine;
Art thou working for them or me?
Nazareth was a little place, and so was Galilee."**
V. Raymond Edman

Additional Treasures:     Psalm 100:2     Mark 10:43-44

# July 25

**"To the law and to the testimony: if they speak not according
to this word, it is because there is no light in them."
Isaiah 8:20**

We live in a thoroughly compromising world. Decades of television
have desensitized Christians to sin, and torn down whatever morals were
operating in the world's population. Hardly anyone wants to commit
himself and state the absolute truth about right and wrong according to
the Word of God. It's not a popular thing to do. However, it is the only
*truth* in this world and the standard that will never change.

**"There is but one standard of the everlastingly right and
the everlastingly wrong, and that is the Bible."** – T. De Witt Talmage

Because God's people are so influenced by the world today, they
have become adept at dressing up sins in a respectable guise.

**Lying**– keeps the "awful truth" from making other people ill at ease.
It is amazing the difference a few decades can make in the standards
and morals of our society. We have come from the practice of men
keeping their word as a sacred bond without a written contract, to one
where a contract can be broken on a whim. Lying is considered a way of
life now, yet it is still what the Bible says, it is an abomination to God:
sin which He hates!
"Remove from me the way of lying..."     Psalm 119:29
**Gossip**– is initiated "because of concern" about others. A person
who will gossip is a detriment to his family or any other group. It is
considered to be 'innocent' chatter over the fence or a cup of coffee but it
has destroyed families, churches, and friendships. Gossiping is like
throwing feathers into the wind. You can't gather them all back up again.
Neither can you undo the effects of gossip. "Whoso keepeth his mouth
and   his   tongue   keepeth   his   soul   from   troubles."
Proverbs 21:23
**Neglect of the Bible** – "I have to work hard, and I'm just too tired
to read or pray. God understands." God *does not* 'understand' for He
holds His Word above His very name! "...For thou hast magnified thy
word above all thy name." Psalm 138:2
We can't possibly keep a right attitude and perspective about the
things of God unless we do read His Word and listen to what He says.
Things are distorted without the clear vision of His truth in our hearts.

Additional Treasures:     I Peter 1:25     Ephesians 6:11-17

# July 26

**"Brethren, I count not myself to have apprehended: but this
one thing I do, forgetting those things which are behind,
and reaching forth....I press toward the mark..."
Philippians 3:13-14**

Anyone could live his whole life regretting mistakes and failures of
the past. All humans have them. It is discouraging to reflect on past
failures, *or accomplishments*, if it distracts the Christian from giving his
whole heart to the present time he has to serve the Lord.

The Apostle Paul wouldn't stop and congratulate himself for all the
great work he had done in the ministry; he continued like each day was
the starting point. He was after the *prize* which was completing the work
God had called him to do.
"I press toward the mark for the prize of the high calling of God in
Christ Jesus." Philippians 3:14

We would do well to focus each day on the things that we desire to
accomplish for the Lord, after we first establish our focus on the Lord
Himself. Each day can be a fresh beginning with old things left behind.

Saints of the past learned that to be happy and unencumbered with
worry and fretfulness, they had to trust the Lord for the past as well as
the present and future. Only God can handle our blunders and keep them
from burying us in a sea of regret.
In that great classic by Hannah Whitall Smith, *The Christian's
Secret of a Happy Life,* she gives some invaluable advice for Christians.

**"Never indulge, at the close of an action, in any self-reflective
acts of any kind, whether of self-congratulations or of self-despair.
Forget the things that are behind, the moment they are past, leaving
them with God."**

Regret keeps us from being as productive in our lives as we can be.
If it is sin that we regret, confessing and forsaking blots it out forever.
"If we confess our sins, he is faithful and just to forgive us our sins,
and to cleanse us from all unrighteousness."
I John 1:9

Additional Treasures:     Proverbs 28:13     Philippians 4:6-7

# July 27

**"...But Jesus stooped down, and with his finger wrote
on the ground, as though he heard them not."
John 8:6**

Wicked men were always trying to trap the Lord in some way. When they brought the woman caught in the very act of adultery, they thought this would be the time Jesus would be on the spot. "Now Moses in the law commanded us, that such should be stoned: but what sayest thou?" John 8:5

**Jesus cut right through their hypocrisy, and judged *the man who was also guilty as the woman*, and the men who had supposedly caught them in the very act of sin. There is a strong indication that it was arranged, to create an impossible situation for the Lord to solve without compromising the law. What fools they were, standing in the presence of God in the flesh!**

"So when they continued asking him, he lifted up himself and said unto them, He that is without sin among you, let him first cast a stone at her. And again he stooped down, and wrote on the ground. And they which heard it, being convicted by their own conscience, went out one by one, beginning at the eldest, even unto the last..." v 7-8-9

What Jesus said arrested their attention right away, *"He that is without sin among you..."* In the presence of the Lord, the conviction of sin was so strong they forsook their plot against Jesus and left, one by one, beginning at the eldest. *He had the most sin, being the oldest!* Jesus forgave the woman and told her to *"go, and sin no more."*

"O Lord, the hope of Israel, all that forsake thee shall be ashamed, and they that depart from me shall be written in the earth, because they have forsaken the Lord, the fountain of living waters." Jeremiah 17:13

We don't know what the Lord wrote with His finger on the ground. It might have been their names, starting with the eldest! They certainly left in that order, oldest to the youngest. Jesus was the fountain of living waters but those religious hypocrites hated Him and rejected Jesus vehemently. The woman is the only one who left there with the water of life. John 8:11

Additional Treasures: John 8:31-32    John 10:27-30

# July 28

**"Marvel not that I said unto thee, Ye must be born again."**
**John 3:7**

Jesus told this to Nicodemus, a ruler of the Jews, who came to talk to Jesus at night. He was startled to hear what the Lord had to say, for Jesus told him exactly what he needed right away.

"Jesus answered and said unto him, Verily, verily, I say unto thee, except a man be born again, he cannot see the kingdom of God." v 3

Then the Lord explained in detail about this *royal birth* which gets one into the family of God. He even tells Nicodemus why and how God provided for it.

"For God so loved the world, that he gave his only begotten Son, that whosoever believeth in him should not perish, but have everlasting life." v16

**A higher birth means a higher life! Children of kings and queens on earth are brought up to conduct themselves as *royalty*, no matter what is going on around them. This intense training sets them apart from the ordinary citizen, and they are permanently fixed in that *royal* mold.**

We are children of the King of Kings and Lord of Lords! We have a royal birth since we were *born again* into His family. Our Lord starts right in at birth training us by putting His Holy Spirit *in us* to teach us all things. Because of that we should stand out and be distinctly different than ordinary citizens of the world. A dedicated Christian is an oddity in our society today. At times they may even draw attention like the royals do when they appear in public. After all, good manners, clean conversation, modesty in dress and deportment stand out in contrast to the ways of the world.

"But grow in grace, and in the knowledge of our Lord and Saviour Jesus Christ." II Peter 3:18

"Behold, what manner of love the Father hath bestowed upon us, that we should be called the sons of God: therefore the world knoweth us not, because it knew him not." I John 3:1

When we eat out at a restaurant, we always ask the blessing on our food before we eat. We don't make a show of it, but just quietly do it. People often stop by and comment to us about it. Recently, a man stopped by our table and patted my husband on the shoulder and said "That's a good witness, Brother."

Additional Treasures:    Ephesians 5:8    Romans 8:16-17

# July 29

**"Whatsoever a man soweth, that shall he also reap."**
**Galatians 6:7**

The law of the harvest has been in effect ever since God created the earth and set it into motion. It not only affects things that are planted and harvested from the ground, but all the dealings of mankind.

We know assuredly that it always works in compliance to God's Word, for the Lord said He would not be mocked.

"Be not deceived; God is not mocked: for whatsoever a man soweth, that shall he also reap." Galatians 6:7

If there was ever a failure, our God could be mocked, *or ridiculed,* but we know that will never happen. Some people ignore the law and feel that the sins they are engaged in will not make a difference in their lives. But when the harvest comes up, what devastation!

Good and kind deeds that we sow will also come up in a harvest to bless and enrich our lives and those connected with us.

**My husband has always shown kindness to people in need and in distress. He has helped many motorists stranded on the highway with flat tires, and especially mothers with little children in the car.**

**One day I was the one in need! I was returning from a visit with my sister and had a blowout on the freeway. As I was getting the car stopped, a young man traveling toward me on the opposite side stopped his car and came across the grassy median and said, "Where's your jack?" He proceeded to fix the flat as though he was sent to the very spot just for that purpose. I felt such gratitude in my heart because God had blessed me with instant help, and I remembered *why*. My husband had sown seeds of kindness and help. When the harvest came, it was wonderful.**

"As we have therefore opportunity, let us do good unto all men, especially unto them who are of the household of faith." Galatians 6:10

"And let us not be weary in well doing: for in due season we shall reap, if we faint not." Galatians 6:9

Additional Treasures:     Luke 6:38     Colossians 3:25

# July 30

**"He that covereth his sins shall not prosper: but whoso confesseth and forsaketh them shall have mercy."**
**Proverbs 28:13**

That verse means that things start falling apart soon enough in the life of the transgressor, then misery of heart and soul sets in. The way back to God is confessing and forsaking the sinful path. This is illustrated in the life of King David after his sin of adultery, and then murder.

"Have mercy upon me, O God, according to thy lovingkindness: according unto the multitude of thy tender mercies blot out my transgressions. Wash me thoroughly from mine iniquity, and cleanse me from my sin. For I acknowledge my transgressions: and my sin is ever before me."

King David was forgiven and restored to fellowship with God. But the seed had been sown, and the king reaped a bitter harvest as a result of his sin of adultery and murder.

The seeds of sin sprout and bring forth a harvest, even though one may fervently hope for crop failure. If regret could reverse the law of the harvest there would be many cancellations, especially in the lives of Christians who have the Holy Spirit present to convict them of sin. The law remains for God's children; in fact chastisement may come speedily.

"Mortify therefore your members which are upon the earth; fornication, uncleanness, inordinate affection, evil concupiscence, and covetousness, which is idolatry: For which things' sake the wrath of God cometh on the children of disobedience..." Colossians 3:5-6

One of my most used and favorite verses is Psalm 51:10. It is a good 'bath-tub' for God's children and they can jump in and out as often as needed in the course of a day. Since even the 'thought of foolishness' is sin, we certainly need a ready prayer verse to cleanse our hearts frequently. Thoughts can turn wayward in a second if some past offense comes to mind, and thoughts are swift to increase to a clamoring host urging one toward anger and resentment. That's the time to stop it by praying "Create in me a clean heart, O God; and renew a right spirit within me." Keep it in mind for ready use.

The Word of God is the deterrent to sin. Read it faithfully!

Additional Treasures:    Psalm 119: 9, 11    Proverbs 11:5-6

**"The fear of the Lord is strong confidence:
and his children shall have a place of refuge."
Proverbs 14:26**

The fear of the Lord is a *loving reverence* for our Lord. We do not deliberately sin against the One we love and revere. Christians should start each day confiding in the Lord the love and respect they have for Him. It would give them the strength and confidence to face the world.

**The devil is constantly discouraging the attitude of *"loving reverence for God"* in us, because he knows there is such blessing and joy in it. Some of his methods continue to be effective.**

**He makes prayer *burdensome*,** and assures us that it doesn't do any good. Don't be discouraged! God hears us every time we utter a word; even before that He listens to our thoughts. Prayer is effective even when we don't feel like it, don't want to, and just go through the motions. I used to feel that way when I worked in our cotton field dragging a long cotton sack behind me pulling bolls. My heart was definitely not in it, but my part helped to get the crop in anyway. Prayer always brings results! We may not see them at all, but rest assured that our petitions are heard by the Lord and He works on our behalf.

**He tempts us to tolerate *respectable* sins,** assuring us that those things are not so bad. White lies are easy to begin with, but it is amazing how many we have to tell to prop up the first one! We may allow sinful thoughts to occupy our minds. No one knows...but God. It does matter what we think for thoughts are the beginning of words and actions. They 'rule' our lives. That's why we are to "Let this mind be in you, which was also in Christ Jesus." Philippians 2:5

**He makes us forget that sin has *wages*.**

We all know what wages are. That's what you get on pay-day. A noted preacher of the last century, R.G. Lee, was famous for a sermon he preached about the wages of sin titled "Pay-Day Someday." Many men and women repented after hearing that powerful message on the consequences of sin. Many sad stories could be told of the suffering that sin brings. Don't let the devil deceive you. Sin *always* collects wages!

Additional Treasures:    Proverbs 8:13    Psalm 104:34

# August 1

**"Whoso causeth the righteous to go astray in an evil way,
he shall fall himself into his own pit..."**
**Proverbs 28:10**

Christians can be led astray. There are many warnings in the Word of God to keep us from being deceived by all the ways and means the devil uses to lead us off the path of faithfulness to God.

"Ye therefore, beloved, seeing ye know these things before, beware lest ye also, being led away with the error of the wicked, fall from your own steadfastness." II Peter 3:17

Christians are influenced and led away by the company they keep more than anything else. Some have found out, too late, that wicked companions can influence them for evil before they can influence their companions for good. Any compromise on the Christian's part will weaken his testimony and delete God's power from his life.
"Enter not into the path of the wicked, and go not in the way of evil men." Proverbs 4:14

**"No one is strong enough and wise enough to be safe in constant company with persons of wrong principle and false religion, any more than one is healthy enough to be safe physically in a malarial or fever-laden atmosphere. Indeed, one who goes by choice into bad company and loves to remain there is already more than half fallen. The only time when one is safe in bad company is when he is laboring to do them good."** Commentary

Not only can Christians be led astray; some of the things we tolerate and pursue affect us in an adverse way. We must be aware of the influence of the computer, television, videos and a constant involvement with other activities that consume time and energy, which are not important. These can eat up the time and then the things that matter are often neglected. A good motto to post somewhere over your 'to do' list for the day is three little words: Don't Waste Time! It helps me to get more done with that reminder right in a prominent place where I see it during the day.

"Abstain from all appearance of evil." I Thessalonians 5:22

Additional Treasures:   Psalm 34:13-14   Proverbs 1:10

# August 2

**"Thy word is a lamp unto my feet, and a light
unto my path."
Psalm 119:105**

For those who have walked through dense woods in the darkest part of the night, the importance of a light for the path is fully known. Without light, one cannot see things on the path that entangle the feet or animals that scurry about or lurk in the underbrush. While neither may be life threatening, it is sensible to avoid these things. Many inexperienced folk have stumbled out of the woods smelling like a skunk!

This world is *dark woods* we are passing through. More than food for our bodies, we need the Word of God stored up in our minds to get us through safely. It is the light that enables us to see things with the wisdom of God. After showing us the way to go, it also has the power to strengthen us as we travel along.

But Christians today are dulled by the things of the world, and easily forget how necessary it is to read and absorb the scriptures. Some think they are reading it, when in fact they are not getting enough of God's Word to keep them fit spiritually. They struggle along defeated, wondering what is wrong, since they are Christians and attend church regularly.

*The Neglected Bible* – **Some men belonging to a Bible Association called upon an old woman, and asked if she had a Bible. She was angry at being asked such a question, and replied, "Do you think, gentlemen, that I am a heathen, that you ask me such a question?" Then calling to a little girl, she said, "Run and fetch the Bible out of the drawer, that I may show it to the gentlemen." They asked that she not take the trouble, but she insisted that they should "see she was not a heathen." Accordingly the Bible was brought, nicely covered. On opening it, the old woman exclaimed, "Well, I am glad that you called and asked about the Bible; here are my eye-glasses; I have been looking for them these three years and did not know where to find them!"** Commentary

"The law of thy mouth is better unto me than thousands of gold and silver." Psalm 119:72

Additional Treasures:     Jeremiah 15:16     Proverbs 6:23

# August 3

**"For our transgressions are multiplied before thee,
and our sins testify against us…"
Isaiah 59:12**

Sins multiply easily and quickly. A little *white* lie is supported by more lies. *Secret sins* force the guilty into a web of compromise and deception until a time when the sins are confessed and forsaken.

"He that covereth his sins shall not prosper: but whoso confesseth and forsaketh them shall have mercy." Proverbs 28:13

Dedicated Christians are not taken in by the temptation to commit some horrible sin. Things that ensnare them are *little* sins.

**The television programs that plant bits of trash in the mind.**

Whatever goes in the 'eye-gate' is stored away forever. That's why the images of trauma and other things we would like to get rid of still stay with us.

Before you can flip the TV channel at times you will see pornographic pictures or violent scenes which make a negative imprint in your mind. Women are more susceptible than men, because they are more emotionally wired to "feel" and experience what they watch. Be selective, and if you want to really make spiritual headway, watch it less and less....

**Missing worship at church without excuse.**

You'd think that would never become a habit, but it can. There are times when every dedicated Christian would like to just stay home. He is tired or wants to catch up on something, or work his hobby...just stay home! That is a temptation coming in that doesn't look like one. Beware. Don't miss church.

**Neglect of personal devotion to the Lord** is something I warn about more than anything else in my teaching. I know how my life changed when I began to study the Bible and get some scriptures in my heart. It is our food and water for the soul and one cannot be healthy, spiritually, without it.

**Reading Christian books *about* the Bible, more than the Bible itself.**

This is a subtle trap, if you like to read especially. With all the years of experience, I still find myself absentmindedly piling up the books on my nightstand and spending a lot of time reading good books and spending less time with God's Word. Ladies the battle never ends. Beware of anything at all which lures you away from daily reading of the scriptures.

Additional Treasures:    I John 5:17    Proverbs 4:27

# August 4

**"Deliver thyself as a roe from the hand of the hunter,
and as a bird from the hand of the fowler."
Proverbs 6:5**

The roe, *the deer*, is swift and wild but can be hunted down if he does not stay out of range. If a bird is not wary it can easily be taken. The fowler conceals his net, and then puts out the food. The little bird flies down for a feast; the net is sprung, and he is caught!

Our Heavenly Father warns us with illustrations that we can easily understand. Sin will trap us and destroy our lives. The devil works tirelessly to entice us into sin so that he, instead of the Lord, can control us.

"...if God peradventure will give them repentance to the acknowledging of the truth; And that they may recover themselves out of the snare of the devil, who are taken captive by him at his will. II Timothy 2:26

**I recently read about how women can be caught up in reading 'romance' novels, and the devastation caused by the addiction to them. Many wives and mothers will escape into a fantasy world by reading, and ignore their responsibilities to their families. Many 'romance' novels are sexually explicit, and fall into the same category as pornography. No woman should put such filth into her mind. It will poison the heart, and take away the ability to think realistically about her relationship with her husband. It is an awful, sinful trap; don't be caught in it.**

Avoid the display racks loaded with books with alluring sensual picture covers. Imagine the devil standing beside it motioning to you. *He is!*

God can break the power of sin if you are in the trap.

"If we confess our sins, he is faithful and just to forgive us our sins, and to cleanse us from all unrighteousness." I John 1:9

Additional Treasures:    Titus 2:4-5    Proverbs 31:10

# August 5

**"Honor thy father and mother; which is the
first commandment with promise…"**
**Ephesians 6:2**

This verse is among the Ten Commandments given on Mt. Sinai.
"Honor thy father and thy mother: that thy days may be long upon
the land which the Lord thy God giveth thee." Exodus 20:12

Obedience in showing respect and honor to one's parents holds a
blessed guarantee. "That it may be well with thee…" Ephesians 6:3

God provided for parents and their children the blessed life with this
unique commandment. It is a provision for parents when they grow old
and the infirmities of declining years take their toll. Their riches are their
loving, caring children.

*Duty to parents.* – **We read in ancient history that a certain city
was besieged, and at length had to surrender. In the city there were
two brothers who had in some way obliged the conquering general,
and in consequence of this, received permission to leave the city
before it was set on fire, taking with them as much of their property
as each could carry about his person. Accordingly, they appeared at
the gates of the city, one of them carrying their father, and the other
their mother.** Commentary

After my mother had a stroke, she lived in a nursing home the last
few months of her life. She was mobile, but unable to verbally
communicate so my sister and I diligently visited her every day, one or
both of us without fail. Mother knew we would be there, and often sat in
the entrance room watching the door. We did various things to amuse her
and one day to see if she would respond to music, we took her to a large
room with a piano and I sat down and played old songs from long ago
that she used to sing to us. That hit the spot! She would sit at the end and
tap the piano with her fingers keeping time with the music. Not only
Mother, but many other residents would come and sit there enjoying old
songs and hymns from another generation.

The truth of God's Word remains. Godly parents, being faithful
and obedient to God, have children who grow up to honor and cherish
them.

"And even to your old age I am he; and even to hoar hairs will I
carry you: I have made, and I will bear; even I will carry, and will deliver
you." Isaiah 46:4

Additional Treasures:    Ecclesiastes 12:1    Colossians 3:20

# August 6

**"For the prophecy came not in old time by the will of man:
but holy men of old spake as they were moved by the Holy Ghost."
II Peter 1:21**

The Bible is not the work of men; God only used their hands to write the divine message. "All Scripture is given by inspiration of God, and is profitable for doctrine, for reproof, for correction, for instruction in righteousness..." II Timothy 3:16

The Word of God is the most amazing power on earth; it can convict a hardened sinner of his need for salvation, and '*birth*' him into the family of God. Men have resisted and wrestled with the Scriptures down through the ages as Jacob also wrestled with the Lord at a turning point in his life. Jacob lost the battle, and came away limping. "And as he passed over Penuel the sun rose upon him, and he halted upon his thigh." Genesis 32:31

Men lose when contending with God, and many prideful, obstinate individuals have had to surrender as the Holy Spirit used the Word to pry open their hearts and reveal their lost condition.

**Long ago, a Christian man stood at the dock and handed out gospel tracts to passengers boarding a ship to cross the ocean. One haughty man took a tract and when realizing what it was, tore it to shreds and threw it on the ground before proceeding to board with his friends. But later a tiny bit of the shredded tract fell out of the cuff of his shirt where it had lodged. It had a single word: *eternity*. That one-word message burned into his heart and he could not escape. It was the means of eternal salvation for his soul.**

Every word of God is potent, and even when shared by the timidest soul, it can deliver such an impression to the heart that a soul can be brought out of darkness into the glorious light of the gospel. We can't understand that kind of power, for only God has it. Just remember that telling someone what the Bible says is never a wasted effort.

"For the word of God is quick, and powerful, and sharper than any two-edged sword, piercing even to the dividing asunder of soul and spirit, and of the joints and marrow, and is a discerner of the thoughts and intents of the heart." Hebrews 4:12.

Additional Treasures:   Jeremiah 5:14   Romans 1:16   Ephesians 6:17

# August 7

**"Man that is in honor, and understandeth not,**
**is like the beasts that perish."**
**Psalm 49:20**

The beasts of the earth do not have souls like human beings, who are made in the image of God. Animals live by their God-given instinct, yet lack the capacity to *know Him*.

Men may attain to the highest level of earth living, and yet refuse to acknowledge God their Creator, and Jesus the Savior who died to redeem their souls from eternal damnation. At the end, they will be like the beasts that perish regardless of their preeminence or station in life.

An inch of time – **"Millions of money for an inch of time!" cried Elizabeth, the gifted but ambitious Queen of England in the fifteenth century upon her dying bed. Unhappy woman! Reclining upon a couch – with ten thousand dresses in her wardrobe – a kingdom, on which the sun never sets, at her feet – all now are valueless; and she shrieks in anguish, and she shrieks in vain for a single "inch of time." She had enjoyed seventy years but like too many among us she had devoted them to wealth, to pleasure, to pride, and ambition so that her preparation for eternity was crowded into a few moments; hence she, who had wasted over half a century, would barter millions for an inch of time. R.T.S.**

"The wicked are estranged from the womb: they go astray as soon as they be born, speaking lies. Their poison is like the poison of a serpent: they are like the deaf adder that stoppeth her ear..." Psalm 58:3-4

We cannot comprehend the love of God for the 'wicked who are estranged from the womb.' He provided a way, a *new birth,* which Jesus secured by His death on the cross in payment for sin. Pride and self-will keeps sinners from coming to Christ, though He is the King of Kings and Lord of Lords!

"And this is life eternal, that they might know thee the only true God, and Jesus Christ, whom thou hast sent." John 17:3

Additional Treasures:    Romans 14:11    Psalm 103:15

# August 8

**"Train up a child in the way he should go: and when
he is old, he will not depart from it."
Proverbs 22:6**

We live in a generation where parents are slack in this admonition from the Word of God. They are too busy, tired, stressed out, and brainwashed by the world to take care of their children in the right way.

Most training that children get today comes from school, their peers and the entertainment world. Christian families will also be guilty of neglect in training their children if they consider the brief time at church and Sunday school to be adequate for *spiritual* instruction. In time, that mindset will prove to be a costly mistake. "The foolishness of man perverteth his way: and his heart fretteth against the Lord." Proverbs 19:3

Many parents have grieved over children and said, "I raised them in church; I don't understand why they are gone astray." But children are raised at home! They pick up all the attitudes and ways of parents. They will love what their parents love, respect what they respect, and generally emulate those that they love most. Parents are the first pattern, and those who endeavor to instill the knowledge of God in their children are wise indeed.

**"The heathen mother takes her babe to the idol temple, and teaches it to clasp its little hands before its forehead in the attitude of prayer long before it can utter a word. As soon as it can walk, it is taught to gather a few flowers or fruits, or put a little rice upon a banana-leaf, and lay them upon the altar before the idol god. As soon as it can utter the names of its parents, so soon it is taught to offer up its petitions before the images. Whoever saw a heathen child that could speak, and not pray? Christian mothers, why is it that so many children grow up in this enlightened land without learning to pray?"** ---Vt. Chronicle

Do your children or grandchildren ever *hear* you pray? Children ought to be taught to pray to God and look in His Word for answers. It is easy when they are in the formative years, but when they are half grown, it is usually very difficult to even get their attention, much less, impress upon them the importance of prayer and reading the Bible. Start early for lasting results!

Additional Treasures:     II Timothy 1:5     II Timothy 3:14-15

# August 9

**"And he said unto them, Set your hearts unto all the words which I testify among you this day, which ye shall command your children to observe to do…"**
**Deuteronomy 32:46**

If a person is really sold on an idea and cannot be persuaded otherwise, he is considered as one having a *mind-set*. I believe God would have His children cultivate a *heart-set* about His Word. The most fruitful, beneficial and certainly the greatest learning time is that which we spend reading the scriptures. "For it is not a vain thing for you; because it is your life…" Deuteronomy 32:47

Those who spend little or no time reading the Bible have no idea what they forfeit by such neglect. They may feel that it is time wasted, but the Lord says it is not a vain thing for you. It is not an empty exercise.

The Lord was speaking through Moses telling the people to set their hearts to His Word and to teach their children. "It is your life" He said. It is that important to incorporate God's Word into your thinking and living. In more ways than we can count, the Lord blesses through His Word.

**The Word keeps us from sin.**
"Thy word have I hid in mine heart, that I might not sin against thee." Psalm 119:11

**The Word has answers to our prayers.**
In praying, we speak to God. In His Word, He speaks to us. Suddenly a verse will reveal the answer to a problem you have prayed about. "The entrance of thy words giveth light; it giveth understanding unto the simple." v. 130

One day when our daughter, Jeanne, was in Bible College, she called with a frantic plea for advice about some problem she and her roommate were experiencing at the time. Since I was so far away and disconnected from the scene my mind was blank about any kind of advice. All I could think of was this verse from Psalms. I told the girls to look it up and then read the Bible with the prayer for enlightenment concerning their dilemma. I remember the incident because Jeanne's roommate protested in the background saying, "Does your mom think we are 'simple'!?" I told them that everyone fits into that category, and we all need understanding from the Lord.

The Bible is earth's greatest treasure, and it belongs to the children of God. They can understand it, but the unsaved cannot.

Additional Treasures:     Isaiah 40:8     II Peter 1:4

# August 10

**"Submitting yourselves one to another
in the fear of the Lord."
Ephesians 5:21**

This verse is referring to the attitude of godly men and women in marriage. People who don't accept the Bible as truth scoff at the Christian's concept of marriage and the different roles of men and women as taught in the scriptures.

"For the husband is the head of the wife, even as Christ is the head of the church: and he is the saviour of the body. Therefore as the church is subject    unto Christ, so let the wives be to their own husbands in everything."

This is the *order* that God set down for the foundation and workings of marriage and family, and He is *not* favoring the man in any case.

"Husbands, love your wives, even as Christ also loved the church, and gave himself for it." v 25

In this world of humanistic philosophy, the main thing is "rights." "I've got my rights." "Your rights come first." It is no wonder that some women turn livid with anger when they hear God's exhortation to "submit yourselves unto your own husbands, as unto the Lord."

**Women, submitted to the headship and leadership of their husbands, are trusting God in the most important issue of their lives and may be pleasantly surprised at the power that comes with submission. God will honor obedience to His Word; wives have nothing to fear. God will take care of the consequences of being obedient to Him.**

"Nevertheless let every one of you in particular so love his wife even as himself; and the wife see that she reverence her husband."
    Ephesians 5:33

If a woman would be obedient to God at first in *choosing* out her husband, she would not have many problems that come with being married to someone who cares nothing for God's order of things. But whatever difficulties you may have, 'go by the book' and trust that God can do something for your life.

Additional Treasures:    Ephesians 4:32    I Peter 3:1

# August 11

**"Likewise, ye husbands, dwell with them according
to knowledge, giving honour unto the wife..."
I Peter 3:7**

When we know the literal meaning of special words that have so much to do with our lives, it opens up a whole new dimension of understanding and appreciation, *especially* in the area of marriage.

Husband and wife. – The word 'husband' literally means 'the band of the house,' the support of it, the person who keeps it together as a band keeps together a sheaf of corn.

There are married men who are not 'husbands', because they are not the band of the house. Truly, in some cases the wife is the husband, for oftentimes it is she, who by her diligence, thrift and economy keeps the house together. The married man, who by his wasteful habits strips his house of all comfort, is not a husband; *in a legal sense he is*, but in no other for he is not a 'house-band'.

The word 'wife' is unique too. It literally means a *weaver*. The wife is the person who weaves. Before our great cotton and cloth factories arose, one of the principal employments in every house was the fabrication of clothing: every family made its own. The wool was spun into thread by the girls, who were therefore called 'spinsters'. The thread was woven into cloth by their mother, who accordingly was called the weaver, or the wife.    Commentary

**A godly husband will be a *house-band* for his home, and a godly wife will be the *weaver* who works happiness all through the fabric of her marriage and family. When a marriage and home has these qualities, it is a pleasure to be present in the family and feel the harmony and happiness which is evident. Every member of such a family can thrive and grow in a healthy atmosphere.**

The battle rages in today's society; there are constant attacks on marriage and the traditional family structure. But it still remains that the happiest, healthiest people on earth are those who live according to God's basic laws in the matter.

"What God hath joined together, let not man put asunder." Mark 10:9

Additional Treasures:    Proverbs 31:25    Genesis 2:23-24

# August 12

**"It is an honour for a man to cease from strife:
but every fool will be meddling."
Proverbs 20:3**

One of the reasons Christians don't realize answers to their prayers is because they aren't looking in the *answer column*: the Bible. The Word of God holds answers to prayer, and unless we diligently open it every day and look, we will miss them.

I discovered this truth for myself many years ago. The bitterness from an old hurt was embedded in my heart. I prayed, but nothing helped until one day I read a certain verse from the Proverbs. "It is an honour for a man to cease from strife…" With that Word, God opened my eyes and I could see what I'd been doing. I was fighting the battle myself and could *never* win. I had to stop striving and allow God to fight for me. *He always wins!*

God answered my prayer before I prayed it, but I wasn't looking for the answer in His Word. After that experience in my learning, I penned the first of a collection of poems titled: *Poems That Sprang From a Verse.*

**Girding on my sword, I sought the familiar battlefield
Where the enemy lurked in the shadows
Anticipating the delight of dancing about just out of reach
Of my slashing sword of anger and frustration.
*The day ended as usual.*
Homeward I trudged, weary with fatigue,
Helpless to quell the hurt of another battle *lost,*
While the enemy scampered back into the comfortable
Recesses of my mind to await another day.
*Then You showed me Your Sword:*
Sharp, two-edged, gleaming from countless victories.
*It pierced my heart*
Cutting cleanly into the wound for healing,
Then with a blow destroyed the enemy, leaving a settled peace.
*Thank You Lord.***

Additional Treasures:     I Samuel 17:47     Psalm 18:3

# August 13

**"...If ye have faith as a grain of mustard seed,
ye shall say unto this mountain, Remove hence..."
Matthew 17:20**

A mustard seed is a very tiny little thing, and the Lord certainly knew what a comparison He made. It means, at best, we don't have much faith. The Lord was never surprised at anything in His dealings with men because He *knew* what was in man, yet the Bible says that He *marveled* at their lack of faith. It was a wonder and astonishment.

"And he marvelled because of their unbelief.  And he went round about the villages, teaching."  Mark 6:6

Since faith is based upon the facts of what God has said, it is incredible that men would have little or no faith. The Bible is the Word of God and it is *truth.* "Sanctify them through thy truth: thy word is truth." John 17:17

Folks offer excuses for not trusting in Christ. One is, "I just don't have enough faith to be saved." In reality, it takes so little faith to believe that Jesus died for your sins, was buried and rose the third day as the Bible says.  If a person believes that fact with a repentant heart...*he will be saved.*  It cost Jesus a tremendous price to save sinners, but He made it so very easy for sinners to be saved.  Just believe the facts in the Word!

**"It is not the quantity of thy faith that shall save thee.  A drop of water is as true water as the whole ocean.  So a little faith is as true faith as the greatest." -Bib. Ill.**

Christians grieve the Lord because of their unbelief. It means they are not taking the Word of God into their minds and hearts, because that is the only thing that increases our faith.

"So then faith cometh by hearing, and hearing by the Word of God."
Romans 10:17

Additional Treasures:    Deuteronomy 8:3    Hebrews 11:6

# August 14

**"And it came to pass also on another sabbath,
that he entered into the synogogue and taught: and there
was a man whose right hand was withered."
Luke 6:6**

No doubt this man was known as the man whose hand was withered, *shriveled up.* The Bible says it was his *right* hand, indicating it was significant; it was his working hand.

It was a glad day when Jesus came to the synagogue and saw him there in the crowd. Jesus told him to stand up and keep standing in the midst of the people, and the man obeyed. The Pharisees were watching to see if the Lord would heal on the Sabbath, hoping to get an accusation against Him. They considered healing to be unlawful on the Sabbath. Jesus knew their thoughts and said: "I will ask you one thing; Is it lawful on the sabbath days to do good, or to do evil? To save life, or to destroy it?

"And looking around about upon them all, he said unto the man, Stretch forth thy hand. And he did so: and his hand was restored whole as the other." Luke 6:9-10

We can imagine the joy of the man with his hand restored to normal. But the Pharisees became insane with anger against Jesus! "And they were filled with madness; and communed one with another what they might do to Jesus."

**The world hates the Lord, and His work in restoration of sinners. They are *not glad* at the salvation of a man or the restoration of a disobedient Christian. When Jesus *restores* in any case, they ridicule the resulting change in peoples' lives. But there is joy for one *stretching forth his withered hands of unbelief*, and allowing God to make them strong again in faith and obedience.**

If people will believe Jesus and obey Him on the spot when He speaks to them, they will see amazing things happen as a result. Once we had a woman in the church who had smoked all her life, had her fingers stained green, and reeked of tobacco. After a revival service one night, she told me that God had convicted her of smoking and she was quitting 'right now'. Doubt was there even as I encouraged her to be obedient. But she absolutely quit smoking and stayed clean the rest of her life. And that was in her home where everyone one else used tobacco! That how the power of God works with obedience.

Additional Treasures:   John 15:18   Jeremiah 31:3

# August 15

**"Then saith he to the man, Stretch forth thine hand.**
**And he stretched it forth..."**
**Matthew 12:13**

This man had a *withered* hand, a serious handicap for a man who must work and care for his family. He was assembled with others in the synagogue when Jesus came into the place. The Lord *knew* about the withered hand, and called the man forth out of the crowd. His obedience to the Lord in the simple command, "Stretch forth thine hand..." brought newness to his life. He would no more be known as the man with the withered hand, but the one whose hand was healed by Jesus.

The Lord knows about the withered hands of His children, who through neglect and indifference to the Word of God grow weak and ineffectual in the things of God. *Their spiritual hands are withered.*

**On the parking lot of a grocery store a limousine stopped near my car. One of the darkened window glasses came down, and a dainty hand holding a cigarette was clearly visible. At a glance it told me much about the owner.**
**She was a privileged lady.** That hand did no work to mar the beauty of it. The skin was smooth and flawless.
**She had a small frame.** The hand was very small and dainty.
**She was a "well-kept" lady.** Her nails were manicured, shaped and polished brightly to perfection. And there was another obvious thing the hand showed.
**She smoked cigarettes.** She held one expertly, as smoke curled out the window of the big car, telling me that the lady with the beautiful hand had clothing that smelled like cigarette smoke. It cannot be hidden!
Our spiritual hands, the way in which we demonstrate our faith in God, are showing. What do others know by observing us?
**Withered hands neglect to hold the Bible to read and pray.**
**Withered hands don't reach out to the lost.**
**Withered hands shy away from fellowship with the church.**
**Hands are withered by sin in the heart and life.**

Additional Treasures:     I Timothy 2:8     Acts 3:7     Mark 9:27

# August 16

**"For sin, taking occasion by the commandment, deceived me, and by it slew me."**
**Romans 7:11**

Sin is very deceptive and people are easily fooled by it. Many lives have been ruined, families destroyed, churches devastated, and strong nations brought low by the deceitfulness of sin.

Sin is the *transgression of the law*. If you do something contrary to what God says in His Word, you have sinned.

"Whosoever committeth sin transgresseth also the law: for sin is the transgression of the law." I John 3:4
"All unrighteousness is sin..." I John 5:17

Calvary shows us the truest picture of the horror of sin. It was there that Jesus the sinless, perfect One died as a substitute for sinners.
"For the wages of sin is death; but the gift of God is eternal life through Jesus Christ our Lord." Romans 6:23

For all the instruction God gives to us in His Word, we are still very vulnerable to sin's deception. We are not *afraid* of it; therefore the devil has an edge. He makes sin appealing and as Christians draw close, the devil springs the trap! Then they begin to see the true nature of sin with its misery and devastation. The pleasure of sin is just for a season, or short duration.

Note – **A horrible torture during the middle ages was that of a cell, which, at the prisoner's first entrance presented an air of comfort and ease; so that it was not until he had been confined for a few days that he observed the dimensions of his cell beginning to contract. But once the discovery was made, the fact became more appalling every day. Slowly but terribly the sides drew closer and the unhappy victim was crushed to death. Such is the deception of sin.** Commentary

"Let not sin therefore reign in your mortal body, that ye should obey it in the lust thereof." Romans 6:12

Additional Treasures: Psalm 107:17   Deuteronomy 28:67

# August 17

**"And the work of righteousness shall be peace;
and the effect of righteousness quietness and assurance for ever."
Isaiah 32:17**

One Wednesday night at church, the preacher gave some instructions concerning happiness and assurance in Christ. With so many today being weak in faith, unable to stand fast in the things of the Lord, we need encouragement and reassurance in the fundamentals of our faith.

### The Blood of Jesus makes us safe.
"Much more then, being now justified by his blood, we shall be saved from wrath through Him." Romans 5:9

The firstborn Hebrew sons in Egypt, on the night of the Passover, may have sat trembling and afraid as the death angel passed through, *even though* the blood was on the door outside as God said put it. But they were safe! The blood applied on the doorposts was what mattered, *not their feelings*.

### The Word of God makes us sure.
"Verily, verily, I say unto you, He that heareth my word, and believeth on him that sent me, hath everlasting life, and shall not come into condemnation; but is passed from death unto life." John 5:24

One of the happiest days of my life was the day the Lord revealed to my heart the fact that, in Christ, I am eternally saved. The Word of God is the key: *God said it, we must believe it.*

### Obedience makes us happy.
"Now therefore, if ye will obey my voice indeed...then ye shall be a peculiar treasure unto me above all people..." Exodus 19:5

Obedience to God brings favor and blessing into our lives more than anything we can imagine. If there is a cloud of unhappiness in your heart, check out the obedience factor. Are you *doing* what the Word of God says to do? There is no other way to peace and well-being except through obedience.

**Reading the Bible daily** gives us an edge in living. The day just goes better when you acknowledge the Lord first of all. Read your Bible!

Additional Treasures:     I Peter 2:9     Romans 6:16

# August 18

**"As we have therefore opportunity, let us do good unto all men,
especially unto them who are of the household of faith."
Galatians 6:10**

The largest family on earth is God's family. We are brothers and sisters in Christ--those who have been born again. There should be no lack of love and consideration among the saved, but in this hectic world it is easy to neglect important things and let opportunities to minister to a needy soul pass by.

A Christian coping with a trial needs an encouraging word. The Lord gives the right words to say if we will ask Him, and *listen.*

"A word fitly spoken is like apples of gold in pictures of silver."
    Proverbs 25:11
One with a broken heart needs love and understanding.
"Wherefore comfort yourselves together, and edify one another, even as also ye do."  I Thessalonians 5:11

It seems hard in these last days for Christians to take time to minister to one another. It is the devil's ploy to keep us frazzled and generally distracted, so that we are ineffective in the caring ministry. But it is important to encourage one another by prayer and helpful deeds of kindness. Everyon is needy, though we can't always see it.

### THE HIDDEN CARE

**Perhaps the need one cannot see;
Life seems perfect as can be.
Yet, maybe there's an underneath part:
A little care hidden in the heart.**

**We pray, then, since God does know,
Any and all concealed from show.
His love overturns the underneath part,
And tends the care hidden in the heart.**

Edna Holmes

Additional Treasures:    II Thessalonians 1:3    Romans 12:10

# August 19

**"And a man shall be as an hiding place from the wind…
as the shadow of a great rock in a weary land."
Isaiah 32:2**

The prophet Isaiah speaks of the Lord as he wrote, being moved by the Spirit of God.

"For the prophecy came not in old time by the will of man: but holy men of God spake as they were moved by the Holy Ghost." II Peter 1:21

**Those who have sought a hiding place from fierce winds threatening destruction of lives and property *know* what an unspeakable relief a safe place can be. Storm cellars are common in certain parts of the country where tornadoes devastate whole communities. Many lives have been saved because of these 'hiding places'.**

Jesus is the hiding place for the soul. He came down and made a permanent shelter for those who will trust in Him. His death, burial and resurrection provide a place of safety for eternity, and peace and calm in this life.

"Be merciful unto me, O God, be merciful unto me: for my soul trusteth in thee: yea, in the shadow of thy wings will I make my refuge, until these calamities be overpast." Psalm 57:1

Calamities are defined as great misfortunes, serious trouble and misery. Such things will come into our lives directly and indirectly, affecting us in an adverse way. Those *in Christ* have a place of refuge.

"The eternal God is thy refuge, and underneath are the everlasting arms: and he shall thrust out the enemy from before thee; and shall say, Destroy them." Deuteronomy 33:27

**The Lord's our Rock, in Him we hide, A shelter in the time
of storm; Secure whatever ill betide, A shelter in the time of storm.**
Charleswoth-Sankey

Additional Treasures:    Isaiah 25:4    I Peter 5:7

# August 20

**"As the shadow of a great rock in a weary land."**
**Isaiah 32:2**

On a trip to Canada, we drove through states we had not visited before and had occasion to see some beautiful scenery in national parks. In one, it had unusual rock formations and the whole area was mostly rocky terrain with the blistering heat of the sun beating down making it almost impossible to enjoy. As we returned from a long walk back into the area, the path came alongside a huge rock towering up and blocking out the sun. It was blissful in that cool shade and I thought of the Lord being as the *shadow of a great rock in a weary land.*

The Lord has such love and compassion for His children. How quickly He will come to us and alleviate our suffering if we will trust Him.

"It is of the Lord's mercies that we are not consumed, because his compassions fail not. They are new every morning: great is thy faithfulness." Lamentations 3:22-23

**In the heat of spiritual battles we must *run to the Rock* and get in the shadow of it. The devil does not fear God's children in the least, but he fears the One who has power to protect them. If you want to make the devil tremble, then go to the Lord in prayer. Nothing on earth can keep you from effectual prayer *that brings results,* except sin hidden in the heart.**

"If I regard iniquity in my heart, the Lord will not hear me."
Psalm 66:18

"Blessed be God, which hath not turned away my prayer, nor his mercy from me." Psalm 66:20

> **Oh, Jesus is a Rock in a weary land,**
> **A weary land, A weary land;**
> **Oh, Jesus is a Rock in a weary land**
> **A shelter in the time of storm.**
> Charlesworth-Sankey

Additional Treasures:    Psalm 69:14    Isaiah 25:4

# August 21

**"Let your light so shine before men, that they may see your good works..."**
**Matthew 5:16**

It is important for Christians to have a *testimony* for the Lord. Men must *see* good works before they will believe saved people are genuine in their profession of faith. In our society today, the world and the church are so blended together; the distinctness is not there as it was a few decades ago. The influence of the church has diminished, along with its testimony.

**"When we went to school we drew houses, horses, and trees, and used to write '*house*' under the house, etc., for some persons might have thought the horse was a house. So there are some people who need to wear a label around their necks to show they are Christians, or else we might mistake them for sinners.**

**Avoid that. How can I know what you believe in your heart? I must hear what you confess with your mouth. '*Speak that I might see you.'"** Spurgeon

Christians may speak volumes without words. Their deportment and appearance are like brightly colored signs hanging round their necks.

If the Word of God is naturally in a person's conversation as a point of reference, it is a telltale sign that he lives by it: a Christian.

"Let the word of Christ dwell in you richly in all wisdom..." Col.3:16

Modesty in dress and speech makes men and women stand out clearly in today's society. But it is amazing to see how Christian women have succumbed to the style today of 'plunging necklines'. Women who scorned to think of such a thing in years past are now revealing their 'cleavage' because it is stylish. The thought of being 'out of style' is more than some women can bear in this decadent society we live in. The word *modesty* in the Bible has been deleted from their minds.

"In like manner also, that women adorn themselves in modest apparel, with shamefacedness and sobriety..." I Timothy 2:9

In an unguarded moment, pretense is forgotten. Make sure that your life measures up to the Word of God, for *His* honor and glory.

Additional Treasures:   I Peter 3:1-2   Proverbs 31:20

# August 22

**"The first said unto him, I have bought a piece of ground,
and I must needs go and see it: I pray thee have me excused."
Luke 14:18**

This is the parable Jesus put forth as He observed people who tried to get the chief places in the house where they had been invited to eat. It was important to be seen in a prominent place at those gatherings. Jesus directed their minds to something greater and of utmost importance.

"Then said he unto him, A certain man made a great supper, and bade many: And they all with one consent began to make excuse..." v 17

People make all kinds of excuses for refusing the invitation of the Lord to accept His gift of salvation. They also make excuses for not being true and faithful in the things of the Lord after salvation.

Nobody would buy some land before they see it! That was a very weak excuse, and so are the excuses that Christians use for not reading the Word of God.

**I don't like to read!**

The fact is that everyone will read what is of interest to them. One must *begin* and *continue* reading the Bible before it can do a work in the heart. So many people stop short of that goal because they get discouraged.

**I don't have time.**

If one has time to eat food for his physical body, he has time to feed on the food that will keep him spiritually well and strong in his soul. It is foolish to neglect either one.

"Seek ye out the Book of the Lord, and read..." Isaiah 34:16

**Some really don't know where to start reading the Bible. They hear it all the time "Read the Bible, read the Bible," and they are thinking, 'Where do I start?' If you don't have a plan, then start reading in the four gospels beginning with Matthew. The first part of the chapter is genealogy but verse eighteen starts the account of circumstances surrounding the birth of Christ. Read with the thought in mind that you are there with Jesus and listening to Him. Follow the Lord through the scriptures and you will learn so much. Make it a daily habit to read and let your heart soak up the wonderful sayings of Jesus. The benefits you will gain will bless your life from now on.**

Additional Treasures:     Colossians 3:16     Psalm 19:8

# August 23

**"Even in laughter the heart is sorrowful;
and the end of that mirth is heaviness."
Proverbs 14:13**

Sin planted the seed of sorrow in the human race in the Garden of Eden as Adam and Eve disobeyed God and fell into sin. It makes no difference how blissfully happy we may be for a moment, the element of sorrow remains in the depths of our hearts.

When Jesus came down into this sin-cursed world to redeem us, He too was touched by that sorrow.

"He is despised and rejected of men; a man of sorrows, and acquainted with grief: and we hid as it were our faces from him; he was despised, and we esteemed him not." Isaiah 53:3

**Sorrow in suffering is one of the greatest assets in our Christian life. It is always the times of suffering of some kind that draw us closer to God. We pray more; search the Word for insight, comfort, and answers. We talk about things of the Lord which encourages and blesses us as well as others. Both blessings and sorrows have their purpose in the Christian life. We like the blessings best, but sorrow is the necessary element which adds 'perspective' to our lives...as the depth and richness of color in a masterpiece painting.**

"Before I was afflicted I went astray; but now have I kept thy word."
Psalm 119:67

God's people have always suffered in this world through all ages. Jesus said it would be that way, and we in this generation have a clear path to follow of those who have gone before us.

Comfort in Sorrow. – **I say there is comfort, real and deep, in thinking that the path of sorrow we tread has been beaten smooth and wide by the feet of the best that ever trod this world; that our blessed Saviour was a Man of Sorrows, and that the best of His Church have been suffered to journey by no other path than that their Master went. Nothing has come to us, nothing will come to us, but has been shared by better men.** – Boyd

"And God shall wipe away all tears from their eyes; and there shall be no more death, neither sorrow..." Revelation 21:4

Additional Treasures:   Job 23:10   I Peter 1:7

# August 24

**"For they are light unto those that find them,
and health to all their flesh."
Proverbs 4:22**

This is a blessed truth to know. The Word of God will also make one physically healthy. God states it clearly in this chapter of Proverbs.

"My son, attend to my words; incline thine ear unto my sayings. Let them not depart from thine eyes; keep them in the midst of thine heart. For they are life unto those that find them, and health to all their flesh." Proverbs 4:20-22

God makes it plain. If we read the Bible for our daily spiritual food and store it in our hearts, it will keep our hearts, *and our flesh,* healthy. Many things affect physical health besides the obvious well known diseases.

**Envy... the rottenness of the bones.**

Envy is defined as 'a feeling of discontent and ill will because of another's advantages, possessions etc.' It can also be defined as 'resentful dislike of another who has something that one desires.' When envy enters into the heart, it keeps company with anger and malice and will keep the mind in turmoil and produce ulcers and other physical ailments. Nothing is harder to handle than envy. "Wrath is cruel, and anger is outrageous; but who is able to stand before envy?" Proverbs 27:4

When the first signs of envy start stirring in your heart, take it right to the Lord for deliverance from that debilitating sin before it turns your life to shambles and spreads 'rottenness' to your bones. "A sound heart is the life of the flesh: but envy the rottenness of the bones." Proverbs 14:30

"Let all bitterness, and wrath, and anger, and clamour, and evil speaking, be put away from you, with all malice..." Ephesians 4:31

**Anxiety and Stress affect the body.**

These conditions can make you sick in a way that the 'flu bug' can't. We all fall prey to anxiety and stress, but the Lord tells us what to do in every situation. *Focus on our Savior.* "And the peace of God which passeth all understanding, shall keep your hearts and minds through Christ Jesus." Philippians 4:7

"Thou wilt keep him in perfect peace, whose mind is stayed on thee: because he trusteth in thee." Isaiah 26:3

Additional Treasures:     Philippians 4:8     Exodus 15:26

# August 25

**"Rejoice not against me, O mine enemy: when I fall, I shall arise; when I sit in darkness, the Lord shall be a light unto me."**
**Micah 7:8**

One of the things which baffles the world is the way Christians can go on no matter what comes into their lives. Their peace of mind and joy can abide undisturbed in the middle of troubles and tragedy.

"The Lord is my light and my salvation; whom shall I fear? The Lord is the strength of my life; of whom shall I be afraid?" Psalm 27:1

"For in time of trouble he shall hide me in his pavilion: in the secret of his tabernacle shall he hide me; he shall set me up upon a rock." Psalm 27:5

Being *personally* acquainted with God through the Lord Jesus Christ affords all that we need in order to endure, even if the way is so dark we can see no light.

"Who is among you that feareth the Lord, that obeyeth the voice of his servant, that walketh in darkness, and hath no light? Let him trust in the name of the Lord, and stay upon his God."
Isaiah 50:10

Christians may be blindly stumbling along at times, and the Lord says in those times: *stay with the Lord!* We are secure in God's love and grace.

"My soul, wait thou only upon God; for my expectation if from Him. He only is my rock and my salvation: he is my defense; I shall not be moved. In God is my salvation and my glory: the rock of my strength, and my refuge, is in God. Trust in him at all times; ye people, pour out your heart before him; God is a refuge for us. Selah."
Psalm 62: 5-8

**"The helm of the universe is held by the hands which were pierced for us. The Lord of Nature and the Mover of all things is that Saviour on whose love we may pillow our aching heads. We need these lessons today, when many teachers are trying hard to drive all that is spiritual and Divine out of creation and history."** Alex. Maclaren. "Unto the upright there ariseth light in the darkness: he is gracious, and full of compassion, and righteous." Psalm 112:4

Additional Treasures:    Psalm 84:11    I John 1:5

# August 26

"For by grace are ye saved through faith; and that
not of yourselves: it is the gift of God."
Ephesians 2:8

The world is religious because men worship. But the gospel of Christ is generally rejected because man wants glory for himself. He will not believe that Jesus provided salvation by His death, and that the only way to get to heaven is to accept it. It is impossible to mix *grace and works*. God redeemed us at an awesome cost, and it is only by His grace that we are saved.

"And if by grace, then is it no more of works: otherwise grace is no more grace. But if it be of works, then it is no more grace: otherwise work is no more work." Romans 11:6

**We should keep salvation truth reinforced in our minds. People will cite good examples about folks who are working to *"make it to heaven."* I've seen some who think their 'being good' is going to impress God and He will let them in. That foolish attitude will doom them forever if they don't repent and trust Jesus only. God's Word can break through any mind-set. When we feel that some cases are 'hard,' we must remember that He saved us and we were dead spiritually as all sinners are. *All without Christ are equally lost.***

No safety in our works. – In the twenty-eighth year of Emperor Tan Kwang, the Yangtze River rose higher than it had been for a hundred years. The loss of property was incalculable. Old Doctor Tai remembered and gave this account, saying that it was much like obtaining salvation from sin. "The rich, who had well-built houses, trusted to them and went to the upper story thinking themselves safe. But the flood increased and the foundations gave way, and the house to which they trusted fell and buried them in the ruins, or a watery grave. But the poor, knowing that their mud-built huts could not stand the rising flood, fled in time to the neighboring hills; and though they lost all yet they themselves were saved." -Martin

**A man may go to heaven without health, wealth, without honor, without learning and without friends, but he can *never* go to heaven without Christ.**

Additional Treasures:    Hebrews 1:3    Romans 5:1-2

# August 27

**"I have gone astray like a lost sheep; seek thy servant;
for I do not forget thy commandments."
Psalm 119:176**

The Lord likens His children to sheep, and one of the characteristics of sheep is their dire need of a shepherd to watch them lest they wander off from the flock.

"Know ye that the Lord he is God; it is he that hath made us, and not we ourselves; we are his people, and the sheep of his pasture." Psalm 100:3

Christians are led off sometimes unawares, because they flirt with sin and consider it to be merely a *harmless flirtation* that amounts to nothing. But a little flirtation can turn into the big sin of adultery, and then the awful grief that comes with being unfaithful to God. We cannot play around with little sins and expect to get by unscathed.

"Ye adulterers and adulteresses, know ye not that the friendship of the world is enmity with God? whosoever therefore will be a friend of the world is the enemy of God." James 4:4

God uses strong language in His Word to make it plain enough for His children to understand. It is *spiritual adultery* to be unfaithful to the Lord. It causes as much grief and heartache as adultery in a marriage relationship. Many unhappy Christians have found that out, and are now reaping the harvest of their harmless flirtation with sin. Sin is *never* harmless!

There are families out of church today that thought it would never happen to them. Someone got careless and flirted with sin until the chains and shackles were slipped around them, and they couldn't get away.

**The sparkle was gone from her eyes
Which did radiate such happiness…in days past.
Even the dew of dormant tears could not imitate it.
How easily we wander from the way,
Into the place of sadness and regret.**
Edna Holmes

Additional Treasures:     Hebrews 10:23     I John 1:9

# August 28

**"For God hath not given us the spirit of fear;**
**but of power, and of love, and of a sound mind."**
**II Timothy 1:7**

The world is full of the spirit of fear but it didn't come from God. Those who live by His Word certainly have nothing to fear, but we are at times very fearful.

Parents are really the targets of fear in our society. The laws of the land are now so set against the traditional structure and values of the family, parents are fearful to discipline their own children and train them up in the way they should go. Still, because they have their children *first* before anyone else can influence them, parents have a decided edge in the warfare. The trouble is that most parents let the formative years slide by without diligently training children from the cradle. Children thrive on love *and* discipline.

**"I am a missionary in my nursery" once observed a Christian mother. "Six pair of little eyes are daily watching mamma's looks, and listening to her words, and I wish my children never to see in me that which they may not imitate." The mother lives again in her children. They unconsciously mold themselves after her manner, her speech, her conduct, and her method of life. Her habits become theirs, and her character is visibly repeated in them. – Hom. Com.**

Once when I was teaching toddlers in Sunday school, I served some treats at the end of class, something simple and not messy for them to handle and eat. While the group was allowed to move about as they munched on their refreshments, one little boy about three years old took his piece of food, put it on a little paper plate and went back, sat down in his place, placed the food before him on the table and then only began to eat it. It showed clearly how that child had been trained at home.

"Train up a child in the way he should go: and when he is old, he will not depart from it." Proverbs 22:6

*Training up a child means:*
*To make skillful by teaching and practice.*
*To bring into a particular position.*
*To direct, point or aim.*
*To educate.*

Additional Treasures:     Proverbs 17:6     Psalm 127:4

# August 29

**"Christ is become of no effect unto you, whosoever**
**of you are justified by the law; ye are fallen from grace."**
**Galatians 5:4**

This verse was quoted to me to 'prove a point' when I was a new Christian and didn't even know the verse was in the Bible. So many folks would love to have positive proof that a Christian *can fall from grace*, and they will snatch at straws to try to prop up their theory.

This verse does not teach that a Christian can fall from grace and be lost again. It simply means that Christ, His death, burial, and resurrection cannot help a person if he insists on keeping the law in order to be saved. He will never attain the grace of God. When people reach for God's grace by their own efforts, they will fall! It is *God's unmerited favor*. No one can ever deserve it or earn it.

"For by grace are ye saved through faith; and that not of yourselves: it is the gift of God: Not of works, lest any man should boast."
Ephesians 2:8-9

**On the ladder of good works, some people are struggling to climb high enough to reach the grace of God. Each rung of the ladder is slippery with false hope; just when one thinks he has attained the height to reach out and grasp God's grace, *he falls!* The teaching of 'falling from grace' or losing your salvation *is* an error that has caused many to throw all hopes aside and turn away from Christianity altogether.**

"The Spirit itself beareth witness with our spirit, that we are the children of God..." Romans 8:16

"My sheep hear my voice, and I know them, and they follow me:
And I give unto them eternal life; and they shall never perish, neither shall any man pluck them out of my hand." John 10:27-28

People who believe the doctrine of 'falling from grace' stumble over the 'sin' factor. They *know* that one cannot be perfect so they must have an 'out' when sin comes into the picture. You get saved again! But that is just gross ignorance or unbelief because the Word tells us that Christians sin, and what to do about it. "If we confess our sins, he is faithful and just to forgive us our sins, and to cleanse us from all unrighteousness." I John 1:9

Additional Treasures:   I John 5:11-12    Romans 10:13

# August 30

**"And the cares of this world, and the deceitfulness
of riches, and the lust of other things entering in,
choke the word, and it becometh unfruitful."
Mark 4:19**

Most sincere Christians are not likely to let the deceitfulness of riches or the cares of this world choke God's Word out of their lives. The little thing that sneaks up on them to make them unfruitful is the lust of other things. *That means a strong desire.* It also means *bad desire or appetite.*

Our hearts have to be tended like a garden to keep out the *other things* which will crowd out the Word of God, and cause us to be unfruitful. The heart is the very core of our lives and naturally affects everything else.
"Keep thy heart with all diligence; for out of it are the issues of life."
Proverbs 4:23

Some of the *other things* that get in and slowly cut off our fruitfulness are so harmless it is difficult to think of them as a hindrance. But the strong desire toward these things can slowly erode our desire to be faithful to God with all our hearts. Christians beware!

**Crafts and other hobbies which consume energy and thoughts.**
Humans have the propensity to become addicted to almost anything! What we like, we want to do more and more until it consumes us. The devil will trap us with anything that works. Beware of time and energy-consuming activities which you are reluctant to stop to attend more important matters.

**Christian books which take the Bible's place.** Those of us who love to read have to watch for this trap. There are good Christian books available everywhere, and you can learn something. However, it takes very little concentration, so we may grab a book instead of our Bible which gives us 'food for the soul'. Beware of that trap.

**Friendships with those who are not saved.** Keeping steady company with unsaved friends can weaken a Christian spiritually before he can influence them for good. We reach out to everyone, but not join their ranks.

Additional Treasures:     Psalm 73:25     Romans 6:12-13

# August 31

*"Cast thy bread upon the water: for thou*
*shalt find it after many days. "*
Ecclesiastes 11:1

The Word of God is so potent it only needs to be proclaimed to do its work. How else could the Lord describe it so that our finite minds can grasp the meaning of its power and wonder?

**He said it was like a hammer, and fire!**
"Is not my word like as a fire? saith the Lord; and like a hammer that breaketh the rock in pieces?"  Jeremiah 23:29

**It is a sword that cuts to the heart without piercing the flesh!**
"For the word of God is quick, and powerful, and sharper than any two-edged sword, piercing even to the dividing asunder of soul and spirit, and of the joints and marrow, and is a discerner of the thoughts and intents of the heart." Hebrews 4:12.

**It has saving power!**
"For I am not ashamed of the gospel of Christ: for it is the power of God unto salvation to every one that believeth..." Romans 1:16

The Word of God is our bread, and after we take it into our hearts, we can then *cast it upon the waters* by sharing it with others. It has power in itself to effect results far and near wherever the restless sea of humanity is tossing about. We are to cast the bread. Throw it out there and someday, in some way you can't imagine, it will affect the souls that receive it with amazing results.

**Bread gleaned by your heart and hand**
**With time and determination to gather,**
**Is rich with promise and strength for the day,**
**And like the manna can't be hoarded away.**
*Cast thy bread...multiplied numbers have never been fed.*
( 'Poems That Sprang from a Verse' by Edna Holmes)

Additional Treasures:      John 17:17      Deuteronomy 17:19

# September 1

"Thou hast brought a vine out of Egypt:
thou hast cast out the heathen and planted it."
Psalms 80:8

We know that Israel was the *vine brought out of Egypt,* and God planted that people in the land of Canaan. Since Egypt has always been a type of the world for the Christian, we can apply these verses in the psalm to the church in the world.

"Thou preparedst room before it, and didst cause it to take deep root, and it filled the land." Psalm 80:9

**The church has always been a marvel in the world. It has remained throughout all the ages since Christ, sometimes under cruel persecution. It is evident even in this present day, as Christians around the world are suffering for Christ's sake that the church continues on and even *thrives* through persecution. Those who would destroy the church do not understand why they are powerless to do so.**

### It is the Body of Christ.

"And hath put all things under his feet, and gave him to be the head over all things to the church, Which is his body, the fulness of him that filleth all in all." Ephesians 1:22-23

The church is the born again children of God, and as the Bible says we are the 'body' of Christ. Therefore, we are His hands, feet, mouth, and other members doing His bidding on earth. That puts the urgency to be faithful to God in perspective. Christ has no other body on earth to do His work.

### It is the Bride of Christ.

"For I am jealous over you with godly jealousy: for I have espoused you to one husband that I may present you as a chaste virgin to Christ." II Corinthians 11:2

Everyone knows how a bridegroom feels about his bride. We cannot imagine with our finite minds how Christ feels about His bride, the church. He laid down His life with anticipation of His bride in heaven with Him. "...who for the joy that was set before him endured the cross...." Hebrews 12:2

Additional Treasures:     Ephesians 5:30     Colossians 1:18

# September 2

**"And he is the head of the body, the church..."**
**Colossians 1:18**

God's children, those born again by trusting Christ, make up the body of Christ on earth. It is a mystery, but because the Lord Himself abides in the Christian by His Holy Spirit, it is so. Jesus is the *head*, and we are His body on earth doing his work. The Bible says that "Christ loved the church, and gave Himself for it." Ephesisans 5:25

The church is beloved by Christ and especially protected in the world that has sought through all ages, to destroy it and its message--the good news of the gospel of Christ.

**The living church. – The true church of God can never perish. It is said that the Baobab-tree – the largest known tree in the world – though stripped of its bark outside and hollowed to a large cavity within its trunk, has the singular power of exuding from its substance a perfectly new bark, which lines both the inner and outer surfaces of the tree. So is it with the church of God. Though pierced and peeled and wounded by the gleaming axes of malicious enemies, it still lives and grows in irresistible productiveness, affording shelter to millions, and stretching its life-giving and healing foliage over all nations.  -Watkinson**

**One of the identifying marks of a Christian is his love for the church.**

"We know that we have passed from death unto life, because we love the brethren. He that loveth not his brother abideth in death."
I John 3:14
**We should faithfully attend the assembly of the church.**
"Not forsaking the assembling of ourselves together, as the manner of some is; but exhorting one another: and so much the more, as ye see the day approaching." Hebrews 10:25
**Teach children and grandchildren to respect the House of God.**
"Train up a child in the way he should go..." Proverbs 22:6

I have six brothers younger than me, all quite small when I got married. My Dad took them to church regularly and always lined them up on the same pew with him. Each Sunday they'd ask the question: "Daddy can we sit anywhere we want to today." He'd answer "You sure can, as long as it's on this pew." That's where they learned to be quiet and behave in church.

Additional Treasures:    Romans 7:4    Philippians 2:15

# September 3

**"And it shall come to pass, that as the Lord rejoiced
over you to do you good, and to multiply you..."**
**Deuteronomy 28:63**

The Lord *rejoices* over His children to bless them out of measure, more than any can actually estimate. He established a unique law that works with amazing results to prosper us. We need only implement its principles in our lives.

"Give and it shall be given you; good measure, pressed down, and shaken together, and running over, shall men give into your bosom. For with the same measure that ye mete withal it shall be measured to you again." Luke 6:38

Those who have learned the blessedness of this principle are indeed happy and prosperous in both material and spiritual assets. For whatever measure is used when conferring benefits on others, is the same measure that comes back to the giver. The more generously someone gives, the more he has in his possession to give!

Generosity of God. – **It was the saying of a certain generous Spanish captain. "There's no way of enjoying one's property like giving it away." It is a joy, a luxury to give. The generosity of God knows no limit. A certain English monarch once threw open his park and gardens to the public. The royal gardener complained to his Majesty that the visitors plucked the flowers. "What," said the kind-hearted king, "are my people fond of flowers? Then plant some more!"**

**So our heavenly King, with lavish hand, scatters on our daily pathway the flowers of blessing, and as fast as we can gather them, in spite of our frequent lack of gratitude, more are supplied.** Commentary

"Honor the Lord with thy substance, and with the firstfruits of all thine increase." Proverbs 3:9

The first step in giving is the 'firstfruits' part. That belongs to God and is the first requirement. After that it is blessings all the way! In over fifty years of obeying the Lord's admonition to 'give' we can testify to the fact that God is faithful to His promises. He has always taken care of us, and now blessed us with a joyful retirement time in our 'older' age. I'm glad that we learned the principle of 'giving' the first thing after we became Christians.

Additional Treasures:    II Corinthians 9:6    Proverbs 11:25

# September 4

"She openeth her mouth with wisdom;
and in her tongue is the law of kindness."
Proverbs 31:26

One who speaks with wisdom *and kindness* is indeed an outstanding individual. There is a measure of maturity ascribed to those who have their tongues under control.

"For in many things we offend all. If any man offend not in word, the same is a perfect man, and able also to bridle the whole body." James 3:2

The words we speak, and the way we speak them tells so much about our character and disposition. Our words affect others and we may, with a word, make someone's day a happy one or a depressing one. Words are very powerful vehicles of thought and we need to be especially careful in our use of them. *Words make lasting impressions!*

**Early in the morning on the day of our daughter's wedding, when she came into the room where I was sitting, I said the first thing that popped into my mind.**

**"Many daughters have done virtuously, but thou excellest them all."**

**Years later Jeanne reminded me of that line from Proverbs I'd quoted that morning, and I confess that I'd completely forgotten what I'd said; I was so distracted with the big event of the day approaching. But she didn't forget it, and it is one of her precious memories.**

What kind of memories are we planting in the minds of others by the words we speak? May they always be those that are *seasoned with salt.* The *salt* is the power  of God's grace that keeps  motives pure, and gives pleasant
savor of sound which blesses and nourishes the listener.

 Speaking Gently – **Speak gently! It is better far to rule by love than fear;**
  **Speak gently – let no harsh words mar the good we might do here!**

  **Speak gently! 'Tis a little thing dropp'd in the heart's deep well.**
  **The good, the joy, which it may bring, eternity shall tell.** – Bates

Additional Treasures:    Colossians 4:6    Proverbs 17:27

# September 5

"But made himself of no reputation, and took on him the
form of a servant, and was made in the likeness of men."
Philippians 2:7

Because Christ *made Himself* of no reputation and became a servant, does not mean He became any less than what He always was and shall be in eternity. He entered the realm of time for the purpose of redeeming man from the curse of sin.

Earth was a foreign place to our Lord but His love for us brought Him down, and in time led Him to Calvary where He died for our sins. Once when Philip asked Jesus to "shew us the Father," the Lord said "Have I been so long time with you, and yet hast thou not known me, Philip? He that hath seen me hath seen the Father..." John 14:9

**Sparta was the most powerful city-state of ancient Greece. It was famous for its military power and its loyal soldiers, and at times in its history, Sparta had more than one king at a time. A king was sent occasionally to some neighboring state in character of a Spartan ambassador. Did he, when so sent, cease to be a king of Sparta because he was also an ambassador? No, he did not divest himself of his regal dignity, but only added to it that of public deputation. So Christ, in becoming man, did not cease to be God. And though He ever was and still continued to be King of the whole creation, acted as voluntary Servant and Messenger of the Father. – Illus. Of Truth**

At a certain time, Jesus came into Jerusalem riding on a colt and the people shouted His praise, "Saying, Blessed be the King that cometh in the name of the Lord: peace in heaven, and glory in the highest." Luke 19:38

Because they did not believe He was God and should not receive such worship, the Pharisees in the crowd asked Jesus to rebuke them. The Lord's reply has always thrilled my heart to read it.

"And he answered and said unto them, I tell you that, if these should hold their peace, the stones would immediately cry out." Luke 19:40

Additional Treasures:     Psalm 50:12     Mark 4:39

# September 6

**"For whosoever shall keep the whole law, and yet
offend in one point, he is guilty of all."
James 2:10**

If men could look at this verse just once with understanding, they would know for certain that it takes the supernatural *grace of God* to be saved. Jesus is the only one who ever kept the whole law--He was the sinless, perfect Son of God.

We know that we could never keep the whole law, *every commandment* in the Word of God, because though we may keep most of it according to our estimation, God looks on the heart. He sees every motive and thought which will invariably keep us from perfection. There will always be that *one point* in which we are failing.

For that reason, our Lord exhorts us to hold back in judging one another.

"Judge not, that ye be not judged." Matthew 7:1

Someone has said that the reason we see faults in others is because we recognize what is familiar in ourselves. According to the Bible, when we judge others by criticizing and condemning, we will also be criticized and condemned by others.

In order to qualify for judging others we would have to know every little detail of all the intricate workings of their lives, every thought and intent of their hearts from the day they were born until the time we judge them. Also, we would have to be perfect! Does that give us an idea of why God tells us to 'Judge not, that ye be not judged.' If we do, we can expect the very same thing done to us. It may not be soon, but it will inevitably come.

**Our church once had a representative of the Gideons speak for us about their work in putting Bibles into public places, such as hospitals and motels, etc. During a question and answer time, I asked if anybody ever steals a Bible from these places. I felt very *self-righteous* at the moment; after all, I would *never* do such a despicable thing!**

**Months later after speaking at a Ladies' Retreat in another state, as I was packing to come home, I unknowingly picked up the Gideon Bible on the table with my books and tucked it away in my briefcase. On the way home, I discovered the "theft" and was horrified. Those people would think I stole it! I was miserable until I got it mailed back with an explanation. I know I was judged, just as I had judged, and it was very humbling.**

Additional Treasures:     Romans 14:4     Matthew 7:2

# September 7

"For none of us liveth to himself, and
no man dieth to himself."
Romans 14:7

We can never say with truth that our lives affect only ourselves. None can make his life begin and end with himself. Nor when he dies, will he take with him all the effects of his life. Everyone, from the most influential to the most obscure, makes an impression on others. It behooves us to consider what *kind* of impression we are leaving in our wake.

Some say when trying to excuse their sin that it doesn't *hurt* anyone but them. But sin makes a wide circle of ripples, which spreads out and touches everything close to it. A man's family, friends, church and neighborhood are affected by his sin, for sooner or later sin *exposes*. That is the hideous nature of it.

"For our transgressions are multiplied before thee, and our sins testify_against us: for our transgressions are with us; and as for our iniquities, we know them." Isaiah 59:12

**Sages of old contended that no sin was ever committed whose consequences rested on the head of the sinner alone; that no man could do ill and his fellows not suffer. They illustrated it thus: "A vessel sailing from Joppa carried a passenger who, beneath his berth, cut a hole through the ship's side. When the men of the watch protested in alarm, "What doest thou, O miserable man?" the offender calmly replied, "What matters it to you? The hole I have made lies under my own berth." This ancient parable is worthy of the utmost consideration. No man perishes alone in his iniquity; no man can guess the full consequences of his transgression.**
--- Spurgeon

Our daily prayer to God should be that we avoid the snares of sin.

"...let not any iniquity have dominion over me." Psalm 119:133

This verse from the Psalms is my 'wake-up' prayer every morning. Once it was a blessing to me in solving a difficulty so I took it for one of my verses to pray the first thing as I'm getting out of bed. In that way, I have a bit of God's Word already planted in my mind even if the day turns upside down and I don't have a quiet time to pray and read. Those kinds of days happen, and we never know when. Get a ready verse to put in your mind early!

Additional Treasures:     Psalm 19:13     Romans 14:12-13

# September 8

**"Even the Son of Man came not to
be ministered unto, but to minister."
Matthew 20:28**

Jesus did not come down into the world with any expectation of being treated as the King of Kings and Lord of Lords, *though He was.* He had one purpose for coming, and that was to do something for mankind: *to minister.* The end of that was His death, which provides salvation for all that believe on the Lord Jesus Christ.

The Lord ministered whether or not He was offered a place to sleep, food to eat, water to drink or any other daily necessity. In His human body, He did have those needs. Once when a certain scribe said that he would follow Jesus wherever He was going, Jesus said:
"The foxes have holes, and the birds of the air have nests; but the Son of man hath not where to lay his head." Matthew 8:20

Though Jesus was pressed without measure by the demands of His work in *ministering* to the people, He endured every discomfort with patience. At the same time He tenderly cared for the disciples' needs.

"And the apostles gathered themselves together unto Jesus, and told him all things both what they had done, and what they had taught. And he said unto them, Come ye yourselves apart into a desert place, and rest awhile: for there were many coming and going, and they had no leisure so much as to eat." Mark 6:30-31
Let us do the work of the Lord in the spirit of obedience, and determine not to be discouraged by the lack of gratitude or appreciation on the part of others. We must go forth *to minister*, and *not* to be ministered to!

"…leaving us an example, that ye should follow his steps.." I Pet. 2:21

Proverbs tells us to "Commit thy works unto the Lord, and thy thoughts shall be established." Proverbs 16:3
Doing things in that order, we won't have to struggle with our thoughts all through the day. It will be settled. What we do is for the Lord and His glory so whatever response we get from others won't deter us. Our thoughts will stay in line with our commitment.

Additional Treasures:     Mark 2:2     Hebrews 2:10

# September 9

**"Take therefore no thought for the morrow..."**
**Matthew 6:34**

The Lord does not want His children to be anxious or uneasy about the needs of life, or to worry. It is incredible that any of us worry after what Jesus spoke in His Word about God's provision.

"...for your heavenly Father knoweth that ye have need of all these things." Matthew 6:32

It is not our needs that we worry about as much as our wants. There is so much to 'want' in this world, and we are bombarded on all sides continually to get more and more earthly possessions. I heard of a missionary who had come back from his field of service for a furlough. He went into a large store with everything imaginable to buy. He said "I'm so glad to see so many things that I don't want." Many missionary wives have told me that it is overwhelming to come back and see what abundance is on display in this country. Some are serving in countries where they can barely get their necessities of life. They experience 'culture shock' when they first get back here.

We are not to entertain worrisome thoughts about tomorrow, whether or not we will have food and clothing or other needs met.

**The birds are a rebuke to our lack of faith in God's care.**
"Behold the fowls of the air: for they sow not, neither do they reap, nor gather into barns; yet your heavenly Father feedeth them. Are ye not much better than they?" Matthew 6:26

**The wildflowers and grass of the fields are a rebuke to our doubts.**
"if God so cloth the grass of the field, which today is, and tomorrow is cast into the oven, shall he not much more clothe you, O ye of little faith?" v. 30

**"It has been well said that no man ever sank under the burden of the day. It is when tomorrow's burden is added to the burden of today that the weight is more than a man can bear. God begs you to leave the future to Him and mind the present."** – George Macdonald

"But seek ye first the kingdom of God, and his righteousness; and all these things shall be added unto you." Matthew 6:33

Treasures: Matthew 7:11    Psalm 37:3-5

# September 10

**"And they brought the young man alive,
and were not a little comforted."
Acts 20:12**

This young man will always be known as the one who went to sleep while the apostle Paul preached! The Bible gives his name, Eutychus, which means *fortunate.* Indeed, he was very fortunate to be where Paul was preaching at the time, or he may not have lived to tell about what happened that night in church.

"And upon the first day of the week...Paul preached unto them, ready to depart on the morrow; and continued his speech until midnight....

And there sat in a window a certain young man named Eutychus, being fallen into a deep sleep: and as Paul was long preaching, he sunk down with sleep, and fell down from the third loft, and was taken up dead.

And Paul went down, and fell on him, and embracing him said, Trouble not yourselves; for his life is in him." Acts 20:7, 9-10

That unusual happening around midnight didn't stop the service where they were saying goodbye to the beloved apostle Paul.

The young man had an excuse to sleep in church because midnight is bedtime, but today church sleepers can hardly excuse their indifference to the Word of God. For many, the cause is staying up so late on Saturday they cannot be alert on Sunday at church. We may also be drowsy with *spiritual sleepiness* when we should be alert and energetic to serve the Lord.

**I fear that some people are not alert in the preaching and teaching on Sunday because their hearts are set on other things which tend to make church seem irrelevant. It is hard to quiet the worldly clamor in their minds and focus on worshipping the Lord. The church has very little effect on the people of God, and the world compared to a generation ago. The world, however, has taken first place in nearly everything. If Christians will focus steadfastly on God's Word, count it as their 'lifeline' every day, and pray to God for strength and fortitude to stay faithful, they certainly will win the victory.**

"And that, knowing the time, that now it is high time to awake out of sleep; for now, is our salvation nearer than when we believed." Rom. 13:11

Additional Treasures:    I Corinthians 15:34    Ephesians 5:15-16

# September 11

"...Man shall not live by bread alone, but by every word
that proceedeth out of the mouth of God."
**Matthew 4:4**

The majority of people in the world today are living on the bread that nourishes physical life, and will have nothing to do with the bread that gives and sustains spiritual life: *the Word of God.*

Jesus made this most important statement in Matthew when the devil was sorely tempting Him to turn stones to bread. He knew the Lord had been without food for forty days and nights and was hungry.
"And when the tempter came to him, he said, If thou be the Son of God, command that these stones be made bread." v. 3

Our text verse is the Lord's answer; he refused to be drawn into the devil's scheme to get him to use divine power to conquer in this temptation. The Lord used exactly what we have today to defeat the devil when he tempts us, the Word of God! In the three attempts Satan made to cause the Lord to go against the Father's will, Jesus answered with, *"It is written."*

Jesus set us an example so we could know how to defeat the devil as we face temptations in this life. The scriptures are as necessary to us for health and happiness as food is to keep us physically fit. After we have obtained eternal life by trusting in Christ, then God's Word becomes our spiritual food for daily living in faith and assurance. We need the balanced diet: every word that proceeds out of the mouth of God.

**It is thrilling when a Christian discovers, personally, that there is power in God's Word. Decades ago another lady and I were visiting our prospects list, and knocked on an elderly man's door who said he was not interested at all. Talking through the screen door, I asked if I might read him a verse from the Bible. I read Romans 10:9 and looked up to see tears coming down his face. Soon the old fellow asked the Lord to be his Savior. It was amazing to me what God's Word did in that moment of time. I learned that day that the power is in the Word of God and not in the one who shares it. We do need clean 'hands and hearts' to do the Lord's work, but the *power* that changes the heart of a sinner is God's Word.**

Additional Treasures:     John 12:48     Job 23:12

# September 12

When we live in obedience to God's Word many pitfalls are avoided. But we soon forget the comfort and wisdom that the Bible has afforded us in difficult times, and our steps will again wander off the path of obedience and steadfastness in the Word. We cannot imagine how uniquely valuable the Bible is for our lives and it is so accessible to us in our country. Many Christians in the world in times past, and even now, do not have the same privilege that we have in possessing the Word of God.

If every family gave the Bible a revered place in the home, the world would have a lot less broken homes and lives because of sin.

Position Wanted – **I would like a job as teacher and advisor to your family. I will never take a vacation. I will never be out of humor. I don't drink or smoke. I won't borrow your clothes or raid your refrigerator.**
**I will be up in the morning as early as anyone in the household and will stay up as late as anyone wishes. I will help solve any problems your children might have.**
**I will give you information that will help you with your job, your family and all of your other interests. In short, I will give you the knowledge that will insure the continued success of your family.**
**I am your Bible. Do I get the job?**      Author Unknown.

A Christian will never appreciate that sacred Word until he has clung to it for an answer, and not given up until it is revealed to him as he diligently searches its pages. Once that impression is made in the heart one will never forget it or cease to talk of its wonders, for he now knows that *God has spoken to him by His Word!*

"How sweet are thy words unto my taste! yea, sweeter than honey to my mouth." Psalm 119:103

"Thy word is a lamp unto my feet, and a light unto my path. 119:105

Additional Treasures:      Jeremiah 15:16      II Timothy 3:16

# September 13

**"That is, that I may be comforted together with you
by the mutual faith both of you and me."
Romans 1:12**

Mutual means *belonging to each respectively.* Mutual faith is indeed a great comfort when people are traveling the globe and happen to be in areas where there are not many believers.

**My brother was a pilot during the Vietnam War, and his duty was to fly military officials to and from their various appointments in the surrounding region. One day when he had some hours to wait in Bangkok Thailand, he saw a man on the street who *looked like a missionary,* and he ran to him to inquire and introduce himself. The man was a Christian, and indeed a missionary in that country. My brother was so delighted to find another believer with whom he could have fellowship for a few hours. It was a precious treasure and great comfort to be in company with a man of *mutual faith* in the Lord.**

Mutual faith enriches our lives, for we have one another as in a family, to rely on in times of difficulty and need. No one understands the nature of the Christian life like another believer. That blessed *mutual faith* binds us together in love and experience.

"And this is his commandment, that we should believe on the name of his Son Jesus Christ, and love one another, as he gave us commandment." I John 3:23

Our mutual faith is the essence of our happiness, and the more we feed the faith in us, the stronger we will be to steadfastly follow Christ. The strength of faith is the Word of God.

**"Faith is not a sense, nor sight, nor reason, but taking God at His Word."** --Evans Quote

As simple as it is, some don't have a ready answer if they are asked "What is faith?" We should all have it written down in our Bibles or some notebook we use: Faith, is believing God. And that is all it is. Faith is based on facts, the facts in the Word of God. It is not a wispy unidentifiable element floating around which can't quite be understood. If a person believes God, he has faith!

"So then faith cometh by hearing, and hearing by the Word of God." Romans 10:17

Additional Treasures: Ephesians 6:16    Hebrews 11:1-3

# September 14

"All that the Father giveth me shall come to me; and him
that cometh to me I will in no wise cast out."
John 6:37

When Jesus stated that He would in *no wise* cast out those who came
to Him, He meant that in no way, manner or fashion would He refuse the
repentant sinner.

"The sacrifices of God are a broken spirit: a broken and contrite
heart, O God, thou wilt not despise." Psalm 51:17

Kings and queens of earth are not accessible to the common man,
but the King of Kings and Lord of Lords *is* accessible to any and all who
will come to Him with a contrite heart: *repentant, sorrowful, humbled.*

The Lord is ever present with His children, those who have been
born again into the family of God, and He is our intercessor in prayer to
our Heavenly Father. That is why your prayers will always be heard if
you aren't trying to hide any sins from God. He knows, of course, and we
waste time when we keep putting off 'coming clean' and confessing our
sins so we can be forgiven and get back in fellowship with the Lord.

"Wherefore he is able also to save them to the uttermost that come
unto God by him, seeing he ever liveth to make intercession for them."
Hebrews 7:25

Christ's willingness to receive. – **It is our melancholy and
miserable misapprehension that we fancy there is some reluctance on
Christ's part that needs to be overcome, some repulse in His mind
that we need to do away with, that we have to persuade and urge
Him to do what we yearn to have done, to forgive us all our sins, and
to blot out all our iniquities. This is a great mistake; ten thousand
times more willing is Christ to receive you, than ever you were to
make application to Him.**-Cumming.

Our brothers and sisters in the last century had a most eloquent
way of writing their teaching and expressions about Christ. How very,
very true that "ten thousand times more willing is Christ to receive you,
than ever you were to make application to Him." It is amazing that we
feel such hesitancy and reluctance to pray and spend time in fellowship
with the Lord. He loves and delights in us with such fervency that He
must allow us only the small glimmers of the light of His love that we
may contain it.

Additional Treasures:    Deuteronomy 4:29    Luke 11:9

# September 15

**"And said unto him, Art thou he that should come,
or do we look for another?"
Matthew 11:3**

We cannot imagine how John the Baptist, that great man of God, could have a lapse of faith, *but he did.* He was discouraged at the turn of events in his life; he was locked up in prison with no hope of release because he had preached against Herod's sin. He heard that the work of Jesus was going on, this One that he had recognized as the *Lamb of God which taketh away the sin of the world,* and also baptized in the river Jordan. He thought that he *knew* beyond doubt, but the doubts came anyway.

John's disciples who carried his message to Jesus were probably prepared to give up their faith in Christ as well, if their beloved leader had such strong doubts about him. We know that the Lord sent an encouraging word and afterwards complimented His servant, John, to those who stood by and heard the exchange with the messengers.

"Verily I say unto you, among them that are born of women there hath not risen a greater than John the Baptist..." Matthew 11:11

Our discouragement touches others, especially when our doubts begin to be verbalized. It is best to go to the prayer closet and the Word of God, and let God reinforce our faith and assurance of His work in our lives.

Influence of doubts on others.—**"I once told my congregation that I had passed through a season of doubt and fear. One of my elders said to me, 'Sir, I am sorry you told the people that. Just suppose you had been swearing or stealing, you would not have told them of it?' 'No,' I answered, 'that would be a terrible thing.' 'Well,' replied he, 'I don't think it is much worse than disbelieving God; and, if you go and tell the people that, you set them a bad example.' And he was right. It is not for the leader in any cause to doubt the success of the enterprise."**—Spurgeon

"I can do all things through Christ..." Philippians 4:13

Additional Treasures:     Romans 14:4     II Corinthians 9:8

# September 16

"And so it is written, The first man Adam was made a living
soul; the last Adam was made a quickening spirit."
I Corinthians 15:45

Through Adam the whole human race fell into sin. What Adam
became by disobeying God was passed on through generations ever
since. We are all *born* sinners because we all came from Adam.

Through Jesus Christ, *the second Adam*, we have redemption
because of His obedience to the Father, which was His sacrificial death
for us on the Cross of Calvary at the end of His earthly ministry.

Redemption.—Once when I was revisiting my native village, I
was going to a neighboring town to preach, and saw a young man
coming from a house with a wagon, in which was seated an old
woman. I felt interested in them, and asked my companion who they
were. I was told to look at the adjoining meadow and pasture, and at
the great barns that were on the farm, as well as a good house.
"Well," said my companion, "that young man's father drank that all
up, and left his wife in the poorhouse. The young man went away
and worked until he had got money enough to redeem that farm, and
now it is his own, and he is taking his mother to church." That is an
illustration of redemption. In the first Adam we have lost all, but the
second Adam has redeemed everything by His death. - D.L. Moody

"Forasmuch as ye know that ye were not redeemed with corruptible
things, as silver and gold, from your vain conversation received by
tradition from your fathers; But with the precious blood of Christ, as of a
lamb without blemish and without spot..." I Peter 1:18-19

If the second Adam, *Jesus Christ,* had not come into the world to
regain for us what our father Adam lost, we would all be without hope in
this world. We should never let thanksgiving slip away from us, but
every day take a moment to thank God for His precious gift of salvation.

"Thanks be unto God for his unspeakable gift." II Corinthians 9:15

Additional Treasures:    Colossians 1:12-14    Hebrews 2:17

# September 17

**"Put on the whole armour of God, that ye may be
able to stand against the wiles of the devil."
Ephesians 6:11**

The armor that God provides for His children is of His miraculous design. It has to do an impossible thing--protect us from the wiles of the devil. The next verse tells us why we need it so badly, and cannot hope to have any success without the armor.

"For we wrestle not against flesh and blood, but against principalities, against the rulers of the darkness of this world, against spiritual wickedness in high places." *v.12*

One Greek scholar translates this verse: "For our contest is not with human foes alone, but with the rulers, authorities, and cosmic powers of this dark world; that is, with the spirit forces of evil challenging us in the heavenly contest." *The New Testament*-Charles B. Williams

The enemy is not something we can see. The spirit forces of the dark world ruled by Satan are not at all challenged by human flesh. We can only contend with what we *see and feel*, and thus we must have God's protection for the spiritual warfare that we face every day of our lives.

**On a mission trip to Germany, we had an opportunity to visit an old castle on the Rhine that was still intact with a few artifacts from medieval times on display. There was a complete set of armor such as the knights of old used to wear in battle. Every part of the body was covered, but only effective if the knight was on his horse. He had to be helped on and off, and if he was knocked off the horse the armor prevented any mobility because of the tremendous weight. He was helpless, for the most part, encased in the armor.**

How unlike the armor that the Lord provides for us! We are only mobile, alert and agile in battle when we *have on His armor*. Without it, we are defeated before the spiritual battle begins. Christians should never assume that the spiritual warfare has slacked off and they can have a "furlough" from the fight. We would be taken 'prisoner' for sure. As long as we're in the flesh, that means still alive, we will be engaged in warfare with the devil. Stay alert!

The Word of God is your power, strength and endurance in the fight.

Additional Treasures:  Ephesians 6:10  Romans 6:13

# September 18

**"Wherefore take unto you the whole armour of God,
that ye may be able to withstand…"
Ephesians 6:13**

We not only are told to use the armor of God so that we may *stand,* which means to *endure, abide, remain upright;* we must also put on the armor so that we may *withstand,* which means that we can 'face, confront, and fight off'. The whole armor of God protects us in spiritual battles.

"Stand therefore, having your loins girt about with truth, and having on the breastplate of righteousness…" *v.14*

**The loins are the part of the body between the ribs and the hipbones: the most *vital, vulnerable* part. When the loins were *girded up*, the long flowing clothing was pulled snugly about the body and fastened securely in the *girdle:* a wide belt made of leather or cloth. Then one was ready for walking or running, or some vigorous activity. Thus, in scripture, the girded loins are a symbol of readiness for service.**

We can only stand, endure, remain upright in the battle against the powers of darkness if we are wrapped up securely in truth. There is strength in our connection and attachment to Christ, the truth, and His Word.

"Jesus saith unto him, I am the way, the truth, and the life: no man cometh unto the Father, but by me." John 14:6

When temptations come into your life, let the scriptures secure your heart and mind for the battle. Pull out that gleaming sword, and start swinging it in all directions! **Speak the Word to the devil.** He hates it, and will get away from the sound of it. If you feel timid to speak the Word to the devil, then sing a song for him to hear. He will flee from 'Nothing but the blood of Jesus' too.

"And take the helmet of salvation, and the sword of the Spirit, which is the Word of God." Ephesians 6:17

Additional Treasures:     II Peter 3:17     Revelation 3:10

# September 19

**"And take the helmet of salvation…"**
**Ephesians 6:17**

Many sports and other activities require helmets for the participants. Even children riding bicycles are supposed to wear helmets to protect them in a fall. Helmets are decorated with emblems and certain colors, especially for various football teams in order to be clearly identified on the playing field.

The helmet of salvation identifies the Christian, if it is worn. The Bible tells us to *take the helmet of salvation,* or do what one does with a helmet to protect the head…*put it on!* Football players do not play the game carrying their helmets under their arms, leaving their heads unprotected. They would all be mortally wounded in that rough sport.

Salvation, that gift we receive when believing on the Lord Jesus Christ, is our first line of defense and *the first* piece of the armor issued to us in the Lord's army. The Bible calls it a *helmet.*

"But let us, who are of the day, be sober, putting on the breastplate of faith and love; and for a helmet, the hope of salvation." I Thess: 5:8

The helmet protects the head, the *thinking* part of us, which is so vulnerable to the crafty wiles or ways of the devil. If he can get our thoughts going the wrong way, he usually wins the battle.

**The only way to control our thoughts and establish them on the right path of thinking is to commit our 'works' to the Lord as it says in Proverbs. Since discovering that verse I make it an early morning practice to do what it says and "Commit thy works unto the Lord, and thy thoughts shall be established."**
**Proverbs 16:3**
**Some of us have vivid imaginations and it's a battle to keep our thoughts from running here and there distracting us all day long. God's Word has such power available to those who believe it and act on its promises. Find the promise that will help you personally and take it for you own.**

Trust Christ personally and you will be eternally saved. When it is fact in your soul, *wear that helmet of salvation.* Let it be known whose side you are on. "Fight the good fight of faith…" I Timothy 6:12

Additional Treasures: Romans 13:12   I Peter 5:8

# September 20

**"Above all, taking the shield of faith, wherewith ye
shall be able to quench all the fiery darts of the wicked."
Ephesians 6:16**

There is a clear definition of faith in the Bible. "Now faith is the substance of things hoped for, the evidence of things not seen." Hebrews 11:1

Faith, *believing God,* is our assurance of what we hope for and the proof of the reality of the things we can't see. How do we *know* about the things of God? We know because of our *faith.*

Faith is a shield between the devil and God's children. With it we can repel and quench, *snuff out or extinguish* the fiery darts that the wicked one hurls at us.

When the boy David went out to meet Goliath, he had no shield except his faith in God's power to give him the victory over this giant who defied Israel's army and God. The giant was wearing heavy armor from head to feet, and also had a man going before him with a shield. David's shield of faith protected him, *though the giant never saw it.* David was not touched in the battle, and Goliath was brought down with a stone from a slingshot!

The wisdom of God was in David because he trusted God and meditated on His Word. When he went out to meet the giant, Goliath said disdainful things to David, and David replied back with the most startling statement the giant had ever heard. All he knew of battles was with gruesome weapons of war and you slaughter the enemy when you can. But this very young man, David, ran out there and told Goliath that "the battle is the Lord's, and he will give you into our hands...." I Samuel 17:47

**That is the secret of success in spiritual warfare. *The battle is the Lord's.* The warfare is in our minds; it is not a tangible thing which can be fought in the flesh. The devil starts the war and keeps it going in our minds. Be warned, and be alert. Go right to God and let Him fight your battles. Keep your mind clear every day by running the Word of God through it. Keep some memorized verses stored up and grab one when you need strength to overcome in the moments of struggling with your thoughts, wanting to think right as the Lord would have you to.**

Additional Treasures:     I Samuel 17:45     II Corinthians 10:4

# September 21

**"For I was envious at the foolish, when I saw
the prosperity of the wicked."
Psalm 73:3**

When the psalmist was at a low point in his life, he spent the greater part of this psalm complaining to God about the wicked who were prospering, and the godly who were suffering. But later he would say with a repentant heart:

"When I thought to know this, it was too painful for me; Until I went into the sanctuary of God; then understood I their end." v. 16-17

Though Christians have trials and troubles in this world and are not always granted prosperity, they have a glorious future in eternity and the presence of God with them in this life.

The wicked at the best are *set in slippery places;* life is uncertain, and in a moment of time they will die and then suffer forever in hell. Their life on earth and whatever riches they possess is all they will ever have.

We must be careful to guard our hearts from the *lust for things* and the envy of those who do have riches. Lust is an unholy desire that can overpower common sense. People can become obsessed with getting more and more, and in turn yield their lives to indebtedness and misery.

Love of Gold. – **An immigrant ship was wrecked on a desert island. The people were saved, but they had few provisions, and it was necessary to make haste to clear and till the ground and sow seed. Before this could be done they discovered gold on the island, and everyone gave himself up to the search for wealth. Meantime, the season slipped by, the fields were left unplowed, and the people found themselves starving in the midst of useless treasure.**

**There are people now who starve their soul and conscience that they may acquire a little more gold and silver.** –Commentary

The rich young ruler that came to Jesus inquiring about salvation was so foolish because he couldn't imagine giving up one particle of his wealth to follow Jesus. When the Lord put him to the test, covetousness showed up in his heart. He wanted wealth, and not Jesus who could save his soul.

Additional Treasures:     Matthew 6:33     Proverbs 13:7

# September 22

**"And he said unto me, My grace is sufficient for thee:**
**for my strength is made perfect in weakness."**
**II Corinthians 12:9**

God's grace is not only the means by which salvation is available to us; His grace is also sufficient for every situation that comes into our lives. We comprehend His strength the most when we are weak and lean hard on God. "...my strength is made perfect in weakness."

This is the human way of thinking—*"If I can do it myself, I don't need anybody."* Christians get into a great deal of sorrow by being independent in spirit, and not relying on God. Some worry whether God has sufficient grace to help them in their dilemma. We grieve Him with our lack of faith.

**My Grace is Sufficient for Thee.** – The other evening I was riding home after a heavy day's work. I felt weary, and sore depressed, when suddenly as a lightning flash that text came to me, "My grace is sufficient for thee." I reached home and looked it up in the original, and at last it came to me in this way, "My grace is sufficient for thee," and I said, "I should think it is Lord," and burst out laughing.
I never fully realized what the holy laughter of Abraham was until then. It seemed to make unbelief so absurd. It was as though some little fish, being very thirsty, was troubled about drinking the river dry and the river said, "Drink away little fish, my stream is sufficient for thee." Oh brethren, be great believers! Little faith will bring your souls to heaven, but great faith will bring heaven to your souls.--*C.H.Spurgeon.*

**Exercise your faith**...and it will grow from *little* to *larger* in scope.
Faith believes God: if you have faith that is what you do: you believe God! Therefore take what God says and act on it. At times I think about the world's situation and it disturbs my peace of mind. One day I read these verses and really listened to what they said. "Trust in the Lord with all thine heart: and lean not unto thine own understanding. In all thy ways acknowledge him, and he shall direct thy paths." Proverbs 3:5-6

I'm to trust God completely. My own understanding is faulty. God knows everything, and I see a small margin of the picture. I'm simply to look and focus on Him, and He will lead me. That takes the worry out.

Additional Treasures:     Philippians 4:13     II Corinthians 9:8

# September 23

"I am as a wonder unto many; but thou
art my strong refuge."
Psalm 71:7

Christians are a wonder; they cause *fascinated astonishment* or admiration in this world. That of course, is contingent upon their genuineness and dedication to God. Those living like the world are usually held in disdain. Even the wicked in the world respect something that is real and genuine.

**I have seen a Christian family having dinner in a cafeteria bow their heads to give thanks for the food, and all conversation around them stop until the prayer is said. There is still some respect for godly people, though it is greatly diminished compared to a few decades ago. In my parents' generation even the unbelievers still kept Sunday as a day of rest, regarding it as the Lord's Day, though personally they rejected Him.**

Today the church and the world are blended in so many ways; a dedicated Christian stands out, and is a *wonder*. It is tempting to compromise because the fear of man and what people may think of us is stronger than our *fear of the Lord,* which keeps our hearts right. We don't have a Biblical concept of God to the point where we possess a reverence of Him which is stronger than anything else in our minds. Our human pride seems to stay well and fit in spite of all the 'truth' that we know about the sin and folly of it. We actually concern ourselves with what people think, when our only consideration should be about our Savior, who loved us and died for us.

The Lord would have us to remember that man is only a mortal being and helpless. He gives a telling comparison: "As for man, his days are as grass: as a flower of the field, so he flourisheth. For the wind passeth over it and it is gone; and the place thereof shall know it no more." Psalm 103:15-16

In another place the Lord also paints another vivid word picture of what our lives are like in view of eternity. "For what is your life? It is even a vapour, that appeareth for a little time, and then vanisheth away." James 4:14

I think of that fact every time my teakettle starts boiling and the steam starts escaping through the spout...immediately disappearing as vapor! That is what my life is like. How am I going to live in the brief time I'll have on earth? It is simple things that God uses to cause us to think seriously.

Additional Treasures:    I Peter 1:24    Hebrews 12:1

# September 24

"Also unto thee, O Lord, belongeth mercy:
for Thou renderest to every man according to his work."
Psalm 62:12

Serving our Lord is not a hard thing to do. Jesus is in the yoke of service with us; He makes it possible for us to be fruitful.

"Take my yoke upon you, and learn of me; for I am meek and lowly in heart: and ye shall find rest unto your souls. For my yoke is easy, and my burden is light." Matthew 11:29-30

**When I was a young child, our farm had no modern machinery for plowing the fields and gathering in the crops. Mules and horses were used with plows and wagons. Two mules were hitched up to a plow; each had to pull his part and a whip was used to make sure the animals pulled together. The plow lines running from the harness around the mules were slipped over the shoulders, and the one plowing was actually yoked up with the team of mules, though he didn't pull any weight at all. Many times I've looked across the field at the wisps of dust stirred by the mules, the birds following the plow, and hear the voice of the plowman and the crack of the whip. My father and brother came in from the fields very tired from *following* behind the plow, but they *never* pulled it themselves. That was not their part in the work of plowing.**

In God's commands of service, He is with us and goes before us, as He did for Joshua when he took command of the people of Israel after Moses' death. "Have not I commanded thee? Be strong and of a good courage; be not afraid, neither be thou dismayed: for the Lord thy God is with thee whithersoever thou goest." Joshua 1:9

It is an honor to be used of God by "following behind the plow" as the Lord performs His work. It makes all the difference when we 'follow' and not try to exert our own power and muscle to make things go a certain way. Such an attitude can cause much heartache and hindrances in our service for the Lord. *God must be in His work.* All else is in vain.

"Faithful is he that calleth you, who also will do it." I Thess. 5:24

Additional Treasures:    Mark 13:34    I Peter 4:11

# September 25

**"I went by the field of the slothful, and by the
vineyard of the man void of understanding."
Proverbs 24:30**

It has always been easy to spot the property of the slothful man. It takes some diligence and determination to take care of fields and vineyards. The lazy man did not get the job done. The results were apparent.

"And, lo, it was all grown over with thorns, and nettles had covered the face thereof, and the stone wall thereof was broken down. Then I saw, and considered it well: I looked upon it, and received instruction."
Prov. 24: 31-32

What kind of 'instruction' do we receive from observing something that has become a wasteland of neglect? Whatever was not kept up appears to be of little worth. We learn that neglect diminishes value and also the appeal of the appearance of things. That translates so aptly to the testimony of a Christian. Some people leave their Bibles in the car, all the time, so they will be handy for church on Sunday. I've seen Bibles ruined by being stashed in the hot sun on the dashboard or over the back window. Apparently they were not used at home. Neglect of God's Word will certainly mean neglect of prayer and all good intentions go downhill from there. A man's testimony can become worthless because of his own neglect of his relationship with the Lord. The wall of 'protection' will be crumbled for the Christian who is lazy in personal devotion to God and he will have *thorns and nettles* causing discomfort and frustration in his life, and he will be easy prey for the enemy.

God's Word is the 'heavenly x-ray' that we have easy access to which will enable us to keep our hearts by being made aware of the area that needs attention. His Word contains the perfect prayer verse for us to use when we can't think of how to approach the Lord to get off that path of neglect and back in fellowship with Him. All we have to do is pray with a sincere heart and confess whatever sins the Holy Spirit uncovers in His search.

"Search me, O God, and know my heart: try me, and know my thoughts: And see if there be any wicked way in me, and lead me in the way everlasting."     Psalm 139:23-24

Additional Treasures:     Proverbs 12:24     I Corinthians 15:58

# September 26

**"Yea, my reins shall rejoice,**
**when thy lips shall speak right things."**
**Proverbs 23:16**

This verse reminds us of the ways of good parents in bringing up their children to be polite and mannerly in conduct and conversation. They have to be *taught* to speak the right things in association with others, so that it becomes natural for them.

God has given us His Word to guide us in all things, and especially how to *say the right words* at the right time in order to be a good witness for the Lord on this earth. Too often the tongue is used in other ways and its purpose, which is to speak in a God-honoring manner, is forgotten as we allow it to have its own way.

It would be time well spent for us to gather all the scriptures about the tongue, its use and misuse! They can make you think long after you close the Bible from reading them. When you 'know what God knows' because of what He has told you in His word, you will be aware of it when actions prove these verses as plain as day. For example, have you ever noticed that a 'know it all' type person can talk the loudest and longest about something he knows little or nothing about? And the person who may be an expert on the subject is quiet and says very little or nothing. The Lord *said* it would be that way. "He that hath knowledge spareth his words: and a man of understanding is of an excellent spirit." Proverbs 17:27

"Where no wood is, there the fire goeth out: so where there is no talebearer, the strife ceaseth."     Proverbs 26:20

A scandal spreads like wildfire, and will go on and on as long as people keep talking. Those who are victims of gossip may feel overwhelmed and utterly helpless. It will stop only when those doing the talking, adding wood to the fire, cease. The talk stops and the uproar will die down and finally cease. The fire goes out.

Let us guard that *little member* that has such a powerful affect upon our lives and of those around us.

Additional Treasures:     James 3:2     Proverbs 13:3

# September 27

"A merry heart doeth good like a medicine:
but a broken spirit drieth the bones."
Proverbs 17:22

We have all heard someone say, "I feel so much better around that person; he is so upbeat and happy." And the opposite is true of the person who is continually downcast and unhappy. Nobody can really enjoy the company of those with *broken spirits and dried bones!*

The Lord made it possible for His children to have peace and happiness in this world. If we would only believe His Word and claim the promises, our hearts would always be spilling over with joy.

"These things I have spoken unto you, that in me ye might have peace. In the world ye shall have tribulation: but be of good cheer; I have overcome the world." John 16:33

We are to be cheerful and have a merry heart. Some folks used to think that godly people were supposed to look sorrowful and go about with a sad countenance. But not so! The Lord says *be of good cheer.*

Jesus once asked two of His disciples, who were walking toward the village of Emmaus what kind of talk they were engaged in that made them so sad. "And he said unto them, What manner of communications are these that ye have one to another, as ye walk, and are sad?" Luke 24:17

The Lord opened their understanding, and they knew it was Jesus alive from the grave. He restored peace and joy to their sad hearts.
"...the joy of the Lord is your Strength." Nehemiah 8:10

One thing that should keep our hearts bubbling over with joy all the time is the fact that Jesus abides with us. *He lives with us!* There is nothing in the world or heaven above that could trouble Jesus. He said "All power is given unto me in heaven and in earth."
Matthew 28:18
Think on these facts the next time your heart seems depleted of joy and a sense of well-being. Sit down and talk to Jesus who is right there with you.

Additional Treasures:     Proverbs 15:13     John 14:27

# September 28

"Oh how I love thy law! It is my meditation all the day."
Psalm 119:97

We cannot imagine an absence of the Word of God because it is always available to us. We cannot see ourselves waiting to get a brief time with the Bible *chained to the pulpit* at church. But in ages past, that was the only way Christians were allowed to read its precious contents.

In earlier centuries there were times when Christians had the Bible or some parts of it, and had to hide in their homes as they read it. If they were caught, it meant prison or death.

In other lands when the natives believe on the Lord and become acquainted with the power of God's Word, their testimonies are inspiring. The joy of having the Word printed in their native language cannot be measured. We saw that demonstrated before our eyes in Papua New Guinea, as the Christians received their New Testaments translated into the common language. They *value* the power and comfort of God's Word in that dark land.

**Dr. Moffat, a missionary to South Africa, tells of a little lad who had been converted by reading the New Testament. One day he came to Dr. Moffat in much distress telling him that their big watch dog had gotten hold of the Book and had torn a page out of it. Dr. Moffat tried to comfort him, by saying that he could get another Testament. But the boy was not at all comforted. "Think of the dog," he said. Dr. Moffat, supposing the boy thought that the paper would do the dog harm, laughed and said, "If your dog can crunch an ox bone, he is not going to be hurt by a piece of paper."**

**"Oh, Papa Moffat," he cried, "I was once a bad boy. If I had an enemy, I hated him, and everything in me wanted to kill him. Then I got the New Testament in my heart, and began to love everybody and forgive all my enemies. And now the dog, the great big hunting dog, has got the blessed Book in him, and will begin to love the lions and the tigers, and let them help themselves to the sheep and oxen."**

**What a beautiful tribute this African boy, out of the simplicity of his heart, paid to the power of the Bible!"**
–Wells of Living Water-Vol.1

Additional Treasures:     Job 23:12     John 20:31

# September 29

"Ponder the path of thy feet, and let all
thy ways be established."
Proverbs 4:26

Many do not *ponder* (give serious thought) to their spiritual walk as they follow the Lord on the narrow path. They are wishy-washy about dedication and cannot be depended upon for faithful attendance in the house of God.

The world is looking on as Christians can't make up their minds and hearts to be truly faithful to the Lord. That is why the Bible exhorts us to ponder, or think about what we are doing. We should leave a clearly cut trail behind us as a legacy, showing others the blessedness of having their ways established to honor God.

## LEGACY

We are leaving a sure legacy
On the path of life we trod.
Is it treasure of the precious kind,
Reminding others of our God?

The legacy that points to God,
A pattern of will and obedient design,
Is beyond wealth gleaned from the earth,
Which cankers and rusts with time.

Make clear impressions in sands of time,
Footprints of love and faith that's deep.
Others following closely in your wake,
Will have a legacy to keep.

"He that saith he abideth in him ought himself also so to walk, even as he walked." I John 2:6

Additional Treasures:     Ephesians 5:15     Galatians 5:16

# September 30

"Praying always with all prayer and
supplication in the Spirit..."
Ephesians 6:18

No doubt, one of the wonders of the spiritual world is that Christians do not enter into their privilege of petitioning the throne of God where Jesus sits on the right hand to make intercession for His own. *We do not pray!*

We should pray *always*, but Christians sometimes go for days or longer without communicating with the Lord through prayer, yet that is where the power for the Christian's life comes from.

**Prayer helps us in times of temptation to stand true to God.**
"Watch and pray, that ye enter not into temptation: the spirit indeed is willing, but the flesh is weak." `Matthew 26:41

**Prayer gets our needs supplied.**
"Ask, and it shall be given you; seek, and ye shall find; knock, and it shall be opened unto you..." Matthew 7:7

**Power of Prayer** -- "In February 1931, our mission district was reduced to a state of famine, and there was yet another month to wheat harvest. We had helped many, and one day when the Christians came for help we had to tell them we had nothing left. I told them that God was a prayer-hearing and prayer-answering God. They proposed to come and join in prayer each afternoon. On the fourth day of intercession I was called out of the meeting to see what was happening. Away in the north was a dark cloud approaching, and as we watched it crossed our district and rained heavily. It was not an ordinary rain, but a deluge of little black seeds in such abundance they could be shoveled up. They asked, 'What is this?' reminding us of the Children of Israel in the wilderness who asked a similar question. The seeds proved edible and the supply so great it sustained the people until harvest. We learned later that the storm had risen in Mongolia and wrecked the place where this grain, called Kao Liang, was stored. The seed was carried fifteen hundred miles to drop on the district where the prayer was being answered."
--Wells of Living Water, Vol.1

Additional Treasures:    John 16:24    I Kings 18:37-38

# October 1

"So she gleaned in the field until even,
and beat out that she had gleaned."
**Ruth 2:17**

Ruth, the daughter-in-law of Naomi, had chosen to come back to the land of Canaan and abide with her mother-in-law. She also declared her faith in the God of Israel.

"…thy people shall be my people, and thy God my God…" Ruth 1:16

Ruth was a young widow who was willing to work in the fields to gather food to sustain her aging mother-in-law and herself. She followed behind the reapers as the poor were allowed to do, and gathered the grain that they had left. We know that the kind owner of the field came to check on his workers and discovered Ruth among the women combing the field for the leftover grain. He gave her kind words and his blessing, and without her knowing it, Boaz gave command to his reapers.

"And when she was risen up to glean, Boaz commanded his young men, saying, Let her glean even among the sheaves, and reproach her not: And let fall also some of the handfuls of purpose for her, and leave them, that she may glean them, and rebuke her not." Ruth 2:15-16

When Ruth was through for the day, she *beat out* what she had gleaned to see what she had accomplished by her work. She was able to take about a bushel, an ephah, of barley home to Naomi so they would have food to eat. She was greatly rewarded for her diligence in hard work and her pure motive for service which was her love and concern for her mother-in-law.

It would be a good question to ask before we lay down for the night to sleep. 'What have I accomplished today for the Lord?' He is the One we are living for and representing in this world.

What have I gleaned? – **It is a good question for us to ask ourselves in the close of every day. "Where have I gleaned today? What improvements have I made in knowledge and grace? What have I done or obtained that will turn to a good account?"** Com.

Additional Treasures:     Ruth 4:13-15     II Corinthians 9:6

# October 2

**"But my God shall supply all your need according
to his riches in glory by Christ Jesus."
Philippians 4:19**

We are delighted, and perhaps inspired, when we read of God's miraculous provision for the saints of old as they diligently prayed and believed God would provide their needs. That Word will *never* change, and it is the same promises that the great prayer warrior, George Muller, relied upon as he prayed for food and other needs for his orphans over a century ago.

The story is told of a day in George Muller's Orphanage at Ashley Downs, when there was literally no breakfast for the children in the house. Mr. Muller led a little child by the hand into the long dining room, and said, "Let us see what our Father will do." The plates and mugs were on the table, but they were empty. There was no food and no money to supply the need. The children were standing waiting for the morning meal, when Mr. Muller said: "Children, you know you must be in time for school" Then lifting his hand, he said, "Dear Father, we thank thee for what Thou art going to give us to eat."

A knock at the door was heard. The baker stood there and said: "Mr. Muller, I couldn't sleep last night; somehow I felt you had no bread for breakfast, and the Lord wanted me to send some. So I got up at 2:00 o'clock and baked fresh bread and have brought it." George Muller thanked the man and gave praise to God for His care, then said, "Children, we not only have bread, but the rare treat of *fresh* bread." No sooner had he said this, than there came a second knock at the door. This time it was the milkman. He said his milk cart had broken down, right in front of the orphanage, and that he would like to give the children his cans of fresh milk so that he could empty his wagon and repair it.
–Selected

"But seek ye first the kingdom of God, and his righteousness; and all these things shall be added unto you." Matthew 6:33

**We must sort out our *needs* from our *wants*, then look up to God in faith and ask Him to supply those needs as He has promised in His Word. It will amaze and bless the Christian who patiently waits on the Lord, as He works all things together in providing every need of his life.**

Additional Treasures:     Philippians 4:6     Psalms 31:19

# October 3

**"The Lord knoweth how to deliver the godly out of
temptation, and to reserve the unjust unto the day
of judgment to be punished."
II Peter 2:9**

As long as a Christian is living on earth, he will have temptations to endure because the body of flesh is so vulnerable to sin. The idea *that temptation itself is sin* is common and adversely affects many lives. We need to keep a realistic view.

### Temptation is the *enticement* to sin.

"Blessed is the man that endureth temptation: for when he is tried, he shall receive the crown of life, which the Lord hath promised to them that love him."     James 1:12

The Word of God will never say, "Blessed is the man that sins" but it does say that the man that endures temptation is blessed. Temptation is always a trial in the Christian's life, *but it is not sin.* It can lead to it if one yields to the enticement or encouragement to sin.

### Sin is the transgression of God's law.

"Whosoever committeth sin transgresseth also the law: for sin is the transgression of the law." I John 3:4

It is the devil's ploy to tempt every Christian to sin against God by being disobedient to Him in some manner. We must recognize it for what it is as the attraction to sin comes into our thoughts, and immediately take up the Word and fight back! Read or quote aloud any verse that applies to the thought. If you can't think of one at all, just start with the first verse in the Bible. *"In the beginning God..."* The name of God has power to calm your thoughts and help you to resist temptation.

"This is my comfort in my affliction: for thy word hath quickened me." Psalm 119:50

A lady told me once that she had such troubling thoughts one day and could not get any peace so she went about her chores just repeating the name of Jesus over and over. Whatever it takes, just fight back as the devil tries to rob you of every particle of joy you have in your heart.

Additional Treasures:     Hebrews 3:13     Proverbs 1:10

# October 4

"For all the promises of God in him are yea,
and in him Amen, unto the glory of God by us."
II Corinthians 1:20

When we forget the promises of God and wander off the path of faithfulness, we are definitely in the enemy's territory and can be taken captive.

It is hard to resist temptation if we cannot recall one precious promise from the Word of God. We must *remember* and often meditate and reflect on what God has promised to those who have trusted in Christ. There are many *giants* among our enemies who are waiting patiently for the opportunity to get us locked up in the place of despair, or doubting.

**"Now a little before it was day, good Christian, as one half amazed, brake out in this passionate speech: What a fool, quoth he, am I thus to lie in a stinking dungeon, when I may as well walk at liberty! I have a key in my bosom called Promise, that will, I am persuaded, open any lock in Doubting Castle. Then said Hopeful, That's good news; good brother, pluck it out of thy bosom and try.**

**Then Christian pulled it out of his bosom, and began to try at the dungeon door, whose bolt (as he turned the key) gave back, and the door flew open with ease, and Christian and Hopeful both came out..."** The Pilgrim's Progress – John Bunyan

How many times has the Giant of Despair locked you up in Doubting Castle and inflicted all kinds of miseries to your mind and heart? He is just waiting for you to wander off into his territory. *But you have the key to freedom!* Keep it in a prominent place in your heart. It is the Word of God.

"Many are the afflictions of the righteous: but the Lord delivereth him out of them all." Psalm 34:19

"Whereby are given to us exceeding great and precious promises: that by these ye might be partakers of the divine nature..." II Peter 1:4

Additional Treasures:     Romans 4:21     Isaiah 43:2

# October 5

"And you hath he quickened, who were dead
in trespasses and sins;"
Ephesians 2:1

Quickened means to be made alive. One who has trusted in Christ has been made alive spiritually. It is the supernatural work and power of God that *regenerates* the lost man and makes him a new creature.

The dictionary gives the definition of *regeneration* as being born again spiritually, being made new. Even with a clear explanation of the meaning, there are Christians who plod fearfully along never quite laying hold of the assurance of eternal life.

Apparently, that has been the case in all ages. In a sermon I read by J.C. Ryle, a preacher in England in the last century, he deals with the question: *Are You Regenerate?* There are some distinctive *new* things about a Christian of which he will be keenly aware in the beginning of life with Christ. It is an entire alteration of the inner man:

His *will* is new, his *tastes* new, his *opinions* new, his views of *sin* are new, his views of the *world, the Bible, and Christ* are new!

A newborn Christian is a *babe in Christ,* and must grow in grace and knowledge of the Word of God. Over a period of time, the fruit of the Holy Spirit will be more evident in his life. However, *from the first day* of regeneration the Christian experiences a change of which he is aware. For many it is the realization of peace in the heart, where before there was misery and guilt.

"Therefore if any man be in Christ, he is a new creature: old things are passed away; behold, all things are become new." II Corinthians 5:17

Are new things evident in your life? Are you a new creature? There may not be all of the distinctive marks of a Christian immediately in a newborn babe in Christ, but there will be an evident change long before he can even name the fruits of the Holy Spirit. When Christ moves in; you change.

Additional Treasures: Titus 3:5    John 5:24

# October 6

**"Whosoever believeth that Jesus is the Christ
is born of God..."
I John 5:1**

In our day of blending the world and the church together in order to gain acceptance in both realms, the distinction of a pure and holy life is hardly seen anymore. Still, there *are* identifying characteristics of a true child of God. In some they are faint, dim, feeble, and hard to discern. In a few others, they are sharp, bold, and unmistakable. It is a joy to meet others that have many if not all of the Christian characteristics obvious in their lives. They are strong in faith and encourage others by their testimony.

In a message by J.C. Ryle (1816-1900), the marks of regeneration are given according to Biblical teaching. The Bible is the textbook on salvation. Today so much doubt and confusion prevails; people need to understand the marks, *identifying characteristics,* of a Christian from the Bible.

**A true Christian does not habitually sin.**

Whosoever is born of God doth not commit sin; for his seed remaineth in him: and he cannot sin, because he is born of God." I John 3:9

Sin will not be the *lifestyle* of the true Child of God. God is a faithful Heavenly Father; He will not allow His children to go on in their sin without correction. The Bible states it very plainly.

"For whom the Lord loveth he chasteneth, and scourgeth every son whom he receiveth." "But if ye be without chastisement, whereof all are partakers, then are ye bastards, and not sons." Hebrews 12:6, 8

The child of God cannot prevent sin dwelling in him; he is in the flesh. But he hates it and has a great desire not to sin at all. He is convicted of sin easily and is never at peace with unconfessed sin, though Christians can be disobedient and become cold-hearted for a time. God tends to that in His own time and way. We should never put off confessing our sins which so easily beset us...for we will not have peace of mind as long as we try to hide them from God. He reads our hearts, searching them, continually.

Additional Treasures:    II Peter 1:10    Titus 2:11-12

# October 7

"But the salvation of the righteous is of the Lord:
he is their strength in the time of trouble."
Psalm 37:39

The work of Christ in the heart at the new birth, of which Jesus spoke in the gospel of John, will definitely make a change in that person's life. We must not forget the reality of regeneration and the distinct marks of a Christian.

As previously stated, a true Christian does not *habitually* sin. That means he cannot live in sin without discipline from God, his heavenly Father, just as parents correct their children when they disobey.

**A regenerate person does not make the world's opinion his rule of right and wrong,** *no matter how many are doing it.*

"For whatsoever is born of God overcometh the world: and this is the victory that overcometh the world, even our faith." I John 5:4

True Christians follow God guided by His Word, and they would rather have praise of Him than that of men. They are not comfortable with going against what the Bible says in the affairs of life.
It is a happy Christian who has settled it in his heart to follow God's Word, as he understands it…*no matter what.*

**A true Christian has a special love for other children of God.**
"We know that we have passed from death unto life, because we love the brethren. He that loveth not his brother abideth in death." I John 3:14

They are kinfolk! The sons and daughters of God cannot help but love one another in a special way. I have noticed in other countries, as we have traveled to mission fields, how that bond of love is prevalent among Christians though they don't speak the same language, and their cultures are worlds apart. In Mexico I desperately tried to communicate with the women as they did also with me. We waved our arms, drew imaginary pictures with our hands and then would finally give up and just hug each other. When we had no one at the moment to interpret, we were a comical sight no doubt.

Additional Treasures:     I John 3:18-19     Ephesians 4:32

# October 8

"Grace and peace be multiplied unto you through
the knowledge of God, and of Jesus our Lord."
II Peter 1:2

Continuing the study of the marks, *identifying characteristics,* of the Christian, we find that the *love for the brethren* is very easy to point out. That is the person who loves to go to church and participate in the worship of the Lord with other believers. He enjoys the fellowship and encouragement gained from that time together. There is something seriously wrong when one professes Christ, but has no desire to attend when the family of God congregates to worship Him and learn together.

**A regenerate man believes that Jesus Christ is the only Saviour by whom his soul can be pardoned and redeemed.**

"Whosoever believeth that Jesus is the Christ is born of God: and every one that loveth him that begat loveth him also that is begotten of him. *I John 5:1*
Although at times he may feel weak as though he has no faith at all, a real Christian will testify that he would not give up Christ for the entire world. He would never trust anything or anyone else.

**A regenerate person is a holy person.**
The saved person endeavors to live according to God's will, to do the things that please God. He is not perfect and knows it. There is warfare inside all the time to draw him away from God but he does not consent to it. That is the reason for the acute need of the Word of God every day, with consistent prayer, to enable the Christian to stand against temptation and the constant harassment of the enemy, the devil.
**Are you regenerate, are you saved?**
That is the most important question you will ever face up to and answer in your entire life. Your eternity depends on it. Pride will fight you like a wild thing! That was my worst battle as an unsaved church member. What will people think? But it finally came down to the awful reality to me that I was the one who was lost and would spend eternity in hell; why worry about what another mere human being may think? Actually, every other child of God will rejoice when another is saved. But the devil uses pride.

Additional Treasures:     II Timothy 2:19     II Corinthians 13:5

# October 9

**"Better is the sight of the eyes than the wandering
of the desire: this is also vanity and vexation of spirit."
Ecclesiastes 6:9**

The reference to the *sight of the eyes* means the enjoyment of what is available to a person. If we constantly long for things that we do not have, then we will fail to appreciate what is already present in our lives to enjoy.

Some marriages are full of unhappiness because of the *wandering of the desire*. It may be a longing for more and better material things that they cannot afford, which causes stress in the family. It is far better to enjoy modest means free of stress and *vexation of spirit*.

**In some cases, men and women alike have a *wandering desire* reaching back into the past for another person they once knew. When they direct their emotional expectation to the deadness of the past, it is a vain exercise and will only bring disappointment. God intends for every couple to enjoy the love and companionship of each other, *in the reality of the present.***

"Drink waters out of thine own cistern, and running waters out of thine own well...Let thy fountain be blessed: and rejoice with the wife of thy youth." Proverbs 5:15, 18

In the context of this chapter in Proverbs, you can readily see that God is *not* just talking about cisterns and wells and fountains. There will be plenty of satisfaction and enjoyment in the relationship one has with his or her spouse. The Lord is saying *drink out of that cistern!*

When one has the inclination to let the *wandering desire* loose, he should consider what a vain thing and vexation of spirit it will bring into his life. God will satisfy the longings of the heart according to His will.

"Delight thyself also in the Lord; and he shall give thee the desires of thine heart." Psalm 37:4

Additional Treasures:     Proverbs 16:3     Philippians 4:6

# October 10

*"Apply thine heart unto instruction, and*
*thine ears to the words of knowledge."*
Proverbs 23:12

So much of the Psalms and Proverbs are given to the instruction for taking in the Word of God. The Lord patiently says it in His Word over and over. He knows that our hearts are prone to wander away from Him with the slightest distraction. In our text verse the meaning is plain. Read the Word of God for yourself, and *listen* when it is taught or preached unto you.

Our society today is so blessed with the *availability* of the scriptures. The saints in past centuries had to wait in line to even *see* a page of the Bible, *which was chained to the pulpit.* It was precious because they did not have it to read and study in the privacy of their homes.

We must never assume that we *will always have* the privileges that we do now as Christians. Let us appreciate the freedom God has allowed us to have in this generation, and make use of it by dedication to the things of the Lord. Priority in Bible reading will keep one's life peaceful, even in the midst of the normal run of trials and troubles, which is common to all.

**Thy Word is like a deep, deep mine, And jewels rich and rare**
**Are hidden in its mighty depths, For every searcher there.**

**Thy Word is like an armory, Where soldiers may repair**
**And find, for life's long battle-day, All needful weapons there.**

**O may I find my armor there, Thy word my trusty sword!**
**I'll learn to fight with every foe, The battle of the Lord!**
Edwin Hooder – Gottfried Fink

The most pleasant surprise a Christian will ever have, personally, is when he develops the habit of faithful Bible reading. He will be amazed at the spiritual understanding and insight which develops in his soul.

Additional Treasures:     Proverbs 22:20-21     Psalm 119:97-104

# October 11

**"Thus saith the Lord; For three transgressions of Edom, and four, I will not turn away the punishment therof..."**
**Amos 1:11**

The descendants of Esau, Jacob's twin brother, were called Edomites. So they were kinfolk of the Israelites, yet they treated the people of Israel with cruelty when they would not allow them to pass through their country on the journey from Egypt. It created hardship and suffering when Edom came out with an army and turned the Israelites away from water and a closer route to their destination. God took notice of that wickedness and in time the judgment came. The Lord names the four indictments.

**Because he did pursue his brother with a sword.**
The old desire for revenge had not died out, even after hundreds of years since Jacob had deceitfully taken Esau's birthright. The spirit of revenge was kept alive by his descendants.

**And did cast off pity.**
Compassion was totally lacking in the Edomites. They were not touched by the needs and suffering of the weary Israelites.

**And his anger did tear perpetually.**
The desire to utterly devastate the Israelites was fed by a well of anger, which stayed fresh and abundant with use.

**And he kept his wrath forever.**
Edom *refused to forgive* his brother, Israel. Generations had come and gone while they stayed entrenched in bitter hatred, which ultimately brought God's judgment on the nation.

These things, which brought the nation of Edom to an end, are the same sins we grapple with today in spiritual warfare. You must keep on the "whole armour of God, that ye may be able to stand..." Eph: 6:11

**Once when reading I came to Psalm 37:8 and it took on a whole new meaning for me as God rebuked me for the anger which was in my heart. It was as though He had His finger under it pointing out each word emphatically. "Cease from anger, and forsake wrath: fret not thyself in any wise to do evil." I was faced with my sin, confessed it, and was cleansed by the Word. What a privilege to be God's child!**

Additional Treasures:    Mark 11:25    Colossians 3:13

# October 12

**"For if ye forgive men their trespasses,
your heavenly Father will also forgive you."
Matthew 6:14**

It is imperative that we learn the blessing of forgiveness, not only as it comes from God to us through Christ, but as a guarantee of continued peace and well-being in our lives after salvation. We must practice forgiveness, *because we will always need it for ourselves!*

**The nation of Edom, descendants of Esau, ceased to exist because of their ill treatment of the Israelites as they journeyed from Egypt. The reason for their cruelty was an *unforgiving spirit*, kept alive and fervent by raging anger and wrath.**

Forgiveness seems to be shrouded in a fog of misunderstanding in spite of all the attempts made to explain it. We may master it for a moment, but the next time we are tested by an offense in our lives the meaning again eludes us, as we struggle with our feelings.

**The dictionary defines *forgive*ness:** to give up the wish to punish or get even with: absolve.
**The Bible tells us how to do that:** give it all to God, and let Him work and reconcile all things involved.

"Dearly beloved, avenge not yourselves, but rather give place unto wrath: for it is written, Vengeance is mine; I will repay, saith the Lord."
Romans 12:19
If we stay out of God's way and God's *business*, then every offense will be dealt with to the good of all concerned. When we try to do it ourselves, the results make more grief than the initial offense that hurt us.
"Cease from anger, and forsake wrath: fret not thyself in any wise to do evil." Psalm 37:8

We all have an unusual capacity for carrying anger and many times we are not aware ourselves that it is lying dormant in our hearts. Some have anger stored from their childhood. Others have stored their anger away and pride themselves on being nonchalant about it, until one day something sets it off and their control mechanism can't hold it in. People can do horrendous things in a moment of unleashed anger! It is best to confess and forsake it.

Additional Treasures:    Ephesians 4:31-32    Galatians 5:13-15

# October 13

"...Not by might, nor by power, but by my
spirit, saith the Lord of hosts."
Zechariah 4:6

The mighty things of men and all the power they can call up is ineffective to accomplish the work of the Lord. Men's efforts prove to be very puny in comparison to the real thing--God's power.

Samson enjoyed numerous victories and acclaim as the champion of the Israelites against their enemy, until he broke his vow of dedication to God when he was tempted by Delilah. It was a pitiful revelation when Samson realized himself that his own power could not deliver him from the enemy.

"And she said, The Philistines be upon thee, Samson. And he awoke out of his sleep, and said, I will go out as at other times before, and shake myself. And he wist not that the Lord was departed from him." Judges 16:20

We know what happened to mighty Samson. The enemy had no mercy; they put out his eyes and made a slave of him grinding at the mill.

The devil is waiting patiently to catch us off guard and unprepared with the Word of God to protect ourselves. He will capture us and render us ineffective in serving the Lord with our lives, which is his aim for everyone who belongs to Christ. His hatred of the Lord knows no bounds.

**In a reunion with veterans of the Korean War, my husband talked with the men who were in the same outfit as he was during some terrible battles, and the time particularly when the Chinese crossed the Yalu River and entered the war. They came in human waves with great loss of lives for their side, and for the Americans. The army had to pull back, fighting a relentless battle for days until they finally got back out of that area, exhausted, and many near frozen from cold of that Korean winter. One veteran expressed it simply:** *"I didn't fear death, I feared running out of ammunition and being captured by the enemy, knowing how they treated prisoners."*

Do we fear capture? The most miserable people are Christians who have yielded to temptation, been drawn into sin and 'taken prisoner' by the devil. He treats prisoners cruelly, and has no mercy. *Be prepared,* and armed with the Word in your heart. Fight! Your life depends on it.

Additional Treasures:     I Thessalonians 5:17     II Timothy 2:15

# October 14

*"But that on the good ground are they, which in an
honest and good heart, having heard the word, keep it,
and bring forth fruit with patience."*
Luke 8:15

In keeping the Word that we hear, we allow the Holy Spirit to produce His fruit in our lives. That is *love, joy, peace, longsuffering, gentleness, goodness, faith, meekness, and temperance.* Every particle of that fruit is cultivated and brought forth with patience.

One definition of patience is willingness to put up with waiting, pain, and trouble without complaining or losing self-control; our pattern for patience and longsuffering is the Lord. His infinite love motivates His 'long patience' which blesses our lives every day.

"Be patient therefore, brethren, unto the coming of the Lord. Behold, the husbandman waiteth for the precious fruit of the earth, and hath long patience for it, until he receive the early and latter rain." James 5:7

Our love and patience is often discouraged when people do not respond to our witnessing, but we should pray diligently for the *long patience* characteristic of our Lord. *He* had patience with each of us who have trusted in Him and we should, in turn, show that patience through our lives as we reach out to the lost.

**In many ways, the Lord gives us tests to check out our progress in the developing patience. It is not for *His* information, but for ours. How do I know I'm becoming a patient individual until it is tested in my life? Oftentimes, I've come from a frustrating ordeal with the realization that I'm not *there* yet! The Spirit has more work to do in my heart.**

I grew up in a family of ten children, seven of which were boys. There was no patience among us. Only our mother had patience. My little brothers, out playing, were always getting into a squabble which grew to an uproar and fighting. They would run tearfully to Mother and start telling on each other etc. She would make them all come in, *be quiet*, and *wait* while each one told his version of things. They tried desperately to make it sound bad. If one said another threw a rock, it was always described as an "iron" rock! By the time the last one told his tale, the whole thing was diffused and they went back to the yard in good humor to play again.

Additional Treasures:     Ecclesiastes 7:8     Hebrews 10:36

# October 15

"Therefore remove sorrow from thy heart, and put
away evil from thy flesh: for childhood and youth are vanity."
Ecclesiastes 11:10

Some adults have sorrow in their hearts connected directly to their childhood and youth. Negative emotions experienced in young children make an impression that may not be easily erased.

**I grew up with *fear*, which was easily triggered by any cross words between my parents. They had a brief separation when I was seven years of age, and though it didn't happen again, I *felt acute fear* when they had the least kind of argument. Even in adulthood, it is disturbing when I happen to hear a couple arguing. That typifies the strength of impressions that emotional trauma, suffered in childhood, makes on the heart of the individual.**

God is the only One who knows and understands all about us, and what kinds of things are burrowed into the depths of our hearts. In this imperfect world, everyone has negative impressions to deal with sooner or later. That's why the psalmist prayed: "Behold, thou desirest truth in the inward parts: and in the hidden part thou shalt make me to know wisdom." Psalm 51:6

When the Word of God registers in the *inward parts,* it begins to root out the sorrow from the heart and continues a steady deliverance as the wisdom gained is applied. Bitterness and hatred must be put away if ever the sorrow is to be dispelled. All this is possible by the power of God through His blessed Word. "...for childhood and youth are vanity."

The past is an empty era. Whatever was *is no more,* and realizing that in the *hidden part* of our being helps us to reconcile all things.

"With God all things are possible..." Matthew 19:26

Sometimes the things people struggle with seem like such a mountain of difficulty that nothing can remove it from its place in their minds. But when God said 'all things are possible' it is true and that's our only hope for relief. Jesus is our Counselor. We can tell Him everything. He can do impossible things to bring about our relief and restoration of joy.

Additional Treasures:     Psalm 139:1-4, 17-18, 23-24

# October 16

**"Let not mercy and truth forsake thee:**
**bind them about thy neck..."**
**Proverbs 3:3**

It is common knowledge that very rich people in the world may keep their most valuable jewels locked up in a vault somewhere, while they wear expensive imitations. The false jewels are worn to make a statement: I own the real thing, but it is too valuable to wear!

The Lord has very valuable things which we are instructed to wear about our necks. No one can ever steal these priceless things from us. We can display them openly, and it is such beautiful adornment. Those things are *mercy* and *truth.*

**Mercy is kindness beyond what can be claimed or expected.**
The highly acclaimed woman in Proverbs 31 was noted for having a merciful tongue." She openeth her mouth with wisdom; and in her tongue is the law of kindness." Proverbs 31:26

Mercy, *kindness,* is a sparkling jewel in one's life that sheds its light on everyone it touches. This jewel is difficult to imitate by human pretense.

**Truth is the fact or facts; matter or circumstance as it really is.**
Jesus proclaimed Himself to be *the truth* "I am the way, the truth, and the life and the life..." John 14:6

Truth is a lovely ornament displayed in one's life. It is the most precious jewel of man's character. *He is truthful.* Anyone who has the reputation of being a truthful person would even be a more credible witness for the Lord in the matter of salvation. Being truthful is the most wonderful character trait.

Truth stands alone and is always enduring while any imitation, *lies,* will ultimately crumble, though they are propped up by many.

In our present day it is appalling how glibly people lie about anything and everything without one spark of disturbance in their conscience. There used to be a time when you could easily tell when someone was lying, but not anymore. There is no nervousness, no blushing, and liars can look you right in the eye and the only thing you see there is possibly amusement as they see that you are probably believing them. But God looks in the heart and knows all. The way of truth is still the happiest way of life. Stay steadfast in the truth.

Additional Treasures:     Proverbs 12:19     James 3:17

# October 17

"Not slothful in business; fervent in spirit;
serving the Lord."
Romans 12:11

How our lives may influence others, or be influenced by others is depicted by an illustration I read.

**"A little clock in a jeweler's window stopped one day for half an hour at fifteen minutes of nine.** School children, noticing the time, stopped to play; People hurrying to the train, saw the clock, and began to walk leisurely; others, rushing to appointments, saw the time and walked slower; Business men, seeing the clock, stopped to talk; Working men and women noted the time and lingered longer in the sunshine, *And all were half an hour late because one small clock had stopped.* These people did not know how much they depended upon that clock, till it led them astray. Many are thus unconsciously depending upon the influence of Christians; you may think you have no influence, but you cannot go wrong in one little act without leading others astray."** Wells of Living Water – Vol.7

Influence is a powerful thing, and it is defined as the power to produce an effect *without using* coercion. A person may have influence by his ability, personality, position or wealth.

The nation's youth looks up to famous sports figures and is influenced by them. Parents may cringe when some of these role models are not such good examples of what men and women should be, for they are seen on television so frequently.

Christians are the most *observed* group of people on earth. The world is both fascinated and irritated by men and women who love God, and live like it. That kind of life is a powerful influence on others. We are exhorted in the Bible to do everything we do for the glory of God. Then we won't have to worry about influencing anyone in a negative way.

"Whether therefore ye eat, or drink, or whatsoever ye do, do all to the glory of God." I Corinthians 10:31

Additional Treasures:     Matthew 5:13     Romans 14:15

# October 18

**"But I say unto you, That every idle word that men shall speak, they shall give account thereof in the day of judgment."**
**Matthew 12:36**

We cannot pretend that we aren't liable for the influence of our lives on others. The Lord said that we are accountable for *every idle word* we speak. The Christian's life is very serious business. We need the power of God's influence on our lives, to make us what we ought to be as His representatives in this world. That influence comes through the power of God's Word and our communication with Him in prayer. People need to see Christians doing the ordinary things of life with the same piety that they display in the church. That has much more influence on the minds of others than many sermons they may hear.

**A consecrated merchant. – When a certain Christian merchant went to his pastor to tell him of his earnest desire to engage in work more distinctively religious, the pastor heard him kindly. The merchant said, "my heart is so full of love to God and to man that I want to spend all my time in talking with men about these things." "No" said the pastor, "go back to your store and be a Christian over your counter. Sell goods for Christ, and let it be seen that a man can be a Christian in trade."**

**Years afterwards the merchant rejoiced that he followed the advice, and the pastor rejoiced also in a generous and open-handed brother in his church, who was awake not only to home interests, but to the great work of missions around the world carried out by the church.-** Clerical Library

My pastor's wife greatly influenced me to read the Bible. She knew so much of the scriptures, and it was a part of her conversation and everyday life. Not only what she said as she taught it, but the way she handled her Bible and referred to it in all situations showed me that she really meant it when she said that she loved God's Word.

God has faithful ones in all walks of life, who are *peculiar treasures.* We know that even movie stars have been saved; and their lives changed a great deal from then on. For some, their careers as movie stars diminished, but their fame and popularity became an asset which they joyfully used for the Lord.

"Who shall give account to him that is ready to judge the quick and the dead." I Peter 4:5

Additional Treasures:    Exodus 19:5    Philippians 1:27

# October 19

"Produce your cause, saith the Lord; bring forth
your strong reasons, saith the King of Jacob."
Isaiah 41:21

In genuine prayer, a Christian should be able to do as this verse says: *Produce your cause...bring forth your strong reasons.* Why do we so often pray half-heartedly when we are petitioning the One that can move heaven and earth for us?

Your *cause* in prayer is the basis or foundation for your petition. *Reasons* are further sensible explanations for your cause. God would have us come boldly to Him in our time of need and bare our hearts in earnest prayer.

"For we have not a high priest which cannot be touched with the feeling of our infirmities; but was in all points tempted like as we are, yet without sin.

Let us therefore come boldly unto the throne of grace, that we may obtain mercy, and find grace to help in time of need." Hebrews 4:15-16

Touched with the feeling.--**Don't you sometimes find it very hard to make even your doctor understand *what* the pain is like? Words don't seem to convey it. And after you have explained the trying and wearying sensation as best you can, you are convinced those who have not felt it do not understand it. Now, think of Jesus not merely entering into the fact, but into the *feeling* of what you are going through. "Touched with the *feeling"* – how deep that goes!**
– F.R. Havergal.

Understanding more of the nature of our High Priest Who intercedes for us in prayer should motivate us to come before Him fervently, ready to present our *cause and strong reasons,* because He is feeling our burden with us. Nothing is too small and insignificant to pray about.

Our best praying is private prayer. Begin the habit now of sharing every burden of your heart with the Lord. He commands us to pray because time spent in the presence of God is of more value to our strength and spiritual growth than we could ever imagine.

Additional Treasures:    I Chronicles 16:11    Romans 8:26

# October 20

**"It is better to trust in the Lord
than to put confidence in man."
Psalm 118:8**

Many Christians have found that truth to be a sad fact in their lives as they have *misplaced* their trust, relying on man rather than God. Our expectations are sure to be disappointed by trusting any source other than God to work out the details of our lives.

*Trust.* -"**Trust in yourself, and you are doomed to disappointment; trust in your friends, and they will die and leave you; trust in money and you may have it taken from you; trust in reputation and some slanderous tongue may blast it; but trust in God and you are never to be confounded in time or eternity."**-D.L. Moody.

Some, at one time or another, trust their own hearts. We may feel that with all the knowledge we have about the things of God, our hearts are stable and trustworthy. *"Trust your heart"* the world encourages. The Word of God says something else about the heart. "The heart is deceitful above all things, and desperately wicked: who can know it? Jeremiah 17:9

Not only can we *not* trust our own hearts that is also the reason we cannot put confidence in others and trust their hearts either! The heart must be kept as a special garden, guarded and tended carefully for a good reason.

"Keep thy heart with all diligence, for out of it are the issues of life."
Proverbs 4:23

"...for out of the abundance of the heart the mouth speaketh."
Matthew 12:34

The heart rules the life; therefore, one must be wise by giving the care of it into the Lord's keeping and *trust Him* in all things. That's *keeping* it and the Word of God is the instruction book which tells us how to do that very difficult thing. We would dread having to keep undisciplined and rebellious children under our roof for any length of time. They could wreck the place and cause extensive damage to our nerves as well. The heart is a 'problem child' and everyone must keep his own. We desperately need help, and the Lord has provided for it. Look in the Bible every day and pull out some powerful word of truth which will keep that heart in line.

Additional Treasures:     Psalm 37:5     Proverbs 29:25

# October 21

**"Thy Word have I hid in mine heart,
that I might not sin against thee."
Psalm 119:11**

Christians have to be motivated *not* to sin. The Word of God stored in the mind is the deterrent. Our hearts can't be trusted to motivate us in any way to do right; hearts are deceitful. What God says motivates us to do right.

**Motivation is the act or process of furnishing with an incentive or inducement to action. So to *motivate* someone, you inspire or give an impulse to prompt or influence them.**

A clear meaning of motivation came to me early in our marriage, when we lived in a West Texas town where my husband worked in the oil fields. We were not yet Christians. Our son was a tiny baby, and my energy was at an all-time low. I barely functioned in the household duties and could see the discouragement in my husband but didn't have the energy to really care.

He worked the evening shift, and one afternoon as he left for work, I *impulsively* said, "When you get back tonight this room is going to look like a new room!" He glanced around the living room wearily and said, "No, it will look just the same." As he drove away, anger and adrenaline rushed through me like a flood! 'I'LL SHOW YOU!' I thought to myself, and immediately bundled up the baby and took him to a grandma neighbor, and ran to the store and bought a package of dye for curtains. Then, I tore into that room like a wild woman! I cleaned and dusted *every* inch of it, vacuumed, and washed and starched the lace panel curtains. My best white sheet was used to make drapes, dyed the color of the rug and dried on the line while I finished polishing *everything* in the room.

When I'd finished that night and put everything in place, that room was the loveliest thing I'd seen in a long time. I barely had time to clean up and be ready when my husband came in the door. The look on his face was worth all the effort, and it was a turning point for me. I worked with renewed energy and felt much better with each day's progress. The motivation that came because of a youthful impulse helped me to get a new perspective which made me feel better in every way.

If we will *listen* to God through His Word, it will motivate us to be obedient and excited about serving Him. It will move us to action!

Additional Treasures:    Psalm 19:8    Jeremiah 15:16

# October 22

**"...and he would have given thee living water."**
**John 4:10**

The woman who came to the well at midday to draw water had no idea who Jesus was sitting on the well waiting for her, since He knew she would come and He would save that poor wretched woman that day. The Lord gave her a drink of *living water* and her life changed from that moment.

"The woman then left her waterpot, and went her way into the city, and saith to the men, Come, see a man, which told me all things that ever I did: is not this the Christ?" John 4:29-30

**"The great river Amazon pours out so mighty a stream of fresh water into the Atlantic, that for miles out of sight of land, just opposite the mouth of the river, the water in the ocean is entirely fresh water.**

**Some years ago a sailing ship left Europe for a South American port and was so long on its voyage, that the water on board began to give out; and though the crew took every care, they shortly found themselves with their last container empty.**

**A day or two later, becalmed in a hot climate, to their great joy and relief they sighted another vessel, and signaled, telling of their piteous position: 'We're dying for want of water.' To their astonishment, the reply which came back quickly, seemed almost to mock them: 'Water all around you; let your bucket down.' Little did they know that they were just then crossing the mighty Amazon's current, and instead of being in salt water they were actually in fresh water without knowing it.**

**Water all around! Fellow traveler, you may be crying out, 'What must I do to be saved?' little realizing that the ocean of God's love is all around you. Oh! 'Let your bucket down!'** Wells of Living Water- Vol. 5.

We who have drunk of the *living water* should offer it to those who have not, for they cannot have life without it. Jesus provided for all that will come and drink of the water of life freely. To refuse to spend time telling the gospel, the precious water of life, it would be something like the sailors knowing of the Amazon's fresh water flowing around the men on the ship who were dying for lack of water, and not telling them. You couldn't imagine such cruelty. Let us keep the Word flowing into our hearts so we will have water to share.

Additional Treasures:    John 7:37-38    Isaiah 43:10

# October 23

*"Jesus said unto her, I am the resurrection and the life:*
*he that believeth in me, though he were dead, yet shall he live."*
**John 11:25**

If Jesus had not come up out of the grave after he died for our sins, we would have no hope. The power of redemption lies in the resurrection of the Lord Jesus Christ. So many times at funerals I have heard my husband comfort the people with this statement: "Jesus went through the grave and made it a pleasant place to wait for the resurrection."

"That Christ should suffer, and that he should be the first that should rise from the dead, and should shew light unto the people, and to the Gentiles." Acts 26:23

The resurrection of Christ from the dead is our hope and takes the fear of death away. "And deliver them who through fear of death were all their lifetime subject to bondage." Hebrews 2:15

**I read a story of a Sunday School teacher who had a little boy in her class whose mother was unsaved, and had such a horror of death that she would not come to church for fear of hearing the subject mentioned. After hearing the Easter lesson taught by the teacher, the little boy ran home and burst into the room and cried, "Mother, you need not be afraid to die, because Jesus went through the grave and left a light behind him!" The words gripped the mother and stayed with her. Shortly after, she accepted the invitation from a neighbor to attend a revival because of her little boy's words. One evening her little boy prayed, "Please, God, make my mamma a Christian, and do it right off quick." That night the mother went to the meeting and gave her heart to Christ.**

When our hearts need reviving in the joy of our salvation, it is time to sit down and read again the account of Jesus' death on the cross and the event of His resurrection on the third day. There is such power in that message to calm all our fears and give perfect peace. If we live our lives on the 'resurrection side' of the gospel, we will have a greater realization of power to withstand the wiles of the devil. That is a blessed truth to meditate on continually.

Additional Treasures:     Matthew 28:6-7, 18-20     Luke 24:6-8, 46-48

# October 24

**"For if we would judge ourselves, we
should not be judged."
I Corinthians 11:31**

The Word of God furnishes such guidelines for our lives, and we could be blissfully happy all the time if we would only listen. The Lord says it plain and simple, "…if we would judge ourselves, we should not be judged."

If we realize what we are doing is wrong, we should stop it immediately and ask God to forgive that sin. Then we won't be judged and punished by the Lord! The Bible is the book of judgment on what is right and what is wrong. Besides that, the Holy Spirit living in us warns us of sin. Our failure to *agree with the Bible* and judge ourselves concerning sin brings the correction of God into our lives, and that can be a very grievous thing.

"As many as I love, I rebuke and chasten: be zealous therefore, and repent." Revelation 3:19

"He that covereth his sins shall not prosper: but whoso confesseth and forsaketh them shall have mercy." Proverbs 28:13

We can have mercy continually flowing into our lives by judging ourselves on the matter of sin, or we can have the chastening, *correction* of the Lord, which we will not enjoy though it does us much good.

"Now no chastening for the present seemeth to be joyous, but grievous: nevertheless, afterward it yieldeth the peaceable fruit of righteousness unto them which are exercised thereby." Hebrews 12:11

The worst situation, which automatically comes into play with our toleration of sin in our lives, is the hindering of our prayers being answered.

"If I regard iniquity in my heart, the Lord will not hear me." Psa. 66:18

This verse may wash right over us without its meaning registering in our hearts. What does it mean? When we are regarding something, we are looking at it! If we have a sin tucked away in the heart, we know it is there, and are looking at it yet won't confess it as sin to God...*He will not hear us when we pray.* It is very important to keep in praying condition, for we never know when we will need to pray *immediately* and not have to take time to do a heart cleaning. Look on sin as God does; He won't tolerate it.

Additional Treasures:     Job 5:17     Deuteronomy 8:5

# October 25

"Understanding is a wellspring of life
unto him that hath it."
Proverbs 16:22

Understanding means *to get the meaning of.* That is a common saying when parents instruct their children. Do you understand what I'm telling you; *do you get the meaning of it?* It is important that children fully understand what their parents are teaching them, and it is very important that we understand what God would have us know from His Word. It will be a wellspring or *continual source* of blessing.

**When I was old enough, my parents would leave my little brothers in my care while they went to town on Saturday to get supplies for the farm and household. Back then it was not a quick trip, and people did not *run to town* to shop. So for most of the day I took care of the children and I knew just what I could and could not do in the line of discipline. Daddy would tell me each time, and then say "Now do you understand?" He meant, *did I get the meaning of his instructions.* If I went beyond that, which rarely happened, I was corrected for disobeying. If the boys didn't mind me according to my dad's word, he corrected them later without fail. Our warning phrase to each other during those days in our childhood was often *"Didn't you understand what Daddy said?"***

The prophet Jeremiah pronounced God's indictment against His people and their sad lack of understanding about God and His Word. They were smart in worldly ways, but ignorant in the things that matter.

"For my people is foolish, they have not known me; they are sottish children, and they have none understanding: they are wise to do evil, but to do good they have no knowledge." Jeremiah 4:22

*Sottish children* were stupid and foolish, drunken. God's people may not be *sottish* from drinking, yet be rendered powerless by the influence of the world and all the pleasures in it to enjoy. As they get wiser to do evil, the knowledge they have of the ways of the Lord decreases.

Keep your wellspring overflowing by the understanding that comes from God's Word. That's where we learn the things that matter. Read it often.

Additional Treasures:     I Corinthians 3:19     Proverbs 15:14

# October 26

**"They that are after the flesh do mind the things of the flesh;**
**but they that are after the Spirit the things of the Spirit."**
**Romans 8:5**

The Lord tells us that we will inevitably reveal what kind of Christians we really are. We will *mind the store.* The things stored up in our hearts will come to light as we give priority to them.

Many times when visiting, I could tell at a glance at the books laying around in the house what kind of storehouse the person was keeping. *Lewdness* stored in the heart slips out in one form or another. Some are so desensitized to indecency; they don't realize that the television programs they watch are not fit for good moral people, much less Christians.

The desire for pleasure and recreation is obvious in the things people surround themselves with in order to enjoy as much as they can in the time they have to do it!

Those who keep a large store for the flesh will always be occupied with it because the flesh will never be satisfied. And there are consequences.

"For if ye live after the flesh, ye shall die: but if ye through the Spirit do mortify the deeds of the body, ye shall live." Romans 8:13

Likewise, the things of the Spirit of God stored in a Christian's heart are obvious because they cannot be hidden.

**There was an immediate change in my husband when he was saved one cold December day many decades ago. From the first, the things of the Lord filled up his heart and whatever else was stored there before was displaced. The most startling change I could see was his interest in reading the Bible. He didn't have much interest in reading before, but overnight he began reading the Bible and couldn't get enough of it! That amazed me. But to him, he was finding out about this wonderful Savior who had made a new person out of Him. He has been storing the Word ever since and preaching it for decades.**

There will be a change when a person becomes a Christian. Reflect on *your* salvation experience. What changes came into your life?

Additional Treasures:    Matthew 16:24    Galatians 5:24

# October 27

**"The Lord, The God of hosts, is his name."**
**Amos 4:13**

The prophet Amos had the calling of God to warn Israel again of the judgment of God. Others before him had faithfully cried out against the nation's sinful and idolatrous ways, but the people had remained hard hearted and stiff necked in rebellion against the Word of God.

Amos was a prophet, *preacher,* with a unique burden. His name itself meant *burden-bearer.* His burden was to convince the people to return to God, and if not, they had better get ready to die!

"Therefore thus will I do unto thee, O Israel: and because I will do this unto thee, prepare to meet thy God, O Israel." Amos 4:12

In their boldness to forsake the ways of God, the people seemed to forget that the Lord God, who brought them out of Egypt into the land of Canaan, also *knew* their thoughts as they began slipping into idol worship. You would think that the people of Israel could never in a million years forget what God had done for them...but they did! It was their association with the people who worshipped idols which got them. Perhaps they assumed that as they were satisfying their curiosity about heathen worship and went to just "observe" at times, that they would not be affected. It never, *never* works that way. As soon as you step into the devil's territory, willingly, you have lost the battle to stand strong in the Lord. Sin weakens us.

**When sin is just a teasing thought in our minds, God *knows it.***

**Let us remember that sin has consequences *every time.***

**Meditate on the greatness of the Lord and His power.**

**Keep thanksgiving and praise fresh in your heart.**

**Tell someone *who does not know* that you are a Christian!**

Additional Treasures:   Job 37:23   Psalm 8:1

# October 28

**"Thou wilt keep him in perfect peace, whose mind is
stayed on thee: because he trusteth in thee."**
**Isaiah 26:3**

Christians are troubled in our world today. The evil that prevails in
every facet of our society is a constant irritant to the righteous. They are
like Lot, Abraham's nephew in Sodom, *vexed* with the conduct and talk
of the wicked.

"And delivered just Lot, vexed with the filthy conversation of the
wicked..." II Peter 2:7

If God did not have His protection operating in our lives continually,
we would be too debilitated to function at all for His honor and glory. He
is the One who gives us strength for each day, and an invisible protection
in which we can have confidence as we trust Him in all things.

Safety in apparent danger. – **A lady was awakened one morning by
a strange sound of pecking at the window; and when she got up she
saw a butterfly flying backwards and forwards inside the window, in
a great fright, because outside there was a sparrow pecking the glass,
wanting to reach the butterfly. The butterfly did not see the glass,
but it saw the sparrow, and evidently expected every moment to be
caught. Neither did the sparrow see the glass, though it saw the
butterfly, and made sure of catching it. Yet all the time, the butterfly
because of that thin, invisible sheet of glass, was actually as safe as if
it had been miles away from the sparrow.** - James Inglis

If we don't keep our focus on the Lord, we will be as afraid as the
butterfly terrified by the sparrow pecking away at the invisible barrier
between them. We are *in Christ*, and we should not be afraid even though
we hear the *roar of the lion.*

"Be sober, be vigilant; because your adversary the devil, as a roaring
lion, walketh about, seeking whom he may devour: Whom resist stedfast
in the faith, knowing that the same afflictions are accomplished in your
brethren that are in the world." I Peter 5:8-9

We are much like the little butterfly when it comes to the 'roar of
the lion'. He can't hurt us at all but he *sounds* like it! He frightens and
that is his ploy. We will run though there is an invisible shield between
us: the blood of our Savior. Remember how safe you are when
temptation comes. Stand firm.

Additional Treasures:     Ephesians 6:12     James 4:7

# October 29

Blessed are the children who are taught the Word of God while they
are in the tender years. That time span is getting shorter for our children
in this generation, because they are subject to the exposure of wickedness
in all forms in our society. Children, at a younger age than ever before,
know about sinful practices in our decadent world.

But children have greater faith than adults; they simply believe what
they are told about God! The Lord implied that when He told the people
that day the condition for entering into heaven: *have faith as a little child.*

Children have a unique way of expression and sometimes amaze us
by their understanding of things and their simple explanations.

**The soul. – A little girl, about seven years of age, was taken with
a brother younger than herself, to see an aunt who lay dead. On
their return home, the little boy expressed his surprise that he had
seen his aunt, saying, "I always thought that when people died they
went to heaven; but my aunt is not gone there, for I have seen her!"
"Brother," replied his sister, "You do not understand it; it is not the
body that goes to heaven! It is the *think* that goes to heaven! The
body is put into the grave, where it stays till God shall raise it up
again. The body returns to dust as it was, and the spirit to God, who
gave it."—Com.**

Timothy was a great man of God due to the influence of the apostle
Paul in his life, but the seed of the scriptures was sown in his heart by a
godly grandmother and his mother.

"And that from a child thou hast known the holy scriptures, which
are able to make thee wise unto salvation...."     II Timothy 3:15

The first verse I heard that made an impression was quoted to me
by a young teenage friend, my age, very studious, who had started
reading the Bible straight through when she was twelve years old! She
had gotten a new one, and that was her goal. She got as far as Hebrews in
about three years, and told me the definition of faith. Neither of us
understood what Hebrews 11:1 meant, but that verse made an impression
that stayed with me. God's Word has power to do that: make a lasting
impression. Share it today.

Additional Treasures:     II Timothy 1:5     Ecclesiastes 12:1

# October 30

**"For whosoever shall call upon the name of the
Lord, shall be saved.
Romans 10:13**

Too often we get involved with other things and forget what the Christian life is all about. We are the body of Christ on earth, doing the work of Jesus the Head. "And hath put all things under his feet, and gave him to be the head over all things to the church, Which is his body, the fulness of him that filleth all in all." Ephesians 1:22-23

We should witness for the Lord and reach out to lost people because that is why Jesus came to die on the Cross of Calvary. He came to save lost sinners, and the whole world was His mission field. He *tasted death for every man!*
"But we see Jesus, who was made a little lower than the angels for the suffering of death, crowned with glory and honour; that he by the grace of God should taste death for every man." Hebrews 2:9

Everyone on earth *can be saved,* if they hear about the facts and will trust Christ personally for salvation. Many on earth have *never* heard of that good news, the gospel. That is the reason for a Church's outreach through the Missions ministry.

Another main reason for being a personal witness for the Lord is the matter of God's will. We cannot be *in His will* and ignore lost souls.

"The Lord is not slack concerning his promise, as some men count slackness; but is longsuffering to us-ward, not willing that any should perish, but that all should come to repentance." II Peter 3:9
I use this verse when I'm praying for lost souls on my list. Since the Lord is not willing that any should perish, it is His will for whoever I'm praying for to be saved! It gives me confidence in prayer when I have such a promise. And we know it pleases God for us to claim His Word: to pray it, to believe it, to quote it often and just feed our hearts on it every day. It is the health of your heart and soul. Nothing is as vital to us as the Word of God.

Additional Treasures:    Romans 10:14-15    Colossians 1:10

# October 31

**"He shall feed his flock like a shepherd: he shall gather the lambs with his arm, and carry them in his bosom..."**
**Isaiah 40:11**

No one is so tender and loving as our Lord is to us. And that is the way we are supposed to treat each other, because He is our example in all things. He showed us by numerous examples while He lived on earth.

"For I have given you an example, that ye should do as I have done to you." John 13:15

In this example Jesus had washed the disciples' feet, *every one of them*. The Lord was showing them how to be humble in attitude and serve each other in humility. He said in essence, "if I can do it, being your Lord and Master, you can do it being the servants of God."

How sobering it must have been for the disciples to submit to His washing of their feet, for Jesus had commanded it. Impulsive, bold Peter protested but the Lord rebuked him.

"...If I wash thee not, thou hast no part with me. Simon Peter saith unto him, Lord, not my feet only, but also my hands and my head." John 13:8-9

Peter was dull in understanding just like so many of us are today. The Lord was talking about *serving with humility, not taking a bath!* He gave us an example of how we are to minister to one another in love, to strengthen and encourage as we walk through life in this sinful world. We should display tender concern for others as a Shepherd does for his sheep.

**A little Chinese boy who wished to join the church gave this touching answer to those who thought him too young: "Jesus has promised to carry the lambs in His arms. I am only a little boy. It will be easier for Jesus to carry me."** – *Selected.*

There is a well-known picture of Jesus carrying a little lamb in his arms while the mother walks by his side with the other sheep. He said His children are like sheep and that tells us how dearly Jesus loves us and looks after us. Sheep are incredibly dumb animals, and cannot live without someone tending them constantly. Thank God for His love and protection of His sheep.

Additional Treasures:   Hebrews 13:20   John 10:11

# November 1

"Let every thing that hath breath praise the Lord.
Praise ye the Lord."
Psalm 150:6

We are entering into the month that holds Thanksgiving, the main holiday of the fall season. It is the most sensible, productive holiday because it reminds people to be thankful to God and that produces joy in the heart.

The world minimizes the theme of being thankful to God, but there are many that still celebrate with that thought in mind and are blessed by it. It is not the decorations and feast on Thanksgiving Day which praises the Lord. It is people whose hearts are thankful, who use the precious breath that God has given to them to praise Him.

Praise for God is so appropriate, and the lack of it so appalling. The Word from heaven is plain:

"Let everything that hath breath praise the Lord."

**All of God's creation praises Him, but our ears do not hear it. We can hear the birds sing and may entertain the foolish notion that because God allows us to *hear* it, they sing for us! However, the praise of everything that has breath, *except humans,* is directed back to the Creator. Man praises God least of all in creation, yet he is the one who is made in the *image of God!***

Perhaps the rocks long to cry out as people go rushing through life enjoying God's gracious mercies without a word of praise and thanksgiving. Jesus said the rocks *would,* if they were allowed to, as He entered into Jerusalem. The Pharisees had objected to the multitude praising the Lord, asking Jesus to stop them. The Lord replied, "I tell you that, if these should hold their peace, the stones would immediately cry out." Luke 19:40

We who have life, *breath,* should praise the Lord and be thankful to Him. Make this month a time of genuine thanksgiving in your life.

Additional Treasures:     Hebrews 13:15     Psalm 9:11

# November 2

**"For the Lord is a sun and shield: The Lord will give grace and glory: No good thing will he withhold from them that walk uprightly."    Psalm 84:11**

The sun beams its glorious light and warmth down every day, but the earth still remains a place of *spiritual darkness.* The natural light, the sun, cannot dispel such darkness generated by sin; only the Son *from* heaven can do that. He sheds His light abroad into every soul who trusts in Him as his personal Savior. Salvation is not a generalized thing; it is a *personalized* gift to anyone who believes on the Lord Jesus Christ. When a person receives the gift of salvation, he comes out of that *spiritual darkness* into the light of the Lord.

"For ye were sometimes darkness, but now are ye light in the Lord: walk as children of light..." Ephesians 5:8

The Lord is not only a sun, *light,* for us but a *shield* to secure and protect us in this world of darkness and danger. He is our *present help* in time of trouble.

"God is our refuge and strength; a very present help in trouble." Psalm 46:1

The latter part of our text verse lets us know how generous and kind our Lord is to His children who live in obedience to His Word.

**"This is a comprehensive promise and is such an assurance of the present comfort of the saints that, whatever they desire and think they need, they may be sure that either Infinite Wisdom sees it is not good for them or Infinite Goodness will give it to them in due time."-** M.Henry

All of us, at one time or another have fervently prayed for a *good thing* to come about. We just *knew*, at the time, that it was God's will for our lives and we felt like the Lord let us down. But later, looking back on the matter, we were so grateful that the Lord refused us the request.

When I look back through the years at what the Lord withheld from us at times as we earnestly prayed, I can only thank Him from my heart full of gratitude. We would have messed up our future for sure if, in the past, God had just given us what we wanted because we kept asking Him so much. He blessed us so much by simply refusing to indulge us like spoiled children.

Additional Treasures:    Philippians 2:15    Psalm 37:3

# November 3

**"...but God is faithful, who will not suffer you to be tempted
above that ye are able; but will with the temptation also make
a way of escape, that ye may be able to bear it."
I Corinthians 10:13**

Sometimes, little parts of a verse may be adopted as Biblical truth even though it is *twisted and turned* to fit. We must be careful to check out what the Bible says, *before* we tell someone it says a certain thing.

The phrase, "God will not put on us more than we can bear," is often quoted to those going through a burdensome trial, as though God piles on the trouble to the breaking point, then stops just short of the Christian's total collapse under the load.

The saying comes from this verse, and *this verse is talking about temptation.* Temptation is the *enticement to sin.* When we are tempted to be disobedient to the Lord, He makes it possible for us to withstand the temptation and escape from it. In that way, *we are able to bear it,* or endure it without sinning against the Lord.

**The Word of God is a mighty help to turn one from temptation.**
**Fervent prayer is the most powerful defense in the battle.**
**Arrow prayers (*help Lord!*) shot up to heaven helps one to escape. *An encouraging word* from a friend may be just the help needed. Sunday's sermon may be the very message for a wavering soul.**

God will not allow us to be *overwhelmed* by temptation, because He will always make a way for us to come out of it, *escape,* as the Bible says. Our part is to keep the right attitude, remembering what the Lord will do.

"Submit yourselves therefore to God. Resist the devil, and he will flee from you. Draw nigh to God, and he will draw nigh to you...."
James 4:7-8

The key to victory is in the 'submit yourselves therefore to God' because with that the devil is definitely resisted by the child of God. You simply run to God's side get safely behind Him. The devil can do nothing with that so he flees the scene. Never leave off the first part if you quote the verse. You not only leave the 'icing' off the cake, you leave the sugar out of the batter!

Additional Treasures:     Hebrews 2:18     II Chronicles 16:9

# November 4

"The highway of the upright is to depart from evil:
he that keepeth his way preserveth his soul."
Proverbs 16:17

The highway or path of life that we travel each day should be the *highway of the upright.* That way leads us straight into the ways of righteousness, and always *away from evil.* When Christians wander off the highway they suffer dire consequences. There is much to be gained by staying on the right road; the soul is preserved!

Here is the way of traveling the highway of the upright:

"Let thine eyes look right on, and let thine eyelids look straight before thee." "Ponder the path of thy feet, and let all thy ways be established." "Turn not to the right hand nor to the left: remove thy foot from evil." Prov. 4: 25-27

**Many drivers have had auto accidents because they didn't keep their eyes on the road. You can't travel down the highway and gaze around at the scenery while you're steering a machine that's moving like a bullet on wheels! Likewise, the Christian must keep his eyes on the road as he travels the *highway of the upright.* There can be a wreck in his life if he is not careful to keep looking straight ahead.**

He must ponder the path of his feet, or think about where he is going. One must be serious about the destination and have a goal toward it. He can *remove his foot from evil* by staying on the road. All around us lays the world with its pitfalls and temptations. *Stay on the road!*

Where does the highway in your life take you each day? For some the briefest stop of the day is the *devotional* time. It is similar to the rest stop while traveling by automobile. The stop is a necessary nuisance, and is done hurriedly so that those traveling can get back on the road and rush on! Don't be deceived. The most important part of your day will be the rest stop with the Lord. Take time out to sit at the Lord's feet and let your heart listen to His Word. We can't estimate the value of time spent with the Lord each day. Just know that His presence gives us strength and joy in our souls. Keep your heart set on Him and rejoice in the privilege of personal time with your Savior.

Additional Treasures:     Proverbs 4:18-19     Ephesians 5:15

# November 5

**"Walk in wisdom toward them that are without, redeeming the time."**
**Colossians 4:5**

The definition of wisdom is knowledge and good judgment based on experience; *being wise.* That means simply: *the right use of knowledge.*

The Bible exhorts Christians to use wisdom in their daily living: *their walk.* Those without Christ are watching, and they need to see something that will cause them to consider Him. It is important; life is uncertain for all and we are to *redeem the time,* or use it wisely while we have time to do so.

Many die without Christ because they put off the matter of salvation, thinking they have plenty of time. Christians are often careless with time and waste it, instead of *redeeming* it as the Lord instructs them to do in His Word.

What is the solemn truth about those who are without Christ, which should cause us to walk carefully and faithfully with the Lord?

**They will be lost forever unless they believe on Christ the Lord.**

"He that believeth on the Son hath everlasting life: and he that believeth not the Son shall not see life..." John 3:36

**Those without Christ do not understand the Bible.**

"But the natural man receiveth not the things of the Spirit of God: for they are foolishness unto him: neither can he know them, because they are spiritually discerned." I Corinthians 2:14

**The unsaved view Christians with a critical attitude.**

"Having your conversation honest among the Gentiles: that, whereas they speak against you as evil doers, they may by your good works, which they shall behold, glorify God in the day of visitation." I Peter 2:12

*You* **may be the only Bible some will** *read.* **What are they reading? They will understand what they** *see* **you do, and** *hear* **you say. Don't give anyone cause to stumble over your testimony!**

Have you ever considered that you may be the only Christian that somebody knows? That may sound strange but the people of God are fast becoming less visible and, to the world, totally irrelevant. Think of that when you step out to face the world each day. *Somebody is reading me...* what kind of message are they getting from my life?

Additional Treasures:   Matthew 5:16   Titus 2:12

# November 6

**"God hath spoken once; twice have I heard this;**
**that power belongeth unto God."**
**Psalm 62:11**

We are so accustomed to the view of the universe through the little window from our planet and the other wonders of creation about us, we fail to consider that the awesome power of God made it all and *sustains* it. Some day when He is through with it, He will fold it all up and put it away.

"And, Thou, Lord, in the beginning hast laid the foundation of the earth; and the heavens are the works of thine hands: They shall perish; but thou remainest; and they all shall wax old as doth a garment; And as a vesture shalt thou fold them up, and they shall be changed: but thou art the same, and thy years shall not fail." Hebrews 1:10-12

**We should meditate on the power of God to enlarge our feeble view of Him and His ability to take care of us. Just as a little child will jump right off a high object into his father's arms, we should trust our Heavenly Father without hesitation. It's a shame to pray and then fret. We *can* trust the Lord.**

Years ago, a Captain commanded a ship sailing from England to New York on a voyage where he had all his family on board. One night, when all were asleep, there arose a sudden squall, which came sweeping over the waters until it struck the vessel, and threw her almost on her side, tumbling and crashing everything that was movable, and awaking the passengers to a consciousness of imminent danger.

Everyone on board was alarmed; and some sprang from their berths and began to dress. The Captain's little girl on board, just eight years old, was awakened with the rest. "What's the matter?" cried the frightened child. They told her a squall had struck the ship. "Is father on deck?" She asked. Yes, father's on deck."

The little thing dropped herself on her pillow again and was soon fast asleep, in spite of winds or waves.

Child of God, shame to your doubts and fears--is not your Father on deck? Remember this when the next squall strikes your life. "I will never leave thee, nor forsake thee." --Wells of Living Water. Vol. IX.

Additional Treasures:   Hebrews 1:1-3    Nahum 1:3, 7

# November 7

**"I am the door: by me if any man enter in, he shall be saved, and shall go in and out, and find pasture."**
**John 10:9**

The dictionary defines a pasture as *any area that serves as a source of food for something.* We know that after the Lord takes us in, He provides all that we need in this life. He *is the door* to eternal life. Going through that door means salvation for the soul. After that, we find that there is *pasture* for us: *rest, food and water.*

**For those of us brought up on the farm in childhood, the word** *pasture* **has a simple, clear meaning. The pasture had water, food, and rest for weary animals after a day of work. It was the grazing place for the cows to spend the day between the milking at morning and night, replenishing that miraculous supply of milk for their calves and our household.**

Do you remember that the struggle and turmoil in your soul stopped on the day you trusted Christ as your Savior? Peace settled in your heart, and that sweet *rest* came into your being. That's the first thing the Lord has for those who trust in Him. *Rest.* They cease from their own works and efforts, and put their faith in the One who died for them.

"Not by works of righteousness which we have done, but according to his mercy he saved us, by the washing of regeneration, and renewing of the Holy Ghost." Titus 3:5

After going through the Door there is a never-ending supply of fresh food *in God's pasture* from His Word, because with the Holy Spirit living in him the Christian can understand it. It is food for the soul. The scriptures are also a well of fresh *water* where the thirst is quenched day by day. *All this in God's pasture!*

"The Lord is my shepherd; I shall not want." Psalm 23:1

Additional Treasures:    John 10:11    Hebrews 13:20

# November 8

"Who passing through the valley of Baca make it a well."
Psalm 84:6

Baca means weeping, or is figurative of sorrow. Our way to heaven lies through the valley of Baca. No matter how well we live it, life holds sadness and heartaches for us. *Before* Adam and Eve sinned in the Garden of Eden, there was no sadness and heartache in the earth. Since that first sin, the earth has not had a day without sorrow. *The legacy of sin!*

A well is made by digging a hole deep into the ground until water is reached, which then springs up and fills the well so that men and beasts can drink and live. That is the natural water, which sustains life in the body.

While we are passing through this life, *the valley of Baca,* we must make wells of spiritual water so that we all can quench our thirst. We dig into the Word of God and find the precious promises, which flow out into our lives and sustain us as water to a thirsty soul. We can make a well in the dreary spots on life's road and share our life-giving water with others.

**Many years ago we had a dear elderly saint in our church that regretfully had to take up residence in a nursing home. She was very upset at first, and we wondered how she would eventually adjust.**

**One day when I visited her she seemed unusually happy and soon I knew why. She discovered that many residents were not Christians, and she found for herself a mission field. "Honey, these old people in here need to be born again!" she said. As she passed through her valley of Baca...***she made it a well.***

Our Lord chose to pass through the *valley of Baca* because of His great love for lost humanity. He endured the heartache and afflictions in the earth, died for our sins, and rose from the dead, leaving a well of living water for all that will drink. Praise His holy name!

"For ye know the grace of our Lord Jesus Christ, that, though he was rich, yet for your sakes he became poor, that ye through his poverty might be rich." II Corinthians 8:9

Additional Treasures:    Psalm 92:12-14    Colossians 1:12

# November 9

**"And he said unto Jesus, Lord, remember me
when thou comest into thy kingdom."
Luke 23:42**

In this month of thanksgiving it is good for our hearts to recall the goodness of God poured out into our lives and *express our gratitude.* It is enlightening to search the scriptures too, and see how the Lord was gracious to those around Him during His earthly ministry.

Imagine the joy of blind Bartimaeus, the beggar who was healed by Jesus, when his eyes were opened to see for the first time in his life! Read that remarkable account in tenth chapter of Mark. Mark 10:46-52

The crowd would have stoned to death the woman caught in the act of adultery if Jesus had not stopped it. He later spoke kindly to her and forgave her sin, sending her away in peace. Do you suppose that she ever forgot the Lord's grace and mercy? Read the account. John 8:4-11.

One of my favorite characters, when thinking on causes for being thankful, is the repentant thief who was crucified with the Lord on that day. It is most remarkable that he exercised faith in Jesus, when he probably never saw the Lord before that day, and all he knew about Him was the fact that Jesus was being crucified like a common criminal. Luke 23:39-43

**There was no outward indication of lordship, there were no insignia of royalty. Jesus was a captive, condemned, insulted, crucified; yet does the dying thief salute Him as a King! King? Where are His royal robes? They have torn from Him even His ordinary dress! King? Where is His throne? That cross of shame on which He hangs!**

**Yet poor, vanquished, insulted, murdered, the dying thief has faith to *recognize Him as a king,* and able to confer royal gifts!**
        —Parker

The thief went from the tortures of the cross he died upon, to the glory of paradise with the Lord. We cannot imagine his praise and thanksgiving!

In His indescribable agony in dying Jesus saved a lost sinner. The thief who trusted the Son of God that day will live forever in eternity with Him. Can we imagine the joy and continual wonder of that man? He chose Jesus.

Additional Treasures:    Revelation 19:5    Psalm 35:28

# November 10

**"Wherefore let him that thinketh he standeth
take heed lest he fall."
I Corinthians 10:12**

Christians will hardly admit to backsliding. In fact, they may be far into it before they are aware themselves that things are not right between them and the Lord. It has a lot to do with the generation we live in today.

The world has succeeded in influencing the church far more than the church has affected the world for Christ. The world has labeled sin for our society as *acceptable,* and Christians for the most part, do not check it out with the Word of God. That kind of neglect allows a kind of *rot* to set in, and we have seen many people of God fall to the world that we thought were strong enough to stand against the wiles of the devil.

The process of backsliding.—**Some time ago, two ministers were walking along the banks of a river, when they came to a tree which had been blown down in a recent gale. It was a mighty, noble tree, tall and substantial, with large outspreading roots and ample foliage. It must have been the growth of the greater part of a century, and anyone who had seen it would have said there was no cause why it should not have stood a century longer.**
**Approaching to examine it, they found it had been snapped off just above the roots; and, on looking still closer, found that there was only an outer shell of sound wood, and that the heart was rotten. Unnoticed, the decay had been going on for years.** –Bowes, Gray and Adams.

The mighty tree would not have fallen in the storm without the rot that had eaten away its strength. So we must put away sin from us, and keep our hearts with all diligence because our hearts rule our lives. If one allows any little sin to stay, which makes a gray shadow on the conscience, he can grow accustomed to it and the rot sets in. We must keep our hearts sensitive and attentive to the Word of God.

"Draw nigh to God, and he will draw nigh to you. Cleanse your hands, ye sinners; and purify your hearts, ye double minded." James 4:8

Additional Treasures:     Proverbs 28:13     Proverbs 4:23

# November 11

**"I am the good shepherd, and know my**
**sheep, and am known of mine."**
**John 10:14**

The analogies the Lord used to make His listeners understand His meaning had to do with what was familiar to them. They *understood* about sheep and shepherds since that was the most common way of life in the region. The Lord says that those who are saved are His sheep.

"Know ye that the Lord he is God: it is he that hath made us, and not we ourselves; we are his people, and the sheep of his pasture."
Psalm 100:3

Jesus said that He *knows his sheep*...every one of them by name, and His sheep *know Him*. They will respond to His voice. By that we are to understand that according to the Bible there is a difference between those who do not believe on Christ, and those who do. Look at who is following after the Shepherd, and those who refuse to follow! Consider the difference.

The Good Shepherd.—**How beautifully the care and compassion of our Savior is illustrated by the conduct of an eastern shepherd. One of my friends traveling in the east, some years ago, met three shepherds with their flocks: each with a large flock of sheep. These three flocks were put together. Each sheep had a separate name; it would not answer to any other name, *or even to its own*, unless called by its own shepherd. Each shepherd knew all his sheep, and also their names. If he saw that one was going in a dangerous direction, he called it back, and it retraced its steps. If the way was narrow or steep, he walked first, and the sheep followed. It is exactly what the Bible says of Christ and His flock: "The sheep hear His voice: and He calleth His own sheep by name; He goeth before them, and the sheep follow Him: for they know His voice. And a stranger will they not follow, but will flee from him: for they know not the voice of strangers." Com.**

How thankful we should be that the Lord gave such a beautiful analogy of His love and care of us. We should add that to our thanksgiving list, and rejoice in the fact that *He knows us, and we know Him!*

Additional Treasures:     Hebrews 13:20     Isaiah 40:11

# November 12

**"Whereby are given unto us exceeding great and precious promises: that by these ye might be partakers of the divine nature..."**
**II Peter 1:4**

Christians are rich beyond description because they possess the sure promises of Almighty God. He tells us in His Word that they are *great and precious.* How happy we would all be if we could fathom their worth, and use them as a wonderful investment to insure peace and well-being in our lives. They are far greater than the precious jewels of rich people in the world.

**The Wonderful Jewels.** —A lady who had lost all her health was reclining on her bed, longing for the society and pleasure that she once enjoyed. She told her sick-nurse to fetch the box that held her jewels, so that she might amuse herself in recalling to her memory the festive seasons when she had worn them to the admiration of so many.

"Now, nurse," said she, "would you not like to have some of these jewels?" "No, ma'am, not at all, for I have jewels much finer."

"Where are yours? You never wear them."

The nurse held up her Bible, saying, "My jewels are in here!"

The lady, thinking that there was some hidden away in the book, said, "Take them out and show them to me."

"Why, ma'am, my jewels are so precious, I can only show you one at a time." Then she opened her Bible and read---"*I have learned, in whatsoever state I am, therewith to be content."* (Phil. 4:11) She told her of the treasure that she had in Heaven; how that, though poor, she had a loving Father, who provided for her, and the great happiness that she had in Him. "Why, nurse, I never heard anything like that; how happy you must be to feel as you do! I wish I could do the same.

The next day, the lady said, "Nurse, I should like to see another of your jewels; the one you showed me was so beautiful."

The nurse again opened her Bible, and read---"*This is a faithful saying, and worthy of all acceptation that Christ Jesus came into the world to save sinners."* (I Tim. 1:15) From the few words that followed, the lady's heart was opened to feel that she was a sinner, and she soon found rest, peace, and joy in believing and trusting Christ Jesus as her Saviour.—Wells of Living Water. Vol. VIII.

If we, who hold such treasures as the promises of God in His Word, were as thoroughly convinced of their value as the nurse was, we might be able to win others to Christ. If God says that they are *precious,* count it so! Be thankful for the precious promises. Store them in your heart.

Additional Treasures:   I Kings 8:56   Romans 4:21

# November 13

*"...for I have learned, in whatsoever state
I am, therewith to be content."*
**Philippians 4:11**

The apostle Paul, in the context of this chapter, speaks about his needs being provided by Christians and his joy in their liberality of giving, knowing how they would be blessed of the Lord. He gives them a general exhortation to always rejoice in the Lord, *be thankful,* because God would always supply their needs.

In whatever circumstance we find ourselves, we are planted there to fulfil God's will and purpose in our lives. If a situation seems hopeless and you can't see past the difficulty, ask God what to do.

**When the renowned scientist, George Washington Carver, was doing research on the peanut plant he came to an end of himself. One night he took a walk under the stars and looking up into the heavens said "God, why did you make the peanut?" It is said that he came back to his lab with renewed energy and purpose. In time, he discovered more than 300 uses for the peanut plant and its fruit!**

BLOOM WHERE YOU ARE PLANTED

The place may be a desert, the middle of a swamp or marsh,
Or a wide, scraggly prairie where breath is stifled by dust.
Life is a unique garden: briars and thorns among delicate things.
It molds us character and patience,
As we are torn, stuck, and soothed again.

Are you planted in a desert place, or wading a murky swamp?
Perhaps you're struggling for fresh air In the plot holding you just now.
Look up out of the tangled growth,
To One who adds fragrance and hue.
Open your heart; let petals unfold.
In the place where you're planted...bloom.

Edna Holmes

Additional Treasures:     Isaiah 58:11     Hebrews 13:5

# November 14

**"And said, O my God, I am ashamed and blush
to lift my face to thee, my God..."**
**Ezra 9:6**

For young girls in my generation, to blush was not an uncommon thing. It had to do with old-fashioned modesty and propriety of girls in that era. Unfortunately, such things are ridiculed now and few experience an old fashioned *blush*. A 'blush' is defined as a reddening of the skin caused by shame, confusion, or excitement.

The prophet, Ezra, tells us why he was blushing. He had been agonizing over the sins of the people and praying for the nation Israel.

"And in the evening sacrifice I arose up from my heaviness; and having rent my garment and my mantle, I fell upon my knees, and spread out my hands unto the Lord my God, And said, O my God, I am ashamed and blush to lift my face to thee, my God: for our iniquities are increased over our head, and our trespass is grown up unto the heavens."
Ezra 9:5-6

Ezra was describing their sins as being piled in a heap as high as the sky. He was ashamed before his God who had brought them out of Egypt, and given Israel the good land of Canaan. They forgot God and turned to idols. In time, they lost their freedom and were taken into captivity as slaves just as they had been centuries ago in Egypt. They *should* blush.

Do we blush over our sin? If we could see ourselves as God sees us, we may as the psalmist pray: "So foolish was I, and ignorant: I was as a beast before thee." Psalm 73:22

The definition of beast is 'any animal as distinguished from a human being.' The difference is humans are made in the image of God, with a soul that will live forever. Animals have only their earthly existence, and they die and go back to the dust. The beasts live by instinct only; they are not conscious of God as humans are. When a man is 'as a beast before God' he lives as though God is not in the picture. He is indifferent to spiritual matters and he lives a carnal life. The beasts are not aware of the wonders of God's creation. They never look up. Their interest is only in the earth to satisfy their animal instincts. May we gaze with wonder at our God, and cherish His Word which is a treasure beyond compare.

Additional Treasures:     Psalm 44:15     Romans 6:12-14

# November 15

**"And no marvel; for Satan himself is
transformed into an angel of light."
II Corinthians 11:14**

If we could see the devil and his frightful appearance, we would not be tempted by him. It would be very easy to refuse his coaxing us to sin, for we would flee his presence immediately! But that is not the way it is in reality. Satan can make himself *and sin* look very attractive. If a Christian is not armed with the Word of God and the discernment it gives, he can be deceived.

**Once when we were visiting friends in Oklahoma, they took us upon a mountain where a brother was the overseer of the area. Wild boars roamed freely, and this man had a boar's head trophy on the wall from one of these animals. It was huge, with two long tusks protruding from its mouth: an absolutely *fearsome* beast! If I'd lived there, I would *never* have gone out at night on that mountain. Just a look at the boar's head convinced me of the danger.**

The devil *knows* that if humans could see him as a wicked being, they would not follow him. So he disguises himself and takes on the appearance of beauty and pleasantness. How many times have we heard people say that they were deceived because something they desired to do seemed so right and good at the time? Soon, they were suffering the consequences of sin.

The Holy Spirit is our warning system, if we are listening to Him. He uses the blessed Word of God foremost, but He also uses other things to warn us of sin's trap. Other Christians may say the words the Holy Spirit wants us to hear. A sermon or a song with a great message all may be used to warn us about sin. We must *pay attention* and be sensitive to Christ in us, the blessed Holy Spirit. He knows what the devil is up to all the time. Listen to Him!

"Howbeit when he, the Spirit of truth, is come, he will guide you into all truth: for he shall not speak of himself: but whatsoever he shall hear, that shall he speak: and he will shew you things to come." John 16:13

"And thine ears shall hear a word behind thee, saying, This is the way, walk ye in it, when ye turn to the right hand, and when ye turn to the left." Isaiah 30:21

Additional Treasures:     Psalm 73:24     Romans 8:26-27

# November 16

**"And I give unto them eternal life; and they shall never perish, neither shall any man pluck them out of my hand."**
**John 10:28**

Jesus paid the penalty of our sins; that is why He could freely give us the gift of eternal life when we trusted in Him. It has been said that *God's grace is free...at His expense.* God gave Jesus, His only begotten Son, to be the Savior of the world. How He could love sinful humanity so much is beyond our understanding. But all that believe it can be saved.

**Nothing on earth that we can experience can adequately impart to our minds what it means to be secure in Jesus Christ. The soul is as safe in Him as if it were already settled in heaven.**

Salvation.—I read of some Russians crossing wide plains studded over here and there with forests. The wolves were out, the horses were rushing forward madly, the travelers could hear the baying; and though the horses tore along with all speed, yet the wolves were fast behind and they only escaped as we say, "by the skin of their teeth," managing just to get inside a hut that stood by the road, and to shut the door. Then they could hear the wolves leap on the roof; they could hear them dash against the sides of the hut; they could hear them gnawing at the door, and howling, and making all sorts of dismal noises; but the travelers were safe, because they had entered in by the door, and the door was now shut.

Now, when a man is in Christ, he can hear, as it were, the devils howling like wolves, all fierce and hungry for him; and his own sins, like wolves, are seeking to drag him down to destruction. But he has got into Christ, and that is such a shelter that all the devils in the world, if they were to come at once, could not disturb a single beam of that eternal refuge: it must stand fast, though the earth and heaven should pass away. --Spurgeon

"For I am persuaded, that neither death, nor life, nor angels, nor principalities, nor power, nor things present, nor things to come, nor height, nor depth, nor any other creature, shall be able to separate us from the love of God, which is in Christ Jesus our Lord." Romans 8:38-39

**We have cause for rejoicing, thanking God for our eternal salvation!**

Additional Treasures:     Romans 8:34     Psalm 46:1

# November 17

**"The law of the Lord is perfect, converting the soul:**
**the testimony of the Lord is sure, making wise the simple."**
**Psalm 19:7**

The Word of God has no equal. No writings on earth can effect a permanent change in a man, except the Bible. God's Word is the sword, which cuts through to the *inside first*, straight to the heart, and then works the effects of its power to the outside where others may see it in the life.

It is evident that God's Word is pure and holy. Those who believe it usually stand out, clearly visible in society for they are the pure and holy on earth. They are not *always* perfect, but what God has planted in the heart makes them *desire* to be. That's what the Word of God will do.

Those who do not believe the Bible and want nothing to do with it are also visible in society. They are the ungodly.

**Long ago a black prince, Naimbana, arrived in England. The gentleman to whose care he was entrusted took great pains to convince him that the Bible was the Word of God. He received it with great reverence and simplicity. When asked what it was that convinced him on this subject, he replied: "When I found all good men minding the Bible, and calling it the Word of God, and all bad men disregarding it, I then was sure that the Bible must be what good men call it, the Word of God."** Gray and Adams--

Many people use the Bible for a showpiece, but have no intention of making it the rule of their lives. They hold it in their hands for various reasons: to get married, to repeat an oath in court, to write down family records to keep, to carry to church because it looks pious, *but the Word of God is blocked from becoming the priority.* That makes all the difference in the Christian's life. Those who are most content in this world are those who have allowed God's Word to control the way they live.

"I have refrained my feet from every evil way, that I might keep thy word...for thou hast taught me."     Psalm 119:101-102

Additional Treasures:     Psalm 119:165     Mark 13:31

# November 18

"And let fall also some of the handfuls of purpose for her,
and leave them, that she may glean them..."
Ruth 2:16

Boaz, the kind owner of the field where Ruth gleaned behind the reapers to get food for her mother-in-law, was aware of this young widow and her new found faith in the God of Israel. He spoke kindly to her.

"The Lord recompense thy work, and a full reward be given thee of the Lord God of Israel, under whose wings thou art come to trust." *V. 12*

By the end of that conversation, Boaz must have been smitten with love! He told the reapers to leave Ruth *extra* sheaves on purpose, not just a few, but *handfuls* deliberately so that she could easily pick them up. Love will do things like that.

**When my older brother discovered the girl that he later would marry, it caused a lot of amusement for the younger children. First, to see how our brother acted as he walked in a daze totally preoccupied with thoughts of his girl. And then, we had an unexpected treat on the Saturdays when we went to town.**

**This lovely girl worked at a drug store that, in that era, had a large soda fountain where sandwiches and ice cream treats were served. When we were introduced and she discovered *we were connected with the object of her love*, she always fixed our ice-cream sodas with *extra* ice cream: *handfuls on purpose!* At the time, we decided it was pretty neat to be kin to our brother.**

God is constantly blessing the lives of His children, because we are connected with Christ, His Son, and our Savior. He heaps on His favors in numerous ways: *handfuls on purpose.*

"For the Father himself loveth you, because ye have loved me, and have believed that I came out from God." John 16:27

Be thankful for the *handfuls on purpose* blessings God gives to you.

Additional Treasures:    Jeremiah 31:3    I John 3:1

# November 19

**"In my Father's house are many mansions: if it were not so I would have told you. I go to prepare a place for you."**
**John 14:2**

Hardly anyone could describe what Heaven is really like. We cannot imagine it because all of our imagination and knowledge is *earth based*! We know what the scriptures say, and readily accept it as the truth, yet we cannot understand heaven as it is in reality. We know that the saved must be changed in order to get into that place, either in the resurrection or *in the twinkling of an eye* as the Lord takes us up in the rapture.

"In a moment, in the twinkling of an eye, at the last trump: for the trumpet shall sound, and the dead shall be raised incorruptible, and we shall be changed." I Corinthians 15:52

Views of Heaven. —**A man of God once said, "When I was a boy, I thought of heaven as a great shining city, with vast walls and domes and spires and with nobody in it except angels, who were strangers to me. Then my little brother died; and I thought of a great city with walls and domes and spires, and a flock of cold, unknown angels, and one little fellow that I was acquainted with. He was the only one I knew at the time. Then another brother died; and there were two that I knew. Then my acquaintances began to die; and the flock continually grew. But it was not till one of my little children went to God in heaven that I began to think I had got a little of myself in. Then several more children and acquaintances entered that place, and by that time I began to think of the residents of that celestial city. Now I have so many acquaintances there, that it sometimes seems to me that I know more in heaven than I do on earth."**

Commentary

"For we know that, if our earthly house of this tabernacle were dissolved, we have a building of God, a house not made with hands, eternal in the heavens." II Corinthians 5:1

No one has lived in heaven and then come to earth except Jesus. He didn't tell us details about heaven which earthlings would dearly love to hear. That was not His purpose. He came to redeem us from the curse of sin and that is what he accomplished. The only people who will see heaven are those who have been *born* into God's family. Make sure you are born again. Nothing else really matters.

Additional Treasures:     Revelation 7:9     Luke 10:20

# November 20

"And the Lord said, Whereunto then shall I liken this generation: and to what are they like? They are like unto children..."
Luke 7:31-32

When adults are likened to children, it is simply implying that they do not behave in a mature manner. The apostle Paul said in one place: "When I was a child, I spake as a child, I understood as a child, I thought as a child: but when I became a man, I put away childish things." I Corinthians 13:11

Immature people sometimes have leadership roles, and instead of making mature decisions, they make childish judgments. It may happen in a church. Those who are *babes in Christ* are put in the places of responsibility, or those who are not dedicated to God are thrust into a place of leadership. In any case, it is like children playing out their little pretend games. I've heard the phrase in reference to some Christians: *"They are just playing church!"* Imagine the detriment to little children when they do not have spiritually mature Christians to emulate.

**When I was a child, *playing church* was one of the most fun things to do. We would pick a spot in the shade of the house, draw some lines for the benches and pulpit then draw straws to see who got to preach first! We had preaching, singing, Sunday school, testimonies, baptizing, the offering and announcements all in the same service. We repeated things we had heard adults say at church and we also copied the mannerisms of the big people! We preached *hell fire and brimstone messages*, pointed at the sinners, and gave emotional testimonies about things that happened in our lives! That was long before the television era, but I have thought of how delightful it would be to have a video of some of our *church services* in the shade of the house so long ago.**

It is not pleasing to the Lord that we remain as children in spiritual things. He has given us His Word to nourish our souls so that we will 'grow up' and be mature in the things of the Lord. Our faith will grow to be strong if we exercise it. "But grow in grace, and in the knowledge of our Lord and Saviour Jesus Christ." II Peter 3:18

Additional Treasures:    I Corinthians 3:1-2    Ephesians 4:14

# November 21

### "...Sirs, what must I do to be saved?"
### Acts 16:30

The Philippians jailer was greatly troubled by the events of that night in his jail, to come to the place of inquiry: "Sirs, what must I do to be saved?" Evidently he'd not had prisoners like Paul and Silas who sang praises to God at midnight, after their backs were lacerated from the beatings, and they were miserably fastened in stocks in the inner prison. They sang and praised God loudly, because the other prisoners *heard* them. God heard them too and sent a great earthquake to deliver them!

"And at midnight Paul and Silas prayed, and sang praises unto God: and the prisoners heard them. And suddenly there was a great earthquake, so that the foundations of the prison were shaken: and immediately all the doors were opened, and every one's bands were loosed."
Acts 16: 25-26

We know by the following verses that the terrified jailer was about to kill himself, knowing that he would be killed if prisoners escaped. But Paul cried out and stopped him in time.
*v.28*

God gave Paul that utterance to save the jailer's life, for Paul certainly couldn't have seen him outside that inner dungeon. It was totally dark, for the jailer *called for a light* to go into the part where they were. There the jailer asked the best question he would ever utter in his life..."*Sirs, what must I do to be saved?*"

**Once I was asked that question. I was reading the Bible each week to an elderly lady who was terminally ill, and her husband was a crude, cantankerous old fellow who showed his displeasure in various ways because I was reading the Bible aloud. The place was small and he couldn't help but hear unless he went outside. That dear lady loved the reading of the Word so much and it comforted her heart, so I felt that I could put up with him for her sake. One day he came in from the outside and sat down abruptly at the table where I was reading and said, *"What must I do to be saved?"* I was stunned! But, I turned to this very part of the Word and showed him the answer. *"Believe on the Lord Jesus Christ, and thou shalt be saved..."*

Additional Treasures:     Acts 16:31-34     Hebrews 4:12

# November 22

**"A fool uttereth all his mind: but a wise man
keepeth it in till afterwards."
Proverbs 29:11**

It is said that you can tell if a wagon is empty coming down the road; it makes a lot of racket! Now we don't live in the horse-drawn wagon times anymore, but that saying is connected with people who rattle on in talking as *"a fool that uttereth all his mind."* Sometimes in their eagerness to express an opinion, people speak without knowledge of the facts.

"He that answereth a matter before he heareth it, it is folly and shame unto him." Proverbs 18:13

"A fool hath no delight in understanding, but that his heart may discover itself." Proverbs 18:2

There are those who do not *listen* where others are talking; they are thinking of what to say when their turn comes again in the conversation. Or, perhaps they are listening to *all the conversation* in a group, and not to the one with whom they are conversing. Let us be careful to mind what the Lord says in His Word. 'The fool doesn't want to understand what you are trying to convey from your heart; he only wants to tell what is in his own!'

Are we considerate in communicating with others? Sometimes it takes *listening* with kindness and sincerity to others before they will ever listen to us share the Gospel of Christ with them.

The only way to keep our verbal communication pleasing to the Lord and appreciated by those around us is to listen to the Word of God on the subject. It has power to hold us back from making fools of ourselves. "Whoso keepeth his mouth and his tongue keepeth his soul from troubles." Proverbs 21:23

A regular reading of James chapter three will be a good reminder of how to use our tongues, and not abuse the privilege of verbal communication. It is a blessed gift and the Lord tells us in several vivid illustrations in James just how cautious we should be with that little member of our bodies. Everything on earth can be tamed...except the human tongue. Beware, be alert, and never let your tongue rattle on making noise like an empty wagon.

Additional Treasures:　　Proverbs 27:2　　Proverbs 29:20

# November 23

**"Against thee, thee only, have I sinned
and done this evil in thy sight."
Psalm 51:4**

This contrite confession on King David's part is what finally brought peace and joy to his heart again after his sin with Bathsheba. He was forgiven, for God will always forgive a penitent heart, but the consequences of that sin rolled on through the years and took its toll on his family.

Sin is *against God!* Somehow that truth eludes us. We not only don't remember that fact; we can hardly *identify sin* today in this corrupt society. It has been played out attractively before our eyes for so long; we have become confused about what is sin and what is not sin. God tells us plainly: "All unrighteousness is sin…" <u>I John 5:17</u>

I heard an illustration about a good criterion for recognizing sin.

**A boy picked up a shirt to put it on, and called to his mother: *"Mom, is this shirt dirty?"* She called back, *"Yes!"* He said, *"How do you know when you haven't looked at it?"* The boy's mother called back a wise answer: *"If it's doubtful, it's dirty."***

If we applied such a rule to our lives, then anything that is doubtful, things we don't feel exactly right about doing, *we would not do!*

Joseph became the ruler in Egypt next to the King himself, because he would not succumb to temptation and *sin against God.*

"…neither hath he kept back an thing from me but thee, because thou art his wife: how then can I do this great wickedness, and sin against God?" <u>Genesis 39:9</u>

Acknowledging the truth of God's Word and keeping it gave Joseph all the strength and resolve he needed to stay right before God.

**Remember: if it's doubtful it's dirty, and sin is against God!**

Additional Treasures: <u>James 4:17</u>   <u>Proverbs 10:19</u>

# November 24

"For where your treasure is, there will your heart be also."
Luke 12:34

Christians must be aware and discerning about the inclinations of their hearts. Whatever preoccupies the heart's affection and attention is the treasure in one's life.

In a crisis, our true character and disposition shows itself. We may not be aware ourselves how vainly we are attached to something in our hearts until it is challenged.

**In our first year of marriage our home burned, and almost everything in it. We were alone in the house, which was out in the country. There were only a few minutes to snatch things and run outside, as the fire started from an explosion in the kitchen and spread rapidly throughout the two story wooden structure.**

**By the grace of God, we were not caught in the kitchen, for we had just walked out of that area into the front part of the house. We were not Christians, so I did not think of grabbing the Bible. I didn't even think of the closet full of nice clothes and shoes I had for the first time in my life; I didn't think of the jewelry in my jewelry box; my thoughts were on the *picture albums*! That's what I grabbed, and ran out with them just in time.**

**Later I would think of that absurd thing and wonder why my thoughts were on photographs, mostly of my husband in the army, when I now had the *real thing*. My foolish young heart was still emotionally entwined around those pictures, and my reaction in that crisis told the fact.**

What kind of treasure is your heart keeping? It will keep what it loves and dote on it continually. The heart that loves the Lord and His Word will preoccupy itself with thinking on Him and reading what He has to say. You cannot be around such a heart very long without discovering what its treasure consists of. We talk about what we love! We are actively involved with our treasures. Let us make them *durable* riches.

Riches and honour are with me…durable riches and righteousness."
Proverbs 10:22

Additional Treasures:    Matthew 6:19    Luke 12:19-20

# November 25

"The rod and reproof give wisdom: but a child
left to himself bringeth his mother to shame."
Proverbs 29:15

Many years ago on this day, the seventh son of my parents was born
into the family. My father was thrilled and not at all dismayed to have the
responsibility of yet another one to train up in his large brood of ten
children. He was simply consistent, and that was sufficient. It *never* was
alright to lie, cheat, steal or be disrespectful to our parents or anyone else.

In my early childhood my parents did not have access to a church.
Preachers occasionally would come through the area and have a meeting
at the schoolhouse, and the country folk would attend the preaching. But
that was an infrequent event. However, the good seed sown in our
father's heart came to fruit in his dealings with his own children. "One
that ruleth well his own house, having his children in subjection with all
gravity…" I Timothy 3:4

**Once, one of my younger brothers was with my father in town. It
was late when they stopped at a market for some groceries, then
drove the ten miles home as it was getting dark. A little while after
they got home, Daddy noticed my brother eating peanuts and asked
where he had gotten them. My brother confessed to picking up a
handful out of the peanut barrel and dropping them into his pocket
at the market. Our father gave the usual correction, and took him
back to town with the remaining peanuts to return them and
apologize to the storeowner for stealing them.**

Many modern day parents would have made light of such an
incident, if they noticed what their child was doing at all. Or they would
have put off making the thing right because of the hour and
inconvenience, but not our father. His children were not to think for a
moment that stealing or being dishonest in any way was acceptable. That
was his old-fashioned way, and how his offspring do thank God for him
today.

The world has a great effect on the average home and the way
parents are raising their kids now. Parents have many things hindering
and working against them; sadly enough, they are the only ones that love
their children and care about their welfare. Stand strong parents! You
have good reason.

"Lo, children are a heritage of the Lord…" Psalm 127:3
Additional Treasures:    Proverbs 19:18    Deuteronomy 6:7

# November 26

**"For by grace are ye saved through faith;
and that not of yourselves: it is the gift of God."
Ephesians 2:8**

In a month of thanksgiving we could spend each day expressing our thanks to God for His gift of salvation, and still come short on praise and thanksgiving to Our Lord and Savior. He is *worthy* of all our praise. If He had not come to save us, we would have no hope in this life or after. Take time in this month to *personally* thank Him for saving your soul. He took the penalty of sin for you and me.

**A young man was asked when he first trusted in Christ and was saved. His answer was, "When the bee stung mother."**

**When he was a little boy he was playing before the door, while his mother was working inside. Suddenly a bee came buzzing at the door, and he ran in to his mother, followed by the bee. She hid him behind her. The bee fastened on her bare arm and stung her severely. She turned round, took her little boy, and showed him her arm. There was the place where she was stung, and there was the bee slowly crawling up her arm.**

**"You need not fear the bee now" she said, "for it has no sting. It cannot hurt you. Its sting is here." She showed her little boy a black speck sticking in the wound. And then she took him on her knee, and told him how the sinner, pursued by God's broken Law and death whose sting is sin, could find no shelter except behind the Cross of Christ; while in Jesus who hung there was plunged the fatal sting. Now all the sinner has to do is *look*, and death is harmless, because all its sting has been exhausted in Christ. Nothing now remains but to bow in thankfulness and praise to the One who is mighty to save. --Wells of Living Water. Vol.V.**

We should be thankful that Jesus took the sting of death, which is the wages of *sin. Remember* the day and time when you personally trusted in Him and realized for the first time the peace with God in your heart.

"For Christ also hath once suffered for sins, the just for the unjust that he might bring us to God, being put to death in the flesh, but quickened by the Spirit." I Peter 3:18

Additional Treasures:    Isaiah 53:5    Galatians 3:13

# November 27

**"Hereby perceive we the love of God, because he laid down his life for us: and we ought to lay down our lives for the brethren."**
**I John 3:16**

We are not to take God's unspeakable gift of salvation and hoard it to ourselves. It is God's plan for the Christian to pass it on, that good news of salvation. After all, He provided for every soul of man that ever was or ever will be on the earth!

"But we see Jesus, who was made a little lower than the angels for the suffering of death, crowned with glory and honour; that he by the grace of God should taste death for every man." Hebrews 2:9

I read an interesting illustration of how shortsighted most Christians tend to be. Some will not get seriously involved in the Missions Program of the church because they can't see past the local level of outreach for the lost. That is a hindering attitude in their lives, of which they may not be aware.

Some people find it very hard to see over their own doorstep with the naked eye. The real story of their lives is this:

**"I had a little tea party**
**This afternoon at three**
**'Twas very small—Three guests in all**
**Just I, Myself, and Me.**
**Myself ate all the sandwiches,**
**While I drank up the tea.**
**'Twas also I who ate the pie**
**And passed the cake to me."**

Their interest is in their own town, or their own church. If that is the extent of their interest, they won't be much involved in the work of the Lord even at home. The man, whose heart is filled with concern for people at a distance on various mission fields of the world, has a heart all the more ready to take upon it the burdens of things nearest. (Com.)

If we would be like Jesus, we cannot be selfish and think only of ourselves. He had the whole world in mind when He died for sinful men.

Additional Treasures:     Revelation 7:9     Matthew 28:19-20

# November 28

"In the last day, that great day of the feast, Jesus stood and cried, saying, If any man thirst, let him come unto me, and drink."
John 7:37

All life must have water; plants, animals and humans. That is common knowledge to men on the earth. The plants and animals go to the supply of water according to their design and instinct. The roots of plants go downward searching out the life-giving moisture in the ground and turn their foliage toward the sun for the nourishment it gives.

The animals instinctively migrate to areas supplying food and water. Mankind employs high technology to ensure that he has plenty of safe water to drink and use on the earth that has gotten so contaminated in recent generations.

Water is a most fitting likeness to The Lord Jesus Christ. He is our very life; without Him we die!

"I said therefore unto you, that ye shall die in your sins: for if ye believe not that I am he, ye shall die in your sins." John 8:24

Jesus also said that He was the light of the world.

"Then spake Jesus again unto them, saying, I am the light of the world: he that followeth me shall not walk in darkness, but shall have the light of life." John 8:12

Everything on earth must have sunlight. It nourishes life according to God's design in nature. The plants and flowers respond, each in their unique way. Just so, we see an amazing change when men come to Christ; He becomes their spiritual light and water.

**In our yard my mother had a "four-o-clock" flower bush. That's all I ever heard anybody call it. In bloom, it was covered with little dark pink flowers, which opened to the sun early in the morning and closed their petals up for the night, *beginning* at four o'clock in the afternoon. I used to wonder with great puzzlement how in the world that bush *knew* that it was four o'clock.**

Additional Treasures:    John 3:18    Romans 10:9,10, 13

# November 29

"Herein is love, not that we loved God, but that he loved us,
and sent his Son to be the propitiation for our sins."
I John 4:10

God's love for us is more than we can ever imagine, and certainly our love for Him cannot compare with that great love. When we give thought to it and search through the Word of God, we must stop at the crucifixion of Jesus and gaze in speechless wonder. *God loved us that much.*

Beloved of the Lord.—Two gentlemen were riding together, and as they were about to separate, one said to the other, "Do you ever read your Bible?" "Yes; but I get no benefit from it, because, to tell the truth, I do not feel that I love God." "Neither did I," replied the other, "but God loved me." This answer produced such an effect upon his friend that he said, "It was as if one had lifted him off the saddle into the skies." It opened up to his soul at once the great truth, that it is not how much I love God, but how much God loves me. --Preacher's Com.

God's love is not weak and faltering in his dealings with His children. He faithfully *corrects* us for disobedience because of that great love.

"My son, despise not the chastening of the Lord; neither be weary of his correction: For whom the Lord loveth he correcteth; even as a father the son in whom he delighteth." Proverbs 3:11-12

Jesus warned Peter that he would fail when he was tempted. Peter didn't believe it, but later wept bitterly as the Lord's words certainly came true. Jesus still loved Peter *after* his sin as much as He ever did, and later would restore him to fellowship.

> "Go tell my disciples—and Peter"
> My heart and my eyes are wept dry.
> That He whom I thrice denied, cursing,
> Should mention a wretch such as I!
>
> "Go tell my disciples—and Peter."
> He knew all my grief and my shame.
> "Go tell my disciples—and Peter."
> Thus, tenderly, speaking my name.
>
> Martha Snell Nicholson

Additional Treasures:     Jeremiah 31:3     John 3:16

# November 30

**"Ye shall dwell in booths seven days;**
**all that are Israelites born shall dwell in booths."**
**Leviticus 23:42**

God had Moses establish a remarkable thanksgiving time for the children of Israel. They were to rejoice and give thanks after gathering in the bounty of their crops by building booths and staying in them for seven days! As they dwelled out in that booth, they were to *be thankful.*

"…and ye shall rejoice before the Lord your God seven days." v.40

When I was a new Christian, I heard a pastor's wife teach a sample lesson in a ladies' meeting about these booths, and I was greatly impressed. I didn't know about this unusual story of Thanksgiving in the Bible, and I never forgot it. There really is *nothing new* under the sun just as the Bible says.

Thanksgiving did not originate with the Pilgrims, as much as we love the story; they simply started a tradition in our country. After struggling to survive through a terrible winter, the pilgrims were grateful to God and decided to acknowledge it in a deliberate way; *just as the children of Israel,* who built booths to dwell in for seven days while they celebrated with thanksgiving.

Every year in November, we should build a Thanksgiving Booth *in our hearts* and dwell there throughout the month giving praise and thanksgiving to Jesus, Who loved us and died for our sins.

We should express gratitude for all the countless benefits He pours into our lives every day. "Blessed be the Lord, who daily loadeth us with benefits, even the God of our salvation. Selah. " Psalm 68:19

Our hearts should fill up with praise, and spill over in testimony to others of the great goodness and kindness of God toward us. Wouldn't we shower praise on someone who had helped us in some tremendous way, and we would tell others so they would also appreciate that person? How much more does God deserve our praise and thanksgiving? Let's build a booth!

Additional Treasures:     Psalm 150:6     I Thessalonians 5:18

# December 1

**"...and a word spoken in due season, how good is it!"**
**Proverbs 15:23**

The most due season in the whole year for speaking a word about the Lord Jesus Christ is the month of December. This time is totally consumed with the celebration of Christmas, the traditional time of our Lord's birth on earth. The order of most of the celebrating is *traditional*, and not *Biblical.*

1. **People exchange gifts with one another though it is regarded as the birthday of Christ.**
2. **It is acceptable to go into debt, putting the family in dire straits financially, in order to have a *good* Christmas.**
3. **Children, who already have everything they desire, are showered with more gifts so that their parents can delight in the glowing feeling of indulgence.**

Statistics show that after Christmas there is a big letdown for many people. They feel depressed; the glow and wonder of Christmas has fizzled out. *That can be avoided.* Celebrate like it was done at the time of His birth!

**A multitude of angels appeared in the night to praise God.**
"And suddenly there was with the angel a multitude of the heavenly host praising God, and saying, Glory to God in the highest, and on earth peace, good will toward men." Luke 2:13-14

**The shepherds saw Jesus, and then told others about Him.** "And when they had seen it, they made known abroad the saying which was told them concerning this child." Luke 2:17

**The Wise Men from the East brought Him gifts.**
"...they saw the young child with Mary his mother, and fell down, and worshipped him: and when they had opened their treasures, they presented unto him gifts; gold, frankincense, and myrrh." Matthew 2:11

Acknowledging the most important One at Christmas time will make the holiday more than just bright lights strung everywhere, and being frantic with the pressures of the season. We should praise the Lord; tell others about Him as the shepherds did, and worship Him with gifts, giving the best that we have to Him first of all.

Additional Treasures:     Isaiah 40:9     Hebrews 1:2-3

# December 2

"For with God nothing shall be impossible."
Luke 1:37

Only God could create the plan which brought the Creator down to earth: born of a virgin, born under the law, to be the Savior of the world.

"But when the fulness of the time was come, God sent forth his Son, made of a woman, made under the law, To redeem them that were under the law, that we might receive the adoption of sons." Gal: 4:4-5

Those of us who know Christ was with the Father in the beginning, and is the Creator of all things, may be surprised at how many people consider His beginning to be at His birth in the stable. I found an interesting story from a preacher, Dr. R.E. Neighbor, of an earlier generation.

**In our sermon we had told of how Christ had come forth from the Father and had come into the world. We told that afterward when He had completed His earthly task, He had gone back to the Father and to the glory which He had with Him before the world was.**

**The next day, aboard train, a gentleman of marked intelligence sought an interview. He told us:--"I have been a prominent churchman and member of a church from my boyhood, and I never knew until I heard you preach last night that Jesus Christ ever existed before He was born of the Virgin Mary."**

**In a Northern city, during a Bible Conference, we told of this occurrence. Following the message, a prominent Christian woman, who must have been in her seventies, astounded us by saying that she had never heard, and never knew that Jesus Christ was God in the eternities past. She thought of Him as having a beginning when He was laid in the manger at Bethlehem.**

We must be diligent, during this season, to tell the truth to children as they see the *Baby Jesus in the manger* constantly before their eyes. Make it the subject of family devotions and teach them what the Bible says about *who* Jesus is and *where* He came from. We can mix learning with joy and gladness in this month's holiday season. It is a golden opportunity.

Additional Treasures:     Luke 1:34-35     John 1:1-3

# December 3

**"And he that was dead came forth,**
**bound hand and foot with graveclothes..."**
**John 11:44**

It is amazing that most people who witnessed the miracles of Jesus did not believe that He was God in the flesh. Surely when He spoke and Lazarus came out of the grave on his own power, *alive*, they would believe. Some did, but not all.

"Then many of the Jews which came to Mary, and had seen the things which Jesus did, believed on him. But some of them went their ways to the Pharisees, and told them what things Jesus had done." John 11:45-46

Those who did not believe on Jesus went from that scene of joy and praise to give an evil report of what the Lord had done. In the remainder of the chapter, the religious leaders of that day made plans to somehow do away with Jesus. "Then from that day forth they took counsel together for to put him to death." V.53

They devised a scheme to kill the One who could raise the dead to life! They were willingly blind to the fact that Jesus was God in the flesh.

**The Strasbourg Cathedral in France is one of Europe's most renowned Gothic buildings. Its famous clock has a mechanism so complicated that it seems to be a work of superhuman skill to the common people. It is said that the clock-maker, being offended and unpaid for his work, came in one day and touched its secret springs, and it stopped. The nation's most skillful artisans could not restore the disordered mechanism and make it work.**

**Afterwards, when restitution was made to him, the maker came again, touched the inner springs, and set the famous clock in motion. There was no doubt, then, that he was the maker and the master of that clock.**

**When Jesus stopped the mechanism of nature, turned it back, and started again the mysterious clock of human life in Lazarus, *who had been dead four days*, it was overwhelming proof that He was God!**

Additional Treasures:    John 10:29-30    Luke 20:38

# December 4

"Pride goeth before destruction, and
a haughty spirit before a fall."
Proverbs 16:18

Pride is defined as *too high an opinion of oneself; conceit.* This attitude in humans has caused more misery than can be measured.

Pride is also defined as pleased satisfaction with what one is, has, or has done, and suggests proper self-respect and personal dignity because of real worth. This is pride in its acceptable context. However, we see it more in the extreme: excessive self-love and arrogance because of imagined superiority.

Satan's subtle suggestion to Eve in the garden, to disobey God and taste of the forbidden fruit, was directed to her *pride.* "For God doth know that in the day ye eat thereof, then your eyes shall be opened, and ye shall be as gods, knowing good and evil." Genesis 3:5

The devil knows our weakness to pride's influence in our lives. Just as Eve, what we *see* we may readily *desire* and then scheme to get what we want in improper ways. God supplies all our needs, but not always the 'extras' that we think would make us happy. Pride wants more and more. Be content!

It is said that a young man from college approached a great London preacher asking him for the privilege of filling his pulpit. As the family was members of his church, he said, "I'll be glad for you to take our midweek prayer-meeting." The young theologian said, "I am not a prayer-meeting preacher, but the best preacher in college. I want the main Sunday service." The pastor granted the request, and after introducing him the following Sunday morning sat down to hear the wonderful sermon which he was promised by the youth.

The college lad arose, dressed in the height of fashion and well groomed. He tried to find his text, but could not. He endeavored to speak, but his words all left him. Embarrassed and ashamed, with drooping head, he left the platform. As he went down, the pastor is reputed to have said, "Young man, if you had gone up the way you are coming down, you might have come down the way you went up."

"Pride goeth before destruction, and a haughty spirit before a fall."
Proverbs 16:18
Additional Treasures:     Proverbs 21:4     I John 2:16

# December 5

"In the year that king Uzziah died I saw also the Lord sitting upon a
throne, high and lifted up... "
Isaiah 6:1

It was a life-changing experience for the prophet, Isaiah. He was
allowed to glimpse a little of the glory of God. He saw the seraphims,
the multi-winged angelic beings who cry *"Holy, holy, holy,"* continually
in the Lord's presence.

"And one cried unto another, and said, "Holy, holy, holy, is the Lord
of hosts, the whole earth is full of his glory." Isaiah 6:3

Isaiah's reaction to the magnificent sight before him lets us know
how we, at best, compare and measure up to the holiness of our God.

"Then said I, Woe is me! For I am undone; because I am a man of
unclean lips, and I dwell in the midst of a people of unclean lips: for
mine eyes have seen the King, the LORD of hosts." v. 5

The Word of God is His cleansing agent for us; it must grieve Him
when we neglect it. Thinking on His majesty and holiness will motivate
us to take our *daily bath* in His Word that we may approach unto such a
one with a clear conscience and pure heart.

**God Revealing Himself. —A star in the far depths attracted the
attention of an observer. It seemed to be a single star, but to his
educated eye it resolved itself into two stars. Those two proved to be
each a star, center of a planetary system like our own. Those two
stars, which seemed but one, were really distant from each other five
hundred times the distance separating our earth from the sun. Who
of us can conceive such sublime spaces as are thus unfolded? What
must he be who walketh among the shining lights, whose throne rises
higher than these stars, whose canopy is gemmed with myriad suns!**

**And if the telescope can put such meaning into the figure of the
heavens, the microscope puts equal meaning into the figure of the
earth. God needs this whole earth for a "footstool." This great
earth, with its giant trees, and inaccessible mountains, and
unfathomable waters, and millionfold forms of life, cannot hold God;
it is but a resting place for his foot. –Pul. Com.**

Additional Treasures:   Isaiah 37:16   Psalm 8:1-9   Psalm 19:1-3

# December 6

**"And mount Sinai was altogether on a smoke, because
the Lord descended upon it in fire..."
Exodus 19:18**

It was an awesome scene when the Lord came down to communicate with Moses on Mount Sinai. The people were terrified to be in *hearing* distance, as well as *seeing* the upheavals of the natural world when God let His presence be known in that place.

"And it came to pass on the third day in the morning, that there were thunders and lightnings, and a thick cloud upon the mount, and the voice of the trumpet exceeding loud; so that all the people that was in the camp trembled." Exodus 19:16

Neither man nor beasts could approach the mountain when God was there. Moses was called up by the Lord to receive His word for the people. They could only gaze from a distance with fear and trembling.

Jesus came into the world *as a baby,* and grew up among humans in the *likeness* of sinful men, to be the Savior of the world. He was approachable, and men were not afraid. *But He was God,* come down to the earth to redeem the fallen race.

**When World War I was over, an artist in New York City was commissioned to sculpt a life-sized statue of a war hero to be placed in Central Park. The work was completed; the figure was displayed on a fifteen-foot pedestal so that all could see that impressive monument as they strolled by in the park.**

**A curator noticed, however, that the people walked around the pedestal and hardly glanced up at the statue. Something had to be done! The officials came up with a solution. They had a two-foot tall replica made of the same statue, placed it at the base of the pedestal with an inscription telling that it was the exact likeness of the larger imposing figure of the war hero above. They could look up and see the real thing, *and they did just that.* The people would stop, look at the smaller figure, then back off and carefully observe the larger likeness.**

"...he that hath seen me hath seen the Father..." John 14:9

Additional Treasures:   John 10:30   Matthew 3:17

# December 7

"The heavens declare the glory of God; and
the firmament sheweth his handywork."
Psalm 19:1

The scriptures tell us that what we see in the heavens in the day *tells* us something, and the nights *show* us something!

"Day unto day uttereth speech, and night unto night sheweth knowledge. There is no speech nor language, where their voice is not heard." Psalm 19:2-3

Those who do not believe in God the Creator are not listening and looking. The heavens declare, *show evidence,* of His glory.

**An Arab, when one day asked, "How do you know there is a God?" turned indignantly upon the questioner, and replied, "How do I know whether a man or a camel passed my tent last night?" His own footprints in creation and providence testify of Him.** –Com.

The heavens also declare the *righteousness* of God. The sun, moon and stars are better witnesses than God's children are on earth; they're consistent and faithful in their appointed role in the universe. If they failed for a moment in the smallest measure, the whole of creation on earth would crumble.

"The heavens declare his righteousness, and all the people see his glory." Psalm 97:6

**In my teenage years my family lived in West Texas. After the day's work we would sit on the front porch enjoying the coolness after the sun went down. I loved watching the full moon rise. The moon was *huge* coming up over the horizon, an optical illusion because of the curvature of the earth. At night the skies would be crammed full of stars! It was an awesome sight gazing into the heavens at something only God has touched.**

In more recent years, I loved reciting the first three verses of Psalm 19 as I did my exercise walking at daybreak, with the sun coming up turning the sky into a kaleidoscope of color. The heavens declare His glory *that He is God* but few see it. Until their spirit is touched by the Spirit of God, their minds are darkened to such evidence. Christians are still the vital "mouthpiece" of God. May we be faithful in giving the Word of God to others so it may enlighten their eyes to 'see' what we see.

Additional Treasures:    Genesis 1:1    Nehemiah 9:6

# December 8

The church is the bride of Christ. Christ loves the church and gave Himself for it. How He loves His bride! Someday, the Lord will come from heaven and take His bride from the earth and back into that blissful eternal place to dwell with Him forever.

"For the Lord himself shall descend from heaven with a shout, with the voice of the archangel, and with the trump of God: and the dead in Christ shall rise first: Then we which are alive and remain shall be caught up together with them in the clouds, to meet the Lord in the air: and so shall we ever be with the Lord." I Thessalonians 4:16-17

I've attended many weddings, which were breathtaking in their beauty. The brides are lovely with a glow seemingly reserved for this important moment in their lives. The tenderness and love in the eyes of a groom gives solemnity to the occasion. Does the Lord allow us to get *a little glimpse* in an earthly wedding? We cannot imagine that heavenly wedding of Christ and His bride, the church; it will be beautiful beyond compare.

Several years after my daughter's wedding the beauty of the event was still vividly fresh in my mind and I was able to capture it somewhat in the third verse of a poem: Three Looks.

**She came down the aisle that day…at last,**
**A vision in white satin, ruffles, and lace.**
**Filmy illusion fell from snowy brim,**
**Veiling the bride's radiant smiling face.**
**It was that once in a lifetime scene**
**For the groom…looking steadfastly at his bride.**
**He guided her gently to their place to vow.**
**We observed the wonder…the look in his eyes,**
**But lack fitting words that look to describe.**

Additional Treasures:    Revelation 19:7    II Corinthians 11:2

# December 9

**"I tell you, Nay: but, except ye repent, ye shall all likewise perish."**
**Luke 13:3**

None are exempt from the vital need of God's salvation. All must be born again; all must repent just as the Lord says in His Word. "Jesus answered and said unto him, Verily, verily, I say unto thee, Except a man be born again, he cannot see the kingdom of God." John 3:3

Repentance means turning from one way to another--changing direction in one's life. Evidence of true repentance is an abhorrence of sin.

I read a very apt illustration in regard to a person's view of sin after he truly repents of it, turning to Christ as his Savior.

**Hatred for sin.** —I once walked into a garden with a lady to gather some flowers. One large bush was bending under the weight of the most beautiful roses. We both gazed at it with admiration, and the lady pressed forward into the thick bush and reached for the one flower, which seemed to shine above all the rest for beauty. As she did this, a black snake, which was hid in the bush, wrapped itself around her arm. She ran from the garden screaming and it was a long time before she could be quieted. Such is her hatred now of the whole serpent race, that she has never since been able to look at a snake even though it were dead. No one could ever persuade her to venture again into a cluster of bushes, even to pluck a beautiful rose.

Now this is the way the sinner acts who truly repents of his sins. He thinks of sin as the serpent that once coiled itself round him. He hates it. He dreads it. He flees from it. He fears the places where it inhabits. He will no more play with sin than this lady would afterwards have played with snakes. -- Com.

**In our generation today, the world has succeeded in conditioning its population to *pet the snakes, not fear them!* Sin has become acceptable, and yet its consequences will always remain the same. Keep faithfully reading the Word of God and *be aware that sin will bite you*, if you get near it. And if that bite comes, look to the One who has the 'cure.' "If we confess our sins, he is faithful and just to forgive..."** I John 1:9

Additional Treasures:　　I Peter 1:23　　Proverbs 11:19

# December 10

"Wilt thou set thine eyes upon that which is not? for riches
certainly make themselves wings; they fly away as an eagle..."
Proverbs 23:5

People whose happiness is dependent on what they possess are
always in danger of being shattered by the loss of it. Life is uncertain; we
never know from one day to the next what will transpire that can cause
an upheaval in our lives. We should keep our focus on the One who
sustains us. "I will lift up mine eyes unto the hills, from whence cometh
my help. My help cometh from the Lord, which made heaven and earth."
Psalm 121:1-2

**A very rich nobleman was reduced to poverty during the French
Revolution and forced to flee for his life, leaving all his home and
inheritance. He escaped and came to New York, where he was forced to
live without servants, and to take care of his own needs, which he had
never done in his entire life of splendid affluence. But he had a cheerful
attitude about his situation and once remarked while doing some service
formerly done by servants, "Had it not been for the Revolution in
France, I should never have known how easy it is to wait on oneself."
Com.**

Christians should not be dependent on anything or anyone other than
God to maintain peace of mind and happiness in life. That will ensure
that they will never have a heartbreaking loss, which will wreck their
lives.

In a comparison to money and wisdom, it is far better to be *richer*
with the latter. "For wisdom is a defence, and money is a defence: but
the excellency of knowledge is, that wisdom giveth life to them that have
it." Ecclesiastes 7:12

Money can leave us as quickly as the eagle can soar up and away from
the earth, *especially at this time of year!* But wisdom is a valuable asset that
money cannot touch. It not only enriches; it gives life to those who have it.
*Wisdom comes from God* and God invites his children to ask for wisdom for
he has plenty and does not 'upbraid' us or 'get on our case' for not coming
sooner or for causing hardships in our lives without it. Only God loves us so
and has patience to teach us the same lessons over and over.
Re: James 1:5

Additional Treasures:    Job 22:25-26    Psalm 31:19

# December 11

**"...whosoever therefore will be a friend of
the world is the enemy of God."
James 4:4**

The world is and shall always be the enemy of God because the world's system *excludes* Him. It is clearly defined in the scriptures.

"For all that is in the world, the lust of the flesh, and the lust of the eyes, and the pride of life, is not of the Father, but is of the world." I John 2:16

For that reason, Christians should not be too caught up in friendship with worldly people for they are *enemies of God*. When one fraternizes with the enemy, he is sure to be affected in his resolve to be faithful to God.

Special Need of Watchfulness. —**When cast by Providence among sinful persons who respect us, we ought to be peculiarly watchful. The hatred of the ungodly, when poured upon Christians in the form of persecution is seldom harmful to their spiritual nature, but the friendship of the world is always to be suspected. We are disarmed by kindness, and it is never safe to be disarmed in an enemy's country. Who can have much to do with sinners and *not* have something to do with their sins? All Philistia could not have blinded Samson if Delilah's charms had not deluded him. Our worst foes will be found among our ungodly friends. Those who are false to God are not likely to be true to us. Walk carefully, believer, if thy way lie by the sinner's door, and especially if that sinner has acted a friendly part to thee.** - Spurgeon

The only way we can protect ourselves from being conformed to the world's ways is to allow God to *transform* us to be like Christ.

"And be not conformed to this world: but be ye transformed by the renewing of your mind, that ye may prove what is that good, and acceptable, and perfect will of God." Romans 12:2

One does not have to be concerned in his relationship with the world if he is genuinely dedicated to Christ. The separation will come naturally. The world cannot be comfortable with godly people. Those who love the world, the world system which excludes God, will not seek a Christian's company.

Additional Treasures:    I John 2:15    Titus 2:12

# December 12

"For we brought nothing into this world,
and it is certain we can carry nothing out."
I Timothy 6:7

In over four decades of ministry we had many funerals for all ages, from newborn infants to a man over one hundred years old. We have realized the truth of this verse in every case, regardless of the status of the individual. Neither the rich nor the poor ever took anything with them into eternity. That makes funerals very solemn. Death is final, and nothing can be changed of the life one has lived on earth, *after he dies*. It is so important that we keep in mind what our real treasures are, and maintain them.

"Let us hear the conclusion of the whole matter: Fear God, and keep his commandments: for this is the whole duty of man. For God shall bring every work into judgment, with every secret thing, whether it be good, or whether it be evil." Ecclesiastes 12:13-14

Sometimes we cling to things which have no eternal value, which distracts us from tending to the main issue of life: *Fear God and keep His commandments.*

**In childhood, at one time, I got caught up with the game of hopscotch. I learned to draw the pattern on the ground, and worked toward the ability to hop all the way to the end and back without making a mistake. One day I found the perfect piece of broken glass to use in the game. It was the thick bottom piece of a jar or dish, fit in my hand just right, and it seemed to glide across the ground into the block I'd aim for each time I tossed it. *I loved that piece of glass.* It became a treasure in my eyes. I'd carefully hide it under a clump of grass at day's end so that no one else would find it and take my prize! I'd run out each morning to see if it was still there. In my childish mind, it was the most valuable thing in my life.**

We smile at the foolishness of little children enamored with worthless things, for they do not know better. But Christians may waste time and money on worthless possessions that draw them away from faithfulness to God. We have heard God's people say, as death was drawing close that they wish they had been more dedicated to God.

Additional Treasures:    Luke 10:27    James 4:14

# December 13

**"Keep my commandments and live; and my law**
**as the apple of thine eye."**
**Proverbs 7:2**

I've heard the expression, *living the low life,* and understood it to mean someone living a life of sin utterly disregarding the Word of God. According to the scriptures, we really have life when we adhere to God's instructions: *Keep my commandments and live.*

Some who have lived the low life will testify to the fact that addiction to perverted ways is a miserable way to exist. Yet some who never experienced such ways, respectable and upright citizens in the world, may also be living a low life because they too ignore God and His Word. In God's eyes there is no difference in people, good or bad, *outside of the Lord Jesus Christ.* Hear the solemn truth from the scriptures.

"They are all gone out of the way, they are together become unprofitable: there is none that doeth good, no, not one." Romans 3:12

There follows in this chapter several indictments of the human race that describes the *good and the bad without Christ.* Romans 3:13-18

**"Their throat is an open sepulchre;**
**With their tongues they have used deceit;**
**The poison of asps is under their lips:**
**Whose mouth is full of cursing and bitterness:**
**Their feet are swift to shed blood:**
**Destruction and misery are in their ways:**
**And the way of peace have they not known:**
**There is no fear of God before their eyes."**

It is a difficult thing getting people to understand that these verses describe everyone outside of the Lord Jesus Christ. It is the human, prideful way to think that their own 'goodness' is going to make a difference in their eternal destiny. The most thrilling words a Christian hears from a lost person is when he admits that he's a sinner: "I am lost." That is the first step toward the new birth in Christ. "I am the way, the truth, and the life: no man cometh unto the Father, but by me." John 14:6

Additional Treasures:    Psalm 58:3    Romans 6:23

# December 14

**"For by grace are ye saved through faith;**
**and that not of yourselves: it is the gift of God."**
**Ephesians 2:8**

Christians may think more about the gift of God in this season, and the world has learned that Christmas is a profitable time commercially. We see the display of the Babe in the manger scene often, though not as much as a generation past. As the time of the Lord's coming draws nearer, there is a falling away from the tradition of having Christ predominantly acknowledged, even at the time of celebrating His birth into the world.

But *wise men still seek Him,* and those who hear the truth about Christ and accept the Gift of God provided by His grace, *unmerited favor,* will forever be enlightened.

**Grace, Free.—When Clara Barton, founder of the Red Cross, was engaged in the Red Cross work in Cuba, during the Spanish-American War, ex-President Roosevelt, *then Colonel Theodore Roosevelt,* came to her to buy some delicacies for the sick and wounded men under his command. His request was refused. Roosevelt was troubled; he loved his men, and was ready to pay for the supplies out of his own pocket. "How can I get these things?" he said: "I must have proper food for my sick men." "Just ask for them Colonel," said the surgeon in charge of the Red Cross headquarters. "Oh" said Roosevelt, his face breaking into a smile, "then I do ask for them." And he got them at once; but you notice that he got them through grace, and not through purchase.**

**If men could buy the grace of a quiet conscience and a restful heart, how the millionaires would vie with each other at such an auction; but no one can have this chain of Heaven's gold except by the free grace of God, which is offered to us every one.**
—Wells of Living Water, Vol. IV.

Learned men have tried to define God's grace in many ways, and yet fall short of words. How can man ever understand the love God has for lost humanity, which put His grace into motion and furnished salvation? We cannot fully understand the Babe in the manger!

Thanks be unto God for his unspeakable gift. II Corinthians 9:15

Additional Treasures:     Romans 8:32     John 4:10

# December 15

**"...for he will speak peace unto his people, and to his saints:**
**but let them not turn again to folly."**
**Psalm 85:8**

Jesus was gracious and very kind to the people he ministered to in various ways during His time on earth. He preached the wonderful truth to them, healed, spoke comfort, and even raised the dead to life again!

He saved notorious sinners and gave them a simple command afterwards. *Go and sin no more.* God does not want His people to *turn again to folly.* He knows that our peace and wellbeing depends on our consistent obedience to Him. When Jesus saved the woman who was taken in adultery, the last thing He said to her was *"Go and sin no more."*

"When Jesus had lifted up himself, and saw none but the woman, he said unto her, Woman, where are those thine accusers? Hath no man condemned thee? She said, No man, Lord. And Jesus said unto her, Neither do I condemn thee: go, and sin no more."
John 8:10-11

The only way to enjoy salvation, the new life in Christ, is to be obedient to the Lord. So often we have a *half-hearted happiness,* and it is because we have kept back some area of our hearts: a little room full of things that are not given over to God yet. If we have rebellion lurking at the door to that room, we will resist every effort The Holy Spirit makes to warn us about the folly of keeping what we should be clearing out of the way.

It is easy to *return to our folly,* if we keep the temptation in storage.

**What keeps you from reading the Bible consistently?**
**Do you struggle with prayer; is it hard to talk to God?**
**Are the church services a joy or just a duty to attend?**

While preparing for Christmas, clean out that part of your heart hiding the sin that has taken the joy out of your service for God. It may be a seemingly harmless interest or activity which has slowly eroded the love and dedication you had for the Lord. If you sincerely ask the Lord, He will reveal the culprit and enable you to remove it.

Additional Treasures:     Psalm 86:5     I John 1:5-10

# December 16

"Blessed be the Lord God of Israel,
who only doeth wondrous things."
Psalm 72:18

The only One who can do a *supernatural* work is God. Men may try in subtle ways to take credit for what God is doing in the church and among His people, but it is the Lord who does His work through those who are obedient to Him in the work. "Faithful is he that calleth you, who also will do it." I Thessalonians 5:24

An experienced preacher of the gospel will tell you that there's a vast difference in preaching when the Lord is in it, and when He is not!

**There was a certain preacher who was engaged to preach several nights in a large meeting. The first night went great. He preached with power and eloquence and the audience was moved by the message. Later, as he drove to his hotel, confident and rejoicing about the preaching, he spoke aloud to himself: "Now that was the *real* you tonight."**

**The next night, he came to the pulpit and began to preach confidently in the same manner, but now he had great difficulty. The message fell flat and as he struggled through it the people just looked at him, obviously unmoved. Later as he made his way back to the hotel, weary and downcast, the Lord spoke quietly to his heart. *"That was the real you tonight."***

In all areas of Christian work, people need the power of God for fruitful service. We eventually learn that, when we struggle to make something work and it will not. But when we pray and ask God's direction and blessing, it makes all the difference. It was a great relief to my heart when I realized that I was not responsible for the *results* of our work for the Lord. *He is.* My responsibility is to be obedient to Him.

"Ye have not chosen me, but I have chosen you, and ordained you, that ye should go and bring forth fruit…" John 15:16

When Christians serving the Lord come to the place of leaving all the results to Him, it takes the pressure or stress out of the work and it's a joy. We cannot produce fruit! We can only gather in the fruit which the Lord has produced. He is the one who gets the glory, not the fruit gatherers.

Additional Treasures:    I Corinthians 3:7    Galatians 6:9

# December 17

**"Many seek the ruler's favor;**
**but every man's judgment cometh from the Lord."**
**Proverbs 29:26**

In the world men offer bribes and may be able to buy off judgment. But with God there is *righteous* judgment, and all will be judged on the same level. "Also unto thee, O Lord, belongeth mercy: for thou renderest to every man according to his work." Psalm 62:12

That is *according to his work*, not according to social standing, riches, influence, poverty, etc., but according to the production of his life. Some people won't give judgment a serious thought until they are staring at death. Sadly, that is too late for most people. Men should think about judgment in their youth; life goes by so swiftly.

"Rejoice, O young man, in thy youth; and let thy heart cheer thee in the days of thy youth, and walk in the ways of thine heart, and in the sight of thine eyes: but know thou, that for all these things God will bring thee into judgment." Ecclesiastes 11:9

The Judgment to Come. —**It was my sad lot to be in the Chicago fire. As the flames rolled down our streets, destroying everything in their path, I saw the great and the honorable, the learned and the wise, fleeing before the fire with the beggar and the thief and the harlot. All were alike.**

**As the flames swept through the city it was like judgment day. The mayor, nor the mighty men, nor wise men could stop these flames. They were all on a level then, and many rich men were left paupers that night. When the Day of Judgment comes there will be no difference. When the Flood came there was no difference; Noah's ark was worth more than the entire world. The day before it was the world's laughingstock, but when the flood came, it was worth more than the whole world.**

**When the Day of Judgment comes, Christ will be worth more than this world—more than ten thousand worlds.** –D.L.Moody

Christians lose sight of these solemn facts when their minds are preoccupied with unimportant things. Reading God's Word will help you keep life in perspective and remember what is important in view of eternity.

Additional Treasures:     Proverbs 24:12     Matthew 16:27

# December 18

**"When I saw among the spoils a goodly Babylonish garment,
and two hundred shekels of silver...I took them."
Joshua 7:21**

The man, Achan, caused a lot of trouble to Israel because he was greedy. All the spoils of Jericho, the first city taken in Canaan, were consecrated to God. The people were not to take anything for themselves.

"But all the silver, and gold, and vessels of brass and iron, are consecrated unto the Lord: they shall come into the treasury of the Lord."
Joshua 6:19

When Achan looked at the spoils, *greed* took control and he hid some things in his tent. With that transgression, God's power departed and in the next battle the enemy defeated them. Joshua, their leader, fell on his face in prayer to God and God told him to get up and get the sin out of the camp!

"...neither will I be with you anymore, except ye destroy the accursed from among you." Joshua 7:12

We know that Achan and his whole family perished because of his sin. It was greed in his heart that leaped out and soon destroyed him.

The Danger of Greed. —**Once a servant of an Indian rajah was ordered to keep away from a cave near the rajah's residence, and to keep all others away. The servant began to consider the probable reason of his having been forbidden to enter the cave. He made up his mind that his master must have great treasure hid there, and resolved to get it. Taking a fellow servant with him to secure the coveted prize, they rolled away the stone at the mouth of the cave, when a tremendous tiger sprang upon them and tore them to pieces!**
–Commentary

*Greed* is extreme or excessive desire. It displays itself frequently at this time of year, *especially* when there is so much advertising and pressure to get things. We should not be greedy and cause others to spend excessively to satisfy our wants, nor should we spend money to satisfy another's excessive desire for things. Keep gift giving in perspective at the Christmas season. Honor Christ first of all.

Additional Treasures:   Proverbs 15:27   I Timothy 6:10

# December 19

**"He, that being often reproved hardeneth his neck,
shall suddenly be destroyed, and that without remedy."
Proverbs 29:1**

Christians lean on the patience and long-suffering of God, ignoring His Word, when they know that in their hearts they court danger of judgment in their lives. God does lovingly reprove us, *correct us,* with the Word; if we do not listen and learn from it, then the wheel of judgment starts rolling, and *there is no stopping it!* Who could stop God? The Bible says that His judgment is *without remedy.*

Consequences of Sin. —**We are told that in Sierra Leone, a small country in West Africa, the white ants will sometimes occupy a house, and eat their way into all the woodwork, until every article in the house is so hollow it will collapse into dust as soon as it's touched.**

**It is so with a deceitful character. It may be honey-combed and eaten through; though for years a person keeps up an acceptable appearance with few people suspecting the extent of the inward decay. Suddenly the end will come. There will be one touch of the finger of God, and a life built on deceit and lies will suddenly fall apart.** *"He shall be broken, and that without remedy."* –Com.

The season of God's long-suffering is limited. Those who defer repentance deceive their own souls, because God's love and faithfulness directs discipline into their lives. It is wise to judge ourselves, *before* that correction comes. We judge ourselves when we admit our sin and confess it to God, asking forgiveness. So much sorrow for Christians could be avoided if they would only practice and do what the Word of God says to do.

"He that covereth his sins shall not prosper: but whoso confesseth and forsaketh them shall have mercy. *"*     Proverbs 28:13

My parents used to correct their children *first* by speaking to them. If we ignored what they *said,* then other stronger measures followed. But we could have usually avoided punishment if we had only listened and obeyed their words of instruction or warning. It is much the same with God's children. If Christians would mind God's Word as He warns of sin and its devastation, they would not have to suffer the consequences of it in life.

Additional Treasures:     I Corinthians 4:5     Luke 12:2

# December 20

"For what is your life? It is even a vapour, that appeareth
for a little time, and then vanisheth away."
**James 4:14**

God describes the brevity of life as it is, like a vapor. The steam that
rises from boiling water disappears immediately, so life is so brief
according to the Lord. If we keep focused on the reality of His Word we
would be more diligent to make our days count for eternal value. It
passes so swiftly; man is young, *and then he is old* and where did all the
time go?

Jacob's assessment of his long life clearly came from understanding
and being acquainted with God. He stood before Pharaoh in Egypt, as
Joseph introduced his father to the king, and made this touching
statement.

"And Pharaoh said unto Jacob, How old art thou?

And Jacob said unto Pharaoh, The days of the years of my
pilgrimage are an hundred and thirty years: few and evil have the days of
the years of my life been, and have not attained unto the life of my
fathers in the days of their pilgrimage." Genesis 47:8-9

Jacob called one hundred and thirty years a *few days!* We should
make our days and years *count worthy* as they rush by like the wind.

**The Vanity of Human Life.—**

**Like to the falling of a star,**
**Or as the flight of eagles are;**
**Or like the fresh spring's gaudy hue,**
**Or Silver drops of morning dew;**
**Or like a wind that chafes the flood,**
**Or bubbles which on water stood—**

**E'n such is man, whose borrowed light**
**Is straight called in, and paid to-night,**
**The wind blows out, the bubble dies,**
**The spring entombed in autumn lies,**
**The dew dries up, the star is shot,**
**The flight is past – and man forgot.**
H. King

Additional Treasures:    I Chronicles 29:15    Psalm 39:5

# December 21

**"Bind them upon thy fingers, write them upon
the table of thine heart."**
Proverbs 7:3

There is a little traditional saying that is common to many of us. When we encourage others to remember something we say *"tie a string around your finger."* It probably originated from this Bible verse.

The things we are commanded to *bind upon our fingers* are the commandments of the Lord. Those are the most important things in the world for man to remember, but he does not value God's Word that much. We don't see anyone going around with *memory strings* attached to his fingers. We rarely see a Christian trying to commit the Word to memory by repeating it over and over until he retains it. That would be *writing it upon the table of his heart.* The Word of God is so rich in meaning!

The Christmas season is a time when people tend to forget important things. They get caught up in the frantic rush of activities, and normal life is set on *'hold'* until after Christmas day. For most people the fact that it's Christ's birthday is irrelevant. Make sure that your family has a deeper concept than that. The saying goes: *Put Christ in Christmas.* How could you possibly take Him out? Folks are spiritually blind if they don't see Him.

**My mother's birthday was on Christmas Day. Somehow, it always got lost in the celebration of Christmas. She was rather like a person that had no birthday at all, since nothing was said of it all year long or at Christmastime either. Later, when the daughters were grown, we separated her birthday from Christmas, and in fact, just made it a big part of the family celebration. It was fun to make sure her birthday was no more forgotten.**

Perhaps we forget Christ in the same way. *It's His Birthday!* Make sure the main thing is not lost in the hustle and bustle of Christmas. It was easier long ago to keep out the clamor of the season before it became so rampant with the craze for buying things and piling gifts under an elaborately decorated tree. That has ruined a generation of youth who do not know how to appreciate simple inexpensive gifts. Pray for a way to make this time of year meaningful for your family.

Additional Treasures:  Psalm 33:8  Luke 2:10-14

# December 22

"Honour the Lord with thy substance,
and with the firstfruits of all thine increase…"
Proverbs 3:9

The Lord commands 'giving' because it is vital to our health and happiness on this earth. One of the chief joys for the Christian is giving unto the Lord because He returns the blessings on our heads! The verse following says:

"So shall thy barns be filled with plenty, and thy presses shall burst out with new wine." V.10

The barns were storehouses of various kinds. The press or winevat was where the produce of the vineyards and oliveyards was rendered out and used for their own needs, sold or bartered for goods. This promise is tremendous, for it assures the believer that all his needs will be met. The trusting soul is always delighted by how amazingly God does this.

**Providential Supply of Food.**—A frontier preacher was preaching on one occasion, in a cabin which was at once a church and dwelling. In the middle of his sermon, his host, who sat near the door, suddenly rose from his seat, snatched the gun from its wooden brackets, went hastily out, fired it off, and returning, put the gun in its place and quietly seated himself to hear the remainder of the sermon. After the service ended, the preacher inquired of the strange behavior of his host. "Sir," said he, "we are entirely out of meat; and I was perplexed to know what we should give you for dinner, and it was preventing me from enjoying the sermon, when God sent a flock of wild turkeys this way. I happened to see them, took my gun, and killed two at a shot. My mind felt easy, and I enjoyed the remainder of the sermon with perfect satisfaction." -Bible Com.

**God furnished enough quail for the children of Israel in the wilderness when they murmured for meat. He poured water out of a rock! He furnished manna for them for forty years. The record of that in His Word is for our benefit, that we may understand that He will never fail to care for us either.**

Pay attention to the *incoming* blessings, and be thankful for them. God gives us so much and we forget most of it immediately. Post a 'thank you' card in your heart and keep it updated day by day by thanking God as you pray and read His Word.

Additional Treasures:    Philippians 4:19    Psalm 128:1-2

# December 23

"For all the promises of God in him are yea,
and in him Amen, unto the glory of God by us."
II Corinthians 1:20

The Gift of salvation is Jesus the Lord from heaven. He did His part to redeem us, and made salvation so simple none will have excuse when they stand before God in the last day. All men must do is *believe on Him and receive the Gift.* God freely forgives sin and saves the soul that comes to Him because Jesus provided for it by His death.

"And it shall come to pass, that whosoever shall call on the name of the Lord shall be saved." Acts 2:21

Earthly gifts may be wonderful, but none can ever come close to a comparison with the Gift of salvation. We associate gifts with love and caring, and we can't imagine the measure of love that brought about redemption's plan--*God's love!* We can't even touch it with words of description. Let us just be thankful, especially thankful at the time when the focus is on Jesus' birth, that God so loved us *He gave Jesus.*

We like gifts and gift giving. For many, it's romantic. We like to express our love in unique ways, but some of the best gifts may not have *romance* attached to them, yet they are the most valuable to us.

**One of the most appreciated gifts my husband ever gave to me would not be considered *romantic*, but I'll always remember his thoughtfulness in giving it.**
**At the time our daughter was born, we were at a low time financially, having just made a major move and change, which took all our savings. But when she was born, my husband managed to buy six weeks of diaper service! That was the era *before* throw away diapers, and it was the most needed and appreciated thing he could have done for me. Every time that little white truck drove up to pick up the dirty ones and leave clean diapers, I was so thankful for the love my husband displayed for me through that gift.**

At this season, try giving some gifts that are *not* wrapped in paper and ribbon. Find a creative way to show your love for family and friends.

Additional Treasures:    John 3:16    I John 3:1

# December 24

"Therefore the Lord himself shall give you a sign; Behold,
a virgin shall conceive, and bear a son...Immanuel"
Isaiah 7:14

This prophecy about Christ certainly came to pass as recorded in
Luke. The *fullness of time was come!* Imagine the astonishment of Mary,
a young girl engaged to be married, when told by the messenger angel
that she would be the mother of the Savior.

**Joseph was the espoused husband of Mary. They were in the
waiting period of the espousal, and not actually married. Yet to
break the pledge between them according to Jewish law, they would
have to be divorced. When Joseph saw that Mary was pregnant, he
thought of quietly putting her away in that manner instead of
making a public scene about it, where Mary could actually have been
stoned according to custom. Of course, God took care of the detail
with Joseph, and revealed the news of the Savior to him also. What a
relief it must have been for that godly man who loved Mary, his
espoused wife.**

"Then Joseph being raised from sleep did as the angel of the Lord
had bidden him, and took unto him his wife: And knew her not till she
had brought forth her firstborn son: and he called his name JESUS."
Matthew 1:24-25

All praise to Thee, eternal Lord,
Clothed in a garb of flesh and blood;
Choosing a manger for Thy throne,
While worlds on worlds are Thine alone!

Once did the skies before Thee bow;
A Virgin's arms contain Thee now:
Angels, who did in Thee rejoice,
Now listen to Thine infant voice.

A little child, Thou art our guest,
That weary ones in Thee may rest;
Forlorn and lowly is Thy birth,
That we may rise to heaven from earth.
Martin Luther

Additional Treasures:    Matthew 1:18-21    Luke 2:8-14

# December 25

"...and when they had opened their treasures, they presented unto him gifts; gold, frankincense, and myrrh."
Matthew 2:11

These gifts that the Wise Men brought to present to the Baby Jesus were *kingly* gifts. They *knew* that he was a king, though they were not Jews. They didn't have the Old Testament scriptures to read the prophecies about Him; yet they knew *because they had seen His star in the East.* They believed *that* miracle more than the Jews would believe the miracles they would see Jesus do, *in person,* in His public ministry. Those Wise Men followed that star, and traveled a great distance to fall down and worship the King and present their valuable gifts to Him.

Christians would probably have more peace and enjoyment of Christmas if they did acknowledge the fact that it is considered to be the Lord's birthday and not just a season for people to franticly exchange gifts with each other. It would do wonders for the heart if everyone did, in some way, give the Lord Himself a gift.

**The Gift**
**Give a gift to Jesus?  What does one give to a King,**
**Who has untold treasure, the universe,**
**And myriad angels who do His bidding?**
**I'm least among His servants...what could I give?**
**Yet...there is one thing He desires of mine.**
**I'm thrilled, but frightened, and tremble at the thought**
**Of laying such a gift at His feet.**
***But His love constrains me.***
**So I take this tattered, rather roughened thing:**
**Dull with lack of courage,**
**Shriveled from lack of nourishment,**
**Slippery with a spidery web of deceit,**
**And I hold it out to the King...with fear and trembling.**
***Lord, I present to you this unworthy gift;***
***I give to you...my heart.***
Edna Holmes

Additional Treasures:     Romans 12:1     Psalm 150:1-6

# December 26

## "Thou shalt not take the name of the Lord thy God in vain..."
## Exodus 20:7

I've heard people argue that the way that Christians are supposed to live is so dull and boring; they can't *do* anything or have any fun. That is ignorance speaking in those arguments, for the life of a Christian is a life of pleasure and satisfaction.

But people object to the *"shalt nots"* and many stay on the outside of the circle, often looking in with envy at the peace and contentment of the Christian life, yet do not desire to give up their sins in coming to Christ.

I read an interesting illustration concerning that line of reasoning.

**A gentleman said to a friend, "I wish you would come down to my garden and taste my apples." He asked him several times, but he did not come, and at last the fruit-grower said "I suppose you think my apples are not good, so you won't come and try them." "Well to tell the truth," said the friend, "I have tasted them. I picked up one that fell over the wall, and I never tasted anything so sour in all my life and I do not particularly wish to have any more of your fruit."**

**The owner of the garden said, "I thought so! Those apples around the outside are for the special benefit of the boys. I went for miles to get the sourest sort to plant around the orchard, so the boys might give them up as not worth stealing; but if you will come *inside* you will find that we grow a different quality there, sweet as honey."**

**All that the world sees on the outside of the Christian life is the "Thou shalt nots" and "Thou shalts" and think it is a dull boring life. But these are only the bitter fruits which helps discourage hypocrites from trying to emulate the children of God.   If you pass by the exterior bitters, and give yourself up to Christ and live for Him, your peace shall be like the waves of the sea. — Adapted from Spurgeon**

We must never be apologetic because the Word of God has its stern warnings about sin, and firm commands for the children of God. There must be guidelines to *protect us, as well as bless us.*

Teach your children the benefits of the "thou shalt nots" in the Bible. It will be a wellspring of knowledge and blessing for them all through life.

Additional Treasures:   Philippians 2:9-11   Deuteronomy 6:24

# December 27

"The Lord is good unto them that wait for him,
to the soul that seeketh him."
Lamentations 3:25

As we turn our minds from the holiday season so prevalent in our thoughts during this month, and look toward the year coming up, we would do well to keep this thought in mind: God has special things for those who wait on Him. Our natural inclination is to run ahead and do what we think is the best thing to do. How many times do we have to backtrack and come back to correct our mistakes in judgment? We must be willing to wait on the Lord, and keep our hearts reaching out to Him in love and devotion.

It's important to be able to discern what the will of God is for our lives. Some stay forever perplexed about it. "What is the will of God?" they will ask over and over without coming to a solution. We need some guidelines that will stay fixed in our minds permanently.

Long ago **at a certain English port the harbor lights were so arranged that when the pilot of an incoming vessel saw them all in line, shining as one light, he knew the vessel was in the deep water channel which would lead him safely into the harbor. Keeping the lights in view, he was able to pilot the ship into harbor, however dark the night.**

It is even so today when the teaching of the Word of God (Psalm 119:105), the inward impulse of the Holy Spirit (Acts 16:6), and the outward circumstances of providence (Acts 16:10) all combine to point in one direction, the waiting servant may 'go forward' (Exodus 14:15), well assured that he is in the right channel. ---Com.

**The Word of God is our guide. Do we agree with the Word?**

**The Holy Spirit speaks truth to our hearts. Are we listening?**

**Are circumstances substantiating the Word and the Holy Spirit?**

What we want to do may *feel* right and be wrong! Line these three up; you have *the will of God.* We won't be confused about it if we will simply listen when we read His Word. That is what it is: God telling us what His will is! His Holy Spirit makes it plain to us if we will, again, listen. It is the attitude with which we sit down with the Bible and read, desiring to know what God has for us to learn and understand about Him each day.

Additional Treasures:    Psalm 143:10    John 7:17

# December 28

**"And all flesh shall see the salvation of God."**
**Luke 3:6**

Christ came and provided salvation to all that trust in Him. He is not willing that any should perish, and He has commissioned the church to reach out to the lost of the world with the gospel message. Gospel means *Good News!* It may be helpful for us to have a clear and simple presentation of that gospel, with which to encourage the lost to listen and receive Christ.

This is a simple guideline. Seven facts the Lost Must Know:

**Everyone is a sinner.**    Romans 3:23
**The wages of sin is death: separation from God forever.**    Rom.6:23
**No sin will be allowed into heaven.**    Revelation 21:27
**There is nothing a man can do to earn a place in heaven.**    Titus 3:5
**Jesus paid for all sin and offers His righteousness.**    II Cor.5:21
**Eternal life is a gift for those who receive Christ.**    Ephesians 2:8
**A man can know he has eternal life right now.**    I John 5:13

If you are timid in witnessing memorize these verses. Being prepared will make you more confident, therefore, more likely to avail yourself of opportunities that will come.

Remember that *someone* told you about Christ. I never personally met the evangelist who preached the night conviction hit my heart like a hammer! My husband and I had taken a group of young people to the city to hear this preacher in a big public auditorium. Though I had to run in and out keeping track of teenage girls, I still heard enough of the message concerning unsaved church members for it to make a startling impression on me. After wrestling all night with that message, the next day I told my husband I was lost, and he prayed with me, kneeling at the couch in our living room. That preacher's name was Rev. Jerry Barnard, and I've often wished I could have met him and told him that God used his message to reach me.

We will never know until we are in heaven what amazing things happened because we told someone the gospel. We rarely see the end results because the Word of God has such power to effect change in hearts long after the one who proclaimed it is gone.

Additional Treasures:    Luke 24:47    I Timothy 2:4

# December 29

"And the Lord direct your hearts into the love of God, and into the patient waiting for Christ." II Thessalonians 3:5

In the year just ahead of us we must keep focused on the reality of truth in the Word of God. We live in troublesome times, with the world system trying to exclude the Lord from every facet of life.

The Christian walk has never been without difficulty, because the world is not a friend to Christ. Jesus said, "If the world hate you, ye know that it hated me before it hated you." John 15:18

The world hates us and the devil may try to defeat us, but the Lord is for us! Following Him we can look ahead with confidence.

## LOOKING AHEAD

You may notice the valleys are deeper
And the mountains seemingly high,
And our steps more plodding with effort
As time rushes crazily by.

Hear the tireless roar of the devourer,
Though toothless and fangless he be.
In the spiritual warfare that's raging,
There's a psychological part you see.

For there is always rattling of the chains,
Though truth has set us free.
It is disquieting to our souls,
And renders us fearful, doubting victory.

But there's a calm in the eye of battle,
Where the conflict ceases to be.
It's a secret place known to very few,
Directly at Jesus' feet.

Courage and strength are there reinforced.
Resolve is polished to a sheen.
And love drives out fear and doubt,
Just lingering in that place with Him.
Edna Holmes

Additional Treasures:    John 15:11    I Peter 3:15

# December 30

"...that ye should shew forth the praises of him
who hath called you out of darkness into his marvelous light."
I Peter 2:9

We should proclaim the praises of God. He delivered us from darkness into the light! "Who hath delivered us from the power of darkness, and hath translated us into the kingdom of his dear Son: In whom we have redemption through his blood, even the forgiveness of sin." Colossians 1:13-14

We should march into the New Year singing *victory,* and keep advancing on being always faithful to our Lord and Savior. We have His Word to hold us steady as the corruption in the world threatens the very structure of our society.

A great Christian lady in England, a hymn-writer, in ushering in the year 1873, penned a stirring bit of poetry for believers in that day. This remarkable lady had many talents and used all her gifts in the service of the Lord. It is said that she committed the entire New Testament and Book of Psalms to memory. It is no wonder that in her brief lifetime she produced so many beautiful poems and hymns.

### Another Year is Dawning

Standing at the portal, Of the opening year,
Words of comfort meet us, Hushing every fear;
Spoken through the silence, By our Father's voice,
Tender, strong and faithful, Making us rejoice.
Onward then, and fear not, Children of the day;
For His word shall never, Never pass away.
Frances Ridley Havergal

What can you do for the Lord in the New Year? *Ask Him!* In order not to fall out before spring, we must settle it with the Lord what we desire to do for Him in the New Year, and keep to it through all the seasons. Read your Bible, pray regularly, if possible the same time early in the day, and be willing to do other practical down to earth chores for the Lord. We had an older man in our congregation who stayed after church every Sunday morning and straightened the hymn books in the pew racks, picked up any trash strewn about and got it ready for the evening service. That task, so faithfully done, was a tremendous blessing to the church.

Additional Treasures:     Colossians 3:16     I Corinthians 15:58

# December 31

**"But thanks be to God, which giveth us the
victory through our Lord Jesus Christ."
I Corinthians 15:57**

We already have the victory for tomorrow and the rest of the New Year. Jesus *giveth* us the victory. That's continual giving in motion. That means we cannot be defeated! The Lord's sword and armor will make us victors in every battle we face. If that truth stayed fresh in our minds, it would give us peace that defies all turmoil. "Great peace have they which love thy law: and nothing shall offend them." Psalm 119:165

Most everyone will get caught up in making a few New Year's resolutions. Some break them right away, for they always do. Others try diligently...for a few weeks, maybe even a few months. In the end, there are few which have the determination to keep a new resolution. They must exert more effort! However, the best resolution you and I could ever make is to be more diligent in our devotion to God. If you have learned *anything at all* this year, then you have an edge! Make a list and look at it. It's proof that you can make progress in your walk with the Lord.

I resolve *every year* to read the Bible more, reading it through once again as my goal. I carry over my old resolutions I have kept, such as keeping my wake-up verses in mind to use. That can be any verse which means something to you, but it is very important to put some scripture in your mind before you get out of bed! That is the only way you will get ahead of the devil.
He is waiting on you.

More time spent in prayer should be everyone's resolution. If we could only grasp a little of what it means to have the privilege of talking to our Heavenly Father, and He listens to us! Remember, nothing can get in the way of you 'getting through' to Him except sin. Confess that, get rid of it, and then tell God everything that's on your mind and in your heart. He *loves* you, you belong to Him, and He will do whatever needs to be done for your good.

I keep a prayer list, making it up fresh each month and by that I can be sure I don't forget what people ask me to pray about, and can see the progress along the way as I pray. I commit each day to the Lord, and it is amazing to me how He smoothes the way through difficult days. I know what my resolutions will be for another cycle of seasons!

May God bless you abundantly in the New Year. Re: Ephesians 3:20

Additional Treasures:     Proverbs 4:23     Psalm 121:2

# ABOUT THE AUTHOR

Edna Holmes grew up, a country girl, the third one of ten children. The rich and varied experiences of her childhood are often referenced in her writing. She married her "soldier home from the war" at an early age and five years later they both became Christians through a personal faith in Jesus Christ. Their focus changed immediately. Years later her husband became the pastor of a church in Grapevine, TX. He would serve faithfully in that pastorate for forty-two years. Within those decades the church grew to be strong in their missions' outreach: contributing to the support of many missionary families serving all over the world.

Edna was privileged to travel with her husband to many countries as he visited the missionaries, encouraging them in their work. She learned from experience that Christian women all over the world, in all cultures, have the same basic needs and desires of the heart. Edna's priority in the ministry was to teach women, at every opportunity, the Word of God and encourage them to make it the guide of their lives. Treasures to Keep was born when the church women encouraged her to write a daily devotional book for them. She produced it in monthly segments, which later were combined and printed into a complete one-year devotional book. In that form, it began to be circulated outside the church to other women. Many lives have been affected by its plain, easy to understand, teaching.

Edna's purpose is to honor the Lord in her writing; that those who read it may learn more of Christ: "In whom are hid all the treasures of wisdom and knowledge." Colossians 2:3.

CPSIA information can be obtained
at www.ICGtesting.com
Printed in the USA
LVOW04s1449131216
517086LV00012B/848/P